NCGE Pacesetters in Geography, No. 1

Series Editor, Merrill K. Ridd

This volume introduces a new series for the Council. Pacesetter Books are designed especially for the teacher. Others concerned with curriculum and teacher training will find the series useful and stimulating, but it is the teacher to whom we speak — that person on the front line who daily faces the students and the questions "what to teach, and how to teach it." Accordingly, attention will focus on viable issues in geography and on presenting fresh and practical ideas for classroom delivery.

MKR

AFRICA:
Teaching Perspectives and Approaches

Editor: John E. Willmer

Cartographer: Joseph Brownell
Assistant: Joan C. Willmer

A National Council for Geographic Education Pacesetter Book

GEOGRAPHIC AND AREA STUDY PUBLICATIONS
tualatin, oregon

Library of Congress Cataloging in Publication Data

Wilmer, John E.
   Africa: teaching perspectives and approaches.

   (Pacesetters in geography; no. 1)
   Includes bibliographical references.
   1. Africa — Study and teaching. I. Title. II. Series.
DT19.8W54   960'.07   75-2222
ISBN 0-88393-050-1
ISBN 0-88393-051-X pbk.

Library of Congress Catalog Card Number 75-2222.

Printed in the United States of America.

PREFACE

For more than half a century the National Council for Geographic Education has been a relatively small band of teachers who have been concerned with matters related to the teaching of geography. To this end they have sought to provide numerous instruments calculated to be helpful to not just their membership, but to all geography teachers. This has included sponsoring meetings, workshops, and conventions where learning, and an exchange of learnings can take place, but it has also included the writing, production, and distribution of a variety of publications designed specifically to be of interest and value to geography teachers. This includes *The Journal of Geography,* our principal and regular communication vehicle, and an array of non-periodic publications. This volume falls into the last category and we are confident that teachers will find a valuable source of ideas here to help their students learn about Africa.

Books are the fruit of real live thinking people, but this book is more than just that. Contained here is a series of essays by foreign scholars, some of whom are Africans, but all of whom have a deep personal experience in Africa. Other parts of this volume were written by people who not only know Africa, but have a concern for matters related to teaching and learning about Africa. To each of these people the National Council for Geographic Education is especially appreciative, since their only reward is the hope that by sharing thought and insight there will be some benefit for many to learn about a dynamic and critical part of the world. But all of this didn't just happen. John Willmer, who has a great concern for Africa as a vital topic for geography teachers, really made it possible for these voices to come together. His many hours of dedication over a course of several years is a task few can appreciate and for which our organization shall remain indebted. We also wish to express our thanks and appreciation to Joseph Brownell who did all of the original cartography for this volume, to John Willmer for her editorial assistance, and to Akin Mabogunje for writing a thoughtful and feeling foreword. To all of these, and the many not recognized here who have contributed in no small way, the National Council for Geographic Education is grateful. We can hope that our reward will be the many teachers and students coming to know the continent of Africa in a new and different way.

JOHN M. BALL, President
National Council for Geographic Education

v

FOREWORD

Ex Africa semper aliquid novi (Something new always comes out of Africa) wrote the Roman, Pliny, in the first century A.D. In the last fifteen years, it would appear that something new always comes out *about* Africa. The spate of publications, whether of books, monographs, pamphlets or journal articles, attests to a renewed interest in the life and conditions of people in the continent. Compared to the quaint ethnographical and pseudofictional literary output of the earlier part of this century, these new writings represent a genuinely scholarly and more objective appraisal of situations in Africa. An African may not always agree with the viewpoints of many of these publications but he would concede that they are at least honest attempts at understanding the complexity of life within this vast area of the world.

Most of these recent writings have usually been directed at the restricted academic world of scholars with African interest or at the more curious and less insular section of the wider reading public. To that extent they differ from the present volume which has been written specifically to aid teachers in their task of imparting to young and still impressionable students some realistic appreciation of Africa and Africans, devoid of the more popular caricatures so much beloved of sensational writers and journalists. Such a goal for a publication while laudable is by its very nature very difficult and very challenging in terms of a strategy for achievement. Yet, it must be admitted that this book has been structured in such a way as to ensure that as much as possible of this goal is achieved.

The book is divided into four parts. The first comprises eleven essays written some by African and some by foreign scholars who have had some experience of life in Africa. They are meant to set the tone for the rest of the book and to provide basic factual material for the later sections. The first of the essays by Nketia of Ghana raises the issue of the meaning of Africa for contemporary American society. He emphasises not only the historical links between the two continents but also the shared traditions in arts, music, dance and literature. The second essay by Turnbull attempts to describe the basic characteristics of the African. Quite naturally, such an ambitious generalization runs the risk of distorting reality through oversimplification but so deftly was the essay handled that its advantage for teaching purposes is preserved. The third essay by Steel assesses the varied physical environments in Africa and the manner in which they have encouraged or inhibited the development of the continent.

The next three essays are concerned with socio-cultural conditions in Africa. Starting with the population, the question is posed whether the continent is already overpopulated. It is argued that given the falling death rate in a situation of a high and unabating birth rate, the rapidly growing population could wipe out any gains from rising levels of production. But this is not a matter of certainty since the interrelationships between population growth and economic development are complex and are far from being fully understood. A useful background to such an understanding must come from a deeper appreciation of the history of the continent. The next essay therefore provides a brief introduction to the sources and major periods of African history. Given the fact that one major source of African history is oral tradition, it becomes necessary to emphasize the diversity and range of such traditions through an appreciation of the language geography of the continent. This is, however, not meant to create the impression of a static linguistic distribution but of languages with continuing histories of migration and change.

Two essays concern themselves with the basic economic situations. Floyd describes some aspects of land-use paying adequate attention to agriculture as the basic user of land in tropical Africa. He examines the various problems of agricultural development and underlines ways in which agricultural practices differ from those in the Western World. He notes that following on the many changes that have taken place in agriculture and in the rural areas of many countries in Africa, there has developed in recent times massive movement of youths away from the land. Thom takes up the story of this rural out-migration by looking at its effects in the urban centres to which the migrants flock.

Although towns and cities are not novel features in some parts of Africa, it is only in the present century, especially in the last twenty years, that urbanization has become a pervasive process with a remarkable rate of growth. The almost sudden rise in the population of many cities creates new problems which are today the major preoccupations of many African governments.

Three final essays deal with the political situations. The first by Paden examines the pattern of political change in Black Africa since the end of the Second World War. It identifies the various sources from which pressure is put on the political structure inherited by different African countries at their independence and the implications of the widespread military involvement in government for the nature of political institutions that may eventually emerge in Africa. Ocaya-Lakidi and Mazrui review the impact of European colonialism on state formation and nation-building in Africa and conclude that this episode in the history of the continent disrupted "a pattern of institutional growth and development which might have led to the formation of more advanced types of institutions comparable to those of modern Europe and America, but distinctively African in content". The third essay by Akpan focusses on the political problems of Southern Africa. Here, minority groups of white settlers have, through reigns of terror, managed to hold the African majority in thrall. Akpan considers the various tactics of resistance pursued by the Africans and evaluates the prospects for a solution of the racial problems in this southern half of the continent.

In a sense these various essays provide a conspectus of current issues and preoccupations in Africa today. None of them is meant to be exhaustive; their role is to tantalize, to serve as a veritable aperitiff whetting the appetite of both teachers and pupils for more. The attempt to satisfy the appetite is not meant to be done in the manner of a gormand but of a connoisseur making his choice with a good sense of judgment and selectivity. To help towards this end, the second part of the volume is concerned with resources and materials available for teaching about Africa. Beyer's contribution to this section reviews the varied sources to which teachers can turn today for material. Specifically, he lists not only textbooks and journal articles but also mass communication media, service agencies such as the UNESCO, embassies of African countries, United States Department of State and airlines with flight connections to Africa. In particular, he stresses the importance of inviting individuals with knowledge of or experience in Africa who are to be found in most American communities today to speak to the students. An equally untapped source of information about Africa is provided by contemporary African literature, and Nancy Hoon explores the different ways teachers can use this source to real advantage.

The third part of the book concentrates on approaches to the teaching of Africa. Should this be on an interdisciplinary basis? Should it concern itself largely with problems of social change or should it focus on the prospects of economic growth and development? How far can some of the new conceptual and analytical techniques of the "New Geography" be applied in these varied approaches? These questions are grappled with in very expert fashion by the four contributors to this section. In each case, the arguments are presented very clearly and various diagrammatic illustrations and charts are offered to reinforce the points being made.

Finally, there is concern with the effectiveness of teaching and to this end *Part Four* of the volume considers some teaching strategies. These range from the very modern strategy of the design and use of simulation to the more time-honoured though no less effective strategy of using sketch maps. In either case, much thought has gone into the presentation. Difficult concepts have been simplified and traditional techniques of doing things have been given a refreshingly striking new look.

It is not the usual purpose of a Foreword to present the reader with a quick survey of the content of a book but I have considered it necessary to do so in this case because of the special importance I attach to this effort at providing teachers not with a manual of what to do or what to know but a guidebook or directory of where to turn in a serious search for knowledge about Africa. This present volume, indeed, does more than this for it is equally concerned with perspectives, with the appropriate attitude of mind which teachers and students must bring to the study of Africa. This, in fact, is the essence of the book and it needs to be strenuously underlined in a foreword such as this.

It is now almost commonplace to speak of a world getting smaller everyday, a world in which distances are being rapidly annihilated and in which we are all becoming each other's neighbour. The vast and almost incredible revolutions in communications and transportation engineering means that today events in any part of the world impinge on our consciousness with an immediacy never before felt in human history. The prognosis is that this individual consciousness of global involvement will in future become more intense and all-pervasive as science and technology proceed on their almost relentless forward march.

The implication of these developments is the increasing interactions between peoples of different lands, races and cultures. There is no reason to expect that such interactions would lead to greater peace and concord in the world; they could lead to greater hostility and destructive confrontations between different groups. Whether interactions lead to one or the other could depend very much on attitudes, ideas and opinions which people have of each other. And it is here that education has such a vital role to play.

The peoples of Africa and of African descent have for long been the victims of calculated misrepresentations in the literature and writings of the Western World. For as long as they were in no position to retort, to insist on more dispassionate and less prejudiced assessment, to protest downright dishonest scholarship many publications of doubtful value passed into popular literature and are in recent times the unidentified basis of much misunderstanding. Today, on both sides of the Atlantic, we of the present generation have an obligation to undo the havoc of the past. More important, we have a responsibility to offer to the young and growing generation of our countries a more wholesome basis for interacting among themselves.

This, to me, is the real significance of this book. There can be no doubt that there are many ways in which it can be improved. There are more essays that it could include; more approaches and strategies that it could suggest. It is, however, not a compendium. What it sets out to do is no less than invite teachers interested in teaching about Africa to make determined efforts to provide their pupils with those types of information which will enable them to develop the right perspective and thereby help them to become better citizens of the world. This is no mean task and I have derived great pleasure in seeing how far the various contributors have managed to accomplish it. It is in the belief that their modest efforts represent a vital contribution to better human understanding that I commend this book to all tachers about Africa in the United States and elsewhere.

AKIN L. MABOGUNJE
Professor of Geography

University of Ibadan,
Ibadan, Nigeria
1st June, 1973

CONTENTS

AFRICA
Teaching Perspectives and Approaches

PART ONE
Essays

1

The Meaning of Africa

J. H. NKETIA
University of Ghana

AFRICA IN REVIEW

Anyone who looks at the map of Africa today and compares it with what it was two decades ago cannot but be struck by what the difference between the two represents. Although the boundaries of the old colonial territories have remained, their significance has changed from boundaries of 'spheres of imperial influence' to state boundaries. Ethnic groups loosely held together by some alien power which exercised benign influence on their chiefs and ruled their land are being welded into new nations by a new political consciousness. The logic of the internal boundaries set up by the old colonial administration is being challenged where the constituent ethnic groups are large or feel that they should reassert their historical status as independent kingdoms and states – a status which they lost during the colonial regime.

It will be evident, therefore, that while freedom from colonial rule has earned for Africa a new place in the community of nations, it has also brought in its wake many new internal problems, problems which are transforming these new nations and re-shaping their identity or individuality. Accordingly, the study of African problems in Africa has assumed a new dimension, for such problems must be viewed not only in terms of ethnic groups as basic components of African countries, but also from the perspective of national, regional, and Pan-African interests. There are also important international considerations to be taken into account in the study of some of these problems, for Africa has of necessity to be sensitive as never before to the pressures and challenges of the international scene.

3

INTERNATIONAL PERSPECTIVE

The response of the outside world to the new status of Africa has been very concrete and seems to follow common diplomatic patterns. The scramble for Africa which resulted in the effective colonisation of the continent by the major European powers has been replaced by a new order in which the scramble is no longer for direct political domination but for friendship and alliances believed to be mutually beneficial.

If you visit some of the new African nation-states like Ghana, Nigeria, or Senegal, you will, I am sure, be impressed by the number of diplomatic missions set up by foreign governments to represent them. Those include both representatives of the former colonial governments and their allies, and those in the opposite camp. These missions seek to protect the interests of their governments and their nationals in the country while serving as outposts of the economic expansionist programmes of their own countries. Those countries which do not have embassies have trade representatives who function more or less as consuls, for friendship with Africa not only brisks up trade but also cements alliances which are beneficial on world platforms.

Foreign aid is offered in all sorts of forms — in loans, in goods and machinery, in weapons of war or in personnel — and African governments, anxious to develop on all fronts, are accepting these offers and concluding one agreement after the other which binds them in a new way to the wider world. From time to time the danger of these 'friendly' gestures is pointed out. The fear that Africa may be tied to the apron strings of benefactors is expressed, but the need for capital and economic development on all fronts seems to impress African governments far more than such considerations, especially where it seems certain that political sovereignty is externally, at least, not too gravely compromised.

There are many subsidiary activities connected with the presence of foreign missions in African countries, particularly those of Eastern and Western countries which appear on the African scene as rivals in the quest for friendship. Programmes for creating the best possible image of their respective countries — including elaborate information services with lending libraries and regular film shows and photographic exhibitions — are laid on. Generous offers of scholarships are made; visiting artists are sent from their countries to tour Africa. All these, which may seem normal diplomatic activities in Washington or London, and which may not attract too much attention in these capitals, assume a different status in a developing country, and some African governments have had to request the closure of cultural centres set up by foreign embassies in their countries.

But it is not only the projection of the image of a country through its foreign mission that receives attention. The collection of all kinds of information, including data of political significance as well as material of academic value, appears to be of great diplomatic interest, and active support is given to African studies in the hope that it will provide a proper basis for determining diplomatic policies. Interaction with Africa must be inspired by knowledge and not by mere suppositions or stereotypes given currency in the western world by romantic writers.

Diplomatic missions are indeed an interesting phenomenon in Africa today and would make an interesting study. They represent on the one hand, what the present day Africa means to the rest of the world, and on the other hand, the extent of Africa's external involvement with the outside world.

Afro-Americans have played a significant role in the changed international scene in Africa, for they have served as diplomats, information officers, cultural attachés and other kinds of embassy officials, or as Peace Corps Volunteers or as business men. To these, Africa must have more than the kind of sentimental meaning held by their forebearers who were caught in the 'back to Africa' movement. They have to see Africa both as American citizens and as persons of African descent. Their attitudes are conditioned by a complex of relations fostered by policies within their own country and by the political climate of the world scene in which their country is active. Their success or failure in Africa depends very much on how they fulfill the expectations of their ambivalent positions, the depth of their knowledge of Africa and the extent to which this is in accord with reality. The meaning of Africa to Afro-Americans must therefore be assessed not just in terms of Africa and America but also in the context of the international scene in which the two continents and their peoples are involved.

HISTORICAL PERSPECTIVE

There is also a historical dimension to this problem, for Africa's involvement with the rest of the world is by no means new. Africa, the birthplace of man (as the archaeologists now tell us), has a history which cannot be separated from the history of mankind. We are told by historians that the continent participated in the major civilisations of the world and that it shared with Europe a common old-world culture at least up to the period of the dessication of the Sahara. Trade with the Mediterranean never ceased after this even when new relations became established with the oriental world as a result of the invasion of Arab culture and Islamic religion. When fresh contact was established with Europe after this, it had to be of a different sort. The new kind of relationship was one in which Africa supplied gold, ivory, and similar commodities as well as manpower — a relationship which led first to the African diaspora, and later to colonialism. Consideration of the meaning of Africa to Afro-Americans must therefore take into account not only present day attitudes but also those inherited from the historical past.

As in the present era, Africa's historical involvement with the external world stimulated two kinds of response: the exploitation of Africa's potential in terms of the needs of a given era, and the exploitation of Africa with a view to expanding the frontiers of knowledge of this continent.

In the Islamic period, Africa attracted not only Arab proselytisers but also geographers and writers who have left records of travels as well as valuable accounts of the great medieval kingdoms and empires of Africa. Islamic scholarship and learning which found its most palpable expression in the African university of Sankore did not cease when the momentum of Islamic conquest halted. Arabic manuscripts recovered in many parts of West Africa show that Africans were writing the histories and traditions of their countries and recording contemporary events or writing poetry and stories. The existence of such manuscripts in places that one would least expect is one of the interesting things that has come out of recent historical research being carried out in West African centres of African studies. The Institute of African Studies of the University of Ghana, for example, now has a large collection of manuscripts in Arabic script written by authors in Ghana from about the eighteenth century. Some of those are in Arabic. A few are in Hausa and Ghanaian languages like Dagbani and Gonja.

During the European period of African history which followed the Islamic period, there was considerable interest in the study of Africa. However, this interest was, in a way, an outgrowth of the European expansionist outlook which created a strong interest in geography leading to the exploration of parts of the globe unknown to the western world. Explorers were supported by groups and institutions in their own countries. In addition to geographers, we have a host of travellers to Africa who have left accounts of their journeys and of Africa as they saw it within the philosophical framework of their times. The concept of the 'savage' formed the framework of their observations and comments. Some of the more astute observers, however, did find themselves appreciating elements of African cultures because they could not ignore the inherent qualities of those cultures which made them different but worthy of admiration.

The image of Africa created by these travellers has been a very difficult one to correct, especially among those newspapermen who still trade on the sensational, or among those who find in it a rationale for perpetrating policies of suppression and theories of racial superiority. The myths and prejudices against Africa still held by ordinary people in the West are in part due to these accounts which are still read and to other agencies which followed explorers to Africa. Today scholars turn to these early accounts not so much for their comments as for what they can accept as statements of fact that can be used as source material in historical studies. The works of men like Clapperton, Speke, Burton, Bowdich, and Cruickshank are consulted by scholars for this reason.

Along with the accounts of travellers and explorers, one might mention the reports and studies of merchants or officers of European trading companies, and of colonial governments which succeeded these companies. For the trading companies, Africa had a meaning which is very different in many ways from what it means today to foreign enterprises based in Africa. Scholars have begun to study the reports of all these not only for factual accounts of African life, but also for data which will enable them to study the psychological responses of colonial countries and the colonial governments to African situations.

One could go on to review what Africa meant in the writings of missionaries and officers of the colonial regimes – the importance which anthopological studies of Africa assumed in academic institutions in Britain and Europe; the advent of government anthropologists; the coming into being of various experts on African affairs who advised their governments; the setting up of societies interested in knowledge of Africa, in particular the International African Institute which attempted to promote international scholarship and provide a clearing house for information about Africa; the setting up of institutes in former French colonies for studying Africa, and so on – but all these emphasize a western-centred approach to African studies rather than a predominantly African-centred viewpoint.

AMERICAN VIEWS OF AFRICA

Although America did not take part in the scramble for African territories and was, therefore, not involved in the colonial problem, she had taken too large a share in the scramble for African manpower not to be involved in a much more serious way with Africa − emotionally, culturally, intellectually, and to some extent politically. The quest for an enlightened attitude to Africa was pursued no less by American scholars than by European scholars. The spirit of missionary evangelism and the desire for economic expansion and colonisation did not escape Afro-Americans. They responded in their own way to this. The Afro-American diplomat of today was preceded by the Afro-American missionary and other men of action inspired by the challenge of the colonial period of African history and the pressures generated within America by racial problems. The challenges have not ceased even though involvement with Africa has taken on new dimensions.

DIVERSE ATTITUDES

Because of the complex nature of American society, there are diverse attitudes and differences in the intensity of responses to Africa, and variations in the meaning that Africa now has for different sections of the population. In this connection there is a marked difference in attitude between some white Americans and Afro-Americans.

There are many white Americans who are excited by Africa and who have an emotional attitude to it because it gives them exotic pleasure − the same sort of thing that some Africans feel about America. Every summer brings several white American tourists to Africa just for this reason. Many of them are excited by African cultures − by African art, African drumming and dancing. There are many tourists for whom these have aesthetic appeal. Indeed there are few western countries in which are found white people who can respond as deeply to drumming as in America, but this is undoubtedly because of the Afro-American contribution to American culture.

Furthermore, many white Americans are attracted to Africa by intellectual curiosity. Some of them, it appears, get particular satisfaction from the knowledge which they acquire of societies and cultures different from their own, and make a conscious effort to learn to understand them. The quest for a knowledge of Africa started while Africa was still a sprawling colonial empire. It has received great impetus in recent years, and America indeed has the largest number of African studies programmes in the world.

Afro-Americans, as Americans, also share in all these but on different levels. Whereas the white American is often motivated by his own interest and does not at any point have to identify himself with Africa, the Afro-American's dilemma is that he cannot always be so detached, for he has an affinity with Africa which he cannot completely ignore. He may, as some have done, deny this affinity and stay aloof. But if he does identify himself with Africa, he cannot look at it simply as an exotic place. His emotional response to Africa may have to be deeper and more intense, and this may raise a few problems for him.

Having no affinity with Africa, the white American, on the other hand, need not make apologies for Africa or care outwardly about Africa's shortcomings or proverbial 'backwardness.' He may be more interested in the authentic or indigenous culture or way of life as he sees it and not in the things which resemble those of his own American culture. Thus his attitude to an African village may be quite different from that of the Afro-American who may show concern for the village − for its modernisation. What the Afro-American considers defects, shortcomings, or backwardness in Africa may disturb him when he identifies himself with Africa.

Afro-American attitudes to Africa have on the whole been rather ambivalent. Attitudes toward Africa during the formative period of Afro-American history, attitudes toward Africa following the liberation, and present day attitudes are not the same. Afro-American history has seen different kinds of movement towards and away from Africa in response to the pressures of the time, the prevailing intellectual climate, the current image of Africa in the western world, and the challenges which American society itself presents. These attitudes show themselves not only among ordinary Afro-Americans on the emotional level but also among scholars, other leaders of thought, and artists both in their normal work and in certain actions that they initiate.

There are Afro-American scholars who choose to look at Africa from a historical angle because they have a personal, emotional response to Africa and are, therefore, interested in re-interpreting African history or re-discovering hidden aspects of African history which will bring out the achievements of the past and the glorious features of this history passed over by western historians and distorted by those whose image of Africa is that of 'the savage who has never contributed anything to civilisation.'

There are, on the other hand, some scholars who do not want to have anything to do with the African past on the grounds that it presents an inferior image of Africa to the rest of the world. They concentrate on modern Africa not just because this is a legitimate field of study but also because they want to bring out to the world that Africa is modernising itself and that is has cities, industries, schools, universities, and modern buildings similar to those found anywhere in Europe or America. The emphasis thus tends to be on all those things that American public opinion – for all that it is worth in this connection – accepts as the marks of a civilised Africa. These marks of civilisation, it will be noted, are shared by the Afro-American and it comes as a shock to him that the transformation of the African has not followed the same swift pace as that of the Afro-American. I have met many people who ask questions about modern developments and who seem to be relieved to hear about them. Contemporary Africa has indeed a lot to show, but it is of course not only the trappings of western civilisation that make Africa of today what it is but its own heritage of the past which has survived the impact of acculturative forces of the West.

Closely related to this are political attitudes which are generated by Afro-Americans who are privileged to see Africa from outside and to think about problems of Africa as a whole (in the same way as they see America and its many states as a whole) rather than in terms of its constituent countries. Africa owes its movement toward Pan-Africanism to peoples of African descent. When Afro-American scholars are inspired by the Pan-Africanist approach, they join in the war against tribalism and they emulate those African leaders who champion the cause of African unity no matter how unsatisfactory their domestic policies might be.

There is to my knowledge also a number of Afro-American scholars who study Africa like all other scholars – as an area within their disciplines – and who are interested in the understanding and insight, and the theoretical implications that the study of Africa brings to their disciplines. There is no reason why the theories of political science, for example, should be based only on the western experience of government, starting from the Greeks. Indeed many Afro-American political scientists and their colleagues are interested in Africa today because it offers a fruitful laboratory for testing their theories and new hypotheses.

THE CREATIVE ARTS

Concern for Africa has also shown itself in the creative arts but along somewhat different lines. In the theatre, for example, some Afro-Americans have been giving their own versions of African dances in creative forms which use vocabulary from traditional Africa. One sees their efforts in night clubs and on the television. Some do this because they have concern for African culture and wish to share their joy and pride in the performing arts of Africa with others. But others do this merely to earn their living because they know that America is fascinated by Africa. The latter unfortunately pander to the taste of their audiences and perpetuate the sensational image of Africa as a continent of fire-eating, superstitious jungle dwellers. When the spectacular aspects of traditional African theatre are divorced from their context and portrayed as the sole content of this theatre, they cannot but give the wrong image of Africa to those who do not already know it.

In the field of African theatre, what is lacking among many enthusiastic Afro-American artists is the proper knowledge of traditional African forms. There is no doubt that there are many who are genuinely interested and would present the authentic forms if they had the opportunity of learning them. Indeed some of them, anxious to do this, have sought help from African students who may be closer to the forms but who are themselves often amateurs in this field.

There are of course a few well-known Afro-Americans in the theatre who have taken the trouble to visit Africa and learn from Africa. But we have the problem of approach and understanding even amongst such people. Some have approached their work as artists and made a good job of it, while others have tried to dress their work up with meaningless ethnographic references and pseudo-African names.

What has been said of dance is true to some extent of music. There are some who are genuinely interested and concerned about African music. Indeed the record collections of African music that some of them have are amazing in size and variety, and show that they have a genuine interest in exploring this music. However, apart from those in jazz, I do not know of leading Afro-American composers who are studying African music seriously. Indeed one leading Afro-American composer confessed to me some time ago that he was not interested. But then he was also not interested in jazz or popular music and had some scathing things to say about them as music. In the academic discipline of ethnomusicology the absence of leading Afro-American scholars in the African field is a very conspicuous one, and one can only hope that this will be corrected.

Interest in African literature has been shown by Afro-American writers and scholars. There appears to be interest in both traditional literature and, for obvious reasons, in modern African writing. Langston Hughes, perhaps more than any other leading writer, identified himself in a personal way with African writers. In his *Treasury of African Literature* he sought to bring Africa to America and the rest of the world.

The intellectual movement of Negritude, which has given birth to a spate of new African literature and which was inspired by creative minds of the New World, has naturally been of great interest to Afro-Americans and has served more than anything else to foster common bonds among intellectuals in Africa and the Americas.

A NEW ERA

I have dwelt at length on the meaning of Africa to the outside world because I think that African and Afro-American relationships must be seen not only in terms of two peoples of common descent or between two continents, but against a wider background of international relations. The search for the meaning of Africa is, in the final analysis, a search for a common humanity and international understanding.

INTERNAL SEARCH FOR IDENTITY

It is significant that at this time of world-wide interest in Africa, Africa itself has awakened to its culture and has become interested in studying itself, for to study Africa from without and interpret it in terms of the experience of the outside world is not the same as studying Africa from within and in terms of the African experience. The new interest in African studies in Africa started on a small scale. During the colonial era African nationalists and educators like Blyden of Liberia (later of Sierra Leone) conceived of new African institutions of higher education which would feature the study of African subjects; Casely Hayford of Ghana in his "Ethiopia Unbound" outlined an imaginary University of Ghana to be based in Kumasi away from the contaminating influence of western culture.

However, when African universities came to be established just prior to independence, it took a long time before the study of Africa in any context was admitted into the curriculum. The universities had special relations with overseas universities and were at first colonial university colleges. When scholars in old British universities asserted that there was no such thing as African history, they naturally posed a difficult problem for their counterparts in Africa, and it took some time before African subjects could come into the fold of academic disciplines.

Independence has made a lot of difference in attitudes to African studies in Africa today. This can be most clearly seen in the status of the arts of present day Africa – the arts looked down upon in the colonial past, the arts neglected as unworthy of the modern Africa. Country-wide festivals of art have now become a feature of cultural life, and political rallies and events of national importance provide avenues for such expressions. There are national dance companies in Ghana, Sierra Leone, Senegal, Guinea, Mali, Uganda and Tanzania; African rituals and cere-monies, folk tales, and other verbal arts are being reinterpreted in terms of drama or re-created for the New theatre.

This new development in the arts is being encouraged by the search for an African cultural identity in the world of today and by the urge to re-assess the relevance of the values of traditional Africa to contemporary Africa. In this movement even the Christian Church which has been hostile in many ways to African culture has not lagged behind. Conferences on Christianity and African culture have been held, and positive encouragement is being given to African music.

INTERNATIONAL COOPERATION

It is unnecessary to review the research work which is inspired by this new interest in the African past and in contemporary problems. There is no doubt that there is a new era in African studies, an era in which Africa can collaborate with the rest of the world in the pursuit of knowledge of Africa and in enhancing the meaning of Africa. It is our hope that this new era will see the development of international cooperation, particularly between Africa and the Americas. For it is clear that the study of Africa cannot be isolated from the history of the Americas if we wish to have a true understanding of Africa and its culture. It is in the light of this that in 1962 when the Institute of African Studies of the University of Ghana was formally opened by the Government of Ghana, the Research Fellows of the Institute were charged among other things not to confine their interest to Ghana and Africa:

> You should not stop here. Your work must also include a study
> of the origins and culture of peoples of African descent in the
> Americas and the Caribbean, and you should maintain close relations
> with their scholars so that there may be cross-fertilisation between
> Africa and those who have their roots in her past.

It is this collaboration and cross-fertilisation that we now seek, and I hope that this conference on the Meaning of Africa to Afro-

Americans will result in the formulation of joint research projects that we can fruitfully undertake in African and Afro-American studies. I am sure that we can achieve understanding and enrich our appreciation of African cultures without prejudice to the status of the Afro-American as an American citizen and without prejudice to the political, social, and cultural aspirations of the new African.

2

The "African"

COLIN M. TURNBULL
Virginia Commonwealth University

It is disputable how far we who are not Africans can generalize about "the Africans" as though throughout the length and breadth of that vast continent there were only one people. In political context, generalizations are frequently made, but in social context, we hear more often of diversity rather than unity. Yet there *is* a unity, and a powerful one, that runs through all African societies, all African cultures, and all African peoples; it may well be a unity that links them with the Black Americans in a way that cannot be explained as a mere political convenience.

SURFACE DIFFERENCES AND SPIRITUAL UNITIES

The diversity is plain enough on the surface, but even there it can be misleading. There is a wide and obvious range of physical type, sometimes with extremes such as the difference in height between the adjacent populations of the Tussi, in Rwanda, and the Mbuti hunters of the equatorial forest in Zaire; the tallest and the shortest people in the world living side by side. The Bushmen of the Kalahari have their own special physiological characteristics (such as the epicanthic eye fold and the steatopygic development of the buttocks) that seem to set them apart from all other African peoples. There is a wide and equally obvious variation in skin colour and hair form and other physical characteristics, all of which lend themselves to the facile assertion of diversity. Yet recent work by leading geneticists shows clearly that there is a strong underlying unity linking Bushmen to Pygmies amongst the oldest populations, and linking both of them to the vast bulk of the Black African population, including both the Bantu and non-Bantu speaking peoples of east, west, and central Africa. The

17

connection with the indigenous Berber of North Africa is still not clear, but this does not justify the regrettably common division of Africa into North Africa and Sub-Saharan Africa, as though the one had little to do with the other.

Frequently outward differences in physical type are accompanied by differences in culture, just as striking and sometimes just as extreme. You have, for instance, Pygmies and Bushmen living as gatherers and hunters with a technology virtually still of the Stone Age, a minimal material culture, and little formal social organization, while close by you have sophisticated and powerful African kingdoms and empires, rich in material culture, with an advanced technology and highly complex social systems. But just as there is a genetic unity underlying the outer physiological differences, so I believe there is a vital unity underlying the cultural diversity.

The unity springs in the first part from the history of the continent and of the growth and spread of its population which resulted in an overall diffusion. In the second part, unity springs from the nature of the physical environment which, together with a minimal level of technology, has everywhere tolerated a subsistence economy. Often the environment is abundant and the climate even, making it unnecessary for a complex industrial technology to develop. But everywhere its adequacy depends upon a sympathetic, adaptive response from the human population, a functioning within the totality of fauna and flora as part of the natural world. This has led to a widespread direct dependence of the African upon his environment. Whereas other cultures have, for various reasons, had to develop an industrial technology and have sought increasingly to dominate the environment and control it, the African throughout the continent sees himself as a part of the natural world and adapts himself and his culture, consciously and unconsciously, to its varied demands. This leads to the apparent diversity of cultures into as many cultural types as there are environmental types.

We shall be using this correlation of culture with environment to look at the peoples of Africa. It will help us to perceive the essential fact that the differences are of a totally different order than the similarities, and that both exist side by side. One might almost say that the differences are material and the similarities are spiritual. A fundamental aspect of the unity that runs throughout all African societies and cultures is that the "African" is at one with Nature, and to this extent is at one with himself.

We are still, unfortunately, only able to make intelligent guesses at the distant past when man began in Africa. We do not know for sure where he had his origins; a new find could always be made tomorrow that would upset all existing theories. However, it is indisputable that man did have an early origin (the earliest known as yet) in Africa; the remains of early man have been found from the south to the north. There is evidence that the Pygmies and Bushmen are genetically closest to the first Africans, and certainly their culture has changed the least. For unknown thousands of years people like them must have roamed the continent in small gathering and hunting bands with little need for conflict since the population was small and the environment generous.

During the early days man almost certainly learned to cultivate certain wild plants, at least to the extent known as "vegeculture" where the plant is not domesticated so much as merely conserved, so that it is able to replenish itself and supply a constant source of food for the hunters in their nomadic cycles. Some hunters today even transplant some wild plants, but being nomadic, they cannot stay long enough to fully cultivate them. Early man may also have learned to domesticate dogs for use in hunting. The sharing of common water-holes between wild animals and hunting bands may have led to an almost symbiotic relationship from which arose pastoralism as an alternative way of life. Then there was the dramatic development of true cultivation, partly the development via vegeculture of the domestication of indigenous crops, and partly introduced from the Middle East. These three major economies — hunting and gathering (and fishing), herding, and cultivation — today still form the three major modes of living.

SIMPLICITY DOES NOT EQUAL DEPRIVATION

These economies, together with the non-industrial technology, and apparently bizarre (to those who have not bothered to try to understand them) social systems, have led some to regard Africans, as they have regarded other non-industrial peoples, as backward or "primitive." The ethnocentric nature of such a judgement does not need comment, but it *is* worth pausing for a moment for each of us to consider how *we* would compare the African — his way of life and thought — with ourselves.

For anyone who has not been to Africa and who has been raised in a modern western culture it would be difficult not to feel that the African is in some way deprived. It is natural for instance to think of material poverty, for we habitually think in terms of material wealth. It is also natural to think of illness and shortness of life, for our ideals include good health and long life. It is natural to think of discomfort and hardship, for we value luxury and anything that makes life "easy." But even so, and even given the common misconceptions about Africa that exaggerate such "deprivations," are we *really* any better off; are factors of physical security, luxury, and ease valid criteria of comparison between cultures?

We are undoubtedly richer in material culture; that is, we have larger and more permanent homes (or better, houses, for they are not always homes), infinitely more personal possessions of much greater complexity, and, having a cash economy, we can horde wealth much more easily than say an African farmer who is not living in a cash economy and can store only a limited amount of perishable grain. But think of the attendant worries we have, and how we are caught up in the vicious circle of this year's luxuries becoming next year's necessities, and the insidious demand for a constant "improvement" in the standard of living which merely increases our worries and demands that much more of us. And are we any more comfortable? When we weigh the mental discomfort and insecurity against the excess of material comfort I would say, "No." And anyone who has been on a picnic knows how easily material comforts can be shed, and the sense of relaxation that comes from this sudden simplication of life. Just the fact that the picnic has become a social institution is significant.

As to health, in which respect nearly everyone would claim that our progress over the African is indisputable, is it worth living longer if our lives are not correspondingly richer and happier? Is it worth being preserved by modern medical science as a human vegetable? Or to be thrown into old people's homes by children who cannot be bothered to care for us? Or to die of old age in a material poverty such as is never found in traditional African society where there is always enough because there is never too much? Medical science, moreover, is to a large extent responsible for the disastrous population crisis; destroying the balance between the human population and the rest of the natural world; making man, in a sense, unnatural, and threatening his future existence. The African, in traditional societies, seems to find purposes in life other than to live long in an excess of wealth and comfort, and finds his security in the natural world which includes other human beings, rather than in technology.

With these thoughts in mind let us now look at some specific peoples and cultures and see in what ways they are different from each other and in what ways they are alike. Then we may be in a better position to make a judgement, not only about their way of life, but about our own.

THE FOREST

It is ironic that many Africans today are ashamed of those who still adhere to the old way of life, particularly those who do not dress in western style (or who do not dress at all) and who do not take part in modern economic and political life. They have begun to judge their own people by the non-African standards just described, in terms of a purely western concept of progress. To understand a people or a culture we *must*, if only temporarily, shed that concept.

In the dense equatorial forest that stretches along the west coast and over half way across the continent at the equator, traditional ways of life still thrive and people who live outside the forest regard its inhabitants with a mixture of scorn and respect, as backward and primitive and somehow dangerous. Even within the forest this is so. In the Ituri forest, of northeastern Zaire, farmers who were forced into the forest from the grasslands a few hundred years ago regard the people they found there – the Pygmy hunters – with respect they try to conceal as scorn. The village farmers offer first fruits from their plantations to the very people they pretend to look down upon, and credit them with supernatural powers.

It is the same throughout the world – people who live in forests, or in isolation, or as hermits, are frequently suspect of being in league with the supernatural. And so they are, in a way, for they are living necessarily close to nature, in league with it rather than hostile to it, making do with what it has to offer. This is the source of their power, and of the respect with which they are regarded, perhaps arising out of envy. For them nature offers all the security they need in terms of food, shelter and warmth – man's most basic needs. Instead of devoting additional time and energy so as to acquire a surplus, which in their forest they could easily do, the Pygmy hunters of the Ituri make do with a perfectly comfortable and adequate minimum and devote the rest of their time to the art of living. This does not mean that they hunt for a few hours and then sing and dance for the rest of the day, as if in a kind of cartoon.

TIME, SOCIALIZATION, SECURITY

To live well, to live at peace with one's neighbors, with one's family, requires time and effort just as much as the more basic activities of food getting, building shelters, and making the necessary material artifacts. To live well requires that man should not only live with his neighbors but should know and understand them and share the same *basic* view of life. If there is no time for socialization, if it is all taken up in the effort to amass a larger and larger surplus, then man lives in ignorance of his neighbor, and society becomes a mere agglomeration of individuals, each seeking his own good.

The hunters and gatherers, by maintaining economic need at a minimum, are free to spend most of each day in socialization. This may take the form of visiting neighboring bands, passing the time at their own family hearths, playing with children, discussing any problems that face them as individuals or as a group, telling legends that express their charter for life so that the young learn the moral code while it is being constantly reiterated for the benefit of adults as well. Above all there is time for discussion, and for everyone to participate in it, and in this way not only is the general course of daily activity mapped out, but the more serious disputes are either avoided or settled peaceably, and major disruption is averted.

This is not to say that life is idyllic, for proper discussion can be as taxing as any physical effort. But there is a sense of wholeness and security that seems idyllic to many who live more fragmented lives, beset with a multiplicity of problems and in less security. There is the security, for the hunters, that comes from living *with* nature instead of trying to control and dominate it, and from the knowledge that given a minimum of effort the basic needs of life will always be satisfied. And there is considerable security that derives from having the time and opportunity for a form of socialization that enables all problems and disputes to be talked to a peaceful conclusion.

It would seem that the Africans learned this lesson early, for as the population expanded and life became more complex and more demanding, as man began to oppose the environment by cultivation and domestication, the people retained a closeness to it and preserved a sense of balance, allowing for a social system that was truly social because they had to socialize and were expected to do so. Thus traditionally there are no legal codes or strictly penal systems by which a man can be speedily and summarily judged and punished because of a given action. Each action has to be assessed in context, and the cooperation of all those concerned is demanded. The focus is on justice rather than on law, and this demands the cooperation of society as a whole. It is not relegated to a few specialists and a jury of twelve, who probably know nothing of the people involved and who are not in any way concerned.

ADAPTATION AND OPPOSITION

We may have seemed to have wandered rather far from a description of forest life, but that is not so. This is all the essence of life for those essentially forest people — the Pygmy hunters of the Ituri — and it is an essence that has been preserved throughout African life elsewhere, however much the outer form of life may have changed. Those who have migrated into the forest from outside came as farmers, with a farming technology and social organization, and they found the forest a harsh and hostile environment. The farmers had to attack, cut down, and burn the forest in order to survive, and having done all this they still had to work long and hot days to keep the forest from growing back. No wonder they regard the Mbuti Pygmies with a mixture of fear and respect, watching them live with apparent ease in the cool shade of a forest that seems to protect them just as it seems to oppose the farmers. So the farmers form a ritual association with the hunters and put themselves in accord with nature in this way, using the hunters as a kind of medium. That is, although they are opposing the forest — opposing nature — by cutting it down for their plantations, they still recognize its pre-eminence and submit to it. The forest, its fauna and flora, form the very center of their ideological and conceptual systems, even though their attitude to it is one of hostility rather than one of devotion.

The same environment, then, can offer contrasting possibilities for human occupation. If man submits to it entirely, as do the Pygmies, then there is no need for a complex technology; in fact a complex technology would destroy the almost perfect balance of nature by making it possible, almost inevitable, for the hunters to over-kill and over-gather. As it is, the hunters form an integral part of the total ecological picture, and their very hunting is part of the mechanism by which nature maintains its balance. The Mbuti are, for instance, the prime mechanism by which the otherwise destructive elephant population is kept in check. They themselves are kept in check by a birth control system which, while quite unconscious, none the less, can be seen as a system arising naturally from their way of life and its demands, and from their recognition of the demands of nature. Infantile mortality, sickness and disease, although relatively slight among the Mbuti hunters, also function for them, as for other African populations, as a means of keeping the living population in balance, giving those who survive a better chance of living healthy and productive lives.

The submissive adaptation of the Mbuti hunters means that, for once, the environment really is largely determinant, whereas at a more complex level of technology it is merely influential. At their level of technology the hunters are compelled to live in small hunting bands, and to live a nomadic life, never settling in one place for longer than a month. This obviously has profound repercussions in the total social system which is only paralleled where others, like the Bushmen hunters, have made a similarly submissive adaptation although to a totally different environment — the desert.

THE GRASSLANDS

In looking at the people of the grasslands we find a similar ideological relationship with the natural world. But since the major economies are cattle herding and cultivation, the adaptation to the environment is less submissive than that of the forest hunters. The grasslands of western, eastern, and central Africa permit of a wide range of subsistence activities, and there are still a few small isolated hunting groups. Since the expansion of the population began with the advent of cultivation in the grassland regions, this open land has been taken over progressively by the farmers, often in competition with the herders who have been expanding at the same time, and at the expense of the indigenous hunters.

The grasslands, like the forest, allow at the least for an adequate subsistence economy — sometimes an ample one — given a stable population living at a given level of technology. Again there is no incentive to develop a more complex technology. It would not only be unnecessary, it would be detrimental in its threat to a total social system that has proven itself perfectly satisfactory by providing the maximum sense of security as well as supplying the minimum, at least, in basic needs. The focus again is on human relations rather than on material wealth, for this is where the most fundamental source of security is to be found; human beings, if effectively related to each other in a coherent social system, are the greatest wealth of all, and afford maximum social security. As with the forest hunters, the herders and farmers of the grasslands are satisfied with what might, to us, appear to be minimal comforts and necessities, because they prefer to devote a great deal of time and energy to maintaining an increasingly complex network of human relationships.

ADAPTATION AND OPPOSITION

In the grasslands, as in the forest, there are two opposing ideological systems — that of the herders versus that of the cultivators. Again, the basis of the opposition is economic. It is openly expressed and is sometimes manifest in ritual acts of aggression, which must not be mistaken for hostility. Opposition may, in fact, be a way of avoiding or resolving hostility. And again the opposition is due to a difference in subsistence activity, leading to different concepts of the same environment. For both peoples the environment is central in their thought, but the farmers might be said to be earth-regarding, while the herders are sky-regarding. The classic example of opposition here is that between the Kikuyu and the Masai, in East Africa. The Kikuyu farmers regard the earth — the very soil — as the source of their well-being. It is their duty to cultivate it, to sow, tend, and harvest their crops. Their notions of an after-life are connected with the soil; they wish to be buried in the ground when they die, where their ancestors were buried before them so that they may partake in the earthy after-life. In this way their attention is centered not only on the soil but, since they are relatively sedentary, on specific places, hills or ridges, where their fathers farmed before them. The geography and topography of their homeland plays a central part in their social organization, as well as in their system of religious belief.

The herders, on the other hand, are nomadic and so are less attached to any one specific limited area. Their interest is not in soil, but in grass and water — the sources of life for their cattle. To them it is a desecration to destroy God-given grass in order to plant "unnatural" foods. To the farmers on the other hand the herders are committing a sacrilege by not tilling the land God gave *them* to plant. The herders look to the sky rather than to the ground, as their source of well being, for from the sky comes the rain that brings up the grass and provides their cattle with food and water.

RESOLUTION OF POTENTIAL CONFLICT

Despite ideological and economic oppositions between grassland herders and cultivators, and forest farmers and hunters, there is a unity in that they each focus on the environment, on natural order, and seek to reproduce this order in their own lives. There is also a recognition of the potential hostility that underlies the opposition and which could (and, in times of population expansion, does) become competitive, leading to open aggression. A great deal of time is given to certain social institutions that have in the past all-too-readily been dismissed as "primitive" or "barbaric" but which exist, in fact, to resolve potential conflict. The opposition is admitted and not concealed.

   Sometimes the opposition is resolved by a symbiotic relationship of mutual interdependence, such as existed between the Tussi
herders and their farming Hutu neighbors. The Tussi, as an immigrant group, established political control, but it was not one of
oppression as has been held. That would have been both unnecessary and uneconomic. There was rather an exchange of goods and
services between two specialized groups. The Hutu supplied cereal
and vegetable foods to the Tussi and helped tend their cattle. This
freed the Tussi for military organization, thanks to which both
populations escaped the ravages of slavery, despite repeated
attempts by the Arabs to penetrate the area. The relationship only
broke down into open hostility in recent years due to the imposition of colonial rule; the introduction of new and more simplistic
concepts of "equality"; and the destruction of the traditional
balance of economy and power.
   The Kikuyu and Masai found an alternative resolution to their
opposition. After their initial violent contact they separated from
each other, and each kept to their own adjacent lands. This of
course is only possible where there is enough land, and it requires
that the opposition be maintained by ritual. By preventing
ideological contact in this way physical contact is also avoided,
and this reduces the likelihood of open competition and warfare.
What was often mistaken by colonial authorities for "warfare" was
actually ritual conflict in the form of cattle raiding. The raiding
had both political and economic significance, but most important
it allowed for an open expression of the latent hostility and
maintained the vital opposition while doing a minimum amount of
physical damage to either side. Lives were lost and property
destroyed, but it was little in comparison with what would have
happened had there been open warfare. In fact the institution
might also have served as a form of population control. This may
seem a rather brutal way of looking at it, but our own wars are
frequently fought with far less justification, and with much greater
passion, violence, and loss of life.
   Where there was not enough land to allow for this dual system
to operate, and where the incoming herders have not established
political ascendency as did the Tussi, assimilation is the third way
in which the problem has been resolved, and the peoples of
southern Uganda are one of the best examples. In the inter-
lacustrine kingdoms of this region it is no longer possible to
separate the invaders from the invaded, though every now and
then certain physical characteristics can be seen that are reminis-
cent of different origins. Ideologically they have become one,
though following the colonial era the opposition between the

pastoral north and the predominantly agricultural south was fanned into open hostility for political reasons.

RIVER VALLEYS

It was in the alluvial river valleys that social organization reached its greatest complexity, and material culture and technology developed most fully. That does not mean that life for the people who lived there was any easier, more comfortable, or secure. If great nations, states, and empires arose in this environmental context it was in response to the conjunction of the needs of an expanding population and the opportunities afforded by this particular kind of environment. The rivers afforded an ease of transport and communication not possible overland, and called for a different kind of utilization of the land. The most dramatic example is Egypt, where the arable land is confined to a narrow fertile strip, sometimes no more than half a mile on each side of the river, seldom more than a mile, set in the midst of an arid desert. This demanded a totally different technology involving methods for raising water from both river and wells, and complex irrigation systems. The population settlement pattern was quite unlike that of either the forest or the grassland farmers, and it called for a totally different kind of social system. Once again, however, the ideological center was the natural world; but rather than being found in the earth or the sky, the river and the sun were the prime foci of attention. The level of political control demanded under such conditions, with a high density of population, was much greater than elsewhere and here it is relevant to look back, once more, to the forest farmers as representing an early form of social organization in which certain basic elements were established and seem to have been perpetuated no matter how society developed in other contexts.

With the hunters there was little need for formal political control; problems were easily settled by group discussion. But it was still necessary to define the social unit within which man owed certain obligations and held certain rights. The biological family provided the natural unit that man took as his model, just as he used natural order elsewhere as a model for social organization. But the biological family, in the social realm, was *only* a model; it was defined in flexible, social terms, not in rigid biological terms. Much emphasis has been laid on "kinship" systems in Africa, and it is often forgotten that really they are social systems following a kinship model, and that it is social rather than biologi-cal relationships that are being defined.

With the Mbuti Pygmies, for instance, the band is the social family, and the biological family serves as a model in that the terms for "mother" and "father" are applied by an Mbuti to any member of his band who is of approximately the same age of either of his biological parents. More important still, he owes almost exactly the same obligations to all those whom he addresses as father or mother as he does to his biological parents. So also with the other age levels, for grandparents and children. Everyone in the band is classified according to one of these "kinship" terms, and social behavior is accordingly determined. This is the basis of the social system, and while there are many types of family that arise elsewhere in response to different needs, tracing descent from both sides or from one side or the other, the function remains the same throughout. Even in the most highly developed states and empires, the supreme ruler is frequently addressed as "father" or "grandfather," because the classificatory system is extended, ultimately, to embrace the entire nation as a single family, ruled by the representative of the founding ancestor (who is, therefore, a classificatory father).

At this level the family is built up from the nuclear family into extended families, lineages and clans; each an enlargement of the basic model, and each determining a different order of social rela-tionships. The emphasis is on the *social* personality of the member, rather than his separate existence as an individual, and this is what provides all traditional African societies not only with order (without law), but with a powerful unity arising from a common sentiment and a common sense of origin and a recogni-tion of mutual interdependence.

THE DESERT

In the same way that the family serves as a model for wider social relationships, so does the social organization of man at the simplest level of technology — living as a hunter and gatherer — seem to serve as a model, in Africa, for the more complex forms of social organization. The desert, which superficially would seem to be the most uncompromising environment of all, provides examples of both extremes of complexity and simplicity. In the Kalahari desert the Bushmen roam, much as do the forest Pygmies, in nomadic hunting bands. Their technology is minimal and their social organization informal. Their adaptation to the desert is a submissive one — that is to say they accept what it offers and adapt their life style accordingly. Of particular note is the fact that, as with the Pygmies, there is an almost total avoidance of individual leadership or any form of centralized authority. Authority is dispersed throughout the band according to sex and age, each with its own sphere of influence though without actual control. In this way the band as a whole is *necessarily* a cooperative unit. Any assertion of individual leadership would destroy this essential cooperativeness which, in the marginal subsistence economy of the Bushmen, is their major source of security. Their sense of sociality is so great, in fact, that if a person becomes injured or ill while on the long trek from one waterhole to another he will voluntarily remain behind, almost certainly to die, so that the others can go on unimpeded and reach the next waterhole before being overcome by thirst. Waterholes may be three days apart, and three days is the maximum that one can survive, in the desert, without water.

In the North African desert the Berber live a very different life, as camel and goat herders, with some seasonal mountain farming done by a caste of serfs. While they spend some time each year in the mountains, overlooking the desert immediately below, their world is that of the desert over which they wander for the rest of the year, in small familial bands with their herds, in search of pasture and water. This dual form of existence — a form of transhumance — calls for a very special form of social organization that provides for order while the Berber are fragmented and dispersed in their desert environment, and also provides for order when they are in their highly concentrated mountain settlements. The situation is further complicated by pressure on the land and, in the past, by the threat of attack by neighbors and by the constant menace of the Arab invaders.

Organization for warfare has become a paramount necessity, yet the Berber have managed to keep remarkably efficiently to the simpler model we have seen established in hunting societies, forest and desert. Their kinship system is much more complex, to allow for the much greater complexity of interpersonal and intergroup relations. But instead of centralizing authority into a hereditary kingship (using the "father" model) as was done elsewhere, the Berber developed an electoral system whereby authority is again dispersed and rotated through various segments of the tribe. Geography as well as kinship is used to define the segments so that they cross-cut each other and prevent any abuse of authority. In this way no one family and no one segment can amass power for long enough to abuse it, yet power and centralization are provided for, as required by the military needs. The system allows easily for the annual fragmentation of the tribe as it disperses into the desert.

Even within the hereditary kingdoms in Africa, where power is centralized in a much more permanent manner, abuse is checked effectively by divers social institutions, and it is frequently said that "the King is to be eaten," meaning that any wealth he amasses is for the consumption of the nation. The king's granaries, filled by tribute, are for distribution in times of famine, and any failure in this obligation or any abuse of his position of authority can lead to his removal from office and replacement by classificatory "kin."

SUMMARY

Wherever one looks in Africa, at whatever level of organization, then, certain fundamental similarities emerge. There is a focus on social personality rather than on individual identity. This is learned in the normal way as a member of a biological family which is itself almost invariably a cooperative economic unit. This same family also serves as a model for wider social relationships, ultimately embracing the whole society be it a band, tribe, or nation. This feeling of "kinship" is complemented by a sense of spiritual unity brought about by the focus of ideological attention upon the natural environment on which is modeled concepts of social and intellectual order. This all leads to societies that are, while by no means perfect or free of disorder, essentially democratic and essentially egalitarian. They are, however, relatively small societies or they are, in the case of the larger states and nations, broken down into smaller societies within which the concept of familial unity is at least approached by the actual knowledge of biological kinship. Almost everywhere you travel within such a society, you are likely to find biological kin, each with its own separate circle of familial economic and political relationships. So everywhere you go, the myth of the tribe as a single biological unit is reinforced by a measure of actuality, and the ideal of familial relationships of obligation and privilege — and affection — is maintained.

It is in part a measure of the size of modern western society, and of some eastern nations, that we have lost this "natural" social order where physical coercion is unnecesary because of the inner, moral coercion that springs from a live sense of social identity and unity. And it is in part a result of our enormous technological complexity, which we are pleased to call progress, that we have been forced to abandon a social personality in favour of the new ideal, individuality, with security resting in a bank balance rather than in one's neighbors and kin. These are some of the essential differences between the traditional African way of life and ours, and this is the major lesson to be learned from a study of the peoples of Africa.

3

The Physical Environment of Tropical Africa: The Human Assessment

ROBERT W. STEEL
University of Liverpool

ENVIRONMENTAL DETERMINISM

Geographers at one time saw man as very much at the mercy and the behest of physical circumstances. Not everyone accepted completely the doctrine of 'determinism' — the belief that physical conditions determined, controlled and dominated human life in all its aspects. Not all geographers or other students of human nature subscribed to what the American writer, Ellen Churchill Semple, stated at the beginning of her book, *Influences of Geographic Environment* (1911):

> Man is the product of the earth's surface. This means not merely that he is a child of the earth, dust of her dust; but that the earth has mothered him, fed him, set him tasks, directed his thoughts, confronted him with difficulties that have strengthened his body and sharpened his wits, given him his problems of navigation or irrigation, and at the same time whispered hints for their solution. She has entered into his bone and tissue, into his mind and soul.

Nevertheless many people have seen mankind as being very far from being a free agent, and very much subject to the influence if not the control of the natural conditions of his environment. Geographers must certainly concern themselves a great deal with the nature of man's assessment of his physical environment and the extent to which he succeeds in adjusting or adapting himself to the circumstances of the habitat in which he finds himself.

AN ALTERNATIVE

There is a very different point of view, one that has sometimes been referred to as 'possibilism'. 'Nature,' one famous French geographer, Vidal de la Blache, put it, 'is never more than an

33

adviser'. Another Frenchman, Lucien Febvre, encouraged scholars to refer to this point of view as the 'possibilist' point of view by stating bluntly, 'There are no necessities, but everywhere possibilities; and man as master of these possibilities is the judge of their use.' Many geographers reckon that no longer can it be said that Nature drives man along a particular road, but it offers him a range of opportunities from among which he is free to select. Increasingly we talk very boldly — and perhaps rashly — of 'Man's conquest of Nature' or more reasonably of 'Man's role in changing the face of the earth.'

The latter is the title of a volume dedicated to 'the countless generations . . . whose skillful hands and contriving brains have made the whole planet their home' and it makes one very convinced of man's ability to transform the appearance of whole landscapes — by, for example, initiating the irrigation of the Nile Valley, by the draining of the English Fenland, by the opening-up of the American West, or by the building of large towns and cities in areas that were once uninhabited.

When one endeavours to apply these concepts to, say, the problems of the Third World, which is situated very largely within the Tropics, one quickly recognizes that the truth lies somewhere between the rigidity of the deterministic interpretation and what sometimes seem the excesses of the possibilistic point of view. With American landings on the moon, and with the development of remote sensing and similar technological innovations, it becomes easy to imagine that the economic opening-up of areas in the tropics calls for little more than the injection of American dollars — or Russian roubles — in the appropriate projects or the employment of Chinese workers to build new railways or to create vast rice plantations. Yet how mistaken such ideas may sometimes be has become very obvious in tropical Africa during the post-war years with its new concepts of aid and development and the greatly increased involvement of the West in the social and economic, if not in the political, development of African countries. There have been all too many failures and fiascos during this period, often at great financial cost. But despite this, there still lingers in the minds of some an almost overwhelming confidence in what science and technology — along with political determination — can achieve.

EARLY BARRIERS

In tropical Africa, indeed, the physical environment plays an important part in influencing and delaying economic development and in inhibiting some forms of progress altogether, and it has always had this effect. There is no doubt whatsoever that the opening-up of the continent was delayed, at least from a European point of view, for a very long period, by the nature of the physical conditions. The great land mass was a formidable barrier between Europe and the fabulous riches of the East. From early in the fifteenth century Portuguese seamen pushed gradually southward round the great bulge of the northern half of the continent and established contact with the peoples of western Africa.

Towards the end of the fifteenth century the Portuguese rounded the Cape of Good Hope and reached the west coast of India across the Indian Ocean and later their routes were followed by the seamen of other European nations. But apart from the occasional traveller and Jesuit and other missionaries, very few made any attempt to find their way into the interior. The European reluctance to penetrate the continent was not only because this would have been a digression, turning them from their major objectives of reaching the East, but also because physical circumstances deterred them. Some of the rivers reached the sea through impenetrable and unhealthy deltas; many of them had rapids and falls not many miles upstream where they tumbled over the edge of the plateau that in most parts of Africa is relatively near to the coast; and in general there were marked seasonal fluctuations in the volume of water in the stream beds so that navigation was difficult at times of low water and often dangerous when the rivers were in flood. Distances over the plateau were generally great and travel was inhibited by the often dense nature of the vegetation, while elsewhere the interior was said to consist largely of barren and inhospitable deserts. There was also a well-developed belief that the inhabitants were hostile to anyone coming in from outside.

All in all, therefore, Africa appeared to be a continent to be circumnavigated not penetrated, to be by-passed not explored; and, although circumstances have changed enormously through the centuries, some of the physical conditions of Africa remain major deterrents to the economic development and social progress in the second half of the twentieth century. The constraints imposed by the environment, particularly the physical environment, upon the progress of the young African nations are very real: some indeed may be insuperable. One of the greatest challenges to the western world during the last quarter of the twentieth century is to discover the ways and means whereby the obstacles to development in tropical Africa can be overcome by a combination of economic aid and political understanding that in no way harms the national sovereignty of the states.

CONSTRAINTS OF THE
PHYSICAL ENVIRONMENT

An assessment of the physical environment of tropical Africa is thus a prerequisite for an understanding of the obstacles that face mankind in this part of the world in their efforts not merely to exist but also to enjoy a reasonable standard of living and to improve the quality of life and the prospects that they and their children may reasonably expect. There is a tendency to emphasize the uniformity of conditions over much of Africa and to equate with this a similarity of the human response to the nature of the environment. But this is a generalization that is justified only in part, and increasingly students of Africa are stressing the very considerable diversity of environmental conditions and the types of economy and society that have developed over many centuries.

TERRAIN LIMITATIONS

Of all the continents, Africa is the most massive in that it covers an enormous land area, much of it forming a huge plateau that rises sharply from a generally narrow coastal plain. There has, however, been considerable elevation and depression of the plateau, and this has resulted in great strains that give rise to some of the continent's most conspicuous physical features. These include the Great Rift Valley of East Africa and its associated volcanoes (the highest, Kilimanjaro, reaching 19,565 feet above sea-level) and, in West Africa, the volcanic peak of Mount Cameroon (13,353 feet). Elevation has also been responsible for the isolation of several large inland seas or lakes which have since disappeared wholly or in large part. There are remnants of such lakes still in the upper Niger Valley, the Lake Chad region, and the central parts of the Congo Basin. (Figure 3-1)

There is considerable diversity over the plateau because of its range in altitude, and its continuity is much more conspicuous in southern and eastern Africa than over most of the west and north. Only limited areas exceed 6,000 feet, though these are especially important because of the varied ecological conditions that they offer and because of the effect that they have had upon economic development in general and upon white settlement in particular. At the other extreme, there are very few real lowland areas that are 600 feet or less above sea-level; and these, in contrast to low-lying regions in other parts of the world, are normally very difficult to develop in the tropics because of excessively high temperatures, the inadequacy of their drainage, or the dense inpenetrable nature of their vegetation. A high proportion of the

Figure 3-1. General Reference Map of Africa.

total area of the continent lies between 2,000 and 6,000 feet above sea-level and consists of the hard, resistant and geologically ancient rocks, usually with their thin and unproductive soil cover, that are particularly characteristic of Africa. The existence of a sharp and steep plateau rim has often checked the movement of travellers and created problems for the railway builders. Most of the rivers, too, are not easily navigable especially as they often fall over the plateau edge at no great distance from the ocean so that their lower courses are often comparatively short.

CLIMATIC VARIATION

Climatically, tropical Africa presents many problems in relation to farming activities and general economic development. Since most of the inter-tropical parts of the continent are warm or hot during the day almost throughout the year, the climatic element that determines the rate at which plants grow and the degree of seasonal change is generally rainfall not temperature. Extensive areas have average totals of more than 100 inches a year, and a very high proportion of the inter-tropical belt receives 40 or more inches each year. One of the wettest places on earth, certainly at sea-level, is Debundja situated near the Gulf of Guinea at the foot of Mount Cameroon and receiving more than 400 inches per annum. At the other extreme is the Sahara in northern Africa and the similar, though smaller, desert and semi-arid regions of southern Africa, where several years sometimes pass without any real rainfall and where average figures are not only very low but have little or no meaning in terms of settlement or agriculture. It is essential, therefore, to consider seasonal distribution as well as annual totals. In consequence, areas with between 20 and 40 inches of rainfall a year, amounts that are, by the standards of most temperate regions, more than adequate for cultivation or for the keeping of livestock, may suffer from severe drought, in some years at least, because of the markedly seasonal distribution of the rainfall or the great year-to-year fluctuations in the total fall or the intensity of either the evaporation or the runoff. A high proportion of the annual total comes in a few torrential downpours that generally occur towards the end of a prolonged dry season when the surface of the ground is sunbaked and very hard, so that little rain penetrates the soil. Worse still, the rain may wash away such soil as there is and aggravate what is already one of tropical Africa's most serious problems, that of soil erosion.

Variability of rainfall has been recognized in recent years as one of the most significant aspects of climatology over much of

Africa and there has, in consequence, been considerable study of it as a basis for the planning of more efficient agriculture and more reliable economic development. An outstanding illustration of the effect of unreliable rainfall is provided by the costly failure, in the years immediately following the end of the Second World War, of the much-publicized East African Groundnut Scheme. The inability of the programme to produce large quantities of groundnuts was based on inadequate planning and on a variety of inter-related factors, but far and away the most damaging was the lack of rainfall. In the Kongwa district of central Tanganyika (as Tanzania was then known), *average* rainfall would almost certainly have been adequate for the successful cultivation of groundnuts. Unfortunately the critical first years of the scheme were all exceptionally dry and the lack of rainfall in successive seasons was directly related to the failure of the crops.

VEGETATIONAL CONTRASTS

Natural vegetation, like climate, is much more varied than generalizations about the uniformity of physical conditions in tropical Africa might suggest. The types of vegetation often reflect the amount and seasonality of the rainfall. Thus equatorial or tropical rainforest is characteristic of the wet areas of the Guinea Coast and the Congo Basin. Its prolific and luxuriant growth suggests greater fertility than is in fact the case over most of the forested area; and, in contrast to a widely-held belief, the area covered by such rainforest, with its tall trees with great buttress roots and an almost continuous canopy of foliage, is less than 10 per cent of the total land surface of the continent. Toward the tropics, and in East Africa across the Equator as well, the usual type of natural vegetation is savanna, a term that covers a wide variety of grasslands. Adjacent to the forest, quite closely-spaced trees surrounded by grass are common but as the length and intensity of the dry season increase the woodland is impoverished and the trees are not only more scattered but are often stunted, the dominant ones being those best able to stand the bush fires that frequently rage through the savanna, especially at times of extreme drought. In still drier areas the grassland is virtually treeless, and this in turn merges into the thorn scrub of the desert margins. In the desert proper, vegetation is generally restricted to the oases where underground water supplies are available. After the occasional rainstorm there may be an ephemeral cover of grass and flowering plants that rapidly wither with the renewed onset of dry and hot conditions. Beyond the desert there are the areas with Mediterranean climate and its associated vegetation in Northwest

Africa and in the Cape Province of the Republic of South Africa, where the environmental conditions are completely different from those characteristic of most of inter-tropical Africa.

SOIL LIMITATIONS

The soils of Africa, like its climatic and vegetational conditions, provide a varied picture though it is noteworthy that more than one-quarter of the total surface of the continent is virtually devoid of soil — principally in the desert areas. Over the remainder, the nature of the soils varies considerably from zone to zone so that generalization is difficult. There are no great areas covered with highly productive soils as in the wheat-producing areas, of Canada or of the U.S.S.R., nor are there large irrigable lowland areas such as the Indo-Gangetic plains in southern Asia. The actual soil cover is often very thin and there is a liability to erosion, particularly in those areas where the end of the dry season is marked by torrential storms that can do enormous damage in a matter of minutes. Many of the soils lack plant nutrients and are especially deficient in potassium, magnesium, and phosphorus. When clearings are made in the forest or in the savanna grasslands for cultivation, the soil's fertility is rapidly used up since most of the valuable nutrients are contained in the vegetation and in the surface layer of humus or organic material. Furthermore, the nature of the rainfall and the high temperature of the rainwater often combine to cause the leaching of the upper layers or horizons, where nutrients would be available to the plant cover, and to give rise to a 'hardpan' that cannot easily be penetrated by the roots of plants.

Soils do little, therefore, to mitigate the physical circumstances of many parts of tropical Africa, and so those Africans who are engaged in the cultivation of the soil — a very high proportion of the total — face a very severe series of environmental hazards with which they cope to only a limited extent in the absence of any great advance in the application of modern scientific methods to their special needs. Those concerned with the keeping of livestock need an adequate water supply and a sufficient quantity of fodder for their flocks and herds — with a willingness to wander in search of these necessities, particularly during the dry season.

THE TSETSE FLY

Livestock keepers are also faced by a further problem, one that is peculiar to inter-tropical Africa, the threat of trypanosomiasis in animals. This disease is borne by the tsetse fly *(Glossina)*, the incidence of which is widely spread throughout tropical Africa both in the forested areas and over much of the wooded savanna. Tsetse live and breed wherever temperature and humidity are high, and they flourish particularly where the bush or undergrowth is thick and shady. The parasite they carry enters the bloodstream of animals — wild game as well as domestic livestock — it weakens the beasts and eventually causes their death. In consequence, domestic animals can barely survive in most of the tsetse-infested areas in both West and East Africa, where, for example, it is reckoned that two-thirds of Tanzania and five-eighths of Zambia are tsetse-infested.

Apart from the absence of meat and milk from the common diet in such areas, it is impossible without domestic stock to encourage the development of mixed farming whereby the soil fertility of cropped areas is maintained by the application of animal manure. The tsetse is, therefore, rightly regarded as one of the greatest scourges of modern Africa, and much scientific and veterinary effort has been devoted to its eradication, so far with only limited results.

HAZARDS TO HUMAN OCCUPANCE

The tsetse is also responsible for sleeping sickness in human beings though deaths from this cause have been substantially reduced in recent years. In tropical Africa there are, however, many other diseases that are responsible for enormous losses of life and particularly for the high rate of child mortality and the generally low expectation of life in many communities. As medical and other health services become more widespread and more effective, the situation may change, though the incidence of poor health is likely to remain high, especially so long as it is matched by a relatively low standard of living. There are many and varied reasons for this state of affairs. The common diet, for example, is generally lacking in protein and often has an excess of carbohydrates. A diet that is far from nourishing, and a food supply that is at times as short in quantity as it is lacking in quality, combine to make people, especially children, far less resistant to disease than would be the case if they were better and more adequately fed.

It must be remembered too that the proportion of children under the age of fifteen is exceptionally high in many of these countries (often a half or more of the total). This means too that the rate of populaton growth is nearly everywhere high with an annual rate of increase of between 2 and 3 per cent which results in the total population doubling in a period of less than thirty years. There is, in consequence, an ever-increasing demand for food, a demand that cannot always be met in terms of either amount or diversity because of the generally simple methods of farming practised.

There are some illnesses that are rarely themselves the cause of death in a patient, yet they may be responsible for keeping a person permanently below par in such a way that he becomes a ready victim for other diseases that, in different circumstances, he might be able to resist. In tropical Africa the outstanding complaint of this nature is malaria which is caused by the bite of the *anopheles* mosquito which, like the tsetse fly, abounds over many parts of the continent. Many young children suffer from malaria at regular intervals – perhaps every three or four days – though as they become teenagers they seem to acquire some sort of immunity to the mosquito, but their general state of poor health makes them very liable to succumb to other illnesses, some of them of a fatal nature. Perhaps it is not surprising, therefore, that the *anopheles* is sometimes described as the greatest killer in tropical Africa. Paradoxically, it has also been called the 'saviour' of West Africa because of its deterrent effects upon European settlement in that part of the continent. In parts of East and South Africa, climatic and other conditions favoured the appropriation of land and agricultural colonization by Europeans in areas such as the Kenya Highlands, some of the more elevated areas in Tanzania, and the plateau districts in Zambia, and in Rhodesia. It is not without significance that political independence after the Second World War came first to West Africa where there was no major European settlement. By contrast, independence in eastern and southern Africa was delayed if not deterred by the complications arising from the tensions and competition between Africans and Europeans.

PROSPECTS FOR DEVELOPMENT

Varied though the physical conditions throughout the length and breadth of the continent of Africa may be, it will be clear that they do not provide an environment in which mankind can flourish easily and make rapid economic progress. Analysts of the past suggest that famine and epidemics controlled population numbers so that a balance was maintained between man and his physical environment. Today epidemics are controlled by the development of health services, and famine is generally avoided by the organization of food collection and distribution as and when the need arises. But other problems — such as the rapid increase in the growth of the total population and the increasing tendency towards urbanization — appear and then intensify as the years go by. The human assessment of the physical environment in tropical Africa should never underestimate the strength of the constraints, even when ways and means for modifying or circumventing them can be seen.

Unfortunately there has been a tendency to ignore or to underestimate the role played by physical conditions among those who study Africa and Africans, especially by those who see development solely in terms of capital investment, the mechanization of farming, or the injection of technical aid or expertise from outside the continent. Those who look realistically at the situation must recognize that the prospects for many of the developing countries in these parts of the world are disappointing and that the rate of economic growth is likely to be low and not in any way commensurate with the rate of population growth that is almost everywhere very high. Since the opportunities for the further exploitation of mineral deposits appear to be fairly limited, outside certain favoured areas such as the Copperbelt of Zambia or the oil-fields of Nigeria, and Africa seems unlikely to become a major centre for manufacturing industry in the forseeable future, it would seem reasonable to assume that future economic development would continue to depend mainly upon agriculture, including the growing of crops and the rearing of livestock. Yet it is precisely in these fields of activity that so many environmental obstacles are encountered, as has been stressed in this chapter and is elaborated elsewhere in this volume. But unless some at least of these difficulties can be effectively surmounted, Africa will have little chance of maintaining even its present generally low standards of living, let alone of coping with rapid population growth or of making a greater contribution to the economic wealth of the world as a whole.

What must be stressed in any study of African problems is the reality of the problems that must be faced by those who are responsible for political affairs and for the organization of economic and social development. How real these problems are can be readily learned by the plotting of certain spatial distributions on a world map or by seeking out the same information in an atlas. Gross National Product, for example, can be a very useful index of the wealth of a people (in a material sense at least), and a world distribution map indicates very clearly that there is a poor and much less developed Third World, with very low scores in Latin America, most parts of Africa, and in monsoon Asia and the

Far East (apart from Japan), and that the rest of the world enjoys much greater affluence and prosperity.

Many other maps indicate the same contrast. There is, for example, the high incidence of disease, coupled with a relative lack of medical and health facilities, in many parts of the tropics. The same areas have inadequate diets that lack protective and energy values — the daily intake of calories is much below the world average. Reference has previously been made to the high proportion of children under the age of fifteen. There will be consequences for governments in terms of educational, health, and other social service services, and in relation to the provision of employment as well as the obvious demographic outcome of a rapid increase in population in the next two or three generations. The later trend will be largely unaffected in the early years by family planning programmes, however well organized, and no matter how strongly supported by governments. Economic distribution maps will reveal further problems of the Third World in Africa such as the general lack of mineral deposits and of manufacturing industry, and the tremendously high percentage of the working population engaged in agricultural activities. Were African agriculture highly organized and markedly productive, it might not matter that in nearly every country at least 65 per cent (and sometimes as many as 90 per cent) of the people are engaged in farming. However, it must be remembered that Africa's total agricultural contribution to world supplies is generally only small (even including commodities that are special to the tropics such as cocoa, sisal, and some types of oil-seed) and that most of the production is of a subsistence character whereby the needs of little more than the immediate family are usually met from all the work done on the family farm plots.

HOPE THROUGH EDUCATION

Tropical Africa presents us with a host of problems, physical, sociological, economic, and political. Perhaps in education — not only in the narrower but in the widest sense of the term — there lie some of the greatest hopes for the future of Africa and its peoples. This essay has sought to stress the importance of the limitations imposed in many directions by the nature of the physical conditions prevailing over much of the tropical parts of the continent. But there are ways of surmounting some at least of these obstacles, partly by the application of modern scientific and technological methods, but also by increasing the ordinary African farmer's awareness and understanding of his environment. This can be done at all educational levels from the rural school to the Faculty of Agriculture or of Georgraphy in the university or other institutes of higher education. There have, of course, been too many failures, some of which have been studied in detail such as the East African Groundnut Scheme and the Mokwa Project in Nigeria. There has often seemed to be a 'false start in Africa' to use the title of a book by the distinguished French agronomist, René Dumont (1966). Progress has in many areas been disappointingly and frustratingly slow with the introduction of new crops, the diversification of cash crops, the use of artificial fertilizers, the development of mixed farming, and the encouragement of cooperative enterprises. Yet overall there are signs that man is learning increasingly to cooperate with nature as well as to understand her more fully; and possibly there is a greater appreciation of the possibilities for international cooperation and, in particular, for the closer association of the more developed and the less developed countries whether through the World Bank and the Specialized Agencies of the United Nations Organization or through a continuation of the economic and political links of earlier years.

How vitally important are these problems of development in areas where development is not always easily organized was recognized by two international statesmen both of whom died in North America during the last few days of 1972. Mr. Lester Pearson, Prime Minister of Canada from 1963 to 1968, and later chairman of the World Bank's study of world development that produced the Pearson Report published in 1969 as *Partners in Development,* saw clearly the dangers if nothing was done to encourage development in every possible way in tropical Africa as in other parts of the Third World. 'No problem faced by mankind,' he wrote, 'is in the long run more menacing than the division of the world into opposing camps of rich and poor.' Harry S. Truman, President of the United States of America from 1945 to 1952, and the instigator of the Marshall Aid programme that rehabilitated Europe after the Second World War, equally recognized the existence of the rich world/poor world dilemma twenty years earlier when he addressed the American people in 1949 and said:

> ... we must embark on a bold new program for making the benefits of our scientific advances and industrial progress available for the improvement and growth of underdeveloped areas. More than half the people of the world are living in conditions approaching misery. Their food is inadequate. They are victims of disease. Their economic life is primitive and stagnant. Their poverty is a

handicap and a threat both to them and to more prosperous areas. For the first time in history humanity possesses the knowledge and the skill to relieve the sufferings of these people.

These two men by their utterances highlight a series of problems that will remain with us for many years but are more likely to be solved by speedy and resolute action than by continued neglect, for only by human initiative and determination can some of the physical problems of the Third World in Africa be mitigated even if they cannot be wholly resolved.

4

Population in Africa South of the Sahara

WILLIAM A. HANCE
Columbia University

The subject of population is of such pervasive importance that it warrants particular attention in this study of Africa South of the Sahara. Analysis of agricultural systems, rural-urban relations, urbanization, economic and social infrastructural needs, economic growth and development, and other topics requires examination of population levels and dynamics. The population factor also intrudes in the cultural and political realms in such phenomena as inter-ethnic (tribal and racial) relations, separation and segregation in rural and urban areas, religious rivalries, political antagonisms and pretensions, integration of nation states, and cooperation among nations. Indeed, the ramifications of the subject form a series of interwoven systems of such complexity as to challenge the finest of minds.

In a brief chapter the reader can only be given an introduction to some aspects of the subject. It is appropriate first to look at the estimated population total for the region and to discuss the accuracy of this and other demographic data on Africa. There follows a discussion of the question – does Africa have too few or too many people? The next section presents data regarding population dynamics – fertility, mortality, and migration – which determine the rate of population growth. Next, the complex impacts of population growth are studied. And finally, there is a brief look at the distributional patterns of population in Africa South of the Sahara.

THE TOTAL POPULATION

The total population of Africa South of the Sahara, which comprises some 48 separate political units – 41 on the mainland

49

and 7 in large (Madagascar) and small (Comoros, Seychelles, Mauritius, Reunion, etc.) island appurtenances – is estimated at about 298 million in mid-1972.* This is about 80 per cent of the population of the continent and 7.9 per cent of the estimated total for the world.

In fact, nobody knows what the total population of sub-Saharan Africa is because the data vary in validity from country to country. In more-developed countries of the world, demographic data are secured from periodic censuses, usually accompanied by more detailed samples, and from birth and death registrations which are required by law. Even then, estimates may be in error (the 1960 U.S. Census total is thought to have been 5 per cent below the actual total). In Africa South of the Sahara only Mauritius has an effective registration system; elsewhere data on fertility and mortality must be calculated from less satisfactory sources. The main reliance for population totals is on periodic censuses, but many of these, particularly in the francophone countries, are taken on a sample basis (not infrequently a 5 per cent sample), and a number of countries have never had a census.

Furthermore, census-taking in Africa is beset by numerous difficulties which affect the accuracy of the results. It is often difficult, for example, to recruit an adequate number of qualified enumerators. To offset this handicap censuses are sometimes held over several days, weeks, or months whereas a count should ideally be as nearly simultaneous as possible. One way of approximating this ideal is to declare a given day, preferably an easily remembered one such as a holiday, as "census day" and to ask respondents to recall who was in the household on that day even though the enumeration may take place some days later.

Other difficulties include: the inadequacy of base maps or aerial photographs making full coverage less than certain; shortage of qualified central staffs slowing the compilation of data and reducing the amount of valuable information actually extracted; failure to collect data so as to permit international comparisons, despite efforts by the U. N. and other agencies; and lack of understanding by some of those being enumerated.

In the past most African censuses have proved to be undercounts not only because of the difficulties just noted but also because many people avoided being enumerated under the suspicion that the purpose of the census was to increase taxes, reduce

---

*Demographic data are taken or projected from: U. N. *Demographic Yearbook* and the U. N. *Statistical Yearbook 1970* (New York, 1971), Population Reference Bureau, *1971 World Population Data Sheet*, and from recent censuses.

polygyny, secure work crews or military recruits, or for some other unwanted goal.

To avoid such undercounts, more recent censuses have been conducted after campaigns designed to inform citizens regarding the value and purposes of demographic enumerations, including their use in the allocation of funds for schools and other social services and for local roadbuilding, and for the determination of political representation. The lesson was learnt too well prior to the 1962 Nigerian Census, which resulted in a serious overcount in some areas. The census became involved in regional politics related importantly to ethnic rivalries and the resultant acrimony even threatened to disrupt the Federation. The 1962 Census was declared null and void and another was taken in 1963; although it has been declared to be the official count, it is considered by some to have given a higher overcount than that of 1962, one of at least 10 per cent.

Despite the many shortcomings, however, censuses in most countries are becoming more and more accurate, and knowledge of African demography will be greatly increased by the current round of censuses. A number of countries are trying to institute compulsory registration of vital statistics though it is realized that it will take years to perfect the operation. In the meantime, experts have devised valuable methods of estimating fertility and mortality rates from incomplete data, and the increased attention being given to the study of population is gradually broadening and deepening the range of information available. Nevertheless, it is apparent that population figures for African countries must be used with considerable caution.

DOES AFRICA HAVE TOO FEW OR TOO MANY PEOPLE?

Questions parallel to this are increasingly being asked in both the more- and less-developed areas of the world. Although very considerable attention has been given to assessment of the population problems of the very densely populated countries of east and south Asia, the question is also pertinent to Africa, despite the common assumption that the continent is *underpopulated.*

The assumption that Africa does not have too many people has frequently been derived by reference to average or crude density figures. (Figure 4-1.) Africa has a lower crude density than any inhabited continent except Australia — about 31.8 person per square mile in mid-1972. But this figure is a meaningless and dangerously misleading one. It is more important to know what

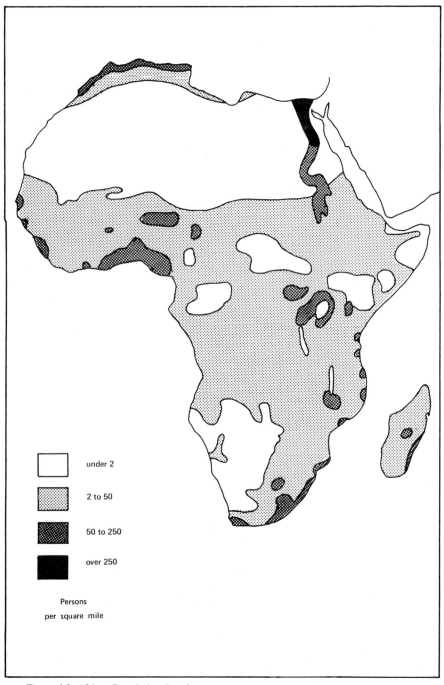

Figure 4-1. African Population Density.

densities people are actually experiencing. In West Africa, for example, only about a sixth of the population lives at or below the crude density, while about two thirds lives at densities more than double the average, and over half of these at densities above 300 persons per square mile. But density figures mean very little unless they are related to carrying-capacity of the land or the stage of economic development. Three persons per square mile can be too many in arid areas, while rich alluvial or volcanic soils with adequate water can support several hundreds of people per square mile at relatively high standards. The Netherlands, with a diversified economy, supports about 840 persons per square mile, a density which would spell hunger and poverty in a less-developed economy with a high percentage of its population in the subsistence sector. The main utility of density figures is in comparative descriptions of population distributions on a regional, not continental scale, though it could be said that unusually high densities in an area might at least warrant a closer look to see whether pressure exists.

Providing an answer to the question — does Africa have too few or too many people? — requires a broad range of information, not just on a national basis but for regions and sub-regions within countries. One needs detailed information on physical factors which affect agricultural production (climate, soils, vegetation, landforms, hydrology, plant and animal pests, and diseases, etc.), on mineral resources, and on the absorptive capacity of the non-agricultural sectors of the economy.

Another problem relates to certain conceptual difficulties. The words *overpopulation* and *underpopulation*, for example, imply that there is some more optimum level. But such an optimum population is difficult to define since it can be based on widely divergent notions regarding an acceptable standard of living; the definition will change with changing technology and stage of growth. Furthermore it is extremely difficult to control population dynamics to achieve a desired optimum level.

Measuring environmental potential is also extremely difficult unless one has information secured from detailed scientific instrumentation (Porter 1970: 187-217). And even if one had such data it would be unrealistic to use it for an area without reference to the technologic skills, social organization, and aspirations of the peoples in that area.

I have tried elsewhere to develop a method to provide at least a preliminary or approximate notion of how much of an area and what proportion of its population are affected *at a given time* by pressure on the land and in urban areas (Hance 1970: 387-89,

417-18). It is based on the proposition that such pressure is revealed by a number of "indicators," given below:

1. soil deterioration, degradation, or outright destruction
2. use of excessively steep slopes or other marginal lands
3. declining crop yields
4. changing crop emphases, especially to adverse soil-tolerant crops such as cassava (manioc)
5. reduction in the fallow period and lengthening of the cropping period without measures to retain soil fertility
6. breakdown of the indigenous farming system
7. food shortages, hunger, and malnutrition
8. land fragmentation, disputes over land, landlessness
9. rural indebtedness
10. unemployment and underemployment in rural and/or urban areas
11. certain types of out-migration.

In using this methodology one gathers information from a wide variety of written sources or from field study to determine just what areas are subject to pressure. Some indicators, taken alone, would not be sufficient to prove the case. For example, out-migration from an area might be motivated by attraction from the destination area, hence it would be necessary to look for signs that it was generated by pressure in the source area before one would conclude that that region was undergoing pressure on the land. Although this method suffers from lack of adequate data in many areas, it is far more workable than systems based on calculating environment potential.

Returning to the original question, there are many people who maintain that Africa has too few people, but most who do so present no rationale for their position. A few scholars hypothesize that population growth stimulates desirable transformations in farming systems (Boserup 1965; Clark 1967), while others suggest that a larger population would aid economic growth by permitting better integration, fuller exploitation of resources, and a larger domestic market. These arguments are subject to serious question in the African context. More densely settled agricultural populations do usually adopt more intensive practices, but adaptations are usually very difficult in the face of the rapid rates of growth prevailing in many countries, and there are more examples of failure to adjust than of success in doing so. Larger markets can better be developed by combining national markets than by increasing numbers of largely subsistent farmers. And I know of no cases where shortage of workers is preventing the exploitation of resources other than low-value agricultural areas which would merely be extensions of subsistence-farming zones. It is true that low and dispersed populations create difficulties in providing and maintaining transport and social facilities, but this does not justify calling for larger populations, as will become clearer after discussion of the impacts of population growth.

Evidence that there are already too many people in parts of Africa, given the present technological levels and stage of economic development, is seen in the widespread existence of un- and under-employment in rural and urban areas and the serious pressure on the land in numerous regions. My estimates are that 37.2 percent of the area of Africa South of the Sahara and 40.2 percent of its population were affected by pressure of population as of mid-1967. Almost all countries have at least small sections under pressure; others, especially in arid countries, have pervasive problems. Many of the highland areas of East Africa and of the smaller island appurtenances are also strongly affected by the indicators of pressure listed above. Although the estimates of area and population experiencing pressure are lower than comparable estimates would be for Asia, they certainly suggest that the myth that Africa has no population problem is erroneous.

POPULATION DYNAMICS

FERTILITY

Africa has the highest fertility rates of any continent in the world. In 1971, birth rates ranged from a low of 27 per 1000 (M) for Mauritius to an estimated 52 per M for Niger, Rwanda, and Swaziland, with most countries having rates from 44 to 52 per M. The median fertility rate, giving the number of live births in the year per 1000 females of childbearing age, is about 175. And total fertility rates, giving the number of children that would be born during the lifetime of each woman experiencing the given fertility rate, range from about 3.5 to 9.1 in tropical Africa, with the median being 6.5. This figure compares with a total fertility rate in the United States of 2.2.

Explanations for the high fertility levels include the following:
1. the typically low age at marriage
2. the high percentage of women who are married
3. the tolerance of illegitimacy
4. the desire for as many children as possible

The last is, in turn, explained in part by the felt need to offset a high death rate and thus assure that some children will survive to maturity and will later provide support in the old age of the parents. Cultural and some religious precepts also strongly favor large numbers of children. The major explanation for lower fertility rates where they do occur appears to be sterility due to the high incidence of venereal disease.

Most experts predict that African fertility rates will not change very much over the next several decades. Factors that would tend to increase the rates include: a reduction of venereal infection, improved health because of the gradual extension of medical and health facilities, prolongation of the average procreative life of African women, reduction of the characteristically very long period of breast-feeding during which there is abstention from intercourse, and, possibly, greater stability in marital relations. A reduction in fertility rates must come mainly from greater interest in reducing the number of children. This appears to show some correlation with rising urbanization, improved educational levels, and higher average incomes, and should develop when there is acceptance that lower mortality rates assure survival of more children. Just when and for what reasons the changed attitude toward numbers of children takes place is not well understood. Recognition of self-interest is doubtless essential, but this recognition may not come until further declines in the death rate make it abundantly clear that children will indeed survive to maturity. Publicity from family-planning agencies is likely to be ineffective unless other factors are operating. Only a few countries have adopted national population policies; only one country, Mauritius, has seen a decline in birth rates of significant proportions.

MORTALITY

Data on death rates are often of doubtful validity in Africa, and up-to-date estimates are particularly difficult due to the remarkably rapid declines which may occur after massive anti-malarial or other campaigns. An average death rate of 20 per M may be reasonably accurate for mid-1971, which is the highest for any world area.

The major explanation for high death rates is the high incidence of disease, with contributing factors being the generally low living standards, the scarcity of medical and health facilities, poor sanitation, inadequate clothing and housing, and malnutrition.

Trends in the death rates are distinctly downward and the U.N. medium estimate for 1995-2000 is 13.1 per M as compared to 22.5 per M for the period 1960-1965. Reductions in infant mortality rates, which range between 100 and 200 per M for most countries, and of child mortality rates, which are also very high, may bring dramatic changes in death rates. It will probably be many years, however, before death rates in Africa are as low as those in more-developed countries because disease rates will probably remain high, and other contributing factors to present high rates place a kind of floor on death rates through which it may be difficult to break.

MIGRATION

The third population dynamic has very little impact on population growth on a continental scale because in- and out-migration is very limited. Within the area, migrations have significantly increased population totals in such countries as Ghana, Uganda, and South Africa, and reduced them in Upper Volta, Angola, Lesotho, and others. Within some individual countries migrations are of importance for certain age groups, occupations, and regions, and may help to explain differential fertility, death, and growth rates. Data on migration levels are less available than for any other major demographic measure.

POPULATION GROWTH

The formula for deriving the population growth rate for an area is:

Growth Rate =
Birth Rate − Death Rate + Immigration − Outmigration

It is usually expressed as a percent rather than on a per M basis. From the information given above it is apparent that Africa has a high rate of growth, probably about 2.7 per cent in mid-1971. This is exceeded only by Latin America, whose higher growth rate is explained by a lower death rate. Since the death rate is declining in Africa and the birthrate is showing no significant change, the growth rate is expected to increase and will very likely be the highest in the world at the turn of the century, perhaps exceeding 3.0 per cent.

These high rates of growth have profound implications for planning, economic growth, population pressure, urbanization, and political stability. They mean that populations will double in 20 to 25 years. Looked at in historical perspective this is a frightening prospect. For Africa as a whole a population of 100 million was not achieved until about 1650; it required 300 years to reach 200 million, 15 years to reach 300 million, and by 2000 it will take only 5 years to add 100 million. By about 2010 the continent may well have a billion inhabitants, equal to the world population only 120-140 years ago. Even if there were not already serious problems of pressure on the land, unemployment, and excessively rapid urbanization, the population growth prospects would soon create difficulties.

THE IMPACT OF POPULATION GROWTH

There are many ways in which rapid population growth may have a deleterious impact in less-developed areas such as Africa.

INCREASED PRESSURES

Increased densities on the land will tend to increase pressure in those areas where it already exits and to subject additional areas to pressure. When it is recalled that populations and population densities are likely to double in 20 to 25 years, the prospects may be better appreciated. In Western Nigeria, for example, about 44 percent of the population is now experiencing pressure at an average density of 941 persons per square mile on about a seventh of the area; by about 1990 half of the population is likely to be residing at densities exceeding 1000 persons per square mile and 27 percent at densities above 2000 persons per square mile.

The consequences of increased pressure on the land are numerous: deterioration of the land, possible breakdown of the farming system, inability to provide adequate amounts and qualities of food, and increased un- and under-employment in rural areas. It should be noted that many parts of sub-Saharan Africa are now affected by seasonal food shortages while diets are generally deficient in proteins and vitamins. The difficulties of modernizing agriculture are also likely to increase. Supposing, for example, that a sample rural area of one square mile now has a density of 100 persons per square mile; 20 percent of the area is in crops, 60 percent in fallow, and 20 percent in wasteland, woods, roads, and settlements. As densities increase there will be pressure to intensify production on the area cropped and to extend the cropped area at the expense of the length of the fallow or resting period. Unless these changes are accompanied by adequately expanded inputs, particularly of fertilizers, land quality will deteriorate and yields per acre will tend to decline even though total production may increase for a time. Introduction of plows or of tractors, instead of having a predominantly favorable impact of increasing production and productivity, may simply expedite the process of deterioration and increase the numbers of unemployed. Provision of inputs to sustain a more modern and more permanent farming may be made more difficult because of inadequate and declining amounts of surplus produce to finance them.

Some people suggest that these difficulties will disappear with application of the Green Revolution to African agriculture. Use of very high-yielding seeds, which is the major base of the revolution, is of great potential benefit, but success requires a concurrent use of other inputs and methods which are not readily introduced to traditional agricultural systems. In any case, the Green Revolution can only provide surcease for a limited period before its benefits are swallowed up by a larger population.

URBANIZATION

As pressure on the land increases, the incentive to migrate to urban areas will increase. Unfortunately, migration to the cities, particularly the prime cities, is already occurring at an excessive rate in relation to their absorptive capacity. Un- and under-employment rates are high in most cities, and projected increases in jobs are not adequate to handle the seemingly inexorable influx. Even in those countries where economic growth has been most satisfactory it has not proved possible to meet the needs for housing or for physical and social infra-structural services. These and other problems are treated in greater detail in the chapters on urbanization and social change.

UNBALANCED AGE-GROUP DISTRIBUTION

Rapid population growth creates what may be considered an unbalanced age-group distribution. African countries typically have relatively high percentages of their total populations in the lower age levels; about 44 percent are under 15 years of age as compared with 24 percent in Europe and 30 percent in the U.S. This means that the ratio of dependents to working population is high, making it very difficult to provide and pay for the necessary social services. Several countries have found it necessary, for example, to postpone the dates by which various attendance levels could be achieved in primary and secondary schools. Nor is it proving possible to provide jobs for the rapidly increasing numbers entering the job market, and eventually it will not even be possible to absorb the growing population in subsistence agriculture. To illustrate the difficulty, it has been estimated that increasing the number of jobs in Nigerian manufacturing by 3 percent would require that sector to invest 18 percent of its income. A subsidiary disadvantage of high population growth rates may also be increased dependence on foreign borrowing.

The impacts of rapid population growth are, of course, felt at the family level as well as on a national scale. The larger families will, in general, have reduced chances for having enough food, an adequate diet, education for all of their children, and for consumption of manufactured products. The health of the mother is also likely to be adversely affected. *In toto,* the opportunities for achieving a better-quality life are likely to be diminished.

ECONOMIC GROWTH

The difficulty of achieving a satisfactory rate of economic growth in face of a rapid rate of population growth may be illustrated in several ways. When it is noted that it requires an investment of about 3 to 4 percent of the national income of a less-developed country to provide each 1 percent of additional population with essentially the same standards as the existing population, it is easier to understand why many countries have not been capable of investing a sufficiently large percentage of their incomes to meet these needs and to achieve a satisfactory rate of economic growth. Indeed, it requires some fast running just to stay in the same place.

A simple model may be used to illustrate the relationships between population growth and economic growth:

	Case A	*Case B*
Assumptions:		
Rate of population increase	3%	1%
Rate of economic growth	5%	5%
Resultant annual increase in per capita incomes	2%	4%
Period required to double per capita incomes	35 yrs.	19 yrs.
In 50 years per capita incomes would increase by about	2.69%	7.11%

The impacts of population growth are now significantly different for more-developed and less-developed countries. Several densely populated West European countries, for example, could now absorb more people than they have, witness the substantial movement of migrant workers from southern Europe and North Africa to France, West Germany, and Switzerland. In these and other more-developed countries, including the United States, the impacts of population growth are more and more measured by increased crowding, growing scarcities of clean water, air, and quietness, burgeoning problems of waste disposal and pollution, and the overloading of public services including education, cultural organizations, recreational facilities, transportation, power, and communications. The immediate argument for reducing population growth in more-developed countries may be more esthetic than economic, though obviously the world as a whole cannot sustain even the relatively low population growth rates of western Europe for more than a moment in geologic time. The major argument for slowing population growth in less-developed countries is now more economic than esthetic, but the concerns noted above for more-developed countries are by no means absent in Africa and their significance will increase with the passing years.

THE NEED FOR FAMILY PLANNING

The many undesirable impacts of rapid population growth suggest that African states should move as rapidly as possible to the encouragement of family planning. While population policies can only be part of overall development plans, the importance and pervasiveness of the population growth variable clearly indicate the potential contribution that can be made by fertility control programs. Unfortunately, knowledge of the best methods for encouraging adoption of family limitation in Africa is very sketchy and the threshold for acceptance of control practices will not be easily crossed.

Given this high threshold and the fact that family-planning programs are either in very early stages of development or completely absent in most countries south of the Sahara, it is apparent that no rapid changes in the fertility rate may be expected. The model comparing 3 and 1 percent rates of growth is somewhat unrealistic from the standpoint that it would take many decades to achieve the 1 percent level. Even under the assumption that fertility rates would decline by 25 or 30 percent by the year 2000, the size of the labor force in a given country would more than double. The marked lag in reduction of the working force is explained simply by the fact that persons who will enter the working-age brackets in the next twenty to twenty-five years are already born or will be before any reduction in fertility can be expected to have a tangible effect. The important differences would be in the then differing rates of increase and the somewhat reduced size of the dependency load.

The number of people in Africa who are cognizant of the overwhelming arguments favoring a reduced rate of population growth is now, unfortunately, very small. Indeed, there is still suspicion held by some that fertility-control programs are a kind of neo-colonialist trick to reduce African population in relation to other world areas. This suspicion has no foundation in fact since actual and projected growth rates in the more-developed areas of the world are well below the comparable rates for Africa. And although one must be sensitive to the fears expressed, remaining silent would surely justify the later criticism that there had been a neo-colonialist conspiracy to sustain poverty in Africa.

POPULATION DISTRIBUTION

The pattern of population distribution in Africa South of the Sahara is dissimilar from that of most continents. It does not show, for example, the marked peripheral concentrations one sees in South America or Australia, nor the marked concentrations in lowland areas one finds in Europe, North America, and Eastern Asia. River valleys, which are often marked by ribbons and nuclei of population on other continents, are much less correlated with such concentrations in Africa, with some exceptions such as the Senegal, middle Niger, and Nile valleys. (Figure 4-2).

The most striking single feature of the gross distributional pattern is the broad, sparsely populated belt associated with the Sahara and adjacent semi-arid regions, mirrored to a lesser degree in the Namib Desert and Kalahari Steppe of southwestern Africa. A second important feature is the widespread dispersion of densely settled nodes, population *islands* often set in seas of sparser settlement. The pattern is, indeed, so varied that one would have to examine each state and each region to secure an adequate understanding of it, an exercise that would require far more space than is available.

FACTORS AFFECTING POPULATION DISTRIBUTION

Population distributions are related to a broad range of factors; sometimes a single factor will provide the major explanation, but often the correlations are too numerous and too interwoven to permit accurate weighting of the various influences.

A few examples will illustrate these points. The emptiness of the Sahara may obviously be related primarily to the single factor of aridity, while several large and numerous small concentrations of population may be explained essentially by the occurrence of mineral resources. An example of more complex correlations is the series of population nodes along and adjacent to the sudan belt in West Africa, a zone where one might expect lower densities because of the long dry period and the fluctuations in rainfall from year to year. Explanations for the population pattern of the belt include the following:

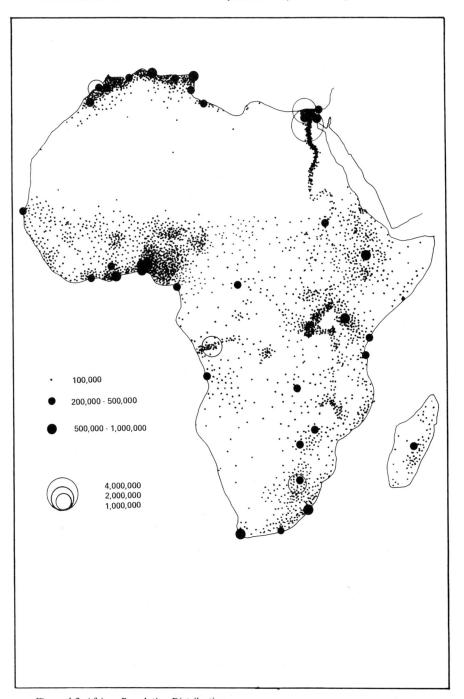

Figure 4-2. African Population Distribution.

1. the ability to grow such subsistence crops as sorghum, millet, peanuts, and beans and such cash crops as peanuts and cotton.
2. the presence of some through-flowing streams and easily-tapped aquifers permitting more intensive production of a wide variety of crops in some portions. Mention should be made of the *fadama* lands, seasonally-inundated floodplains, which are used to produce catch, or quick-growing, crops or provide pasture after the waters have receded in the dry period.
3. the availability of some reasonably good soils.
4. the use of some relatively advanced agricultural techniques, including the application of manures and household waste, particularly in the close-settled zones around the large cities such as Kano and Katsina in Nigeria.
5. the relative ease of movement along the belt, which presumably facilitated early settlement and filling-in.
6. the development of important commercial nodes, dating from about 1000 A.D. and the significance of these nodes not only for regional but for trans-Saharan traffic.
7. the buildup of artisan activity in these nodes, supporting a considerable number of the urban residents.
8. the more recent provision of improved transport to specific centers (e.g., rail lines to Bamako or Kano, and all-season roads to more and more centers). The western end of the belt, focussed on Dakar, enjoys the atypical advantage of having easy access to the sea.
9. the existence for some centuries of powerful states, permitting and sustaining the economic development required to support dense populations.
10. rather opposite to the last point, the settlement of some easily-defensible hill and plateau areas by peoples seeking refuge from the more powerful groups (e.g., the Dogon on the Bandiagara Plateau in Mali).
11. two negative factors important in restricting migration away from the belt are aridity to the north and presence of the tsetse fly to the south.

Although space prohibits looking more closely at population distribution it is important to note that a knowledge of national patterns is essential to planning for transport, the social infrastructure, tactics for economic growth, etc. These patterns may also have important impacts on the degree of economic, cultural, and political integration existent in a given country. An extreme example of a dispersed pattern of population and economic nodes is seen in Madagascar, where integration is so poorly developed as to produce flows more akin to those found in an archipelago than on a giant island. In Uganda, on the other hand, integration is much easier, especially in the densely populated and most productive regions north of Lake Victoria, although Uganda, too, has remote population nodes in the southwest (Kigezi) and the northwest (West Nile Province).

It has been possible in this chapter to touch only on certain aspects of population. Others are referred to elsewhere in the book. It should be apparent, however, that the population factor is highly complex and pervasive and that it presents actual and prospective problems of very great significance to Africa South of the Sahara.

5

An Introduction to African Historiography

HARRY A. GAILEY
California State University, San Jose

History in the traditional Western view has two definitions. One attitude held most strongly by European historians a century ago was that their written accounts were faithful recreations of that which actually happened. Most twentieth century historians are more modest. They believe their histories, based upon the best available evidence, are still subjective accounts of the past. Thus, an objective total recreation of past events becomes a goal which most consider unobtainable. Nevertheless, a good historian will use all available data in his attempt to reconstruct events of an age removed in time from his own.

HISTORICAL SOURCES

The most reliable historical sources are written records. Formal historical training in the twentieth century has concentrated upon the methods of collection, validation, and use of written sources. Historians have also made use of other sources such as architecture, household items, clothing, and art. A few European or American historians have also sparingly used oral tradition and myth. The bulk of history until quite recently has been political history, and most Western historians normally have not found it necessary to consult anything but written sources. Thus, while a small minority of historians have used other disciplines and non-written source material, the majority were not prepared for the seeming unorthodoxy required of most contemporary students of African history.

The study of African history is a projection of the discipline as developed in Europe. Most persons who have done research in Africa are either Western historians or Africans trained in

European or American universities. Each of these has, by training, a preference for written sources. Africa, however, is not rich in written artifacts. Most African languages had no written forms until about the mid-nineteenth century when the missionaries and linguists began producing them. In some areas converted to or conquered by Islam, a significant body of written documentation had been left behind. This was particularly true in the savannah lands just south of the Sahara and in the coastal territories of East Africa. However, even in those areas time, disuse, and natural forces have taken their toll, and aside from the few histories and travel accounts produced in the middle ages, Arab written documentation is very scanty. All this means that the historian of Africa is required to go beyond mere written source materials.

Historical accounts can be divided into two broad categories—the general and the specific. Because of the lack of written sources of all types available to the historian, the bulk of the accounts of Africa prior to the nineteenth century are of the general variety. In certain areas of Africa such generalized events as movement of peoples, construction of new administrative structures, patterns of trade, and trends in foreign policy can be reconstructed with considerable accuracy. However, when the historian dealing with such subjects tries to be specific then he is normally asking the reader to accept his various hypotheses based upon a few ascertainable facts because he feels the projections seem reasonable. Statements concerning such items as the types of slavery and the methods of collection and the volume of the slave trade among the Nyamwezi peoples in the years 1710-20, for example, would be very questionable. Students, therefore, should always be on guard against over-generalizations about Africa, particularly those couched in or based upon statistical data.

Historians who focus upon late nineteenth and twentieth century Africa can, by referring to public and private documents, be more accurate when detailing specifics of political or even social and economic history. Their dependence upon oral tradition and such associated disciplines as linguistics or anthropology is normally less than that of their colleagues whose subject areas are earlier.

Most of the new histories which comprise the flood of writing on Africa since 1960 fall into the time period of the late nineteenth and twentieth century. The major problem confronting students or general readers of these more specific, later studies is that of separating the polemical from the probable. Some of the accounts, particularly those related to events of the past two decades, were designed not merely to inform but to propagandize.

In both general and specific accounts, the students of African history lean more heavily upon associated disciplines than would be true of those writing about European, American, or even Asian history. He must be familiar with the most important studies in his area in the fields of anthropology, sociology, and linguistics. The historian must use the pertinent information from these sources and blend it with the oral history of the people and the extant written records in order to write his history. This does not mean that the African historian is liberated from researching the written record. The range of his tasks and responsibilities has simply been extended to other disciplines, particularly when treating of subjects where written documentation is minimal.

PEOPLES OF AFRICA AND EARLY HISTORY

The present day complexity of African peoples can only be understood by surveying the generalized settlement patterns of past populations. One must then consider three different races which form the bases of today's population. These are the Bushmanoid, Negro, and Caucasian.

BUSHMANOID AND NEGRO BEGINNINGS

It appears that the bulk of Africa prior to 5000 B.C. was inhabited by Bushmanoid hunters and fishermen. Because of the lack of guaranteed food supplies, their population density in any given area was small. Some of these Bushmanoid groups could be isolated from contact with neighboring groups for centuries. It is theorized that this isolation over a long period of time resulted in the creation of distinctively different types of people because of the restricted gene pools. In the western Sudan there evolved from the Bushmanoid a small number of Negro people who were larger, stronger, and without such Bushmanoid characteristics as peppercorn hair or steatopygia. In time the Negro population abandoned hunting and adopted agriculture as the major source of its livelihood. This change in mode of living produced surplus food which allowed for a substantial increase in population which in turn forced an expansion into lands which had been Bushmanoid territory.

The movements of the Negroes were aided by iron technology. It enabled them to fashion more deadly weapons, but more important, they developed more efficient farming implements. Population pressure upon a given living space could thus be relieved by some groups moving into and clearing virgin woodland, recreating in the new place a duplicate of the society they had left.

Patterns of expansion were very complex and continued for many centuries. The most dramatic and obvious of these Negro movements were the Bantu migrations. Bantu expansions seem to have begun from the vicinity of the northwest Cameroons. They continued for almost 2000 years until the whole of central, east and southern Africa were populated by people of the so-called Bantu linguistic and cultural complex. Today there are hundreds of different groups of people speaking mutually unintelligible but related languages. They live according to various economic modes—nomadic and semi-nomadic herding and sedentary farming—in scattered political settlements and in centralized kingdoms. Such differentiation occurred through continuous separation of one group from another and the adoption of various means of making a living.

Similar shorter range Negro movements resulted in the population of all the savannah lands adjacent to the coast of West Africa. Here, before the year 1000 A.D., were the ancestor groups for such modern nations as the Wolof, Mandingo, Ashanti, Yoruba, and Ibo. A reverse migration of East Indian foodstuffs such as yams and bananas reached the west and central African savannah agriculturists at differing periods after 500 A.D. These crops allowed the settlement and exploitation of the forest lands. Migrations into the forests came very late and in some parts of Africa were still occurring when the first Europeans arrived. Figure 5-1 outlines some of the main movements of peoples on the continent of Africa.

The ancient Bushmanoid population was forced to retreat by the complex Negro expansions. In some instances the Bushmanoids were killed or absorbed by the more dominant Negro population. In other cases they retreated before the migrations. Presumably in the virtually inaccessible areas of the Congo Basin, the specialized group of Pygmies evolved from a restricted Bushmanoid population. By the thirteenth century large numbers of undifferentiated Bushmanoids had reached southern Africa. Here they developed into the two present day Khoisan speaking groups—the Hottentots and Bushmen. The reduction in the physical size of the Bushmanoids seems to have occurred after the arrival of significant numbers of Khoisan speakers south of the Limpopo River.

CAUCASIAN INVASIONS

Caucasians came to Africa as invaders in a long series of unconnected invasions which began before 5000 B.C. They came across the land bridge from Asia; this ancient population formed the base

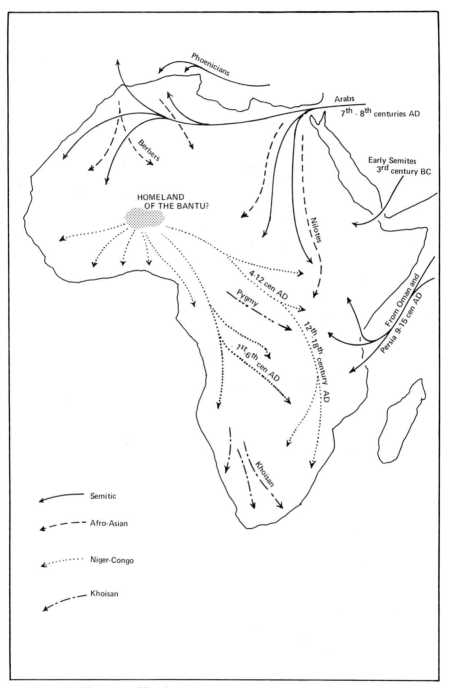

Figure 5-1. Movement of Peoples.

for the Egyptian and North African populations of the ancient world. During the period from 1000 B.C. to 500 A.D. a myriad of Caucasian people settled along the southern coast of the Mediterranean. The Carthaginians, Jews, Romans, Vandals, and Byzantines all left their economic, cultural, and genetic mark upon the older Caucasian population. The descendents of the mixture of Caucasian groups are today called Berbers. Some of the Caucasians, even during the Carthaginian period, had moved into and south of the Atlas Mountains where they became nomadic pastoralists. After the Arab invasions of the seventh century, more refugees from the settled coastal areas moved southward and learned to exist in the vastness of the Sahara Desert. Other early Caucasian invaders were the few Semitic invaders from Yemen who established themselves along the Ethiopian coast of the Red Sea. This population with later reinforcements was the ancestor group to the modern Ethiopians.

The most important Semitic invaders of Africa were the Arab followers of Muhammad. By the opening of the eighth century all of northern Africa was under their control. North Africa thus became in the medieval period a part of the most advanced culture west of China. In the five centuries following Muhammad's death, Muslim armies and Islamic traders carried the faith up the Nile and across the Sahara to the major towns of black Africa. The new faith of the Arabs profoundly altered the fabric of society in the savannah belt of Africa. Along the east coast of Africa, Persian and Arabic Muslims came to trade with the recently arrived Bantu. By the thirteenth century the Muslims had established themselves as the dominant force in coastal and island towns such as Mombasa, Kilwa, Pemba, and Zanzibar. For the next six centuries these Arab merchant-rulers extended their trade far into the interior of Africa. They not only deeply influenced the economics of interior people, but managed to convert large numbers of black Africans to the faith. From the mixture of Bantu-speaking peoples and Arabs along the coast there developed a distinctive Swahili culture, complete with its own language spoken by a racially mixed group.

There have been few European colonists in Africa. There were only four areas where there developed significant European settlement. The oldest and most successful venture was in the most southerly part of Africa where after 1652 the Europeans seized the land from the Africans. Today over three million Afrikaner and English-speaking whites hold political and economic power over the fifteen million black majority in the Republic of South Africa and Rhodesia.

Portugal sent colonists in the seventeenth and eighteenth centuries to Loanda and Mozambique. Along the lower reaches of

the Zambesi River there had developed by 1800 a mixed Portu-
guese-African population which ruled the great plantations or
Prazos. A later influx of colonists in the nineteenth and twentieth
centuries gave the Portuguese the necessary numbers to maintain
their control over Angola and Mozambique. The third area of
European settlement was North Africa where after 1830 the
French encouraged the settlement of southern Europeans in their
newly conquered possessions of Algeria. The last area of significant European settlement was in Kenya in the twentieth century
where a few thousand Europeans occupied the highland areas. In
each of the four areas where there was a considerable European
population there developed extreme friction between the politically and economically dominant Europeans and the indigenous
people.

Mixing of differing peoples was more marked along the middle
and upper reaches of the Nile than elsewhere. Over centuries there
evolved a number of separate groups whose kinship ties were to
the Kushites, Nubians, Bantu, and Semitic invaders. These polygot
groups have been given the name Nilotes. This name is a general
one and should not be taken to mean an identity of cultures or
racial types since the term Nilote refers to people as politically
disparate as the Nuer and Shilluk are from the Masai and Nandi.

GENERAL POLITICAL SYSTEMS

African farmers and pastoralists came to a compromise with
their environment once they learned an efficient method of
providing food. They did little experimenting with untried
methods because any miscalculations could bring starvation and
destruction to their group. In most African societies all of the
institutions serve to sanction this conservative economic posture.
Political, social, and religious institutions are in their many different forms thus survival mechanisms.

THE FAMILY UNIT

However varied the political and religious institutions
observable today among tropical African agriculturists, there are
certain general features which they share. The family is the most
important unit in the society. From this kernel, relationships are
broadened to admit loyalty first to the extended family, then the
clan, next the tribe, and finally the nation. It is probable that the
most viable political and social organization in Africa prior to the
establishment of kingdoms was the clan which formed the basis
for the village. In all African societies one finds always that there

are heads of families, clans, and tribes whether the society is matri-lineal or patrilineal. Generally these leaders are the eldest or most senior men in the family, clan, or tribe. There are numerous varia-tions in what constitutes seniority, but most societies choose their leaders by elections from a group which is considered superior or senior to others. Thus traditional village and tribal politics is determined by both heredity and election.

African political leaders, even those of large states such as Oyo or Ashanti, normally were not totalitarian. Their powers were checked by councils, secret societies, age-sets, and the imperatives of religion. Religion which permeated every section of an African society was particularly powerful in checking the ambitions of many rulers to increase their authority. Nevertheless, the potential for centralized rule existed in each of these smaller political units. Under the pressure of danger from within or without, it was possible for a strong leader to take power at the expense of the institutions designed to prevent one-man rule. This was probably the major reason for the creation of small states which combined a number of different clans. Some of these states could then later be combined into a rudimentary nation-state.

SUDANIC STATES

There are certain similar institutional patterns in African king-doms which have led some observers to conclude a common point of origin for these practices. They have given the name *Sudanic state* to these polities. Each of these states had a ruler who was believed to be divine or semi-divine and whose health was considered to be of vital importance to the well-being of the state. His face was never viewed by the populace, and his participation in certain harvest ceremonies was necessary for the success of the crops. In these states the positions of Queen-Mother and Queen-Sister were also very important. Ceremonies connected with court life were amazingly similar in polities separated from one another by thousands of miles. Each of these Sudanic states had a well-ordered government bureaucracy appointed by the King which was responsible for the details of governing the large complex kingdom. States such as Ghana in the western Sudan, the kingdom of the Monomotapas on the Zambesi River, the Luba-Lunda king-doms of the Congo, and the Bunyoro kingdom of East Africa were all Sudanic states. The African states which resisted European expansion most effectively in the nineteenth century such as Dahomey, the Mossi, and the Zulu were centralized polities of the Sudanic type. Figure 5-2 locates the major Sudanic states of West Africa in the fourteenth century.

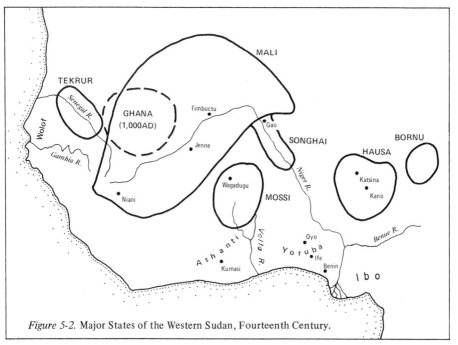

Figure 5-2. Major States of the Western Sudan, Fourteenth Century.

The introduction of Islam to many Sudanic type kingdoms caused some major modifications. Kings could no longer be considered divine, and in theory, law and justice had to be administered according to practices dictated by Muhammad and the learned commentators on the law. However, many of the older ceremonies honoring the King and the Queen-Mother were retained as were many of the festivals. The bureaucracy was even strengthened by the introduction of new patterns of organization adopted from the larger Muslim world. The King's power in these modified Sudanic states was as great as before the introduction of Islam. The most important of such semi-Sudanic states were Mali, Songhai, Kanem-Bornu, and the many Hausa city states of northern Nigeria.

The early nineteenth century witnessed a revival of Islam throughout Africa. In West Africa, purified Islamic states were established in the Futa Toro, and the Futa Jallon. The Fulani religious leader, Usuman dan Fodio, began a revolution in northern Nigeria which unified the old Hausa states. In the 1850s and '60s, Al Hajj Umar led a similar movement which created the Tucolor empire in the western Sudan. In East Africa, Sultan Sayyed Said established his control over the coastal cities, and under his urgings Swahili merchants penetrated deep into Africa searching for ivory and slaves.

EARLY EUROPEAN CONTACTS

European voyages of discovery along the coast of Africa were put in motion by the Portuguese Prince Henry who hoped to find a new route to the Indies which would by-pass the Mediterranean. He hoped also to join the fabled Prester John of Africa in a new crusade which would liberate the Holy Land from Muslim control. By the time of Henry's death in 1460 his navigators had sailed past the coast of Sierra Leone. In slightly more than a generation the Cape of Good Hope was rounded and the Indian Ocean opened for Portuguese trade. Following quickly upon the early voyages of exploration came the traders and missionaries. Very soon the Portuguese decided to limit their activities in Africa to the most profitable areas. In West Africa they built the trading fort of São Jorge da Mina (El Mina) in 1482 to tap the important gold trade of what became the Gold Coast. The Portuguese also concentrated much activity among the Bakongo near the mouth of the Congo River. Then in the early sixteenth century they shifted most of their efforts southward to the territory behind the new town of Loanda. The Portuguese, however, avoided the extreme of southern Africa which they called the Cape of Storms, preferring to dominate Swahili trading states such as Sofala, Kilwa, and Mombasa of East Africa as a part of their plan to monopolize the Indian Ocean trade.

European rivalry soon brought other competitors to Africa. British captains such as John Hawkins in the sixteenth century poached upon Portuguese areas and both the French and British created short-lived chartered companies to trade with Africa. But it was not until the seventeenth century, when the Portuguese and Spanish crowns were briefly linked, that there was a serious challenge to Portugal's trading monopoly in Africa. European rivalry heightened by religious wars resulted in the Dutch Republic seizing Portugal's trade stations on the Gold Coast and eventually driving Portugal from dominance in the Indian Ocean trade. Portugal managed to retain Loanda on the west coast and the city of Mozambique on the east coast. These stations became the nuclei for the later Portuguese territories of Angola and Mozambique.

SLAVE TRADE

By the opening of the seventeenth century the slave trade in western Africa had almost ended the trade in any other goods. Relations between Europe and Africa were largely governed by the mechanisms of the trade. The only territories controlled by the Europeans were the French stations at St. Louis and Gorée in Senegal, the Dutch and British forts along the Gold Coast, and the Portuguese settlements of Bissau, Loanda, and Benguela. Recruitment of slaves to be shipped across the Atlantic was done by African merchants operating within the friendly context of their political systems. Slave raiding was the exception rather than the rule. Continual wars between African groups provided the bulk of those who were sold to Europeans. Another method of obtaining slaves was for coastal merchants to barter with interior people for persons convicted of minor crimes or who were considered by traditional authorities to be expendable. Only when a major state became desperate would it recruit large numbers of its own citizens to be sold. Such practices presaged the downfall of Oyo and the degradation of Benin in the nineteenth century. The kingdoms of Ashanti, Dahomey, Oyo, Benin, and some of the Hausa states by the eighteenth century had come to depend heavily upon the trade. Some states such as Bonny, Brass, and Calabar reoriented their societies because of the slave trade. In the three centuries before the trade was outlawed by European countries, millions of Africans were transported. Most of the slaves were taken from the area between the Gold Coast and the Cameroons, and from northern Angola. In all that time, however, Europeans had hardly penetrated even the immediate interior. African merchants did not wish to share their slaving grounds with any competitors. Even in areas such as the Gold Coast where the Europeans had forts they still depended upon the Africans for slave recruitment.

A LOOK AT THE INTERIOR

Despite the long trading associations, there existed a profound European ignorance of Africa at the opening of the nineteenth century. Various European scientific and business oriented groups, particularly in Britain, at about that time became interested in learning more of the African interior. This new interest can partially be explained by the curiosity of scientists and geographers to fill in the blank spaces on their maps. These geographers and later the missionaries, however, were concerned also with economic advantage and were looking for new and valuable interior markets. Questions concerning African rivers, therefore, became of paramount interest to the European sponsors of expeditions. Thus the first major explorations by Park, Lander, Caillié and others were focused upon the Niger River. Later in the century European concern shifted to questions related to the Nile

River and the great lakes of East Africa. Richard Burton, John Speke, Samuel Baker, David Livingstone, and Henry M. Stanley in a series of explorations filled in much of the geographic data which had been missing on the maps of Central and East Africa.

These explorations took place when European trading interest in Africa was at an all time low level. The abolition of the slave trade had left behind an economic vacuum. There was little of value in Africa for European traders. The trade in such economically valuable products as palm oil, peanuts, and rubber did not become important until the 1870s and then only in a few locations. The adventurers and explorers, however, created public interest in Africa, romanticized the African people, and presented their culture in a simplistic way. Christian missionaries first came in large numbers to West Africa in the 1840s and '50s and their impact on some African societies such as the Fante, Yoruba, and Ibibio was very great. Livingstone and Stanley had urged that missionaries be sent to East and Central Africa and these requests were soon answered. By the end of the 1870s, missionaries were especially active in Buganda and in the lands adjacent to Lake Malawi. They encountered the Swahili slave trade which was one of the dominant economic factors in the areas east of the great lakes. Powerless to halt the trade, the missionaries began to pressure their governments to intervene and break the power of the slavers. This in turn would aid them in spreading the Gospel. Figure 5-3 shows the extent of European occupation prior to the "Scramble".

THE SCRAMBLE FOR AFRICA

Interest in Africa began to revive among European political leaders shortly after the close of the Franco-Prussian War. France, its pride wounded by defeat, sought ventures which would recapture some of its lost glory. In addition, its government was convinced of the necessity for protection of its industries, and some influential men wanted to establish an economically self-sufficient empire. Because of such reasons the French began a tentative series of movements into the interior of Senegal and Guinea in the 1870s, and they subsidized the efforts of the explorer, de Brazza, in Central Africa. In the 1880s the French advance in Africa picked up momentum: most of Senegal had been claimed by 1890; French agents were actively seeking territorial cessions in the interior of the Ivory and Grain Coasts; and the Berlin Conference of 1884-85 had granted French claims to the west bank of the Congo River. The catalyst which speeded up

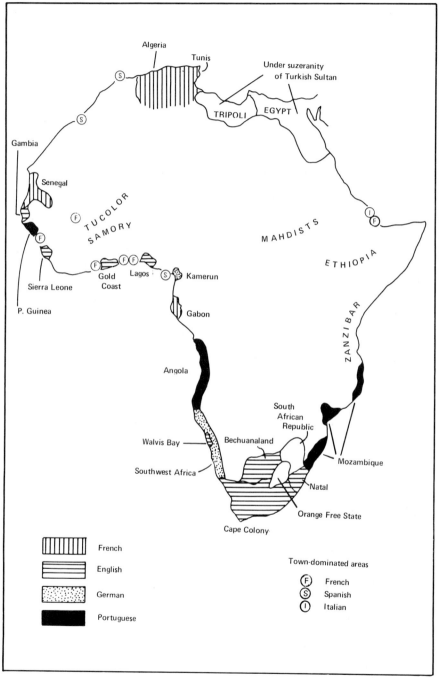

Figure 5-3. Areas of European Occupation, 1884.

European occupation of Africa was King Leopold II of Belgium. Taking advantage of the humanitarian spirit of the age, he helped create the Congo International Association whose mission was to "civilize" and "Christianize" the African. Leopold obtained the services of Henry M. Stanley who agreed to establish the Association's claim to the territory he had discovered in the lower Congo. Stanley for the Association and de Brazza for France began a scramble for territory in this area which was still claimed by Portugal. These European rivalries threatened to get out of hand and the German chancellor, von Bismarck, called the Berlin Conference in 1884. This Conference, which assigned France the area west of the Congo, awarded Leopold's Association the bulk of the lower basin. Portuguese claims were discounted because of a lack of "effective occupation." Leopold soon converted Association rule in the Congo Independent State into a type of personal rule. Some of the worst atrocities committed by Europeans against Africans were done by his agents in the Congo. Public opinion forced Bismarck to recognize the colonial ambitions of the Germans. Against his own feelings, he sanctioned in the mid-1880s the occupation of the coastal areas of the Cameroon and Togo, Lüderitz in South West Africa, and large sections of territory in East Africa.

Britain, which had dominated African trade for over a century, found its spheres of influence threatened by the territorial acquisitions of its rivals. Reluctantly it entered the scramble, and in a series of treaties secured the boundaries of its protectorates along the Gambia, the Gold Coast, and in Sierra Leone and Nigeria. A treaty with Germany drew the boundaries between rival claims in southern and East Africa. Cecil Rhodes, Prime Minister of Cape Colony, and one of the great imperialists, used his money and influence to secure for Britain the vast area of central Africa later known as Rhodesia and Nyasaland. These moves forced the Portuguese to accept boundaries for their protectorates of Angola and Mozambique which denied their hopes of linking the two areas. By 1895 Britain was openly expansionist and soon used the excuse of protecting the Suez Canal and the Nile River to crush the Mahdists in the Sudan. This imperialist spirit was also the major reason for British policy in South Africa which led to the costly Boer War and the military campaigns in Ashantiland, Northern and Southern Nigeria, and in Uganda.

The French in 1890 launched a series of wars designed to bring the huge area of the western Sudan under their control. The campaigns against the Tucolor empire of Ahmadu were successful by 1896. The war against Samory in the Guinea highlands dragged on until 1898, but the bloody conflict with Dahomey was completed by 1894. Borders of the areas claimed by France were regularized by a series of treaties with Germany and England in the 1890s. By the end of that decade, the French were in control of a huge African empire dwarfing in size even the British territory. Figure 5-4 shows the division of Africa into colonial empires.

In a period of less than three decades European attitudes had changed from policies of non-intervention to open annexation. Despite the French, British, and Portuguese military campaigns, most African territory had been acquired peaceably. African rulers ceded their territories by treaty, not knowing what they were signing when they made their marks, or else being overawed by the might and power of the Europeans. Where they chose to fight, they were decisively defeated. The verse of Hilaire Belloc expresses very well the military relationship between Europe and Africa. He wrote,

> *Whatever happens we have got,*
> *The Maxim gun and they have not.*

COLONIAL ADMINISTRATION
AND NATIONALISTIC REACTION

The boundaries drawn by the European powers were totally arbitrary. They divided African tribes or nations, and constrained many different peoples, many of whom had been enemies for centuries, to live together in the same polity. European administrators preferred to assume that the African would not be able to rule himself in the Western sense for generations or even centuries. Thus the mechanisms designed to govern Africans were generally paternalistic and direct. European governors, their staffs, and European officers in the field decided upon policy and required the African chiefs or councils to see that these decisions were carried out.

French territories were grouped together in two large federations—that of West and that of Equatorial Africa. The government was highly centralized with most of the decisions made in Paris or at the federal capitals of Dakar and Brazzaville. African chiefs under the French system were considered as low level civil servants, fit only to carry out orders. The Belgians in the Congo and the Portuguese in Angola and Mozambique used variations of this direct paternalist type of government. British governors had more individual power and were not forced to produce a single standardized system. Britain's boast, however, was her method of

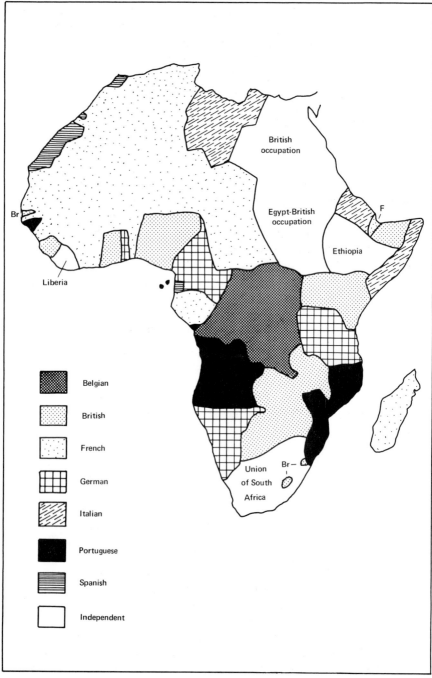

Figure 5-4. Africa Colonial Empires, 1914.

"indirect rule" whereby a great measure of autonomy was given to traditional rulers. Although much of indirect rule was a myth, it did work well where there was a politically centralized African group such as the Fulani Emirs of Nigeria or the bureaucracy of the kingdom of Buganda. Elsewhere it was but a variant of direct rule.

THE ROLE OF EDUCATION

During the early decades of the twentieth century, the African political picture was one of a mélange of ethnic groups held together by European governors, European-led police, and colonial systems of law and justice. Europeans involved and conversant with African policy at this time would not have credited the fact that within a scant two generations the African colonies would be granted self-government and shortly afterward, independence. One factor that brought about political change was education. An increasing number of Africans were educated or trained either because the economy or the government needed trained personnel, or because wealthy, influential Africans saw education as a way of advancement for their sons. Always small in number, educated Africans became dissatisfied with the roles assigned them by the Europeans. They began to demand the liberties and opportunities of which the European states were so proud. After the 1920s they formed political associations and attempted to gain more power at the expense of traditional African rulers. World War II shook the confidence of Europe, and undermined the economies of the imperial powers. The "Age of Imperialism" had passed, and most French and British territories in Africa, instead of being economic assets, became a drain on the reserves of the "home" country. Meanwhile, wars of liberation had broken out after 1945 in Indonesia, Indo-China, and Algeria. These and the more pacific examples of Indian, Ceylonese, and Burmese independence movements were some of the factors which inspired the small nationalist elite throughout Africa.

In the decade following the end of World War II, mass nationalist movements had developed throughout the continent of Africa. Always led by the educated elite and generally centered on one man, these movements sought to appeal to the masses of Africans to cast off the twin yokes of European control and traditional authority. Kwame Nkrumah of Ghana, Julius Nyerere of Tanzania, Nnamdi Azikiwe of Nigeria, Leopold Senghor of Senegal, and Felix Houphouët-Boigny of the Ivory Coast are examples of these new charismatic political leaders. The British,

French, and Belgian governments acceded to rising demands for self-government while Portugual, whose economic life was more closely bound to its possessions of Guinea, Angola, and Mozambique, chose to suppress the nationalist movements. Only the expenditure of great amounts of money and effort has enabled Portugal to retain control of its colonies.

The British led in the devolution of power, and the Gold Coast, which became Ghana in March 1957, was the first African state to receive its independence. In the next five years there was a veritable flood of constitution-making, and most of the European territories became independent states under the leadership of European-educated Africans. Most of these leaders were at first closely aligned with the former imperial power. Only in multi-racial areas such as Kenya, Rhodesia, and the Portuguese territories was there any great conflict between the aims of the nationalists and the imperial powers. Rhodesia, Mozambique, and Angola have remained firmly under the control of Europeans despite the persistent efforts of African guerrilla forces which are particularly active in the Portuguese territories. Only in Portuguese Guinea have the African nationalists been successful in driving the Portuguese out of the largest part of the countryside. The Republic of South Africa, with its population of over three million whites mostly committed to the support of *apartheid,* or separate-ness, is the strongest bastion of white supremacy in southern Africa. The white minority's power over Africans is greatly magnified by its control of manufacturing, mining, and banking in this, the only industrial state in Africa.

In all the new African states, the chiefs or traditional rulers were relegated to secondary roles immediately after independence was gained. Tribal diversity and jealousy, poverty, lack of enough educated personnel, and many other factors have made the path of independence a thorny one for most of these new states. Civil wars wracked Rwanda, Burundi, the Congo (Zaire), Chad, the Sudan, and Nigeria, and the political instability of civilian regimes brought the military to power in countries such as Ghana, Uganda, and Dahomey. Despite such strains, the African states have progressed much further than European observers in the 1930s would ever have dreamed. European education had produced enough men who could, with outside economic aid, begin to attack the tremendous problems of tribalism, nationalism, economic insufficiency, education, health, and unemployment. The brief interlude of European control after the scramble worked a revolu-tion in thought and behavior throughout Africa almost without the Europeans being aware of its happening. There was only a very short transitional period between autocratic European control and the launching of democratically based independent African states. It would be naive to believe that all African leaders in all African states are in control of all the divisive and negative forces in their states. It does, however, appear that most African polities have passed through the most difficult stages of the maturation process and that the next decade will witness more stability and progress than that apparent during the troubled period since independence.

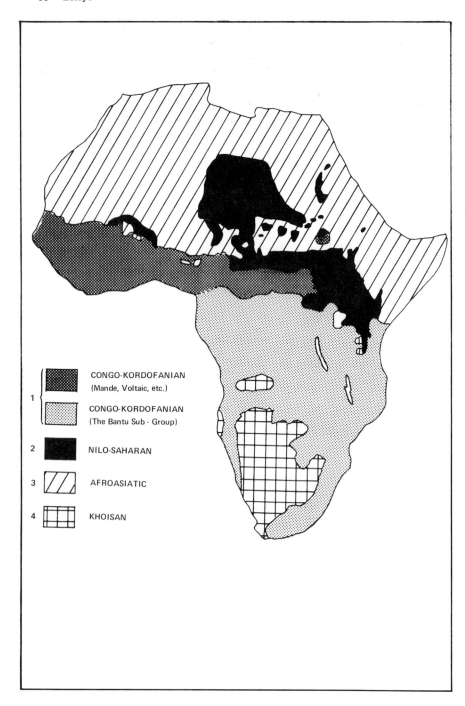

6

A Language Geography of Africa

REED F. STEWART
Bridgewater State College, Massachusetts

LANGUAGE EXAMPLES AND CHARACTERISTICS

Among the rice-growing Vai of the forests of Liberia and Sierra Leone, one can hear conversations such as this:

VAI*	FREE TRANSLATION	LITERAL TRANSLATION
Ndiamoh, yakuneh.	"My friend, good morning."	"Friend, are you awake?"
Mm, yakuneh. I seh.	"Yes, good morning; greetings."	"Mm," (an agreeing sound). "Are you awake? Greetings."
I kpoloh?	"How are you?"	"[How is it in] your skin?"
Kasey bey kamba mai. Ohh i kpeh i kpoloh?	"I'm fine, and how are you?"	"There is no rust on God, and your-self, [how is it in] your skin?"
Kasey bey kamba mai. I seh. Mbey ko beh nu?	"I'm fine, too, thank you. What's the news where you come from?"	"There is no rust on God. Thank you. Is there any bad thing there?"
Ko nyama bey nu. Mbey ko beh nieh?	"Everything's OK. How are things here?"	"There is nothing bad there. Is there any bad thing here?"
Ko nyama bey nieh.	"Fine."	"There is nothing bad here."

*All vowels are pronounced separately and all have roughly the values of the vowels in Spanish; *h* and *y* have been added to the *e*'s and some *o*'s to suggest a modification of the sound.

87

Of course, a literal translation makes the conversation sound absurd, but it must be remembered that even in one's own language a literal interpretation of every word that is spoken may lead to unforeseen results, as many comedians have shown. The important points to be taken from that dialogue and its translations are that the Vai have rather different ways of thinking from those of English-speaking people; that their speech uses different combinations of sounds than do most languages with which we are familiar; and that a pattern can be seen in the Vai arrangement of words, which is to say that the language has a definite grammar. Such a short sample of Vai gives only a hint of the complexity of that grammar, the range of sounds used, and the extent of the differences of thought.

By way of emphasis, one could examine the opening sentences of a corresponding dialogue among the cattle-herding Masai of the savannas of Kenya and Tanzania:*

Apáayiâ! Óê! Súpá! Ípá!

"Mister!" "[responsive sound]" "Greetings!" "The same to you!"

The Masai speech illustrates better than does the Vai, the use of relative pitch, called tonal variation by linguists. Tone is far more important in most African languages than it is in English, and the high, low, and falling tones (´, `,ˆ) give necessary distinctiveness to the words so that their meaning is separate from other words with the same vowel and consonant combinations. English is somewhat a tonal language, as can be illustrated by the difference between a spoken question and a spoken statement. In fact, when English-speakers try to speak a language which is not tonal, such as Kiswahili, they have difficulty, as they do when listening to English spoken in a monotone. Vai is somewhat more tonal than English, but a person who reads the Vai dialogue as if it were English will not be too far off in intelligibility. He will be almost completely misunderstood if he does the same with the Masai conversation.

A second major difference between the Vai and the Masai languages is exemplified by the fact that the Vai dialogue could properly be spoken by any two persons, no matter what their respective ages, occupations, or sexes. The Masai dialogue, however, could only occur between adult men of approximately the same age. Different sets of words would be used between older and younger men, two girls, a man and a women of the same age, a

---

*All said emphatically. Here the *a, o,* and *e* are as in Spanish, as is the first *i.* The underlined *i* sounds as in *sit,* the underlined *u* as in *full.*

man and an older woman, a women and an older woman, etc. It is important in speaking Masai, as it is in speaking many African languages, to know precisely the relationship in which one stands with his or her audience. The variation often extends, not just to pronoun form and slightly to verb and adverbial form, but deeply into the make-up of the nouns, verbs, adjectives, and adverbs. The variation of form is related to gender, often just as arbitrarily as in German, for instance, but the variation is also related to other kinds of classification. Kikamba, spoken in Kenya, distinguishes between animate and inanimate entities, such as a lion and a stone; between the ordinary and the diminutive in size or status, such as a lion and a cub; and between indigenous words and those from other languages. This noun-class approach is characteristic of a large proportion of African languages.

By definition, each language has its own vocabulary. In part, this distinction refers to different words for the same concept: *i seh* means *súpá* means *greetings,* though one should notice that *i seh* also means "thank you." *Greetings* also has a variety of meanings in English, however. Differences in vocabulary also stem from concepts unique to particular cultures. The Masai have a single word for the action of taking off wire bracelets, *a-nyadú.* That same word can mean the warlike action of surrounding in a pincer movement. The Kikamba word *nza* means a cattle corral inside a village, while *kyengo* means "a corral outside a village." The Vai *tehteh* means "exactly in the middle." The last example shows another characteristic of many languages in Africa—the use of repetition to emphasize or even to change the meaning. *Teh* by itself, means "in the middle"; the duplication brings precision. On the other hand, in Luganda, spoken in Uganda by the Baganda, *bafumba* means "they cook", while *bafumbabafumba* means "they are pretending to cook."

WRITING SYSTEMS

With the varieties of languages in Africa, it would be surprising if Africans had not developed a number of writing systems. Most people realize that Egyptian heiroglyphics are African, but do not realize that there had to be centuries of development of writing in and near that corner of Africa before hieroglyphics could attain a widespread acceptance along the Nile. Perhaps it was that background which later assisted the spread of the Punic writing—a distant descendent of Egyptian writing—from North Africa south into the Sahara where the Tuareg women still use it. In the last century and a half, about twenty writing systems have been developed; some based in part on very old ideograms and pictograms, some alphabetic and some syllabic in design. These range from the Osmania script of Somalia to the Vai script of Liberia. To them should be added, of course, the scripts of Ethiopia, of Arabic, and those of European use and derivation. As of 1968, approximately 400 languages and dialects of Africa had been written in variations of the Latin alphabet, mostly in characters of the international phonetic alphabet and mostly through the work of religious groups.

NUMBERS AND DEFINITIONS

The last paragraph raises questions as to how many languages there are in Africa, what an African language is, and perhaps, what a language is. To none of these questions is there a single, simple answer. We are concerned here with means of human communication which are primarily oral. Systems of speech are said to be distinct languages when they are mutually unintelligible, as for instance, English and Sioux. They are said to be dialects when their respective speakers can understand each other fairly easily. Scottish English and the English of New Orleans are different enough to be called dialects of the English language, but they do not prevent intercommunication and so are not separate languages, yet.

MORE THAN ONE THOUSAND LANGUAGES

The more widespread a language is, the more likely it is that there are distinct dialects of it. Africa has many far-ranging languages, such as Hausa, Peul, Kiswahili, and Mbundu, and has, then, a number of languages in which there are dialects. It has, also, an astonishing number of distinct languages, well over 1000. Since the definitions of language and dialects are not precise, the counts vary, and since the names of languages vary according to the language of the person doing the naming, there is substantial duplication in many lists of African languages. Murdock (1959) gives some 6075 names of peoples, without intending to say that each group has its own language or that his list is free from overlapping. Greenberg (1966) shows only the 722 languages for which he has data, without pretending that his list is all inclusive. Taking areas of Africa of which the present writer has some knowledge, centering on Liberia and Kenya, establishing a ratio of duplicated names to the total listed in Murdock for those areas (166:415), and applying that precarious ratio to the rest of Africa, the estimate was made of 2671 languages. That seems too high, but it is the basis for the statement that there are well over 1000 distinct languages in Africa.

The question as to what languages are African is equally hard to answer, primarily because languages do not respect boundaries. People move around, taking their languages with them; they also readily learn the languages of their neighbors.* The result is that one cannot readily match languages with other phenomena. Occupation, climate, a particular human physical characteristic, nationality, religion, location, *tribe* (a particularly elusive term), may each, in one instance, be correlated with a given language spoken as a mother tongue, but usually another instance will upset easy generalizations. A good example of this is with the language family of which the Arabic and Ethiopian language groups are members. Those languages are certainly African, if antiquity on the continent and numbers of speakers are criteria, yet various ancient and some modern languages in southwest Asia, such as Aramaic and Hebrew, are of that same family. This does not make Aramaic and Hebrew into African languages, however, it merely points up the difficulty of classification.

Another difficulty in defining African languages is that a particular characteristic of a group or family may not be found in all its members, nor is that characteristic confined to a given group. Relative pitch (tone) is a Bantu characteristic, yet Kiswahili, one of the most important of the Bantu group, is not a tone language, while a neighboring language, Masai, depends heavily on tonal variations although Masai is not a Bantu language. On the other hand, tone languages are found in many areas of the world outside Africa: in China, for instance.

Earlier, in dealing with the characteristics of African languages, examples were used which accord with a definition of them as belonging to language groups not widely spoken off the continent and not of strongly European origin. That definition would exclude Arabic and Ethiopian and is clearly an arbitrary definition. It would also exclude Afrikaans and Krio as owing much to off-the-continent languages in vocabulary and grammar, yet both languages owe much of their present form to their development on the continent. In fact, as may be apparent by now, there can be no single, technical definition of African languages and an empirical grouping will be used: those languages which are spoken as a

---

*The author knows of a man in Liberia who has never learned to read or write but who can speak five languages and understand another three.

mother tongue by a significant portion of the population of a major political unit on the continent.

LANGUAGE FAMILIES

The map, Figure 6-1, shows the distribution of languages according to families, a term which is not much clearer than is *language* or *African. Family* is used here to mean the largest grouping into which related languages can be placed. Just as German can be placed in the same family as can French, so can Hausa and Somali be included in one family. The drawback is that knowledge of the languages of Africa is still far short of what a linguistic taxonomist would wish for, and there is room for differences of opinion as to what a given similarity between two languages really signifies. There can be, therefore, differences as to the position of some languages in any family classification. The one used here is based on Greenberg, but some linguists challenge him on various points.

Language families can be subdivided into groups of more closely related languages. Some of the groups have many members, some just a few, but those few are so different that they require classification by themselves. Of the groups, perhaps the most famous is that of the Bantu — a subdivision of a subdivision within a group of a language family. There are so many languages within the Bantu subdivision, and they cover so much of tropical Africa that Bantu is often used, imprecisely, as a synonym for African. As might be expected, the Bantu languages are further divided — the classification scheme varying with the approach of the linguist doing the work. Some specialists, such as Guthrie, base much of their historical work on linguistic analysis, deriving migration patterns from the relation of one language to another.

Before dealing with the history behind the present language distribution, it should be remembered that migrations of languages are not necessarily the same as migrations of whole peoples, nor can it be taken for granted that linguistic similarities correlate with other aspects of culture. People may travel and take their knowledge of agriculture or metal working with them, but lose most of their language in the midst of a more numerous population. Conversely, a people may find themselves in circumstances where much of their previous culture wilts away and only the language structure remains. Of course, under those circumstances, the vocabulary is bound to change as well. A comparison might be with the language of small townsfolk in the United States as of 1872 in contrast with the language of the people in those same

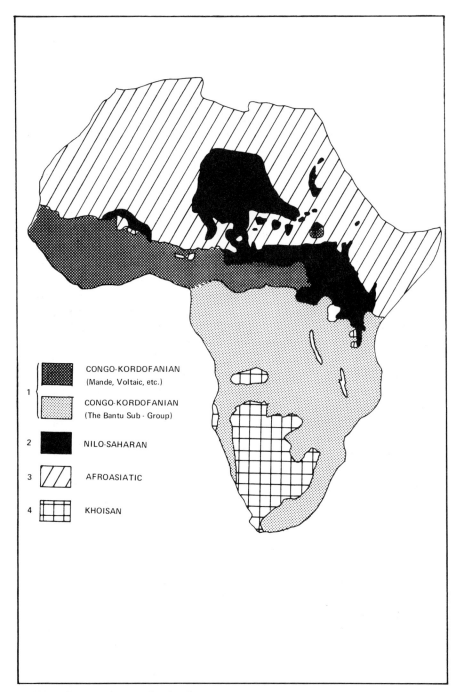

Figure 6-1. Language Families in Africa.

communities in 1972. The vocabulary of the livery stable has given way to that of the service station, so to speak.

LANGUAGE DISTRIBUTION HISTORY

The present distribution of languages throughout Africa is clearly the result of millenia of population movements and language changes, but that is about the only clear statement that can be made without a challenge coming from a linguist, an historian, or an anthropologist. It is frequently impossible, for instance, to equate a postulated ancestral language with a particular cultural complex. For example, it seems fairly clear that people who may have been ancestral to the southern African Bushmen were widespread in eastern and even in northern Africa, but we do not at all know that they spoke any language which might have been ancestral to the present Khoisan languages which the Bushmen speak. There are very small groups in Tanzania which do speak languages of that family, but the points of physical resemblance between them and the Bushmen are not at all overwhelming. From the evidence of those Tanzanian groups, the Sandawe and the Hatsa, and from associated archeological data, one can be fairly safe in saying that the Khoisan languages once spread over a larger area of Africa than they now occupy, perhaps over most of Africa east and south of the Congo rainforests. That early occupance was by a small number of people, it seems — only a few score thousands at any one time.

It also seems probable that the Congo rainforests have been inhabited for some thousands of years by Pygmies, some of whom may also have lived in the forests of western Africa. Although Pygmies now number well over 100,000, their former languages have not been recorded; each small group of Pygmies having adopted the speech of its symbiotic partner group of agricultural people, to the loss of its own language.

Another language group which seems of great antiquity in eastern Africa is the Cushitic, which is presently found on the Red Sea coast and in the Horn of Africa, with small numbers of peoples, isolated from other members of the language group, in central Tanzania. It seems that there was once a more continuous spread of the Cushitic languages over what is now an interrupted range. The wider coverage appears to date back some 3000 years, with the most southerly expansion occurring something over a thousand years ago. Perhaps the Cushites replaced the earlier Khoisan speakers in what is now Kenya and Tanzania, but other groups, unidentified as to language, such as the Capsian culture groups, were also in the area before the Cushites. The Cushitic language group is part of a family which extends over most of northern Africa and also has representatives in southwestern Asia.

Again in eastern Africa a different language family seems to have replaced the Cushitic speakers with members of one of its groups, the Chari-Nile group of the Nilo-Saharan family, which has also pushed into central Tanzania. That area, which has Khoisan, Cushitic, and Nilo-Saharan speakers, also has Bantu speakers, of the Congo-Kordofanian family and thus presents a living exhibit of the complex of African language families, especially when one includes the English, Indian, and Pakistani speakers who now live in Tanzania.

To return to the Nilo-Saharan speakers, the language map suggests that as they were expanding — possibly from an origin in the Darfur vicinity of what is now the Sudan and Chad — Afro-Asiatic speakers were spreading into the home area of the Nilo-Saharans. In some places one language was first on the scene and is still dominant, while in another area that same language group was submerged by a second group. Again, it should be remembered that fairly small numbers of people were involved at a given time; perhaps the total population of Africa was only three to four million as of two thousand years ago. It should also be remembered that the ways for a language to spread and change are many and varied. Trade, migration, inter-marriage, technological change, conquest, and religious change are some of the paths to language variation, producing new dialects and eventually new languages, always with definite family relationships to be found by diligent and lucky linguists.

As Figure 6-1 shows, the Nilo-Saharan family spread to the west as well as to the south and east of the postulated homeland, with the Songhai as a flourishing, if isolated, group along the Niger. Perhaps the Songhai and related languages were in that area before Afro-Asiatic speech arrived. Western Africa, though, may be the area of origin of the fourth family, the Congo-Kordofanian, a group which may antedate the coming of the Songhai. It has been suggested that peoples living in the central part of western Africa, in what is now the Sahara, migrated south about seven thousand years ago as the climate became drier. They may have been the early speakers of the Congo-Kordofanian languages. Of course, the languages diverged with the years and with distance. Some migrations can be rather clearly traced by those divergences, as of the Mande languages into areas previously covered by West Atlantic speakers, both groups being of the Congo-Kordofanian family. Another such shift has been the southward one of the Kwa group toward the Atlantic coast.

Perhaps the most influential language migration, at least for the language map, was that of the Bantu speech of some two to three thousand years ago from the area inland of the Bight of Biafra. Opinions differ as to whether the Bantu speech began to move from the Adamawa highlands between Nigeria and Cameroon or from the area now comprising the Central African Republic, and opinions differ as to whether the spread was rather like ripples on a pond from a point of origin or whether Bantu speech may have quickly passed south through the Congo basin to the Benguela highlands in what is now Angola, to spread out from there in all directions, including back north into the forests of the Congo basin. At any rate, the results can be seen on the language map as an area of Bantu speech that includes most of Africa south and east of the Nigeria-Cameroon border.

There is no certainty why African language movements took place but in the case of the Bantu it does seem to have been associated with a shift in agricultural practice and an increase in metal working. At the risk of being repetitious, it should be pointed out that the movement of a language does not require the mass movement of all of its speakers. What is required is that those people who do migrate, perhaps in short stages, generations apart, be sufficiently influential for their language to supersede the speech of the people who may have been in the area. That influence may be due to social organization or agricultural productivity rather than to initial numbers.

As with other migrations of languages, that of the Bantu sub-group was in progress when Arabs and Europeans began to leave written records about Africa. In southern Africa, Bantu speakers such as the Xhosa were moving southward toward the Cape of Good Hope as the Europeans were moving away from that cape northward in the early 1700's. Both groups had been expelling Khoisan speakers from their areas of advance (though both had picked up elements of Khoisan in their own speech) and both were newcomers to the vicinity where they met near the Great Fish River in the present Cape Province in the 1770's.

Of course, European languages had been in contact with African languages long before that date (since the late 1400's in western Africa) and would increase that contact until almost the entire continent was politically controlled by speakers of European languages. To this day, migrations of African languages have continued and changes are still going on. The brief sketch of migrations above accounts for the general outlines of the language distributions in Figure 6-1 which shows the situation as it was, ignoring incursions from without.

LANGUAGE CHANGE

Those effects are to be discussed now. When two languages are in prolonged contact, changes seem to be inevitable. Words are borrowed by each from the other and sometimes whole phrases are adopted. Kiswahili is an example of a Bantu language which has kept its basic Bantu structure minus the tonality, while borrowing a large proportion of Arabic words and modifying them to fit the Bantu kind of grammar. The name comes from the Arabic *sawahili* meaning "coastal" and has a Bantu-type of prefix, *ki,* which puts it in the class of inanimate things.

With Kiswahili as one example, Afrikaans can be another. Here the basic structure is that of a Germanic language with the vocabulary altered in the direction of Khoisan and Bantu languages, though not nearly as radically changed as was the Bantu of Kiswahili towards Arabic. Afrikaans is the result of a language developing in isolation from its source. Many strangers learned to speak it which helped to effect a rapid rate of change. In addition, cultural and physical environmental demands contributed to vocabulary changes.

A third example of language change, perhaps even more rapid than that of Afrikaans, is Krio of Sierra Leone. It seems to have a grammer with elements of English and of western African languages, and a vocabulary taken from western African as well as from several European languages, largely English. Krio is a result of peoples of many languages learning just enough of yet another language to get along in trade with each other. English was the language which was partially adopted, pieced out with vocabulary from Sierra Leone languages and from the languages of freed slaves from all along the Atlantic coast of Africa who had been put ashore at Freetown. Krio has developed into a complex system of expression with an extensive use in education, government, and commerce.

In Liberia, in Cameroon, and in the former English colonies in West Africa there have developed dialects of English which are greatly different in pronunciation and intonation from *standard* English, and have a markedly varying vocabulary. The development of *coast* English has occurred alongside the teaching of standard English in the schools, therefore coast English has not a great chance of coming into widespread use. A major difference between coast English on the one hand and Kiswahili, Afrikaans, and Krio on the other is that the latter three are the first languages of a large number of people in their respective areas, while coast English is largely a language of convenience, not to be used in the home or school except in rare instances.

LINGUA FRANCA

Krio, Kiswahili, and coast English have developed in part as languages of commerce among peoples of widely different native languages and are widespread. The term *lingua franca* is sometimes used to describe such a language which serves as a medium of communication between peoples of different tongues. There are *coast* versions of Portuguese and to a lesser extent of French in the areas which those two languages colonized, but they are not widely used. Kiswahili, however, is one of the farthest ranging languages in Africa, as Figure 6-2 shows. The same map shows other trade languages which differ from Kiswahili, they are the unmixed languages of people who are major traders. Their languages have been learned by other peoples wishing to do business with them. Hausa, Fulani, KiKongo, Amharic, and Arabic are examples. Some of the trade languages are also national languages, Arabic and Amharic, for instance, or Kiswahili in Tanzania and Sango in the Central African Republic.

NATIONAL LANGUAGES

As Figure 6-3 shows, many countries have adopted the languages of the former colonial powers as national languages, although a few have chosen an indigenous language. When it is remembered that some countries have fifty or one hundred languages spoken among their populations, the difficulty of choosing a national language becomes clear. A general rule might be that when the country has one overwhelmingly dominant language, such as Arabic in Morocco, that language is the choice; when no one language has a commanding position or even a great deal of influence, then a trade language such as Sango or Kiswahili may be adopted; when there is intense rivalry among the indigenous language speakers, as in Zaïre, then the colonial language may be the choice – at least one can say that it offends all equally.

Practically, there are much more positive aspects of using a colonial language such as French, English, Spanish, Portuguese, or in using Arabic. A European language is what the secondary schools and universities used before independence so that the

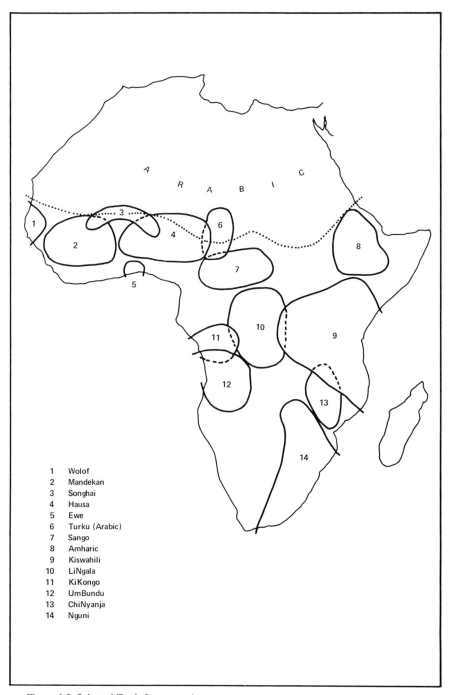

Figure 6-2. Selected Trade Language Areas.

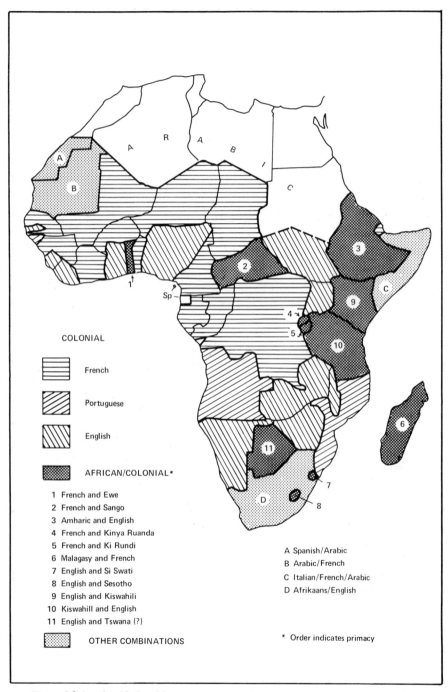

Figure 6-3. Legal or National Languages.

people educated in the western manner, as distinct from those educated in the Koran schools or the traditional tribal upbringing only, have a common language and access to a wide library of texts. In most instances, the colonial language was the one which the pre-independence government used, so that the legislation and the court rulings are in that language. International assistance and commerce may be more easily arranged through an international language, and even pan-African conferences can be more readily conducted in colonial languages than in Hausa or Kiswahili. Knowledge of the colonial language is widespread even among people who have little or no formal western education, but who have worked with and for those who did have that education. The colonial language is also, usually, the speech of the police and armed services. All of these factors help explain why the colonial language has so often been retained as the national language.

At the same time, it should be realized that the adoption of a single national language does not mean that all others will quickly atrophy. It is reasonable to suppose that where the national language is an outsider's speech and spoken by only a few as their mother tongue, the indigenous languages will continue to transmit the local cultures for many generations.

There are problems with any choice of language for national use even assuming that there are no political complications within the country because of language rivalry. At what grade in formal schooling should a national language be introduced? In how many languages can radio or television programs be broadcast to the schools or to the country as a whole? What language is the best vehicle for national writers? Does a local politician need to learn the national language before running for a wider regional office outside his home area? Some of these points are more easily settled if there is widespread adoption of a single national language. There is no uniform answer to any of these problems because of the number of varying and unique language situations among the states of Africa.

Some countries, as noted on Figure 6-3 use a widespread local language as one national language with an international language as a second officially sanctioned means of communication. Lesotho uses both Sesotho and English, for instance. Countries which use a colonial language as the only official language make provision for speakers of indigenous languages to use them in court, through interpreters. Somalia uses three international languages, Arabic, English, and Italian, but does not officially approve the use of Somali, which almost all the population speaks as its first language.

CONCLUSION

An attempt has been made to suggest the richness of African language geography — the diversity and distribution of languages in Africa with some of the reasons for that variation and arrangement, as well as to give some of the consequences of the complicated pattern, perhaps the most complicated continental pattern in the world. It has not been possible to do more than touch on ways of speaking or on the characteristics of the languages of Africa, but many schools and colleges in the United States are now teaching one or two of the more widespread languages such as Kiswahili, Hausa, and Yoruba and a great deal of information can be obtained from such schools. More and more attention is being given to African languages as their importance is forcing itself on a rather surprised world.

FURTHER READING ON
AFRICAN LANGUAGE GEOGRAPHY

The material readily available seems to be either very generalized such as may be found in most texts on the geography of Africa, or rather specialized, dealing with classification questions, or with a particular language group. There is no lengthy treatment of the geography of language, still less is there one on Africa's language geography, apart from the pure classification and mapping of *The Languages of Africa* by Joseph K. Greenberg, Bloomington, Indiana University, 1966. Another map, in much greater detail, is that which accompanies *Africa: Its Peoples and Their Culture History* by George P. Murdock, New York, McGraw-Hill, 1959. Murdock uses Greenberg's classification, but modifies the nomenclature substantially. Much of the material in the present article was derived from "The African Language Picture," which appeared in *The Linguistic Reporter,* supplment 26, summer ·1971, issued by the Center for Applied Linguistics, Washington, D.C., and was by William Gage. A paper that the present writer wishes were in print is a mimeographed one, *A Background in African Languages,* by William E. Welmers, 1963-64, U.C.L.A. Malcolm Guthrie has written a four volume *Comparative Bantu,* London, Gregg, 1969, the second volume of which deals with Bantu prehistory. Articles by Guthrie and others in the *Journal of African History* are valuable in summarizing issues and bringing out new findings. Histories of Africa deal with migrations as well as with current language problems in terms of political tensions. One such is *A Thousand Years of West African History,* edited by J.F.A. Ajayi and Ian Espie, London, Nelson, 1965, with an excellent modification of Murdock's language map on the endpapers. *Zamaini,* edited by B. A. Ogot and J. A. Kieran, Nairobi, East African Publishing House, 1969, is good for East Africa and brings the current language problems more to the fore. Three works not dealing with Africa solely are interesting with reference to worldwide language distribution and with the complications of translation. *God's Word in Man's Language* by Eugene Nida, Harper and Row, 1952, is fascinating reading, while the other two are valuable references. *The Gospel in Many Tongues,* London, British and Foreign Bible Society, 1965, shows specimens of 872 languages, many in scripts other than the Latin alphabet, while *Scriptures of the World,* New York, The United Bible Societies, 1968, lists 1337 languages of the world, alphabetically and by area.

7

Some Aspects of Rural Land Use in Tropical Africa

BARRY N. FLOYD
University of Durham

This overview of agriculture in tropical Africa is intended to identify certain spatial characteristics of land and animal husbandry considered significant in any geographical appraisal of rural land use in Africa. In view of the areal spread and predominance of smallholder farming activities, the focus is on traditional agriculture and its advancement. The commercial and export sector, featuring plantation or estate agriculture, and the large farms of European settlers and other foreigners, is not examined in this study.

OBJECTIVES OF AGRICULTURAL GEOGRAPHY

A conceptual model for the geographical study of agriculture appears in Figure 7-1. The spatial manifestations of the innumerable physical and socio-economic factors operating within the agricultural system may be considered as falling within the domain of the agricultural geographer. His task is to describe, analyze, and attempt to explain the areal patterns of rural land use, including linkages and flows between various sectors of the farming operation.

In addition, the modern geography of man's husbandry of the land involves studies of the diffusion of innovative strategies, and prediction of future farming activities in the spatial organization of agriculture. The most recent developments in rural land use geography feature perception studies, or attempts to establish the personal vantage point from which a farmer views the "living tether" binding man, earth and rural society. Decision-making within the perceived or behavioral environment, and the probable reaction of an individual cultivator to a given situation, is a further facet of contemporary geographic studies of agriculture, particularly relevant in tropical Africa.

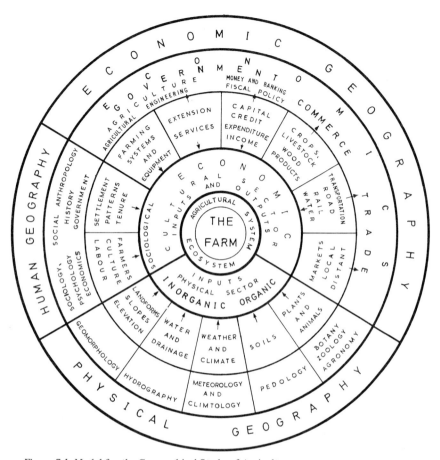

Figure 7-1. Model for the Geographical Study of Agriculture.

AGRICULTURE: THE KEY TO
ECONOMIC DEVELOPMENT IN AFRICA

The less-developed or "fallow" regions of the world are faced with a plethora of economic problems; Africa is preeminently the fallow continent. The broad picture has been painted thus:

> Emerging African states face new demands on the part of their people for accelerated economic development. The major problem in Africa is the reorganization of all sectors of economic life so that accelerated African economic growth can be achieved. Many obstacles are faced. Rapid population growth, stagnation of agricultural production, absence of large internal markets, lack of African entrepreneurs and trained cadres, and balance of payment problems all add to the complexity of the tasks at hand. (Benveniste and Moran 1962:3)

Even when the "stagnation of agriculture" is removed for special study, there remains a set of problems fully as intractable as those in the various other sectors of the economy. Yet, for many, the answer to the well-nigh Sisyphean task of economic advancement lies in the realm of agriculture. When more broadly efficient and productive modes of living are established in the African countryside, a chain reaction of socio-economic benefits may confidently be expected. An economist concerned with African affairs has written:

> The key sector for economic development in most of Africa is still . . . agriculture. So far, only a few African countries have found and developed mineral resources, the only alternative way, at this stage, of earning foreign exchange. For most African countries, then, it is agriculture that must be depended on: to raise the standard of living of the people initially, to provide the minimum market necessary for manufactures to get a foothold, to earn the necessary foreign exchange to pay for imports, and to provide the revenues to finance needed government services. The improvement of agriculture must be the central part of any development program. (Kamarck 1967:89-90)

Assuredly there will be no easy harvest of higher-yielding, more nutritious crops and fatter livestock, but the successful application of *package* inputs, based upon remarkable recent advances in tropical agronomy and global low-latitude research in many fields, can result only in an enhanced agricultural and material life for the mass of Africa's peoples. At the same time, there should be no misunderstanding, on the part of readers familiar only with farming activities and rural living conditions in North America, of the tasks ahead. The lot of the average African cultivator or herdsman is, at present, among the meanest and most meager on earth. According to T. Balogh, primitive African cultivators are members of

> the most disinherited, oppressed, exploited, wretched and physically most ailing class in the world . . . living in primeval misery at a time when the privileged population are able to flourish while wasting an untold mass of resources on national rivalry in the arms and space-age; resources amply sufficient, if well applied, to lift Adam's curse and to eradicate poverty from the face of the earth. (Dumont 1966:2)

Dumont affirms that African farmers are among the true proletarians of modern times and urges a massive agricultural effort internationally assisted, to bring them out of stagnation and on to the road of accelerated socio-economic development. Clearly the academic interest of American geographers in African agricultural systems should be set alongside a deep humanitarian concern for the welfare of the mass of rural Africans.

AGRICULTURE IN AFRICA: SOME BASIC FACTS

The agricultural uses to which this vast continent is being or can be put are many. They cover almost every type of farming organization found in either the Old World or the New, and the raising of every crop in the farmer's book. The greater part of Africa's raw material wealth stems from agriculture. Farming is the principal occupation, and rural living the main social experience, of the majority of Africans. The typical African is still a crop cultivator or cattle herder.

While reliable statistics are lacking, some three-quarters of the continent's population are thought to be involved in agriculture (in some countries, estimates rise as high as 90%), and crop and livestock production account for two thirds or more of the national income of many states. The bulk of Africa's exports are, in fact, agricultural in origin, and provide the main source of foreign exchange earnings. They include bananas, cocoa, coffee, cotton, groundnuts, hides and skins, palm products, rubber, sisal, sugar, tea and tobacco.

At the same time, perhaps one half to two thirds of the total cultivated land area in Africa is used mainly for subsistence cropping, i.e. to feed the immediate farm family or the local populace. Subsistence food crops include bananas and plantains, beans, cassava (manioc), cocoyams, corn (maize), cucurbits (gourds, pumpkin, squash), groundnuts (peanuts), millets, rice, sorghums (Guinea and "kaffir" corn), and yams. Large quantities of produce fail to enter the formal marketing pattern where a record of output can be kept; they are traded instead (bartered or sold) at the local level – in the ubiquitous village markets. In East Africa, it has been estimated that at least 60% of agricultural production does not enter the exchange economy. Productivity on the land is, in general, distressingly low, whether measured as output per acre or per capita. An accelerated transformation from elemental subsistence to surplus-producing commercial agriculture is thus one of the basic goals of rural economic planners in Africa.

DIVERSITY IN AFRICAN AGRICULTURE

The essence of rural Africa, if there is one, is diversity, not similarity. The complexities of African habitats and land use techniques are, indeed, legion. Tremendous contrasts occur from area to area, in both physical and cultural terms, and often over relatively short distances.

> Africa has always been characterized by the diversity of its techniques, forms of production, and degrees of productivity. In the course of time, different modes of life were combined and many economic adaptations and transformations took place. Often a remarkable balance between different economic orientations was realized. The greatest diversity of techniques and development occurs in the sphere of agriculture. Agricultural systems range from extensive and fortuitous methods to shifting cultivation, with different fallowing procedures and to permanent and fixed agriculture. (Biebuyck 1963: 53-54)

The intensity of developmental problems and the prospects for change are just as varied.

ECOLOGICAL CONSTRAINTS

The challenge of expanding agricultural production at all levels is a formidable one, due to a host of physical, social, and economic difficulties.

A major obstacle to the desired break-through to improved systems of land use is the unaccommodating, and in places uncontrollable, ecological conditions. In tropical Africa, the primitive husbandman is still largely at the mercy of his environment; his tools and techniques of cultivation are too rudimentary to afford him mastery over it. There are climatic disabilities: marked seasonality of rainfall, resulting in scarcity or over-abundance of water for crops and livestock, excessive heat and humidity, high winds, and squall-line storms. About 75% of Africa south of the Sahara has scanty, often unreliable precipitation, a serious natural hazard for farmers. Contrary to the popular image, only about 8% of Africa has a tropical rainforest climate, but the ten to twelve month rainy season means that these areas are invariably too wet for optimum human utility in terms of agriculture.

The luxuriant rainforests, heavily-wooded savannas (forest-savanna mosaic), scrublands, and tropical steppes present formidable problems of clearance and management for permanent fields or improved pastures. Many of the savanna grasses have a low nutritive value for domesticated livestock. The soils of Africa are notoriously intractable: heavily leached and easily eroded in some areas, poorly structured with low nutrient status in others. Good soils are the exception in most African states; there are proportionately fewer young and fertile alluvial soils than in any other continent. It is against this physical backdrop that the low levels of productivity on the part of traditional cultivators, and the efforts to raise yields on the part of improved farmers, must be placed.

Nevertheless, the limiting effect of environmental factors such as inadequate moisture and poor soils need not be exaggerated. Many indigenous agricultural systems do, in fact, display remarkable adaptations to both these deficiencies. Modern techniques of water conservation and soil improvement, wedded to empirically derived skills of traditional African cultivators, can go far towards overcoming these handicaps. Figure 7-2 shows how increasing human measures of management can shorten fallow time and improve soil productivity.

In particular, local water supplies can be regularized and augmented by small-scale irrigation schemes and other hydraulic works which are relatively cheap and easy to construct.... Similarly, although much remains to be learned about African soils, there is little doubt that the fertility of many of them can be substantially raised by the judicious application of appropriate modern artificial fertilizers. (Hodder and Harris 1967:16)

SOCIOLOGICAL CONSTRAINTS

The characteristics and distribution of the population, together with customary, tribal traditions and social institutions among African peoples, are often further obstacles to enhanced productivity on the land. Like farmers the world over, the rural African does not fit into a single mold but, as in most national and cultural groups, it is possible to recognize certain dominant traits in behavior and attitudes. The expression, *farmers,* when applied to African cultivators may be misleading to North Americans. Due to the scale of their operations, many African cultivators are gardeners rather than farmers in the western sense of the word. They till small, often dispersed and temporary plots of land, rather than cultivate large, clearly demarcated fields.

It is important to recognize that land use in Africa, as elsewhere, revolves around behavioral patterns and decision-making processes which take into account as many of the ecological and socio-economic variables as a farmer is able to perceive and comprehend in relation to his own situation. The sum wisdom of the rural residents, and their perception of the advantages or hazards involved in pursuing various farming activities, is at the heart of the agricultural *modus operandi.*

The application of this approach to African rural land use has been pithily expressed:

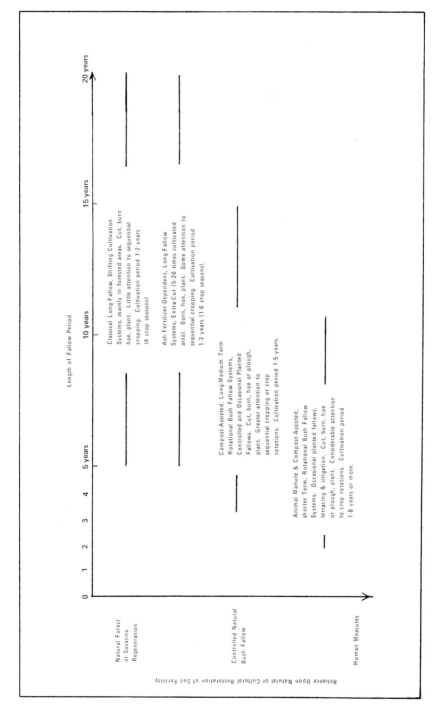

Figure 7-2. Some Land Rotation Systems of Crop Husbandry in Tropical Africa.

... the environment should be processed and refined to an appropriate form, an environmental mode that is accessible to the mind of the man who interacts with it. In fact, the environment is so processed. A man does not say, 'Here I am, a teenage shifting cultivator, living on dark red latosols with a mean annual rainfall of 67.4 inches; the bush I'm standing in has rested for nine years which is the fallow period in my community; ah well, time once again to plant beans.' The farmer 'reads' the vegetation and the sky; he remembers last year's yield. He consults the empirical wisdom of his father, his neighbors, perhaps the local diviner, and possibly the local agricultural officer. His decisions are based on his assessment of the relative chances of success among a number of choices. (Porter 1969:261)

In elaboration of the behavioral theme, many African cultivators place a high priority on "leisure" or, more accurately, on time to pursue activities other than those directly related to the production of food: discussions of tribal or national affairs, administration of local justice, entertainment, ceremonies associated with births, taking a bride, funerals, and so forth. Indeed, it is invariably wrong to view the residents of the African countryside as totally committed to agriculture. G. Kay (1969:497-498) goes so far as to suggest that

the rural African is not a farmer or a fisherman or any such specialist – he is a 'villager' whose polyfunctional life should be viewed as a whole.

In any case, few rural residents cultivate as much land as even their limited techniques or access to natural resources allow, but expend only as much labor as is necessary to satisfy their wants, or to produce such surpluses as they estimate can be satisfactorily sold, exchanged, or given to friends or dependents. In social science jargon, they are "satisfiers," not "optimizers."

The model of a rational *economic man*, responsive to western type incentives to maximize yields and profits from farming, must therefore be used with caution in African land use studies and planning. The notion of *bounded rationality* should probably be substituted for the supposedly omniscient rationality of *economic man*.

SECURITY

Traditional subsistence cultivators in tropical Africa are much concerned with security. Living close to the datum line of poverty and malnutrition, with lives at stake if errors are committed on the land, the African farmer will depart from empirically tested practices only if convinced that the new techniques are absolutely safe.

> It may be possible to show that if he plants his crops each year at a certain time he will get better average returns, but if this includes the risk of crop failure in *one* year, he will prefer to adjust to the variable rainfall in Africa, minimize his risk, and plant the crop over a number of days. (Kamarck 1967:102)

Similarly, the pastoralist feels more secure if he can enlarge his herd during favorable years, then loose or sell off cattle during a bad year. He deems this more sensible than limiting the number of cattle to an average or minimum number he can carry in good years and bad. In any case

> if there are a large number of competitors for scarce grass, and the individual herder cannot rely on the others to behave 'sensibly' and so restrict the total number of cattle to the optimum carrying capacity, then he, like the others, will try to increase his own cattle as much as possible, even though this will mean that the land is over-grazed. (Kamarck 1967:102)

The importance of security reflects also in the traditional settlement patterns of many rural Africans. Nucleated hamlets and villages, with closely-spaced huts set in defensive sites on ridges or hilltops, along water-courses, or in the heart of the forest, were characteristic of rural settlements in earlier centuries. The socio-logical, if not the military, advantages of "near neighbors" have persisted to the present as have the nodal patterns themselves; in order to cushion the impact of innovations, the spatial organiza-tion of modern agricultural settlements in Africa is obliged to take this social factor into account.

LAND TENURE

Security of land holding in traditional African societies was reflected in the various systems of tribal or communal tenure. These were based on the right of access to farm land, and the harvesting of its *fruits* (usufructuary rights), on the part of all members of the community. Permanent individual ownership of a piece of tribal territory was not customary; instead, the land was periodically re-allocated to farmers by their chiefs and other rulers. As long as the population remained small, and shifting techniques of cultivation prevailed, there was no cause to change this procedure. With increased numbers of people and restrictions on access to additional farm land, traditional systems of tenure have proved an obstacle to economic progress.

With fixed or permanent farming, it is important for cultivators to have secure rights to a piece of land. They must invest
labor and capital to build up the quality of the soil, protecting it
from erosion by contour banks, draining it with ditches, or
planting crops in rotation. Capital is required for improved
implements, seed, fertilizer, insecticides. Low-interest loans to
finance these inputs are required, but to borrow money the farmer
needs good credit; the best collateral is the pledge of land.
Security of tenure for himself and his descendents is thus essential.
Many writers have urged tenurial reforms in tropical Africa.

> Traditional communal land tenure was . . . a good adaptation for
> common security within the given conditions. But let there be no
> mistake; it is possible to appreciate, even with a certain admiration,
> the complexity of a culture so intricately adapted to its limitations,
> but the limitations are preposterous and the culture is desperately
> poor. Better methods have still to defer to soil and climatic
> conditions but in many areas will demand a revolution in land
> tenure. (Hunter 1962:101)

Elsewhere, an agricultural economist has written:

> It is clear that the root cause of the economic backwardness of
> various African territories . . . lies in the failure to modify customary
> control of land occupation and tenure, which has prevented the
> emergence of land use and ownership compatible with modern forms
> of commercialized production in a money economy. The failure to
> make of the land a viable economic factor of production has
> condemned the peoples on it to eke out a precarious existence.
> (Frankel 1960:7)

Patterns of land ownership are thus a further factor in the
geographical analysis of farming systems in Africa which require
careful consideration; the spatial variance in tenurial forms can
have a profound effect on landscape patterns and farming
procedures.

MIGRATIONS

Still another characteristic of rural Africa to be noted is the
remarkable level of mobility of the population. Movements are a
time-honored feature of African peoples and

> have resulted from such factors as demographic growth, social
> calamities, search for better lands or water resources, migrations of
> animals, social and political disaggregation, transhumance, nomadic
> ways of life. (Biebuyck 1963:57)

In more recent times, young men have been lured to centers of
mining, the towns, and commercial agricultural areas (including

expatriate farms) in search of paid employment. The extent of migratory labor in Africa has, in fact, been impressive. The copper mines of the Zaire Republic (formerly Congo Kinshasa) and Zambia, the gold and diamond mines of the Republic of South Africa, much of the industry in South-Central, East and West Africa, the tobacco farms in Rhodesia, the tea estates in Malawi, the sisal estates in Tanzania, the large coffee farms in Uganda, the Gezira cotton lands in the Sudan, the cocoa farms of Ghana and Western Nigeria, the groundnut producing areas of Senegal, Mali and Northern Nigeria: all participate in this migrant labor system.

Men may leave their villages for periods of a few days at a time to several months or even years. Some engage in part-time or weekend farming; others participate seasonally, at peak periods, in such activities as clearing the bush or harvesting; still others abandon agriculture as an occupation altogether. As a means of raising capital to invest in farming through better housing, tools, fertilizers and seed, part-time wage labor has been an asset, and the incentives of *economic man* have infiltrated into rural society. But the prolonged absence of adult males can be highly disruptive of the social fabric of a community.

> While migrant labor was probably necessary at one stage of African development, with time it has become clear that the gains have been exhausted ... with the migrant moving back and forth between the money economy and the farm, he is unable to increase his productivity as an industrial worker or as a farmer but becomes stuck on a plateau of relative inefficiency in each case. And the costs in terms of time and energy wasted in shuttling back and forth are high. (Kamarck 1967:106)

What is required ideally is for most migrants to settle permanently in their new positions, while those with the capital assets and aspirations to become progressive farmers should return to their homelands under improved arrangements in the way of tenure, crop sepcialization, and modern techniques of production and marketing. However, to persuade those who have left their villages for paid employment in industry or towns to forfeit their claim to farming rights at home is not easy. Even in the most economically advanced areas, the majority of migrant workers are reluctant to sever ties with the land completely. Traditional forces still bind people strongly to their birthplace, despite the obvious weakening of kin and family associations in recent years.

THE GEOMETRY OF AFRICAN AGRICULTURE

It is important for North Americans when attempting to visualize agricultural landscapes in tropical Africa, to erase their mental images of large, square or rectangular, clean-tilled fields and regimented rows of cash crops. Only over rather limited areas are permanently demarcated, intensively cultivated and geometrically organized fields a dominant feature of the landscape. Elsewhere, more often than not, "fields" are small irregular patches in the bush or forest, imperfectly cleared by burning, cultivated only by hand implements and frequently weedy, and containing a layered mixture of crops planted in what appears to Westerners to be complete random disorder. Even experienced observers find it difficult at times to differentiate garden plot from bush or abandoned clearing.

The reaction of Western observers to the farming methods of shifting cultivators in Africa has been graphically described.

> When one enters a Zande homestead for the first time, the impression is that of complete chaos. The courtyard is shapeless or roughly circular or oval. The huts in it are scattered. Crops, food and household belongings may lie about the courtyard, or be piled on to the verandah of a hut in what seems to be a most disorderly fashion. Worst of all, no fields can be seen. The thickets of plants surrounding the homestead seem as patchy and purposeless as any wild vegetation. It is impossible to distinguish a crop from a weed. It seems altogether incredible that a human intelligence should be responsible for this tangle. This first impression very often decides the whole attitude of the [Westerner] towards primitive agriculture. It fills him with the desire to put things straight and, before he makes any effort to learn the African's conception of order, he starts teaching him his own conception as expressed in straight lines and right angles. . . . It can be seen that the seeming disorder of Zande fields and courtyards is due to the fact that the Zande embroiders his agricultural activity on a canvas and pattern provided for him by nature. He is not free to do otherwise. The seeming disorder is the expression of a rigid order which he has not yet overcome. In comparison, our conceptions of order, our straight furrows and wheel tracks, the even height of well-spaced wheat, the parallel rows of sugar beets and the enclosed fields of a permanent rotation, are achievements of centuries of labor to overcome the limitations of nature and to domesticate the soil. They are the expression of a higher degree of freedom from coercion by environmental limitations rather than of a stricter order. (de Schlippe 1956: 101, 107)

It is a mistake therefore to assume that traditional African farming is as crude and inefficient as its casual and unplanned appearance might suggest. African techniques are, in fact, well adapted to the physical and cultural environments in which they have developed, and changes in them should be undertaken only after a most careful consideration of the ways in which the traditional systems operate. The apparently chaotic arrangement of fields and crops meets the challenge of the environment in several ways. The small separated plots are more easily re-colonized by vegetation under natural bush-fallowing techniques than larger ones. The spread of plant diseases is much more difficult than it is in the vast, monocropped blocks of North American farmlands. Mixed and sequential cropping maintain a constant vegetational canopy to protect the soil from heavy rain and excessive insolation.

> It also provides protection against total crop failure when the mixture is made up of varieties having different moisture and soil requirements and with differing tolerances of drought, wind and pests. (Jones 1961: 9)

More productive, commercial systems of farming in Africa may well require greater attention to geometric regularities in shape and size of fields and other infrastructural features, also distances and directions relating to the circulation of inputs, throughputs and outputs. But such model layouts must clearly be weighed against the costs of combatting the natural hazards of the tropical *milieu,* as well as ameliorating social resistance to change among traditional African communities. Plans for the more efficient spatial arrangement of African farming systems will require comprehensive and co-ordinated effort on the part of many: agronomists, natural and social scientists, administrators and politicians.

CONTINUITY AND CHANGE IN AFRICAN AGRICULTURE

Pronounced changes in traditional agricultural land use in Africa are, of course, underway – and have been so for many years – with the tempo of change quickening particularly since independence. The impression should not be given then that traditional cultivation methods such as those of the Zande are to be found unmodified across Africa. Figure 7-3 suggests a modernization scheme with potential application to much of Africa.

COLONIAL EFFORTS

The colonial governments – British, French, Belgian – made many efforts to improve the agrarian systems within their dependent territories. Kimble (1960:169) writes:

> The schemes that have been put into operation during the past thirty years and more are of many kinds. In scope they range from small-scale pilot projects costing next to nothing beyond the effort of mind and muscle that went into them, to mammoth, multi-

CROP & LIVESTOCK SPECIALIZATION	TRADITIONAL Pre-industrial, subsistence, low per capita productivity	TRANSITIONAL Old industrial types, innovation techniques, increasing com- mercialization, higher per capita productivity.	MODERN New industrial types, new production techniques, commercial high per capita production
CROPS DOMINANT	Land rotation systems of extensive subsistence farming. Rudimentary sedentary, fixed field agriculture.	Plantations, especially tree crops. Intensive sedentary system: crop rotation, soil erosion measures, use of organic and chemical fertilizers. Floodland cultivation.	Modern plantation or estate agriculture scientific pro- cedures. Horticulture. Market gardening for fruits, vegetables, etc.
MIXED FARMING	Land rotation systems (shifting cultivation). Crop and livestock farming, crude unintegrated techniques.	Commercial crop and livestock farming. Attention to im- proved varieties of crops, rotations, fertilizers.	Dairy farming. Manufactured feeds and feed substitutes.
ANIMALS DOMINANT	Nomadic herding. Primitive pastoralism. Transhumance.	Livestock rearing. Upgraded stock, improved pastures. Controlled grazing, paddocking.	Livestock ranching. Feed lots. "Zero" grazing. Intensive pig, poultry, egg production.

Figure 7-3. A Matrix Classification of Agriculture in Africa (Modified from R. Abler, J. Adams, P. Gould, *Spatial Organization.)*

million-dollar, TVA-type excursions into 'social engineering'; from one-man campaigns for the resiting of villages to quasi-military operations calling for the making over of whole countrysides into the likeness of blueprints, and using the armory of weapons – financial, technological, political and scientific – available to Western democracy. Some have been inspired and undertaken by governments, some by private organizations. Some have been directed to the needs of the African, some to the needs of the European, and some to both. Their geographical location has been as varied as their scope, for they have been tried out in forest and veld, swamp and desert, plateau and plain.

Needless to say, many of these programs were over-ambitious and ill-designed, due to inadequate funding and expertise, and a lack of knowledge of the African environment and rural popula- tions. Indeed, the catalog of abortive agricultural projects in tropical Africa is disturbingly lengthy. Among the most ignomin- ious failures were the British-sponsored groundnut scheme in Tanganyika (Tanzania), the Niger Agricultural project at Mokwa in Nigeria, and the Damongo Settlement in the Northern Region of the Gold Coast (Ghana).

Programs which showed greater promise of success, but have since foundered or been much modified, include the peasant settlement or *paysannat* schemes of the Belgians and French in equatorial Africa, peasant colonization schemes in Portuguese Angola and Mozambique, the Office du Niger irrigation project in the Niger Valley of the French Soudanese Republic (Mali), and the Native Land Husbandry program in (Southern) Rhodesia. Only a few of the large-scale, colonially-inspired schemes to transform traditional African agriculture may be said to have succeeded, among them the Gezira irrigation scheme for cotton and food crops in the Republic of the Sudan, and the Swynnerton Plan or Land Consolidation scheme in Kikuyuland, Kenya.

SINCE INDEPENDENCE

Agricultural development schemes incorporating a wide spectrum of projects have been launched since independence in many African states. Some have met (or are meeting) with little more success than those initiated by the former colonial authorities. Others show greater promise of effectively grasping the nettle of rural poverty and backwardness, and bringing about a transformation of traditional agriculture.

A controversial feature of the new Africa is the state-supervised, large-scale unit of production, modelled after socialist forms of agricultural organization, and undertaken with the help of foreign experts from such countries as Israel, the states of Eastern Europe, the U.S.S.R. and the Chinese People's Republic. As examples, we may cite the former state farms and the large-scale cooperative farm settlements in Ghana during the Nkrumah era, and comparable projects still flourishing in Guinea; the farm settlements of Nigeria; cooperative Ujamaa ("family-hood") villages in Tanzania; and the cooperative or community farms in Zambia. In contrast to these centralized, capital-intensive schemes we may note the program of the Kenya government to break up large expatriate properties in the former "White Highlands," and to settle African husbandmen on their own individually-owned farms.

These ambitious programs have been well-publicized in National Development Plans, the annual reports of Ministries responsible for their implementation, and the popular press. And since they are comparatively well-documented, in contrast to the traditional areas of indigenous agriculture, the big politically-motivated projects have tended to receive a disproportionate emphasis in recent academic studies. Yet, it is probably premature to pass scientific judgement on the success or failure of these schemes since most of them have only been launched over the last few years.

Innovative planning in the years ahead must obviously build on the lessons of the past. At the same time, the striking advances in agronomy elsewhere in the world, particularly the development of high-yielding hybrid wheat, rice, and maize, and the breakthrough in plant chemotherapy (the chemical treatment of plants to alter their environmental requirements) must also be taken into account in future African agricultural schemes. The so-called *Green Revolution* could have a profound effect upon land use planning for African farmers at all stages of technology.

THE INDIVIDUAL FARMER

Nevertheless, at the grass- or savanna-roots level, it is still the individual cultivator or pastoralist who must be won over to the reforms which are proposed on his behalf. Ultimately all the problems of land use center around the farmer and his family. If their attitudes and views are not taken sufficiently into account, their ways of farming will never be improved. African planners must never ignore the fundamental observation that it is the people who matter, not the soil, the crops or the livestock – except in their relation to the prosperity and happiness of the people.

Meanwhile, the democratic options to enhance agriculture are as numerous as ever, even if there is no short-cut to full productivity on the land.

> Simple persuasion and advice, the use of monetary incentives or rewards, communal projects and self-help schemes, organized and directed programs, and cooperative societies may all have their place, depending on the physical, human, and economic conditions that exist in different regions. (Hance 1967:53)

The way ahead for African farmers is neither clearcut nor smooth, and we are merely at the beginning of dealing with the problems which must be solved. One can only hope that a real measure of improvement in the livelihood of Africa's rural population may be achieved before the century is through.

8

Urbanization in Africa*

DERRICK J. THOM
Utah State University

Too often Africa is perceived as a continent of villages and its rural nature is emphasized to the neglect of the dynamic processes at work in the urban centers. While the majority of Africa's population do in fact live in villages, increasingly the cities of Africa represent the aspirations for economic advancement of millions of rural dwellers. Moreover, urbanization is playing an important role in the development of the new states of Africa. In order to understand contemporary Africa, it is necessary to be aware of the process of urbanization that has created an urban *explosion* since World War II.

The cities of Africa are not as significant for the total number of people residing in them as they are for the overriding political, social, and cultural change they bring to Africa. Only 12 per cent (31 million) of Black Africa's population resides in urban centers of 20,000 or more. Africa remains the least urbanized of the inhabited continents, but compared to other regions of the world the rate of urban growth is greater than elsewhere. Africa's urban population is now doubling every 15 years and this phenomenal rate of growth is creating social, economic, and political problems. Since urbanization is playing such a dynamic role in bringing modernization and social change to Africa, it is important to understand the background of African urbanization, the problems associated with increasing urban growth, and the morphology of African cities.

BACKGROUND OF AFRICAN URBANIZATION

INDIGENOUS AFRICAN CITIES

A common misconception is that prior to the European intrusion cities did not exist in Africa. There is ample evidence to

*The author would like to acknowledge the assistance and cooperation of Dr. James W. King, University of Utah, for the suggestions and criticisms he has made in the preparation of this chapter.

123

disprove such a notion. The cities of the Nile Valley were among the earliest urban centers in world history. North Africa developed important cities before the time of Christ and in Africa south of the Sahara, numerous cities emerged prior to the era of European discovery.

A line drawn eastwardly from the coast of Cameroon to the Horn of Africa provides a useful but rather crude generalization to demarcate *urban Africa* from *village Africa* (Figure 8-1). North of the line many of the societies developed an urban tradition where pre-industrial cities became the focal point for the development of important indigenous African kingdoms. The area south of the line can be generalized as *village Africa* where cities were not such a common feature, although ruins such as Zimbabwe in Rhodesia and the early trade cities of the East African coast challenge the validity of the generalization. Nevertheless the degree, intensity, and persistance of an urban tradition was much greater north of the line than south.

In the Western Sudan several important cities developed on the southern fringes of the Sahara. Cities such as Bamako, Timbuktu, Jenne, Gaya, Kukia, Kano and Katsina became front ports of Black Africa functioning primarily as important administrative and trade centers. (Mabogunje 1970:335) These cities were located at the termini of the trans-Saharan trade routes and were points of cultural contact between the Arabs to the north and the forest peoples to the south. The earliest of the great Sudanic cities emerged in the third century but the majority developed between the eighth and twelfth century. The significance of many of these cities persisted until the time of the European intrusion in the late nineteenth century.

The cities of the Western Sudan were usually located on a site that provided some natural defense whether on a hill such as Kano or on the bank of a river such as Timbuktu. As an added defensive feature the cities were surrounded by high mud walls. Their situation was ideal with regard to trade routes and location between two different cultural and ecological zones so that with the trade these cities functioned as entrepôt centers. The trans-Saharan trade brought prosperity and cultural enrichment to the Western Sudan and encouraged the growth and development of strong political organization and city-states whose influence extended over vast areas.

The Hausa states which were located in what is today northern Nigeria were typical of the highly organized city-states that dominated the Western Sudan from the third to the twentieth century. Using the Hausa city-state as an example, a theoretical

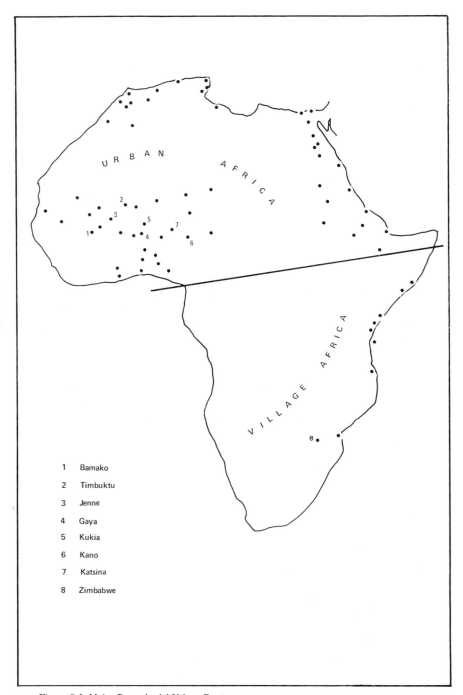

Figure 8-1. Major Pre-colonial Urban Centers.

structure can be applied as a model, in its broad outline, to other Sudanic kingdoms.

Early in the history of the Hausa people the concept of a city-state arose in which a city's rulers gained control over the population of a territory. The city-states that emerged, even prior to the introduction of Islam, produced a ruling elite, a strong administration, and the nucleus of the later Emirates. The city was the nodal point of the state, and the state and people, more often than not, adopted the name of the principal city—the people of Katsina for example, became known as the Katsinawa.

The form and function of most of the Hausa states were very much the same, and the ideal Hausa state can be viewed theoretically as a series of concentric zones radiating from the central walled city or *birni*. (Figure 8-2). This walled city, as a central place, was a commercial, religious, and administrative center. Within the city walls as much as two-thirds of the land was devoted to agriculture; the remainder was devoted to the normal functions of a city, such as commercial, residential, and administrative quarters. A significant function of the *birni* was defense against attacks from neighbors; the vast expanse of agricultural land enclosed within the city walls made laying a successful siege to the city extremely difficult.

Immediately surrounding the walls of the city was a zone of intensive agriculture from which the city's produce was drawn. Usually this zone of intensive agriculture extended for a distance of no more than three or four miles beyond the city walls. Quite often those who cultivated the land resided in the city, and those

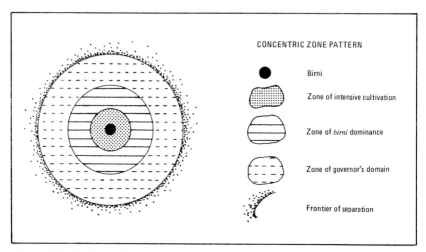

Figure 8-2. Ideal Hansa State.

farming on the periphery of the zone might reside temporarily on their farms during the growing season.

Lying beyond the zone of intensive cultivation and extending for an indeterminate distance that depended upon the strength of the state, was a zone controlled by the city. The peoples living in this zone resided in hamlets, villages, and small walled towns producing agricultural products and crafts for the city, and in turn the products of the city percolated through to this zone. Control of the zone was directly from the *birni* with the inhabitants being subject to direct taxation by the Emir.

A fourth zone, again of indeterminate distance, was one whose population was only loosely bound to the city. This was a zone over which the Emir had gained control through conquest; peoples residing in this region were required to pay tribute. Control of this zone was in the hands of governors appointed by the Emir, but they resided within the *birni* forming part of the Emir's elaborate court. The responsibilities of the governors lay in collecting the assessed tribute and safeguarding the trade routes that passed through their territory. Finally beyond the zone of the governors' domain lay the frontier of separation, a zone that separated one Hausa state from the other. This zone was regarded as *no-man's-land* and was quite often inhabited by pagan (i.e., non-Islamic) Hausa or other ethnic groups. This zone was a source region for the state's slaves and in some instances became a depopulated frontier of separation between adjacent city-states.

To the south of the Sudanic cities important forest kingdoms developed among the Ashanti, Ewe, Dahomey, Yoruba and Benin peoples. Each kingdom focused upon large urban agglomerations that functioned as administrative and trade centers. The Yoruba of south-western Nigeria were probably the most highly urbanized people in Black Africa.

In some respects the Yoruba cities such as Oyo, Ogbomosho, and Ile-Ife were similar in size and lay-out but significantly different in organization and function from the Sudanic cities. Unlike the Sudanic cities the Yoruba urban centers were not created as a result of the trans-Saharan trade but for the purpose of an immigrant population using cities to control the indigenous population. (Mabogunje 1968:76) The primary function of Yoruba cities was administrative although trade based on agriculture and craft production provided the economic base for the cities.

Internal difficulties that eventually led to war in the nineteenth century resulted in the coalescing of several Yoruba towns and the emergence of new towns such as Ibadan and Abeokuta as armed military camps. By the turn of the century Ibadan and Abeokuta each had over 100,000 population and several other Yoruba cities came within the 50,000 to 100,000 population range. Although these were cities in terms of population size they were in effect, like their Sudanic counterparts, large *Agrotowns* where the majority of the population were farmers.

East Africa did not experience the intensity and concentration of urban centers that was found in West Africa. However, towns have existed along the coast of East Africa for over two thousand years. Most of the pre-colonial cities of East Africa were port cities that flourished on trade between East Africa, the Middle East and India. The heterogeneous make-up of the population of these East African port cities included "indigenous Bantu-speaking African peoples, Yemenite Arabs, Persians and Malays. Gradually these peoples evolved into the Swahili people of today." (Mabogunje 1970:336)

Following the rise of Islam in the seventh century and the domination of the East African coast by Islamized Arabs, several city-states developed. The domination of East African coastal cities lasted until the sixteenth century when Arab control was challenged by the Portuguese and later by German and British infiltration in the nineteenth century.

EUROPEAN INFLUENCE AND CITY GROWTH

As European control spread into Africa from the sixteenth to the nineteenth centuries, its influence upon the traditional African cities was varied. The Europeans initially established small trading posts such as St. Louis, Gorée, Conakry, Abidjan, Lagos, and many others along the coast of West Africa. The diversion of West African trade to the coastal areas caused a marked decline in trans-Saharan trade and a subsequent decline of important Sudanic cities such as Timbuktu. At the same time the diversion of trade to the coast enhanced the growth and expansion of indigenous forest cities such as Kumasi, headquarters of the Ashanti, and the cities of Yorubaland such as Oyo.

The European coastal trading posts gradually developed into important port cities and became springboards for European expansion into the interior. As European influence spread and colonial boundaries were established, the port cities became a vital link between the colony and the metropolitan powers. In the interior some of the traditional cities declined when the colonial transportation system by-passed them; the future of others such as Kano was assured when roads and railroads connected them with the port cities and they were drawn into the expanding transportation network and the emerging colonial economy.

The period from 1862 to 1917 was one of establishment of new European settlements, many with specialized functions. During this period more than 50 new towns were laid out with only three located on the sites of indigenous centers. (Hance 1970:215-216) The specialized functions of these urban centers included commercial, mining, transportation and administrative headquarters.

Several of the old trading towns such as Kano and Kumasi retained their commercial function by becoming centers for the marketing of cash crops such as groundnuts and cocoa. Numerous mining towns were constructed to exploit the wealth of Africa and fill the rising demand for minerals in Europe. Cities such as Jos and Enugu were founded to exploit Nigerian tin and coal. Lubumbashi (formerly Elisabethville) was established by the Belgians to exploit the copper of Shaba (Katanga). Cities of Rhodesia located on the highly mineralized Great Dyke included Que Que, Gatooma and Gwelo. The copperbelt towns of Zambia included Mufulira, Nchanga, and Broken Hill. In South Africa diamonds encouraged the growth of Kimberly at the confluence of the Vaal and Orange Rivers while the gold of the Witwatersrand spawned Johannesburg. Many of these mining towns were located in sparsely populated areas which necessitated migration in order to fill the need for labor.

The colonial powers also established towns that functioned as administrative headquarters or regional capitals. The city of Kaduna was created by the British to function as the regional administrative headquarters of Northern Nigeria. The Germans founded Buea in the Cameroons and the French established Niamey in Niger for similar administrative purposes. Many of the port cities came to function as capital cities and usually grew to be the largest and most important urban agglomerations. These cities were able to attract investment for the development of incipient industry. Outside of South Africa and Rhodesia there are no industrial cities *per se,* although industrialization is proceeding at a rapid pace in cities such as Abidjan, Lagos, Tema, Port Harcourt and others.

PROBLEMS OF AFRICAN CITIES

Since the 1920's the proliferation of new towns by the European colonizers has declined, resulting instead in a rapid growth of existing urban centers. Following World War II the rate of urban growth has accelerated at an increasing rate. This trend has resulted in a high concentration of urban population in only a few large-sized cities and in very few medium-sized cities. According to the U. N. Economic Commission of Africia (1969:130), it is estimated that 68 percent of Africa's urban population resides in cities of over 100,000. (Figure 8-3) Furthermore many countries have more than half of their urban population concentrated in a single city which exerts a disproportionate influence on the country's cultural, economic, and political activities. (Table 8-1)

URBAN GROWTH

Cities in Africa are growing at a phenomenal rate, 5.4 percent annually, a rate which is twice the natural population increase. The rate of growth in cities of over 100,000 is even more astonishing; it averages 8.6 percent per year, with cities such as Kinshasa and Abidjan increasing at annual rates of 10 percent and 11 percent respectively. It is estimated that over 60 percent of urban growth is due to migration, where migrants from rural areas arrive in search of economic opportunities. The rural incomes are one-half or one-third less than in the city; this makes city life very attractive to the rural inhabitant. Furthermore, better services, schools, and hospitals are more readily available in the city and further encourage a rural to urban migration.

Migration is either temporary or permanent. Where migration to the city is temporary it is usually young males who find work in order to accumulate cash for bride wealth or to purchase a specific commodity. The journey to, and residence in, the city by young men is viewed as an initiation rite by some societies, an induction into manhood which brings great prestige in return to the village. Although many arrive in the city and become permanent residents, most entertain ideas of retiring to their villages and consequently maintain strong ties with their village home area.

As a result of the rapid population growth of African cities, physical expansion is causing problems for some of them. Constricted sites, poor drainage, inadequate water supply, and physical hazards seriously restrict the growth of some African cities.

Many of the early sites chosen by Europeans were on offshore islands and narrow peninsulas. In some instances the islands were easily joined to the mainland and urban sprawl spread onto adjacent land. Cities such as Lagos and Mombasa survived and grew in this manner although congestion on the bridges joining outlying areas to the central city creates problems of circulation.

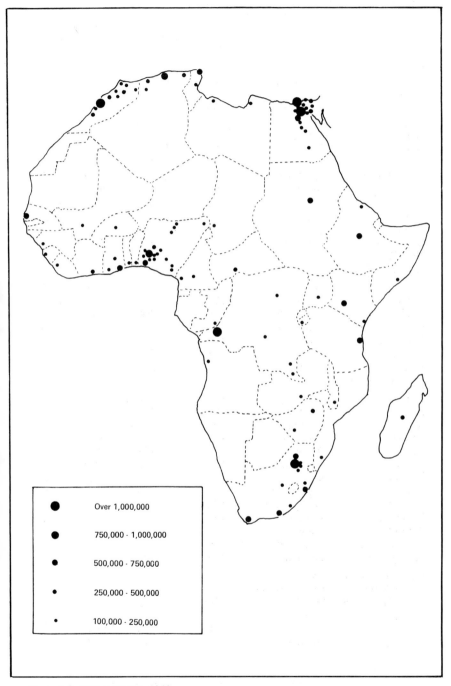

Figure 8-3. African Towns, 1968.

TABLE 8-1
PRIMATE CITIES OF AFRICAN COUNTRIES; THEIR PERCENT OF TOTAL
URBAN POPULATION AND OF RESPECTIVE NATIONAL POPULATION

Country	City	Year	Population (thou.)	% of urban pop.	% of national pop.
WEST AFRICA					
Mauritania	Nouakchott	1966	22	35.5	2.1
Senegal	Dakar	1960	374A	50.1	12.0
Mali	Bamako	1965	165	38.4	3.6
Upper Volta	Ougadougou	1966	110	34.2	2.2
Niger	Niamey	1968	71	36.0	1.9
Gambia	Bathurst	1966	43	100.0	12.8
Guinea	Conakry	1967	197A		2.4
Sierra Leone	Freetown	1963	163A	55.8	7.1
Liberia	Monrovia	1962	81	64.8	8.0
Ivory Coast	Abidjan	1967	400	45.4	10.8
Ghana	Accra	1960	338	21.1	5.0
Togo	Lome	1966	129	39.4	7.7
Dahomey	Cotonou	1965	120	32.1	5.1
Nigeria	Lagos	1963	665A	19.4	1.2
MIDDLE AFRICA					
Chad	Ft. Lamy	1962-63	100	38.0	3.2
C.A.R.	Bangui	1967	150	38.1	10.3
Congo (B)	Brazzaville	1968	200	59.5	22.9
Gabon	Libreville	1968	62	67.4	13.0
Cameroon	Douala	1963-64	187	23.9	3.7
Congo (K)	Kinshasa	1966	508		3.2
Angola	Luanda	1960	225A	47.8	4.7
EASTERN AFRICA					
Ethiopia	Addis Ababa	1966	600A		2.6
Somalia	Mogadishu	1966	170		6.6
Kenya	Nairobi	1962	315A	47.7	3.7
Uganda	Kampala	1959	123A	56.9	1.9
Tanganyika	Dar es Salaam	1967	273A	42.2	2.3
Zanzibar	Zanzibar City	1967	95A	81.9	26.9
Rwanda	Kigali	1967	25	73.5	0.8
Burundi	Bujumbura	1967	100		3.0
Malawi	Blantyre-Limbe	1966	108	69.7	2.6
Rhodesia	Salisbury	1961-62	310A	42.4	8.1
Zambia	Lusaka	1966	152	19.6	4.0
Mozambique	Lourenco Marques	1964	300		4.4
Madagascar	Tananarive	1964	322	42.0	5.5
SOUTHERN AFRICA					
South Africa	Johannesburg	1960	1,153A	17.5	7.1
South West Africa	Windhoek	1960	35	51.4	6.9
Botswana	Gaborone	1968	19		3.1
Lesotho	Maseru	1966	18	100.0	2.1
Swaziland	Mbabane	1966	14	58.0	3.7

A = agglomeration

Source: William A. Hance, *Population, Migration and Urbanization in Africa* (New York: Columbia University Press, 1970), p. 232.

Cities such as Dakar, sited on a peninsula are restricted in their
direction of growth while others such as Freetown and Capetown
with mountainous hinterlands have constricted sites and are hard
pressed to accommodate increasing urban sprawl.

Where drainage is a problem only considerable investment by
the city can relieve the situation, an expense that many cities can
ill afford. The availability of adequate water supply is also a
critical factor, especially in the drier savanna lands. Katsina, for
example, is forced to ration its water during the dry season by
turning off the supply during the daylight hours. Such measures
are not uncommon where drought and limited water supplies
prevail. Unless alternative water sources are found, economic and
urban growth is greatly restricted.

The increasing rural to urban migration, the attractiveness of
only a few large cities, and the physical restrictions of some cities
compound the problems of overcrowding and poor urban living
conditions. The basic and fundamental problem of African
urbanization is the rapid growth and expansion of the cities.
(Table 8-2) The inability of most cities to absorb the great number
of migrants and to provide adequate housing, jobs, and public
facilities causes social, economic, and political unrest.

TABLE 8-2
GROWTH OF MAJOR AFRICAN CITIES 1940-1970

City	1940	1950	1960	1970
Cairo	1,307,000	2,100,000	3,348,000	4,961,000
Alexandria	682,000	925,000	1,516,000	2,032,000
Kinshasa	–	208,000	402,000	1,288,000
Johannesburg	286,000	880,000	1,111,000	1,152,000
Lagos	180,000	230,000	449,000	875,000
Capetown	187,000	594,000	746,000	807,000
Ibadan	387,000	459,000	627,000	746,000
Addis Ababa	150,000	402,000	449,000	684,000
Accra	73,000	140,000	388,000	758,000
Dakar	165,000	230,000	374,000	581,000
Nairobi	100,000	112,000	267,000	535,000
Salisbury	51,000	120,000	270,000	390,000
Kano	89,000	130,000	295,000	351,000
Port Elizabeth	125,000	148,000	274,000	290,000
Abidjan	–	127,000	180,000	282,000

Source: *United Nations Demographic Yearbook* (New York: United Nations 1970) pp.
432-435.
Figures refer to nearest census or population estimate available.

PHYSICAL AND SOCIAL CONDITIONS

The rapid increase of urban population obviously creates a number of social problems. The inability of the city to provide sufficient facilities and amenities results in deplorable conditions where crime, health hazards and many of the social ills of modern urban life obtain.

Since migrants are largely age and sex selective there results in the city a preponderance of youth and males, few children, and very few aged. In South Africa the situation is even more critical in that African families are specifically barred from the city unless the wife has employment. Such conditions contribute to the rising crime rate, prostitution, social diseases, and family difficulties caused by separation.

These social conditions are further compounded by economic conditions caused by high unemployment and underemployment. The inability of the city to generate sufficient jobs to absorb the number of newcomers causes dissatisfaction, unrest, and a politically volatile situation. Unemployment rates in cities like Lagos, Accra, Nairobi, and Kinshasa are 15 to 25 percent of the labor force, making unemployment a very serious problem in most African cities. The highest rate of unemployment is among youth who arrive without any specific skills and only a rudimentary education. They vie for the few available jobs and soon become disenchanted with city life, some turning to crime, others becoming political dissidents agitating for change.

Because of high unemployment rates, many are unable to pay for adequate housing. Consequently, every major city is characterized by sprawling squatter settlements or *bidonvilles* on their margins. These shanty towns are constructed from any available material; everything from crates, corrugated tin, grass, and cardboard is used to construct some form of shelter. Where such housing conditions exist public services are virtually non-existent. Sewage and garbage is discarded at any convenient place nearby. These conditions are compounded during rainy seasons when the space between shelters becomes a veritable quagmire and the inhabitants find themselves living in constantly damp conditions. In Dakar, the medina is a *bidonville* that houses 30 percent of the city's population. About 30 percent of the population of Dar es Salaam and 27 percent of Lusaka live under similar circumstances.

Every large city in Africa is plagued with housing shortages, high rents, and extremely overcrowded conditions. Even in areas where housing is permanent and of better quality, overcrowding persists. One official estimated that in a housing estate in Nairobi where 400 rooms were available to house 1,200 people there were in reality over 3,000 inhabitants. (Oram 1965:24) Overcrowded conditions such as these increase the susceptibility to communicable diseases and one of the most frequent causes of death is tuberculosis. Because of unhealthy and unsanitary conditions dysentary, typhoid, and intestinal diseases are not uncommon. Shantytown residents are also subject to poor diets that result in malnutrition. In some instances the reluctance to spend hard earned cash on nutritious food is a principal cause of malnutrition.

The poverty of the average African urban dweller, the high unemployment rate, and the persistent demands for improved conditions: better housing, modern water supply systems, sewage systems, and electricity—out of reach of most cities because of their limited tax base—cause considerable unrest. Major political problems are caused by the poor quality of urban life and high unemployment, which make city administration a difficult task. The political problems are compounded by the diversity of the urban population which encourages the proliferation of political groups based upon tribal or ethnic background.

COMPLEX URBAN ETHNICITY

One of the interesting characteristics of African cities is the diversity and heterogeneous make-up of the population. This diversity is well illustrated in the small city of Kisumu, Kenya, (24,000) where 25 ethnic groups and citizens from 12 countries reside. (Hanna and Hanna 1971:116-117) In Kisumu approximately 60 percent of the population is African, 35 percent Asian, 2.5 percent European, and 1.5 percent Arab. From this example the heterogeneity of the population is readily observable and while the percentages may vary from city to city the dichotomy between African and non-African on the one hand and among Africans on the other is well illustrated.

Expatriate Europeans, Middle-Eastern peoples, and Asians usually make up a small minority of African city population, but their influence on administration, trade, and commerce is much greater than their numbers indicate. This control has been a source of resentment for the mass of Africans who find the more profitable job opportunities in small business and retail trade closed to them. In East Africa Asian control of the retail trade has caused in part, the expulsion of many of them from Kenya and more recently from Uganda. In West Africa, Lebanese, although certainly never as numerous as the Asians in East Africa, function in a similar role in trade and retail business. The expatriate population remains an educated, wealthy elite, residing in comfortable residential areas with all the conveniences and amenities of modern urban living. Only the expatriates and a few prosperous Africans can afford such luxuries. These residential areas are far removed from the conditions of urban living in the shantytowns.

While there exists a dichotomy between expatriate and African, there is also another, more disruptive cleavage among Africans themselves based upon tribal or ethnic affiliation. The feeling of ethnic solidarity is carried over into the city and, instead of *detribalization* occurring, a *supertribalization* may develop whereby ethnic associations based on common kinship assume primary importance in the city. The intensity of rivalries among different ethnic groups in the urban environment creates tensions that have been likened to the racial tensions experienced in the United States. (Hanna and Hanna 1971:105)

The diversity of African urban populations developed as a result of the growth of the city. Initially the city grew in a particular place and the population was drawn from adjacent areas and usually comprised a single ethnic group. Over time, as the city continued to grow, it attracted different ethnic groups from greater distances and as these peoples arrived they were referred to as *strangers*. The cleavage between the indigenes and *strangers* encouraged residential segregation, and sections of towns tended toward ethnic and linguistic homogeneity. *Strangers* quarters – referred to by various names, such as *Sabon Gari* in Northern Nigeria, or *Zongo* in Ghana – emerged to house the African, non-indigenous population. Since each ethnic group tended to associate, reside, and work with their *own kind* there is evidence of ethnic division of labor – a tendency for a particular ethnic group to monopolize certain jobs in the city. Thus the Hausa protected their domination of the cattle and kola nut trade in the cities of Southern Nigeria while the Ibo, prior to the Nigerian Civil War, tended to occupy positions in civil service and transportation in Northern Nigeria.

Since most of urban growth is the result of rural to urban migration, it might be anticipated that the cities would be wrought with stress and anxiety as the migrants endeavor to adjust to their new surroundings. While adjustments have to be made, the transition from a rural existence to urban living is facilitated through the extended family which recognizes familial obligations to the newly arrived. Relatives already residing in the city provide assistance and support until the migrant finds employment and adjusts to the urban environment.

The transition is eased further through the numerous voluntary unions where association with people of the same ethnic group facilitates adjustment to the city. These voluntary associations provide the newcomer with information about the city, political education, and adult education. In addition to providing this useful service, voluntary associations also look out for the interests of the ethnic group they represent, protect business advantages, and provide politicians with a valuable base of support.

In contrast to the voluntary associations which function to promote the well-being of the urban dweller there are also Improvement Unions in the city which are organized to promote improvements in the home village areas. Funds are collected and lobbying carried out in order to secure roads, schools, and hospitals in the rural homelands. Since most migrants plan to retire to the home village, they retain a vested interest in seeing that adequate modern facilities are made available.

The result of urban growth, urban conditions, and ethnicity has produced a distinctive African urban landscape. In many respects the cities of Africa are similar to those of Europe or the United States. Usually a planned modern Central Business District is identifiable with outlying residential areas, differing in quality of housing, services, and amenities. This, however, is only in the broad outline; in specific details, African cities differ markedly from their European or American counterparts. Several types of African cities can be identified. This provides a useful framework whereby the layout, internal structure, or morphology can be explained.

THE MORPHOLOGY OF AFRICAN CITIES

Professor Akin Mabogunje, a prominent Nigerian geographer, has proposed a fourfold typology of African cities based upon the organization and character of the city: the Traditional City, the "Rejuvenated" Traditional City, the Colonial City, and the European City. (1970b: 345-347)

THE TRADITIONAL CITY

The Traditional Cities are located in areas where indigenous urban settlements prevailed prior to the colonial experience. These cities have retained the basic traditional social, economic, and spatial structure and have not been fully integrated into the developing economy of the new independent states. Those cities that have been by-passed by modern communication networks, where urban growth has been retarded, where out-migration is characteristic and where the traditional, haphazard layout prevails are identified as traditional cities. Ethnically the Traditional City is relatively homogeneous with only a small *stranger* and expatriate element present.

The city of Katsina (population 90,000), a Hausa city of Northern Nigeria, is typical of the traditional African city. The town was founded in the twelfth century and gradually rose to prominence as a great entrepôt and center of learning between 1600 and 1800. The rise of Katsina as a great commercial center can be attributed to two important factors relating to the site and situation. First, the site of the city on the divide between the Niger and Chad basins provided ease of access during the wet season. Second, the location of Katsina within the zone of exchange between the forest lands to the south and the Mediterranean lands to the north gave Katsina a position of nodality on the trans-Saharan trade routes. The relative decline of Katsina in the nineteenth century was caused by repeated attempts on the part of traditional Hausa leaders to regain control of Katsina from the Fulani usurpers who had taken over in 1807.

The arrival of the British and the establishment of Katsina as provincial headquarters reinforced the administrative function of the city. Its commercial function was re-established when Katsina became a collecting point for groundnuts (peanuts), the dominant cash crop of northern Nigeria. Despite these stimuli, Katsina was never fully integrated into the expanding economy and transportation communications. Katsina remained very traditional within the city walls. The British established their Provincial Headquarters and their residences (Governmental Residential Area) approximately five miles outside the city, and European stores or canteens were established on the road leading into the city. (Figure 8-4)

Within the walls of the city the traditional layout has been preserved. At each gate leading into the city there is a hamlet or *ungwa* which traditionally functioned to protect the gateway in time of emergency. Almost 50 percent of the area enclosed by the walls is vacant land and much of it is cultivated. [refer back to pages 000 for description and model of Hausa *birni.*]

It is difficult to apply models of western urban land use to Katsina since no readily identifiable functional areas have been laid out. One would be hard pressed to identify a Central Business District although a commercial strip of small businesses has emerged along the main road leading south. The traditional market place is located in the northwest sector of the residential area and the Emir's Palace is located to the northeast. Government and school buildings are scattered throughout the city in an apparently unplanned fashion. Only the residential area can be readily identified. This area has retained the traditional layout and Hausa

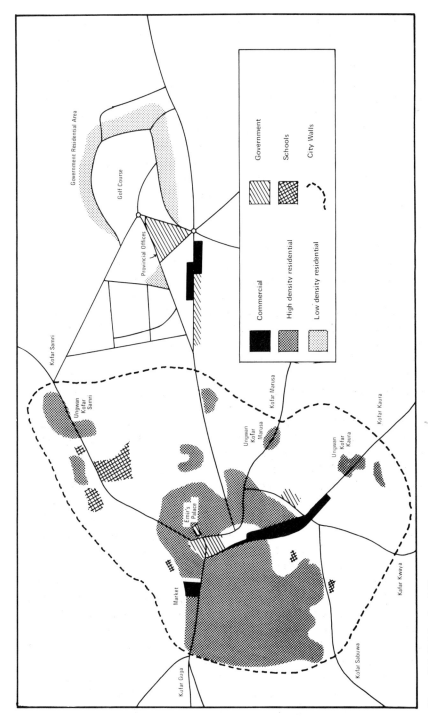

Figure 8-4. Katsina Land Use.

architecture. There are no planned streets between the tightly packed compounds or *gidas* which are constructed of sunbaked mud.

The population is overwhelmingly Katsinawa with only a small *stranger* element residing within the city walls. Expatriates and higher ranking civil servants live in the Government Residential Area outside the walls of the city. The majority of the population is engaged in the traditional craft industries, trading, and farming. Since economic opportunities are limited there is an out-migration of young employable males and consequently, Katsina has not grown as rapidly as those traditional cities that have been integrated into the expanding economy.

THE "REJUVENATED" TRADITIONAL CITY

In contrast to the Traditional City, the Rejuvenated Traditional City is in reality two cities, the old town and the colonial township established immediately adjacent to it. The old town is characterized by its traditional layout and organization, whereas the adjacent new town is usually the product of European urban planning characterized by an identifiable Central Business District and functional areas. Since this city type was incorporated into the colonial economy it became a node for transportation and communication networks and its prosperity resulted in urban growth and the attraction of a diverse and heterogeneous population. This heterogeneous population resided in the new town. Residential segregation of the *stranger* and expatriate was a common feature, although this residential exclusiveness has been breaking down since independence.

The city of Kano, Nigeria (population 295,000) is representative of the Rejuvenated Traditional City. Originating in 999 AD on the site of Dala Hill which provided iron stone for local blacksmiths and a panoramic view of the surrounding plains, Kano grew to be the "greatest commercial emporium in Africa." (Lugard 1902:18) The prosperity of Kano, like that of Katsina, was based upon the role the city played as an entrepôt center for trans-Saharan trade. The city is also located in a rich agricultural zone which supports one of the densest population concentrations in sub-Saharan Africa. With the arrival of the British in 1903 and the extension of the railroad from the coast in 1912, the continued importance of Kano as a commercial center was assured and Kano entered a new phase of development.

Within the city walls the traditional features of a Hausa urban center have been retained although modern services and amenities now serve many of the adobe compounds. Outside the walls, Kano

Township was established by the British to function as the administrative, residential, and commercial quarters of the expatriate and *stranger* population. (Figure 8-5)

The European quarters were established to the east of the railroad in the districts of Nasarawa and Bompai. Today these residential areas still house the expatriate population although the strict observance of residential segregation no longer persists. In the northern section of the Township is Sabon Gari, the residential quarters of the *strangers* who were primarily Ibo from the time of its founding in 1925 until the commencement of the Nigerian civil war in 1967. Separating the European and *stranger* residential quarters are the railroad tracks and a European type Central Business District where European, Syrian, Lebanese, and other expatriates operate their stores, banks, and trading companies. A market exists in the Sabon Gari and has grown to be almost as large as the traditional market located in the old town. Between the Sabon Gari and the walls of the city is the Hausa *strangers* residential area known as the Fagge district. Textile mills, groundnut oil mills, shoe factories, and a wide variety of consumer oriented industries are located primarily in the northeast section of the township.

The present-day city of Kano is a bustling, prosperous metropolis, a rejuvenated traditional city that has become a focus for northern Nigeria. The morphology of the city presents an interesting contrast between the traditional city with its un-planned streets and crowded residential areas on the one hand, and the planned geometric layout of the more spacious residential areas of the Township on the other. The designated functional areas and the heterogeneous population further differentiate the two cities and present an interesting dichotomy between the traditional and modern.

THE COLONIAL CITY

The majority of African cities can be classified as Colonial Cities. The Colonial City is the product of colonial administration and is characterized by a planned symetrical layout, designated functional areas, and segregated residential quarters. Mining towns, railroad towns, port cities, and administrative cities founded and laid out by the European colonial powers and designed for African settlement are classified as Colonial Cities. These cities emerged as nodes of commerce, mining, and administration, and were oriented to export activities.

The internal structure of the Colonial City includes a modern Central Business District and sections of the city designated for industrial and residential functions. The population is predomi-

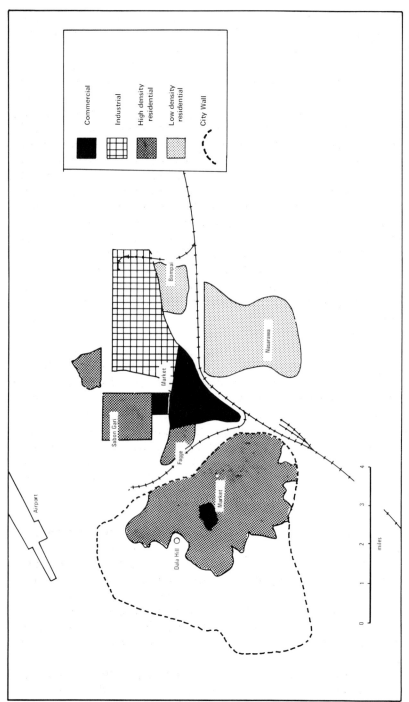

Figure 8-5. Kano Land Use.

nantly immigrant with considerable diversity among the indigenes, *strangers,* and expatriates. These cities are troubled with excessive immigration and, consequently, shantytowns on the periphery are a common feature.

Nairobi, the capital of Kenya, is representative of the Colonial City. Founded in 1899, as a railroad town on the line constructed from Mombasa to Lake Victoria, Nairobi has profited from its strategic location midway between the coast and Lake Victoria. The situation of Nairobi with regard to the productive Kenya Highlands and Uganda, enhanced the commercial function of the city since all exports to the coast passed through Nairobi. In 1907 the growth and development of Nairobi was further assured when British colonial administrative headquarters were transferred to Nairobi. Nairobi grew gradually, and for the first thirty years of its growth African settlement was restricted. Following World War II the city has grown from an estimated 100,000 in 1940 to 478,000 in 1969.

In 1948 Nairobi established a master plan and through controlled planning has restricted industrial sites to the periphery, and established spacious parks. It maintained residential segregation until the time of independence in 1963. The central city is characterized by a modern Central Business District with high rise buildings, modern public buildings, railroad facilities, and retail establishments. (Figure 8-6) The retail establishments vary from modern department stores with a wide range of luxury goods to the small general stores or *dukas* operated primarily by Asians. Beyond the central city to the east is located the high density residential area housing 71 percent of Nairobi's African population. (Figure 8-7) To the north and west is a zone of medium residential density known as Parklands-Eastleigh district where 80 percent of the Asian population resides. (Table 8-3) The growth of the Asian population and the restriction of the spatial growth of the Asian quarters in the Parklands-Eastleigh district led to the establishment of new Asian residential quarters in South Nairobi.

A distinguishing characteristic of Nairobi is the extensive area devoted to low density residences. These were at one time reserved exclusively for European housing on quarter acre, five acre, ten acre, and even twenty acre lots. (Halliman and Morgan 1967:105) The low density residential area is located to the west on the higher elevations in the district known as Upper Nairobi. This residential area is made up of scattered clusters of residences separated by open space and quite often very rugged terrain.

Since Kenya's independence, residential exclusiveness has broken down, wealthy Africans and high ranking government

Figure 8-6. Photograph of Nairobi.

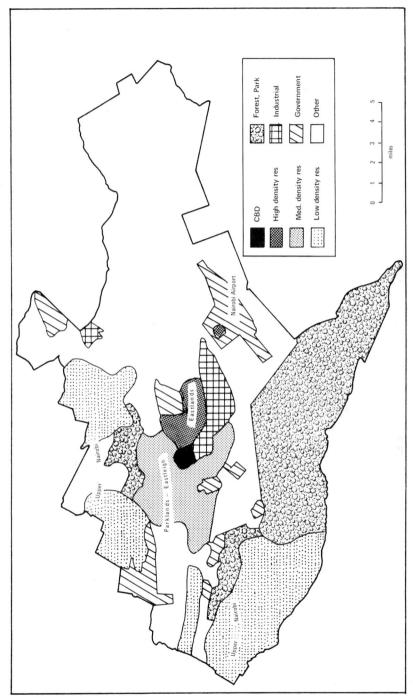

Legend:
- CBD
- High density res
- Med. density res
- Low density res
- Forest, Park
- Industrial
- Government
- Other

Nairobi Airport

Eastlands

Nairobi

Upper

Parklands — Eastleigh

Upper — Nairobi

0 1 2 3 4 5
miles

Figure 8-7. Nairobi Land Use.

officials reside in areas once reserved for Europeans. Where Asians have vacated housing in the Parklands-Eastleigh district, Africans have moved in, and in the high density district of Eastlands older buildings have been replaced by new apartment buildings.

South of the Eastlands district is the industrial district. Immediately south is the extensive Nairobi National Park, a game reserve within sight of downtown Nairobi. This park is an important tourist attraction especially for travellers in transit with a few hours layover in Nairobi. In 1963, anticipating rapid urban growth, Nairobi annexed and created the New Nairobi area to the east of the city. This area is primarily open space with only the modern Nairobi airport located within the area.

Today Nairobi continues to function in its traditional role as a node for transportation and communication networks. Additionally, the city is the most diversified industrial city of East Africa and is playing a significant role as a regional center for economic integration.

THE EUROPEAN CITY

In contrast to the Colonial City which was intended for African settlement, the European City is reserved almost exclusively for European habitation. The city is European in structure and layout with residential segregation strictly enforced through

TABLE 8-3
CITY OF NAIROBI: RACIAL COMPOSITION

	Upper Nairobi	Parklands and Eastleigh	Nairobi South	Eastlands	Industrial	Central	Total
African	18,513	15,900	2,745	110,227	3,668	4,335	155,388
Arab	42	630	12	230	16	52	982
European	17,686	2,262	435	95	86	912	21,476
Goan	153	3,431	672	3	105	886	5,250
Indian	672	45,780	6,322	19	1,034	15,665	69,492
Pakistani	210	9,695	690	13	369	735	11,712
Somali	15	764	–	36	17	26	858
Mixed Coloured	35	132	60	20	–	8	255
Other	148	725	162	19	14	61	1,129
Not Stated	47	112	11	58	3	22	253
Total	37,521	79,431	11,109	110,720	5,312	22,702	266,795

Source: Dorothy M. Halliman and W.T.W. Morgan, "The City of Nairobi" in W.T.W. Morgan, *Nairobi, City and Region* (Nairobi: Oxford University Press, 1967), p. 107.

legislation. The African population is confined to the outskirts of the city or in townships beyond the city's boundary. In most instances the African is discouraged and even restricted from migrating to the city. The European City is an anachronism in modern Africa and prevails in white dominated South Africa and Rhodesia where strict social and residential segregation is enforced. According to the philosophy of apartheid (the practice of racial territorial segregation in the Republic of South Africa) the city is the domain of the white man; the African, being a rural inhabitant, is permitted into the city only to work and reside temporarily on the outskirts.

Johannesburg, the most diversified industrial city in South Africa, provides a good example of a European City. Founded in 1886 when gold was discovered on the barren high veld, Johannesburg has grown to a population of 1.1 million and has become the regional center for the most highly urbanized area in Africa. Within a radius of 30 miles of Johannesburg there are at least seven cities with a population of over 50,000 forming what is referred to as the Witwatersrand conurbation.

The internal structure of Johannesburg is characterized by several zones of occupation. The modern Central Business District with high land values and high rise buildings functions as the commercial heart of this diversified city. Adjacent to the Central Business District is the railroad and industrial zone, and immediately to the west is the Asian and Coloured residential area. (Figure 8-8) To the west, separated by open space and a cemetery, is the more spacious residential area reserved for European habitation. To the south of the Central Business District are the mining area and industrial sites.

The African quarters are located on the periphery with large African townships or reservations located beyond the boundary of Johannesburg. Townships such as Soweto (Southwest Township), which has a population of over 370,000, are reserved exclusively for Africans who form the bulk of unskilled labor required for working in the mines and of domestic help demanded in the European residential area.

Johannesburg is a thriving metropolis and although gold mining remains an important activity the city has evolved into a diversified industrial city, a commercial center, and a focus for transportation facilities in South Africa. The strict enforcement of residential segregation and the restriction of African movement within the city gives Johannesburg a distinctive European flavor, not only in the layout of the city but also in the population makeup.

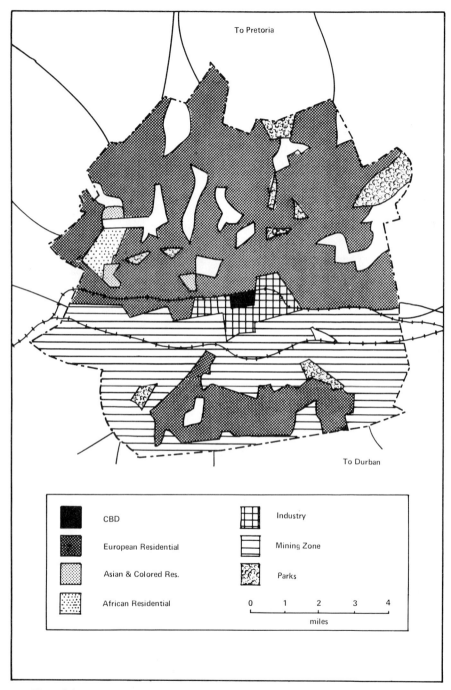

Figure 8-8. Johannesburg Land Use.

CONCLUSION

The cities of Africa appear to be facing insurmountable problems. Rapid urban growth, poor urban conditions, diversity of population, unemployment, and lack of urban planning are among the most pressing problems. City officials are faced with the problem of providing services and amenities from a limited tax base. Financial support from the central government is an invariable necessity, but is often unavailable. The resolution of many of these problems appears to lie in stemming the ever increasing rural to urban migration and in developing comprehensive plans. The accomplishment of both these objectives will be extremely difficult. Improvement of rural conditions may slow down migration to the city but will never entirely stop it. To date African cities have not developed comprehensive plans but have relied on partial planning. Frequently where plans have been drawn up they have been done by expatriate firms with little experience in African urban problems. Often housing projects for the upper income and middle income population have been emphasized and low income housing, where the need is greatest, has been neglected. Despite the many problems, urbanization in Africa is still at an incipient level. There is yet time for the problems to be identified and resolved.

By virtue of the functions which African cities perform, the city is the node of modernization and social change. Functioning as the focus for transportation, communications, commerce, manufacturing, and administration, the city is the major recipient of outside contacts and influence. It is a point of diffusion for new ideas and knowledge, and a vital link between the rural areas and the modern world. In this capacity the cities of Africa will continue to influence the direction and development of the countries to which they belong.

9

Black Africa: Patterns of Political Change

JOHN N. PADEN
Northwestern University

Within the 20-year period 1945-65, most of the states of Africa organized nationalist parties and achieved independence from colonial rule. This pattern of rapid political change has continued in the years since independence. Party systems have come and gone in many areas; military regimes have been through several stages; and out of the crucible of the first decade of independence has emerged a clear sense of the problems of political structure, political performance, and political representation. What will be the pattern of the future?

There are 42 states in the African continent that are members of the United Nations, constituting more than one-third of the world community of nations. These states range in size from Nigeria, which with nearly 57 million people is among the ten largest nations of the world, to mini-states such as Lesotho, Congo-Brazzaville, Botswana, Gabon, Gambia, Swaziland, and Equatorial Guinea, with populations of less than one million each. The focus in this essay will be on independent black Africa, excluding the Arab states of North Africa and the white-dominated states of Southern Africa. (Figure 9-1). All but two of the independent states of black Africa—Liberia and Ethiopia—have a history of formal colonialism.

The year 1960—when most of the West African states achieved independence, to be followed during the next few years by most of the states of East and Central Africa — may be said to mark a turning point in African political history. This essay tries to assess the patterns of political change in contemporary black Africa and to evaluate the two major tasks of independent political regimes — economic development and nation-building.

The problems of economic development and nation-building clearly have been interrelated. Economic development entails an

151

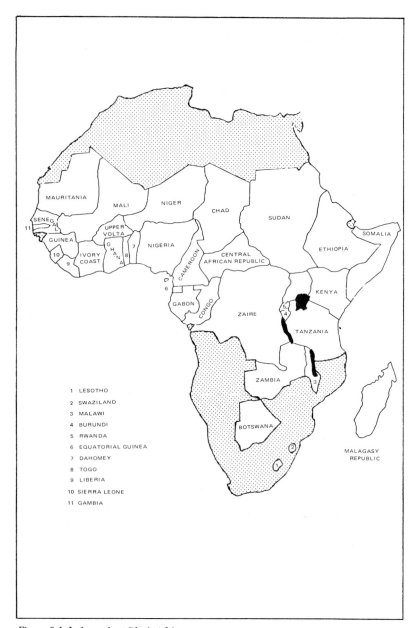

Figure 9-1. Independent Black Africa.

assessment of resources, rational planning, building economic and infrastructural bases for development, providing the educational growth necessary to mobilizing populations and facilitating communications, and increasing productivity to accommodate urbanisation rates which are among the highest in the world. Nation-building requires a reconciliation of diverse ethnic elements within a country and the reinforcement of a national identity which up to the time of independence had often been little more than a colonial designation. Nation-building also requires the adaptation of inherited political systems to the particular needs of each country. In the event political systems often broke down and were replaced by military regimes. In other cases states were plagued by civil war. The question of political representation took on primary importance, and until this issue was resolved, elections often became a breaking point in the fabric of political life.

Out of the efforts of African states to achieve economic development and forge nationhood, patterns of political change may now be discerned. These patterns are best seen from a comparative perspective, looking at all of the independent black African states, rather than just a few. The statistical basis of such comparisons is only now becoming available, as researchers working from theoretical perspectives have been able to devise indicators of change appropriate to Africa and susceptible to cross-national data analysis. The statistical patterns presented in this essay are drawn from a data bank in which is coded more than 1200 variables on social, economic and political change in each of the African states. The data bank is co-directed by the author of this article and is located at York University in Canada. The data are composited from country sources, United Nations sources, and from case-study materials. Comparisons are made among the 32 states that had achieved independence by 1966, thus excluding Swaziland and Equatorial Guinea. The island state of Malagasy is also excluded from consideration here.

ECONOMIC DEVELOPMENT

Four categories of socio-economic change are particularly important in assessing economic development: demographic change, educational change, income and production changes, and changes in trade and investment.

DEMOGRAPHIC CHANGE

The great range of estimated populations in the independent black African states from nearly 57 million in Nigeria to 357,000 in Gambia, is shown in Table 9-1. While in relation to their size most African states are under-populated rather than over-populated, it should be noted that there are severe overcrowding problems in urban centers and that much of the land is not yet arable. Despite improvements in health facilities and education, the rate of natural increase of population in the post-independence period averaged only 2.6 percent per year, which is modest by Third World standards, being 3.7 percent at its highest in Somalia

TABLE 9-1
ESTIMATED POPULATION, 1969

Rank	Nation	Population
1	Nigeria	56,700,000
2	Ethiopia	24,769,000
3	Zaïre (Congo Kinshasa)	20,564,000
4	Sudan	15,186,000
5	Tanzania	12,926,000
6	Kenya	10,890,000
7	Uganda	9,526,000
8	Ghana	8,546,000
9	Cameroon	5,680,000
10	Upper Volta	5,278,000
11	Mali	4,881,000
12	Malawi	4,398,000
13	Ivory Coast	4,195,000
14	Zambia	4,056,000
15	Niger	3,909,000
16	Guinea	3,890,000
17	Senegal	3,780,000
18	Chad	3,510,000
19	Rwanda	3,500,000
20	Burundi	3,475,000
21	Somalia	2,730,000
22	Dahomey	2,640,000
23	Sierra Leone	2,510,000
24	Togo	1,815,000
25	Central African Republic	1,518,000
26	Liberia	1,150,000
27	Mauritania	1,140,000
28	Lesotho	930,000
29	Congo Brazzaville	880,000
30	Botswana	629,000
31	Gabon	485,000
32	Gambia	357,000

and 0.9 percent at its lowest in Gabon. Details are given in Table 9-2. Most of the African states are predominantly rural rather than urban, but rates of urbanization have started to accelerate. Several of the large capital cities have almost doubled their populations since independence, and one of the effects of the increase in city populations has been to create political pressure within the cities while necessitating a rural base for most politicians within the country.

TABLE 9-2
PERCENTAGE INCREASE IN POPULATION, 1967

Rank	Nation	Percent Increase
1	Somalia	3.7
2	Niger	3.5
2	Rwanda	3.5
2	Zambia	3.5
5	Kenya	3.4
6	Lesotho	3.3
7	Sudan	3.2
7	Tanzania	3.2
9	Dahomey	3.1
10	Togo	3.0
11	Ghana	2.9
12	Central African Republic	2.8
12	Guinea	2.8
12	Uganda	2.8
15	Ivory Coast	2.7
15	Senegal	2.7
17	Botswana	2.6
17	Malawi	2.6
17	Nigeria	2.6
20	Zaire (Congo Kinshasa)	2.5
20	Upper Volta	2.5
22	Burundi	2.4
23	Cameroon	2.3
23	Mali	2.3
25	Gambia	2.1
25	Mauritania	2.1
27	Liberia	2.0
28	Ethiopia	1.9
29	Chad	1.7
29	Congo Brazzaville	1.7
31	Sierra Leone	1.5
32	Gabon	0.9

EDUCATIONAL CHANGE

Literacy rates in Africa have been among the lowest in the world. Few of the colonial regimes did more than educate a handful of Africans to staff civil-service positions and/or semi-skilled occupations in the civil service. In virtually every African state the enrolment figures for primary education increased dramatically after independence, as is illustrated in Table 9-3. It is clear that independent African states have set education

TABLE 9-3
PRIMARY EDUCATION ENROLLMENT, 1966
(Per Thousand Population)

Rank Nation		Enrollment
1	Congo Brazzaville	221
2	Lesotho	195
3	Gabon	169
4	Ghana	163
5	Cameroon	133
6	Zaïre (Congo Kinshasa)	130
7	Botswana	124
7	Zambia	124
9	Central African Republic	105
9	Kenya	105
11	Liberia	101
12	Ivory Coast	98
13	Togo	94
14	Uganda	73
15	Malawi	71
16	Tanzania	63
17	Senegal	61
18	Burundi	57
18	Rwanda	57
20	Dahomey	55
21	Sierra Leone	52
22	Chad	51
22	Nigeria	51
24	Guinea	46
25	Gambia	42
26	Mali	35
26	Sudan	35
28	Upper Volta	22
29	Niger	21
30	Mauritania	19
31	Ethiopia	16
32	Somalia	11

as a priority and that they have been moderately successful in attaining this goal at the primary level. Virtually every African state has its own university, and some states such as Nigeria – which already has five universities – are planning to double their university facilities in the next decade.

INCOME AND PRODUCTION CHANGES

During the period 1960-65, the average rate of growth of *per capita* real gross domestic product in Africa was among the lowest in the world, 1.4 percent per annum. This is slightly less than the average for Africa in the decade 1950-60 and perhaps reflects some of the problems of economic development in newly independent countries. There is a considerable variation, however, among the African states in *per capita* GNP, ranging in 1968 from U.S. $310 for Gabon to $50 for Malawi, Upper Volta, and Burundi, with Zambia at $220, Mauritania at $180, Botswana at $100 and Ethiopia at $70.

TRADE AND INVESTMENT

Directly related to GNP are the patterns of capital formation and investment. In some cases these figures have decreased since independence, and in other cases they have been increased. Two major trade patterns have been relatively constant in the post-independence period. First, many of the African countries remain 'single-crop' economies, the average state being dependent on its principal export for about 53 per cent of its total export. At the top of the list the percentage goes over 90 with Botswana and Zambia, and over 75 with Burundi, Chad, and Senegal. Kenya, Malawi, and Tanzania have low percentages ranging from 26 to 19, for their principal export as part of the total exports. The second trade pattern, dependence on a metropolitan country as major trading partner, continued into the independence period, although a number of states have consciously tried to diversify their trade relationships. Importantly, many African states have begun to increase their trade with other African countries; some of this statistical pattern, however, reflects differences in accounting systems, particularly for products in transit from land-locked states.

The second critical problem facing the independent black African states, that of creating nations out of numbers of diverse language and ethnic groups encompassed within artificially delineated national boundaries, is without precedent in recent world history. The continent of Africa has the highest number of language groups in the world—well over 1,000 distinct languages, out of a world total of 2,500 languages. (Table 9-4). Traditional socio-political patterns vary enormously, ranging from areas with a heritage from mediaeval centralized kingdoms, such as Ghana, Mali, Songhay—states which were often larger and more complex than their European counterparts during the same period—to those with a history of very small-scale societies without regular patterns of leadership. It is impossible to designate definitively the number of 'ethnic' groups in Africa; ethnicity depends on social definitions

TABLE 9-4
SEPARATE LANGUAGES SPOKEN

Rank	Nation	Number of Languages
1	Sudan	171
2	Nigeria	125
3	Zambia	69
4	Ethiopia	63
5	Zaire (Congo Kinshasa)	61
6	Ivory Coast	57
7	Tanzania	56
8	Cameroon	50
9	Central African Republic	41
10	Ghana	37
11	Liberia	29
12	Upper Volta	27
13	Uganda	24
14	Chad	22
14	Guinea	22
14	Kenya	22
17	Togo	16
18	Dahomey	15
18	Gabon	15
18	Mali	15
21	Niger	14
22	Senegal	8
22	Sierra Leone	8
24	Congo Brazzaville	7
25	Malawi	5
26	Botswana	2
26	Burundi	2
26	Gambia	2
26	Lesotho	2
26	Mauritania	2
26	Rwanda	2
26	Somalia	2

and is a constantly changing phenomenon. It is possible, however, to state that with a few exceptions (Botswana, Lesotho, Swaziland), African states have an average of four or five major cultural groupings per country and an even larger number of languages are spoken.

NATION BUILDING

Not surprisingly, the political institutions that France and Britain—both with relatively homogeneous populations—had developed for themselves proved a less than adequate legacy within the multi-ethnic African context, where political communities are perhaps more comparable to Switzerland, Belgium, or Yugoslavia. Problems of representation arose early in the histories of the new states, and institutions for the resolution of conflict failed entirely. The overwhelming number of new African states have responded to the challenge of creating national unity by fostering single party systems, whether of the pragmatic type or the authoritarian type. Even so, these single-party systems were often unable to meet the challenge of nation-building, and as early as 1963 two major patterns of political instability had begun to emerge: *coups d'état* and inter-ethnic conflict. The problems of ethnic and language pluralism, party development, and elite instability and inter-ethnic conflict are discussed below.

ETHNIC AND LANGUAGE PLURALISM

Ethnic pluralism presents problems of political representation and is particularly susceptible to internal conflict. Language pluralism presents problems of mass communication within a nation, and languages may become symbols of ethnic identity. Since it is less difficult to quantify language distribution than ethnic distribution, the former will be used to indicate the extent of pluralism within the African states. Perhaps more important than the number of languages spoken is the extent to which people within a country can speak or understand a major language of wider communication. The African propensity for multilingualism has probably increased since independence, and in several countries *lingua francas* are emerging. Thus, for example, Tanzania has a large number of language groups but with the post-independence establishment of Swahili as the national language, an increasing number of Tanzanians can communicate with one another in that language. In the face of extreme language pluralism, most of the African states have retained French or English as the official national language (especially for use in education, commerce, and government) in the post-independence period. Many states, however, have found it useful to employ vernacular languages in adult literacy programs and in some radio broadcasting services. On this issue, the goal of economic development (which requires mass mobilization and literacy) may conflict with the goal of nation-building (which may require more stress on a single national language). National language policy has often been a political issue in the post-independence period, and a number of states have official vernacular languages (Somalia, Nigeria, Mauritania, Tanzania, Central African Republic, and Zaïre are examples) in addition to French and/or English.

The colonial legacy has affected ethnic and linguistic pluralism in several ways. From an early point British administration was identified with the policy of indirect rule, by which the British governor and residents worked through traditional authorities with regard to taxation, law, succession to leadership, and community boundaries. This system had the effect of incapsulating traditional communities and preserving traditional cultural values. Many civil servants in British areas administered territories using traditional methods and often operated in their vernacular languages. This pattern has often continued in the independence era, and may have intensified ethnic consciousness—and hence inter-ethnic conflict—in some areas.

By contrast French rule is often described as direct. The French established administrative units which cut across traditional political and cultural boundaries, recruited local leadership from outside of the traditional hierarchy, stressed the use of the French language at all levels and centralised government in the West African and Equatorial African federations. An African meritocracy was created consisting of those Africans who were assimilated into French language and culture and who had severed many of their traditional cultural and linguistic ties. Perhaps as a consequence, French-speaking African states have had less difficulty in terms of ethnic conflict, and more difficulty in the independence period in terms of a 'mass-elite' gap, that is, a breakdown in communications between the political leadership and the citizenry at large.

The initial premise of Belgian colonial policy was 'company rule', in which large portions of the Congo were allocated to European mining and agricultural concerns, and the companies were held responsible for administration and development of infrastructure within their areas. The abuses of this system were so great that the Belgian parliament took over direct control of the Congo and administered it in an authoritarian manner but without reliance on either traditional elites or an evolved meritocracy. The Belgians stressed the use of vernacular languages in primary education and did little to break down ethnic identities. Thus the Congo came to independence in 1960 with all of the problems of ethnic and language factionalism, and none of the advantages of an integrated national elite. Since independence, the Congo has established four official vernacular languages: Lingala, Swahili, Luba, and Kongo.

POLITICAL PARTY DEVELOPMENT

By the end of 1970, six of the 32 independent African states had multi-party systems, five had military regimes, and 20 had single-party systems. One state—Ethiopia—was a monarchy with no party system. Even in those countries with multi-party systems, in most cases one party predominates and these states thus have many of the characteristics of a single-party system. The clear pattern in the independence period, with regard to types of political regimes, has been an overwhelming tendency toward centralised authority, whether based on a single-party system, a one-party dominant system, a military regime or monarchical principles. Elections are used to confirm this authority, and only in two instances (Somali and Sierra Leone) has a party in power been defeated.

Within the French-speaking areas, this type of authority structure is a natural adaptation of the Fifth French Republic model, with its heavy stress on presidential powers and a weak parliament. Within the English-speaking areas the authority structure is a development from two aspects of the Westminster model—the sovereignty of parliament and rule by cabinet. Interestingly, the political device of federalism, which has been adopted by three African states (Nigeria, Cameroon, and Tanzania) is in all cases combined with strong centralised leadership. Given the problems of economic development and nation-building, it was perhaps inevitable that such centralization would occur.

This centralization had its roots in the colonial era and is part of the colonial legacy, being a combination of the authoritarianism of metropolitan political institutions and hierarchial cultural patterns widespread in traditional Africa. The colonial experience with regard to elections, however, was one of multi-party competition (with the partial exception of the Congo, where there were no party systems at all until 1958). In British Africa, parties often represented regional or ethnic constituencies while in French Africa parties tended to represent ideological or socio-economic constituencies. In the post-independence era, these factions were submerged within the single party structure. As groups felt excluded from government, however, these pre-independence multi-party constituencies often formed the basis for coups or inter-ethnic conflict within the new nations.

ELITE AND INTER-ETHNIC INSTABILITY

During the independence period (through 1970) there were 26 successful *coups d'état* in 14 independent black African states. In some cases, the military returned power to a civilian government (as in Ghana and Sierra Leone). In other cases the military transformed itself into a political party (as in Zaïre and Congo-Brazzaville). In still other instances the military governed through martial law. Some countries have experienced recurrent instability (Dahomey, Sudan, Zaïre, Togo, Congo-Brazzaville, and Burundi, for example), while other states have experienced no elite instability (these include Botswana, Gambia, Mauritania, Tanzania, and Zambia) (Table 9-5). There is of course no single-factor answer to the question why *coups* occur. In English-speaking Africa they seem to be more related to underlying ethnic conflicts than to the inter-elite conflicts which have characterised former French areas. Within French-speaking areas, most *coups* have been relatively bloodless and have frequently resulted in return to civilian rule.

The basis of inter-ethnic conflict within the new African states is often related to perceived inequities within the structures and institutions of government, often a direct consequence of colonial policies. The most serious form of ethnic conflict is civil war, and six African states (Sudan, Ethiopia, Zaïre, Nigeria, Chad, and Burundi) have experienced such wars. Other forms of ethnic conflict include rebellion—efforts on the part of an ethnic group to achieve more autonomy, as with the Tiv in Nigeria and irredentism, the desire of an ethnic group that has been divided by an international boundary to reunite its peoples, as with the Somali, or the Ewe of Ghana/Togo.

Given the fact that at least 150 major ethnic/language groups in Africa have been severed by international boundaries, instances of irredentism have been surprisingly few. Likewise the extent of ethnic rebellion has been minimal, given the considerable potential for developments in this area. The question of civil war may be a transitional problem in nation-building but one with long-lasting consequences, as it was in the United States. Thus, for example, the civil war in Nigeria from 1967 to 1970 preserved the union but the post-war problems of reconstruction and reconciliation are considerable. Significantly, one result of the Nigerian civil war has been to slow down the process of centralization and to allow each of the 12 new states considerable autonomy in matters of development. Most civil wars occur partly as a result of represen-

TABLE 9-5
POLITICAL INSTABILITY SINCE INDEPENDENCE

		Party system (1970)	Post-Independence election	Coups	Civil Wars
1	Botswana	multi-party	1969		
2	Burundi	single party	1961;1965	1966 (July) 1966 (Nov.)	Hutu-Tutsi (1965)
3	Central African Republic	single party	1960;1964	1966	
4	Cameroon	single party	1961;1970		
5	Chad	single party	1962;1963; 1969		northern areas (in progress)
6	Congo Brazzaville	single party	1963	1963;1968	
7	Zaire (Congo Kinshasa)	single party	1965;1970	1960;1965	Katanga (1960-64)
8	Dahomey	military rule	1960;1964	1963;1965; 1967;1969	
9	Ethiopia	monarchy	–		Eritrea (in progress)
10	Gabon	single party	1961;1964; 1967; 1969		
11	Gambia	multi-party	1966;1970		
12	Ghana	multi-party	1960;1964; 1969	1966;1972	
13	Guinea	single party	1963;1968		
14	Ivory Coast	single party	1960;1965; 1970		
15	Kenya	single party	1969		
16	Lesotho	multi-party	1970 (many earlier elections)	1970	
17	Liberia	single party	1961;1965; 1969		
18	Malawi	single party	1969		
19	Mali	military rule	1964	1968	
20	Mauritania	single party	1965		
21	Niger	single party	1965;1970		
22	Nigeria	military rule	1964	1966 (Jan.) 1966 (July)	Biafra (1967-70)
23	Rwanda	single party	1965;1969		
24	Senegal	single party	1963;1966; 1970		
25	Sierra Leone	single party	1962;1967	1967;1968	
26	Somalia	military rule	1964;1969	1969	
27	Sudan	military rule	1958;1965; 1968	1958;1964; 1969	southern areas
28	Tanzania	single party	1965;1970		
29	Togo	single party	1961;1963	1963;1967	
30	Uganda	single party	1962	1966;1971	
31	Upper Volta	multi-party	1965;1970	1966	
32	Zambia	multi-party	1968		

tation problems, and the matter of regional representation will continue to be a political issue in African states. The current civil war in Chad, for example, is not unrelated to the fact that the northern Muslim peoples in the country (who constitute almost 50 percent of the population) have been almost completely stripped of political representation at the national level.

ASSESSING POLITICAL CHANGE DURING
THE FIRST DECADE OF INDEPENDENCE

Many of the problems of establishing viable political institutions in independent black Africa are related to the enormity of the challenges of economic development and nation-building, as discussed above. The colonial legacy provided little positive contribution in dealing with either of these problems. It is premature to assess whether the first decade of independence will be a transition to more stable and suitable types of political institutions or whether the underlying problems are so great that they will continue to invite military action. In assessing political change during the first decade of independence, however, several observations may be made.

First, political structures emerging in French-speaking Africa have not been significantly different from those in English-speaking Africa, despite their different colonial legacies. Of more importance, perhaps, is the fact that West Africa has probably had more political experience over the years than East or Central Africa and that, with the notable exception of Tanzania, the process of political mobilization has gone farther in West Africa than in other parts of Africa.

Second, the relationship between economic development and political change is relatively clear. Countries which have more economic resources and countries which are more developed have had more instances of political instability than the less developed states. There probably exists a curvilinear relationship between economic development and political stability; in the initial stages of development there is little conflict; in the middle stages there is likelihood of conflict because people are competing for resources but without firmly established "rules of the game"; in the higher stages of economic development the likelihood of conflict diminishes because new institutions of political representation and the resolution of conflict have usually been developed. An example of this third category is Nigeria, which was driven to civil war partly in response to competition for access to the country's enormous oil resources, and as a result of the war, Nigeria is now fashioning new political institutions (such as the 12-state system) to deal with problems of representation.

Third, with regard to nation-building and political stability it appears that the number of language groups is probably less important in the development of a nation than the number of cultural groups. To some extent, cultural patterns are a product of the environment and hence culture zones tend to be closely identified with environmental zones. Thus, virtually every state in West Africa is plagued with reconciling northern peoples (savanna-land agriculturists and pastoralists, usually with a Muslim heritage) and coastal peoples (with rainforest agricultural skills and usually representing Christian or traditional religious cultures). While ethnic conflict has been more prevalent in English-speaking Africa than in French-speaking Africa, it has been most prevalent in the former Belgian areas of Zaïre, Rwanda (in the pre-independence era), and Burundi. Civil wars, however, are most common in the very large states, regardless of colonial legacy. The observer is led to conclude that colonial policies toward ethnic groups have had an important influence on matters of ethnic relations in the independence period. At the same time, the policy of recognizing traditional cultural/language groups may be an important step towards dealing with the problem of political representation, which clearly will continue to be a major issue.

Given the importance of formulae for political representation, three distinct models of political development may be said to have emerged.

The Tanzanian model informally tries to insure representation throughout the country on the basis of political party cells, but prohibits any reference to ethnicity in such representation.

The Ivory Coast model is common to the Franco-phone area, which is essentially elitist, is characterised by interest group representation, and is less concerned with mass representation.

The Nigerian model more explicitly recognizes the nation to be a multi-national entity based on states which in most cases have a recognizable ethnic base. Because Nigeria has such a large population, and because it has the potential to become a power of international stature (with a standing army of 300,000 soldiers—more than the rest of all African states combined—and with the economic potential of the petro-chemical industry), the Nigerian model may well come to be the most important. Significantly both Tanzania and Nigeria are federations (Ivory Coast in some respects is in a *de facto* federation with the *Entente* states), and both are relatively progressive in their internal and external relations. The future of the mini-states in Africa is not yet clear.

Since economic development seems to require economies of scale, it seems probable that some form of regional integration will occur. Such regional integration will inevitably have political consequences both in terms of the structures necessary to coordinate economic decisions and in terms of the problems of political representation and ethnic pluralism.

SUMMARY

The first decade of independence in Africa has seen rapid urbanization, with its attendant problems and political pressures, but also its potential for modernization; significant increases in educational levels; a modest decline in real terms in rates of economic growth and a continuation of certain colonial trade patterns. The political consequences of these patterns put pressure on the political structures which were inherited from the colonial powers. Despite the high degree of ethnic and language pluralism in the African states, there was a clear tendency to centralized authority. This, in turn, often exacerbated the issue of political representation, and groups which were excluded from government (either elites or ethnic groups) frequently tried to take power or opt out of the system. The second decade of independence may well see further creative adaptations of political institutions to meet African needs, but the precedent of military involvement in government is clearly established and the military will probably be used as a foundation to whatever political institutions may emerge.

SENGHOR
NYERERE
IDI-ADMIN ADDA
ZIMBABWE
KAUNDA
CABRAL
NKRUMAH
GOWAN
KILWA
MOBUTU
OBOTE
BENIN
KUSH
MBEKI
KACHINGWE
SISULU
OJUKWU
ISANDHLWANA
HOUPHOUET-BOIGNY
BONGO
MONDLANE
MALI
SERETSE KHAMA
BANDA
GHANA
KUMBI SALEH
MANDELA
BOKASSA
TSIRANANA
FANON
AZIKIWE
CESAIRE
MATABELE
SITHOLE
LUMUMBA
KENYATTA
MBOYA
HAILE SELASSIE
KONGO
ZULU
SONGHAI
SEKOU TOURE
ASHANTI
BALEWA
DADDAH

10

State Formation and Nation Building in Africa

DENT OCAYA-LAKIDI AND ALI A. MAZRUI
Makerere University, Uganda

It is possible for a developed society or even a nation to exist without a government or a state. It is also possible for a people to have both a government and a state; but to fall far short of true nationhood. Human history has ample illustrations of these phenomena; and Africa in its several centuries of history is no exception.

The history of Africa (which for our purpose must be defined to include the present) falls into three major periods in this connection. First there is the Africa before the white man came. This is the Africa of great empires, of big and small states and – in some cases – of nation-states. It is also the Africa of easily recognisable nations. Some of these had states (nation-states); some of them did not; and some were so small as to deserve the name *tribe* rather than nation.

Then came the white man. As long as he settled in relatively "empty" areas as just one more society in Africa; or even where he merely traded but without settling permanently; he contributed to the disorganisation and breakdown of African nations and states indirectly. But suddenly at the close of the last century there was a great rush from Europe to Africa not to trade more actively or to settle more in empty areas; but to acquire territories to control and exploit. Nations, nation-states, states, and tribes became dismembered only to be incorporated in various bits and pieces into new different states.

The final historical phase begins with the *formal* independence of these states from the foreign controlling powers. But note: the independence is that of the units created by colonisation, not of its various pre-colonial units individually. Now, the colonial powers had been able to maintain these various units together within the same state. Would the new black leaders be able to do

169

the same easily? And another thing: the colonial powers had allowed the various tribal units more or less autonomous existence. There was very little, if any, attempt to integrate the tribes into a single nation. What would the new rulers do? Would they be content with several tribes and several tribal identities or would they now require each individual to identify with the single state in order that it grow into a new nation?

These are some of the questions we shall touch on in this essay. We will first take the state and look at how it has changed from pre-colonialism to the post-independence period. We shall then do the same thing with the nation. In the process of doing this we hope to answer questions such as: Are nations really created or do they grow naturally? How viable are the newly created African states? Is Africa likely to unite into one great federation? etc. etc.

THE EARLY INDEPENDENT STATES

To take a look at the map of Africa today is to be met with an obvious yet very significant fact: there is no bit of territory in Africa today that one could call a "no-man's-land." To stand anywhere on the continent is to stand within some state or other.

It is this total division of the continent into states which is new and significant. But the existence of states as such goes back earlier than the white man's knowledge of Africa. One can do no better than quote *African Kingdoms* on the location of some of these states which were, more correctly, civilisations. African history, it notes:

> . . . covers a wide spectrum of belief and thought, action and co-operative enterprise. The high civilisations of the ancient Nile have their place in it — Kush, whose kings and queens challenged Egypt: Axum, a continuous stronghold of Christianity from the fifth century. So too do the strong states and empires that flourished beyond the Sahara during Europe's Middle Ages and Renaissance — mysterious Zimbabwe, whose massive stone walls enclosed the temple homes of divine rulers 'chosen . . . for their equity'; Kilwa, an island fortress whose trading contacts reached far away India and China; Songhai, whose powerful kings encouraged scholarship as well as commerce; Ashanti and Benin, whose sculptors created a religious art of impressive power . . . (Davidson 1966:22)

The book goes on: "But the record of achievement is not confined to big political systems alone. . ."

With these achievements, these parts of Africa went far beyond what is normally required for laying claim to the title of statehood. These are, first, that there is clearly defined territory;

and second, that there is an authority capable of maintaining order within and able to protect the territory from threats without. To do this a state must have a structure of government able to carry out orders from the centre and also able to "listen in" on the people who form the basis of it. It must be able to collect taxes to support such a structure, and to provide for its external defense and to provide the people with *certain other basic* services.

Some of the empires and civilisations mentioned above were admirable examples of the state. Let us take an example: the Zulu of Central Africa. They were a nation; but this nation developed only within the context of a state that was viable. And viability itself, according to Max Gluckman, centred around two things: a powerfully organized army and centralisation of political power in the king through his ownership of all the land. Gluckman says of the growth of the power of the state under Shaka, for example, that:

> Cattle raids were frequent, but there were no wars of conquest. By 1775 the motive for war changed, possibly owing to pressure of population. Certain tribes conquered their neighbours and small Kingdoms emerged which came into conflict. In this struggle Shaka, head of the Zulu tribe, was victorious; by his personal character and military strategy, he made himself, in ten years, master of what is now Zulu land and Natal and his troops were campaigning far beyond his boundaries. . . (1967:25-6)

Of centralisation of political power through land ownership he says: "The king also owned the land. All who came to live in Zulu land had to acknowledge his sovereignty." (1967:29)

Here then you had a viable African state. It was able to protect itself from its neighbours; in fact it was able to extend itself. It had a central authority to whom allegiance was owed. It had ways of resolving internal conflicts. It was more or less stable.

With minor exceptions, most of the African states were like this. There was usually a central authority based on descent or conquest, and it made itself felt through a graded hierarchy of authorities down to the lowest man. While in the case of the Baganda of East Africa a single tribe or nation only was involved; in most other cases a large state incorporated many different tribes. It tended to be a federation or even a confederation.

THE DENIAL OF STATEHOOD

When the European powers, in a great scramble at the end of the last century, divided up Africa among themselves; they were engaged in three things at the same time.

First, they destroyed the unity of tribes, nations, states and federations. Sometimes this was done very easily; a consequence of the fact that there had been a great weakening of the African institutions due to contact with European traders, missionaries, and explorers. Also the Europeans were the more superior in technology of war. But sometimes the conquerors met very stiff resistance, as they did with the Zulu of South Africa.

Second, they were simultaneously creating new states. Present day African states were thus created out of existing entities — states, empires, nations and tribes.

Finally, there were in the old Africa, tribes and nations without states. The Nuer of the southern Sudan are a good example, and of them E. E. Evans-Pritchard has written:

> . . . We must recognise that the whole Nuer people form a single community, territorially unbroken, with common culture and feeling of exclusiveness. Their common language and values permit ready intercommunication. Indeed, we might speak of the Nuer as a nation, though only in a cultural sense, for there is no common political organisation or central administration. (1967:279)

Most of the pastoral tribes were like this. What the colonial state creation did was to place them firmly for the first time within the confines of one state or another. There was never, after colonialism, a "no-man's-land" in Africa.

CONSEQUENCES OF COLONIAL STATE FORMATION: THE INTER-STATE DIMENSIONS

A number of consequences flow from the facts that present day African states were formed in the European scramble to colonise, and developed a viability under colonialism.

The European powers in carving up Africa were concerned solely with the balance of power among themselves. They paid very little, if any, attention to African ethnic geography. William Zartman (1966:108) writing about inter-African relations has demonstrated that the frontiers of Ghana, for example, cut through seventeen major tribes. This is generally true of Africa as a whole. What is the significance of it? There are two. We may use Uganda in East Africa to illustrate the first of these. The western boundary of Uganda cuts through the Alur tribe. Some Alur are thus in the Zaire Republic to the west and some in Uganda to the east. The same is true of the Acholis at the Sudan/Uganda boundary to the north, and of the Banyankole at the Tanzania/Uganda boundary to the south. Such a set-up is an easy basis for claims and counter claims for the return of territories or populations to where they 'rightly belong.' It can be the basis of inter-state tension, if not of outright conflict and hostilities.

Uganda has so far managed to escape this eventuality as have many other African states. Not least because there is a general recognition of two things: that it would have been hopelessly impossible for colonialism to have followed ethnic boundary lines in carving out states*, and that – even had this been possible – the milk has now been spilled and it is impossible to gather it up again. It would mean the total reorganisation if not disorganisation, of Africa. The consequences would be more destructive than constructive. This is why the Organisation of African Unity, at its founding in 1963, accepted state boundaries in Africa as drawn by the colonial powers.

Despite these obvious facts, Africa as a whole has not been able to avoid territorial and population claims or even physical combat to solve such claims. When Morocco became engaged in sporadic hostilities with Algeria and Mauritania in 1962, it was in part to regain historical unity by recovering land and population lost during colonial state formation. Other obvious examples of border clashes are those of Somalia with Kenya on the one hand and with Ethiopia on the other.

But the fact that a single ethnic group comes to be shared among several states need not inevitably lead to inter-state conflict. Beyond merely accepting the status quo, this very same fact can be used positively to argue for peace among the neighbours in a situation where hostilities might have existed. It can also be an argument for greater regional unity.

Thus Uganda's President Amin recently engaged in intensive exercises in persuading his neighbours that the peoples of Eastern Africa were brothers who, therefore, should not fight one another. With a threat (real or imagined) of guerrillas attacking Uganda from the Sudan and Tanzania to reinstate Uganda's deposed Milton Obote to power, Amin has been telling his neighbours that they are ethnically of the same substance as their Ugandan brothers. Should fighting erupt between Uganda and Tanzania, or between Uganda and the Zaire Republic, or with the Sudan; the Banyankole, the Alur and the Acholis would be fighting their own people. Under such circumstances it makes sense to have a peaceful border.

*There would have been many more states in Africa than now exist were it to be said that each tribe should have its own state. Some of these would have been too small to be viable. And to combine whole rather than fractions of tribes into a few large states would have required working out carefully which tribes naturally went together. Given the haste in which the colonies were formed and the fact that the future could not be read; this could hardly be done.

THE INTERNAL DIMENSIONS

Consequences of colonial state-formation are also to be observed within the respective states themselves. For one thing formerly stateless tribes have found themselves within the jurisidiction of a state, something to which they were not accustomed. But more important, state creation brought together within the same country many different peoples.

Now whereas the colonial rulers were outsiders in relation to the collection of tribes which they dominated; this could no longer be true of the new rulers of Africa. Colonial rule had been exempt from intertribal rivalry for positions and power. How are African rulers to secure the loyalties of the other peoples? How can they appear neutral when the label they carry is still very much *tribal*? These issues have grave consequences for the stability and the viability of the state.

An obvious course of action is, of course, to treat all residents within the state as individuals with equal rights, rather than to base authority on ethnic sentiments and loyalties.

A good beginning was made in this direction during the fight for independence but, like so many other good things of this life, it carried with it its own difficulties. What were some of these?

One was the undermining of the rather undemocratic colonial structure and (in the case of the British colonies) of the colonial preservation of tribal institutions and sentiments. Education and the introduction of modern economic practices had already gone a long way in this direction. But now nationalist Africans started to demand the realisation of the ideal of one-man-one-vote and national self-determination. On the face of it the exercise appears quite unrelated to the future stability and viability of the independent African state. But let us look again. The key to the link is the colonial administration and how it successfully kept law and order. Though there were significant differences between the British, the French, and the Portuguese colonial administration, we shall focus on British colonial rule as an example, and constantly compare it with the position of an independent African government today. Our concern is simply to demonstrate how nationalism and the movements connected with it, set the stage for conflict, instability, and insecurity for the African independent state at the same time as the basis for internal stability and security was being worked out.

Those who argue that African political independence has been merely the replacement of white faces and white rulers by their black counterparts (Fanon: 1963) would probably see in the present day African executive president the continuation of the colonial governor. On the face of it the parallel is true and complete; for the governor was the most important of all powerful autocrats in the colonial setting. In the eyes of many, this is the direction in which the African executive presidency has been evolving. But there are important differences between the African president and the British colonial governor – differences which have grave consequences for the problems of loyalty and legitimacy in present day independent African states.

PRIMORDIAL LOYALTY

First, the colonial governor, being an outsider to the collection of indigenous societies over which he came to rule, was naturally exempt from the tribal rivalries and jealousies of the type the African president cannot avoid. Unless the boundaries of the ethnically homogeneous society from which he comes and those of the state he heads are one and the same, the African president comes from one tribe in the state of multiple tribes. This is the source of what has been termed *the crisis of political legitimacy* in Africa today; those who claim to speak and act for the whole country are still very tribally identifiable. In their thinking the citizens tend to automatically add this identification to the president's name and official title; e.g. President Jomo Kenyatta of Kenya, a Kikuyu; President Amin of Uganda, a Kakwa; Benedicto Kiwanuka, former Chief Minister of Uganda, a Muganda.

This is why it has been said that prior to the crisis of legitimacy there is a more telling one: the *crisis of identity.* People tend to identify too closely with their own tribes, not enough with the nation-in-creation; but even worse they identify public officials tribally.

But Africans should not jump to the conclusion that this sort of identification and its characteristic accompanying loyalty – primordial loyalty – is universally bad simply because in the African context at the moment it plays havoc with nation-building. One major reason for the stability and law and order under the colonial governor was simply that the loyalty accorded him was largely primordial. In the colonial situation it operated at two levels; a higher *European level* and a lower *native level.* What the governor had was, simply stated, his white tribesmen (i.e. any Englishman) in all key positions in the administration. He could be sure of their loyalty as much as an African chief in the traditional society could be sure of the loyalty of his tribesmen – they all shared primordial or primary sentiments.

The British colonial administrative structure was, of course, not entirely staffed with Britons from the governor to the last administrative officer in the village. Somewhere along the line below the level of the District Commissioner the line of Britons stopped and the line of African administration began. Now what ensured loyalty at this point since Britons and Africans did not share primary sentiments? The governor could be sure of the loyalty of the entire structure (more or less) down to the lowest administrative Briton, but how was this lowest man to secure African loyalty? To this question we shall return in due course. It suffices at this stage to say merely that *if and where* this could be done, the line of sure loyalty stretched from the individual African in the village to the man next to the governor; for the African structure, too, centered around primordial loyalty to the family, the clan, the tribe. To have the *true* head of the tribe loyal to the British becomes, in essence, to have the tribe loyal to the British colonial governor.

PERSONAL LOYALTY AND LAW AND ORDER

The colonial governor had on his side, as we shall see, additional advantages far beyond primordial loyalty in securing obedience and ensuring law and order. Many of these advantages were not to be available to his black African counterpart – the president. What this means is that the president would, in his search for loyalty, come to rely on and need primordial or tribal loyalty even more than the governor.

The initial essential need is for the African president to find people who will be loyal to him personally. The directive issued by President Banda of Malawi on June 19, 1966 is illustrative of this search. It said, in part:

> . . . From now on, I want it to be known and realised that Resident Secretaries and District Secretaries are, in their district or provinces, my *personal* (emphasis added) Civil Services representatives; and that I am charging them with . . . specific responsibilities. (Tordoff 1968:539)

Banda was being much more open than some others of his colleagues have been; but they too have been doing more or less the same thing. The most elaborate system of *personal loyalty* structure that has appeared to date is probably that in Ghana under Nkrumah. (Bretton 1966)

The crucial areas that heads of state have paid the greatest attention to, have been the security forces – prisons, police, secret police, and army. Here recruitments on tribal and regional lines and promotion on the basis of personality has tended to remain the same as during the colonial period. The colonial powers had also recruited from this or that tribe depending on how loyal to the government the tribe was supposed to be.*

Fortunate for the colonial governor, this kind of recruitment could be done without generating too much tribal rivalry among the tribes. In the case of Uganda, for example, some tribes simply did not consider military life up to the high image of sophistication they had of themselves. They had no reason whatsoever, therefore, to resent British colonial recruiting patterns.

With the president of an independent African country there is now a general awareness by almost all of the tribes within their states that power grows out of the barrel of a gun and that no tribe can afford to look down upon becoming army men. Thus in the Ugandan case during the Jinja barrack disturbances a Member of Parliament charged in the National Assembly:

> . . . I believe that if Government wants to bring back stability in
> our Army, this army must be broad based. At the present our Army
> is composed of people mainly from one region . . . things seem to be
> very much Northernsided. Even the Military Council . . . is com-
> posed of only Northern region people . . . (Uganda Government)

The African executive head of state, then operates in an atmosphere where there is sensitivity about tribal and regional recruitments into key positions in the country – something the colonial governor never had to contend with. But his difficulty is much more than merely pressures for equitable distribution of key and sensitive positions among the tribes. He also operates under obligations – many of them created by himself and his colleagues – to promote equality, democracy and progress. The people, in order to acquire these things, were asked merely to vote him and his colleagues into office.

Were it that, like the colonial governor, he had to concern himself merely with law and order, the African leader's task would still be more difficult than the governor's. But now he takes the reign of power amid promises to develop the country. This has consequences for his being able to maintain stability.

---

*See Morris Hanowitz (1964) *The Military in the Political Development of New Nations.*
On p. 52 in the footnote he lists the following recruiting pattern by the British: –
India: mainly from the remote Sikhs; *Pakistan:* mainly from rural tribes, especially Punjab and Pathans; *Sudan:* there was a strong imbalance of northern Arab officers; *Nigeria:* with strong representation of remote northern Moslem tribes (e.g. Benue and Ilorin); *Ghana:* northern tribes till 1961 supplied 80% of the NCO's; *Uganda:* the Acholis; *Kenya:* the Kamba and Kalemjin, etc.

GOVERNMENT BY 'GODS'

The upper structure of the British colonial administration, as we have seen, came more or less intact from London. That is, the governor could be sure of the loyalty of almost everybody in this sector of his administration because they shared primordial loyalty to the English nation. The question we raised earlier was how was loyalty to be secured from the heads of African tribes?

I think we have to look at history for an answer; and this constitutes a third major area of contrast between the governor and his African counterpart. We find it in British demonstration of *general mastery* and mastery over the Africans. The first time he ever came into contact with the white man, Central African evangelist Sithole has vividly recorded:

> ... The African was simply overwhelmed, overawed, puzzled, perplexed, mystified, and dazzled. The white man's 'house that moved on the water'; his 'bird that is not like other birds'; his 'monster that spits fire and smoke and swallows people and spits them out alive'; ... and many new things introduced by the white man just amazed the African (Sithole 1959:146-7)

The same picture is dramatically painted by the Nigerian novelist Chinua Achebe in *Things Fall Apart* and also in *No Longer at Ease.* In the former, the news that the white man had wiped out an entire clan is enough to dampen the spirits of even the most courageous of the warriors though at least one of them, Okonkwo, was not to be deterred from challenging the white man single handed.

In the latter novel, a retired soldier could go regularly to a market in the neighbouring village and help himself to whatever he liked. He went in full uniform and no one dared touch him. It was said that if you touched a soldier, Government would deal with you.

The governor had the military might to "subdue the natives," and therefore he could legitimately chant Hilaire Belloc's couplet:

> *Whatever happens we have got*
> *The Maxim gun and they have not.*

But only to some extent; for it is a well known fact that in establishing their colonies abroad the British suffered from scarcity in men, materials, and money. There is no better evidence of this scarcity than the British colonial system of indirect rule. It arose not out of British ingenuity but was forced on them by necessity. It was also, of course, expedient for other reasons such as solving communication problems between the British and the African.

What came to be instrumental in colonial control of the *native* was, thus, in the final analysis, not British might but the image they managed to project of being powerful. And the white men, from the time they first took over in Africa, never allowed the illusion of their great power to waver among the African population. To quote Sithole again:

> Conscious of the magic spell they had cast over the Africans, they did everyting to maintain it. They demonstrated their control of the lightning by firing their guns regularly . . . there was hardly anything that the white man did that had no god-like aspect to it . . . [and] the African, who never argued with his gods lest their wrath visit him, adopted the same attitude to the white man . . . Woe unto him who argues with the new gods from over the seas. (Sithole 147)

The white man captured the minds of the African not only as gods who could do wonders with technological gadgets; but also as the high priests of the Christian God. Religion was instrumental in winning African loyalty to the colonisers. Later, some District Commissioners came to rely on their own personality to extend the boundary of their authority even further. *Prestige and bluff* — both drawing their strength from the days of pacification — as well as *personality,* then, played a large role in ensuring African loyalty.

But *bluff* can succeed only under certain conditions. First, it can succeed where the subjects on which it is to be used are ignorant of the actual situation prevailing. Is it any wonder, then, that with the spread of formal education, British rule became increasingly difficult?

Secondly, under conditions of ignorance on the part of the subjects, the kind of bluffing that succeeds is the kind that threatens *reprisals* for certain actions, i.e., those which are prohibitive. They demand *non-action.* While appropriate in a situation of preoccupation with law and order, they cannot be of much use in a situation that is seeking that people should do things.

GOVERNMENT BY 'MERE MEN'

For independence to come to black Africa the colonial gods had to be unmasked. This was done by African nationalist leaders by making their people politically conscious. But in doing this they were, at the same time, making certain that the techniques which brought the British colonial governor loyalty and stability would never be available to the African executive head of state.

First, the African president ascends to the position of power in a situation of changed attitude in the population. This change was, of course, necessary if he and his colleagues were to bring independence. The people have been told that it is in the power of the rulers to improve material conditions, that the reason that change has been slow is because those who occupied positions of authority were aliens. The people come to expect dramatic changes after independence. They have been told during pre-independence election campaigns that they can govern themselves and should not be pushed around by people in authority. They come to resent any stern measures that an African government may find it has to undertake in the name of law and order.

Second, the African chief executive head has been drawn from among the Africans themselves. He is a mere man; whereas the British had descended from *above* the collection of tribes. They were *gods*. The chief executive has to rely on his actions, especially in the area of economic progress, and on his personality to bring him loyalty.

Third, to make concrete improvements in the economic conditions of his people so as to retain their loyalty, drastic actions are required to break the foreign exploitation of the Africans. But to take drastic action he must first of all have a secure power base from which to operate. A multi-tribally constituted political party has tended to be unequal to the task; and so has a multi-tribally constituted army command. There has consequently been a tendency to resort to tribal or primordial loyalty; and to emulate the British colonial governor in appointing members of the ruler's tribe to key positions in the administration and the army. The governor ultimately had to go, because the Africans came to realize that though the British claimed to have brought *civilisation* and *democracy* to Africa; the British *tribe* were being given most of the best things the land could yield and the best positions in government.

And so it has tended to be with the African chief executive. He may be genuinely convinced that he must develop the country, but soon finds he needs a sure base of power – a loyal power base to do it. He turns to the group whose loyalty to him he can more or less take for granted – his own tribe. But this becomes his undoing because now he is open to charges of tribalism. His image declines. He may soon find himself out of power like his counterpart, the colonial governor.

We have said so many things about the African state. Indeed we seem to have taken too much time over it to the neglect of a discussion of the nation. We think that this is as it should be. First, because the nation in the European sense, if it is developing in Africa, is still in its embryonic stage and therefore difficult to study. Second, before the nation emerges within the context of the present day African state, the respective African countries involved will need to have solved a number of inevitable social, economic and political problems; some of which we have already outlined in our discussion of the state. The important thing to grasp is that the state and its leaders are going to play a crucial role in the solution of these problems. The state, then, is the basis of the nation.

PROBLEMS IN NATIONAL INTEGRATION

The process of national integration itself, which may lead to the evolution of the nation, involves four stages of interrelationship between the different ethnic or cultural groups in the country. These are co-existence, contact, compromise and coalescence.

CO-EXISTENCE

Mere co-existence is characteristic of the colonial period. While the central colonial government had direct dealings with each of the tribes within the state, the various tribes had very little contact with one another. A situation in which the tribes were insulated one from the other meant that intertribal conflicts were almost non-existent, since there was hardly any contact. And this was the way the central authorities wanted it. Their aim was not integration, but stability.

CONTACT

But some contact among the different tribes did occur, even during the colonial period. Four things tended to facilitate this. First, there was the Second World War which brought together within the same army peoples from different tribes. Other central governmental services, e.g. the Civil Service and other branches of the armed forces, are increasingly having the same effect on the country's population today. Second, there was a system of education which allowed pupils to go to any school of their choice at the higher level. In parts of Africa this has provided for contact not only among different tribes within the same state, but also among peoples from neighbouring states. Third, we must mention politics, especially during the struggle for independence. Though political parties tended to be, for the most part, tribally based; they increasingly had wider and wider bases, incorporating more and more different tribes. Finally, labour movements cut across tribal and state boundaries and this proved to be an important means of facilitating contact among peoples of different tribes.

With improvement in communications services and with general development of the economy, increased mobility among the population of a given African country should follow, and with it, increasing contact. At the moment, those locked in their traditional tribal communities – without contact with peoples of other tribes (except for government officials, traders, etc.) – are still sizable in number. Contact and mobility go together.

COMPROMISE AND CONFLICT

It is among the mobile that there is contact, and – following from this – conflicts. Such conflicts may take one of several forms. There may be no specific grievances at issue, but instead a diffused sense of hostility because certain tribes have always been traditional enemies. It could also be a case of rivalry for central political power or against the hegemony of a particular tribe in national affairs. The Luo and the Kikuyu in Kenya, and the northern and southern tribes in Uganda have displayed this kind of disposition from time to time. In Kenya, for example, the Kikuyu under Kenyatta have continued to concentrate *political* (though not necessarily *economic*) powers in their own hands with the Luo envious of this and, sometimes, even restive. In Uganda things have not been so straightforward. Before Obote came to power in 1962, the Baganda, especially, were clearly the favoured tribe of the Protectorate and tended to dominate in all aspects of the territory's life. They were the envy of the northern tribes even if sometimes looked down upon by the same tribes for being so conservative. But with Obote, the north took over the control of the country's political affairs. This position still holds under General Idi Amin's Military Government. But the Baganda are still a formidable force in the country's bureaucracy as well as in trade and commerce.

Another form of conflict may involve a specific issue in dispute. Often border claims are the source of the dispute as in the case of the famous *lost counties* issue between Buganda and Bunyoro in Uganda. Just before independence the Banyoro insisted that the Baganda be made to return to Bunyoro part of the latter's territory given to them by the British in recognition of their military assistance during British penetration and pacification of the area.

But the two related phenomena which have drawn the most attention from those who study Africa are simply tribal *nationalism* and separatism. Tribal nationalism itself may be assertive as in the case of the Ibos of Eastern Nigeria. That as many as 30,000 of them may have been killed in Northern Nigeria – away from their own eastern homeland — is an indication of how assertive the Ibo were in pursuing employment and trade opportunities in other parts of Nigera.* This assertive nationalism ultimately turned to isolationism when it became clear that compromise as a means of settling conflicts among the Ibos and other Nigerians was not working out satisfactorily.

In the case of the Baganda of Uganda it has been a more conservative, less assertive, brand of nationalism at play. The Baganda have sought to resist integration into the larger Ugandan society, thus placing the Ganda society itself, as an entity, in jeopardy. The crushing of Baganda by force was an indication that peaceful means of settling inter-group conflict had failed. Further evidence of the failure of compromise as a process in integration may be seen in the phenomenon of the *expulsion of aliens* by independent African states: Ghana deported Nigerians in 1958; in 1967 Senegal expelled Guineans, and Cameroon ordered out Nigerians (Peil 1971); in East Africa, Milton Obote of Uganda was beginning to make a similar move against Kenyans and Tanzanians in 1971 shortly before he was removed from power in a military coup.

THE STRATEGY OF INTEGRATION

The expulsion of aliens, secession, separatism, and the use of naked force to bring a community to heel are all indications of the failure of compromise in conflict resolution. It is not necessarily an indication of the failure of integration. For, though compromise recommends itself as the best, being the least painful means of integration, force can be an equally effective means.

In Uganda one had to choose between leaving the Baganda alone in their autonomy by compromising with them, or forcibly reducing their political and *military* power as a first stage in integrating them into the larger community. Obote carried out the forceful reduction; it is now President Amin's task to complete the process of integrating the Baganda fully in the mainstream of Uganda's national life by peaceful means.

The strategy of integrating various tribes within the single state must be related specifically to the nature of the ethnic groups with which one is dealing, and also to their sizes. In Nigeria, for instance, Ibo assertiveness might have made compromise between two of the country's dominant peoples work, but the Notherners' conservatism was probably the factor that effectively reduced the

*The Ibo were not the only peoples killed in Northern Nigeria, but they lost far the largest number.

possibility of its working. In Tanzania, Nyerere (1966: 1) has claimed, with truth, that they have been lucky because "no one tribal group dominated all others in size, wealth and education." What this means is that there are countries in Africa such as Tanzania where tribal integration need not be the highest item on the list of priorities.

Where it is a high priority, however, three methods are possible to deal with the problem of tribal co-existence and integration. First, it is possible to have no policy at all on the matter. Kenya illustrates this best. Here the Kikuyu are more or less in control and are likely to keep this position for a long time. The next largest tribe, the Luo, are becoming restive. But there is no specific policy of integrating the tribes as tribes into Kenya's national life. Even the nomadic Masai are being left alone. Full integration when, and if, it finally does come, will have been the result of natural processes rather than of *social engineering.*

K.A. Busia of Ghana has attempted to argue for nation-building on the basis of tribal communities. This is the second alternative available for integration. Busia's position is that Africa should not seek to destroy the tribe first and then build the nation. The tribes themselves are to be building blocks for the nation. He argues that attempts to contain or even destroy tribal loyalties and the tribe as a community in order to make way for the new nation have tended inevitably to create tensions instead (1967:31). But might not the avoidance of intertribal conflicts be at the same time a denial of opportunity for the integrative process to move forward? Without conflict there can be nothing to compromise about; and without a built up tradition of conflict resolution there can be no deep sense of shared national history, and therefore no nation.

In Uganda, Milton Obote chose a road exactly the opposite of what Busia recommended, namely a direct and indirect assault on the tribe in order to liberate the individual for nation-building. In the first document for "moving to the left" the assault was on a particular kind of tribal organisation — those with kings at their heads. Perhaps rather than an assault, it was really a victory speech — Buganda had recently been crushed and other kingdoms had been abolished. District local governments, which in Uganda coincided with the tribe, had long since been reduced to nothing. The Charter could thus say, as it does in its Article 10:

> ... So long as feudal power was a factor in the politics and the economy of Uganda, it could not be disregarded ... It must be ... noted that in a society in which feudalism is an important and major political and economic factor, that society cannot escape being

Rightist in its internal and external policies. With the removal of the feudal factor from our political and economic life, we need to do two things. First, we must not allow the positions of the feudalists to be filled by neo-feudalists. Secondly, we must move away from circumstances which give birth to neo-feudalism or general feudalistic mentality . . . (Obote 1968)

But the feudalistic communities differed from other tribal communities only by being larger and politically (as well as militarily in the case of Buganda) much more powerful. In their pull on individual loyalty and therefore in their competition with the nation-in-creation they were all the same. Consequently a method had to be found to deal with not just certain, but with all tribes. All of them had now lost almost all their constitutional autonomy. What was needed now was for the tribal sentiments to be destroyed.

The program for this came in the form of Document No. 5: *Proposals for New Methods of Election of Representatives of the People to Parliment.* * Those aspects of the proposals relating to the reduction of the effect of tribalism on the political system were so simple in conception as to be startling in originality. Each prospective Member of Parliament was now to contest the election not in one but in four constituencies – one in each of Uganda's four regions: Northern, Eastern, Western and Buganda. The aims were that representatives of the people in parliament should be elected by a cross-section of the people as a whole, to foster the unity of the country, to make sure that no one can rely on just his tribe in order to get elected into parliament and, once there, to do away with

. . . [the] kind of attitude and practice [whereby] the role of the members of Parliament to deliberate upon all matters affecting the Nation as a whole becomes secondary, and the rest of the people, not being citizens in one's constituency or District, become 'other people' to be served, perhaps, after 'my people' have been served. (Obote 1970)

We are not concerned in this article to assess the merits or demerits of Obote's Document No. 5 as a strategy for tribal integration, but wish only to note that it was one measure due to be tried in an African country that might contribute to integration. The Military Coup of January 1971 unfortunately cut the experiment short.

*Circulated to Members of the Ugandan Parliament on July 17, 1970.

VERTICAL INTEGRATION

Formal education has not been a very effective means of reducing tribalism. It has provided for some contacts and conflicts as
well as for conflict resolution among the elite; but it has failed to
change attitudes and sentiments, especially as they relate to
loyalty to the tribe.

But even were it an effective method, it carries with it the
possibilities of creating further integrative problems. Formal education has been most effective in creating social classes in society
(Mazrui 1970:61-72). Now, not every African country sees this as
an integrative problem requiring as much attention as tribal integration. But African countries who have declared themselves
socialistic have displayed varying amounts of concern about the
problem.

It has been a central concern of Nyerere (Tanzania), Senghor
(Senegal) and Obote (Uganda) since 1968. Article 26 of *The
Common Man's Charter* describes the problem succinctly:

> ... We need only to stretch our eyes not to the distant future but to
> the years immediately ahead of us, taking into account the fact of
> our present expanding economy, to recognise that if no new strategy
> is adopted now, inequalities in the distribution of income will
> change dramatically the status of millions of Africans, and might
> result in our having two nations – one fabulously rich and living on
> the sweat of the other, and the other living in abject poverty – both
> living in one country . . . (Obote 1968)

The one urbanized and educated; the other peasant and un-
schooled. How is this vertical and regional gap to be closed?
Uganda, despite the clear recognition of the problem as indicated
above, has done little to close the gap. Tanzania has gone furthest
both in attempts to close the vertical gap and also in rural development by way of the Ujamaa* strategy.

NATION-BUILDING

Viability, reasonable stability, and security are necessary if a
state is to attempt with reasonable success, the solution to some of
the problems presented above. But the effective solution of these
problems is not, by itself, nation-building. A nation is ultimately
all these things, which we may call *social integration* and *effective
conflict resolution.* But it is more.

---

*Ujamaa – a Swahili word literally meaning "family-hood," used to convey the idea of
mutual involvement is Tanzanian socialism [editor].

There must also be *cultural* and *normative fusion*: which is largely a natural growth; and *shared national experience,* which can only come about after a long period of time. It is only then that one has arrived at the stage of complete coalescence.

It would be a mistake to imagine that these processes occur either uniformly over the whole of a given country, or that they occur in distinct stages one after another. Integrative conflicts may occur along the vertical dimension among groups that already share a common life style. On the other hand, the acquisition of a common life style which may give the impression of being the crowning phenomenon signifying the completion of coalescence may, in fact, contribute to integration, at least in some of its aspects.

Swahili in Tanzania is both a shared language and also, in a way, a shared culture. Yet it is one of the means the Tanzanian government is employing for nation-building. It needs to be emphasized that one is dealing here not only with a language *qua* language, but with something which is cultural as well. Something which evolved *naturally* over time.

Cultural and normative fusion calls for more than merely imposing the same language across the state, or for more than indoctrination in certain chosen and desired values. These things must grow slowly with the people.

> . . . it is not enough that people should interact economically; it is not enough that they begin to share cultural traits; it is not enough that they should socially evolve a multiplicity of institutions for resolving conflict, there is a fundamental dimension required to pull these other four together and focus them towards the centre. This fifth dimension might be the collective cumulation of shared nation experience . . . (Mazrui 1972)

"National memory" of this nature must be distinguished from short-lived consensus and the equally ephemeral collective, national-will, to act together. Both of the latter can be politically induced given the right moment and the right issue. A clear external threat to national security, or a natural disaster may play into the hands of the statesman and lead to the creation of national solidarity – the will to act as one. But the solidarity soon melts. What is necessary is, of course, a series of such solidifications and thawings in a dialectical movement. They accumulate to form the nation's memory. It takes time.

What this means is that the building of the nation as such is impossible and, in any case, ought not to be the central preoccupation of African statesmen. The nation will grow more or less naturally. The way to influence the nature of this growth is indirectly through the building of a certain desired kind of society. The basis for all this is a reasonably stable state.

CONCLUSION

There were both states and nations (in the modern sense of these terms) in Africa before the white man colonised the continent. The effect of colonisation was to disrupt a pattern of institutional growth and development which might have led to the formation of more advanced types of institutions comparable to those of modern Europe and America; but distinctively African in content. This opportunity is now lost forever. With the intervening colonial years, African states in their struggle to create distinctively African societies and nations will always have the colonial experience squarely against them.

South Africa is the richest country in Africa, and could be one of the richest countries in the world. But it is a land of extremes and remarkable contrasts. The Whites enjoy what may well be the highest standard of living in the world, whilst Africans live in poverty and misery. Forty per cent of the Africans live in hopelessly overcrowded and, in some cases, drought-stricken Reserves, where soil erosion and the overworking of the soil makes it impossible for them to live properly off the land. Thirty per cent are labourers, labour tenants, and squatters on White farms and work and live under conditions similar to those of the serfs of the Middle Ages. The other 30 per cent live in towns where they have developed economic and social habits which bring them closer in many respects to White standards. Yet most Africans, even in this group, are impoverished by low incomes and high cost of living.

The lack of human dignity experienced by Africans is the direct result of the policy of White supremacy. White supremacy implies Black inferiority. Legislation designed to preserve White supremacy entrenches this notion. Menial tasks in South Africa are invariably performed by Africans. When anything has to be carried or cleaned the White man will look around for an African to do it for him, whether the African is employed by him or not. Because of this sort of attitude, Whites tend to regard Africans as a separate breed. They do not look upon them as people with families of their own; they do not realize that they have emotions — that they fall in love like White people do; that they want to be with their wives and children like White people want to be with theirs; that they want to earn enough money to support their families properly, to feed and clothe them and send them to school. And what 'house-boy' or 'garden-boy' or labourer can ever hope to do this?

Africans want to be paid a living wage. Africans want to perform work which they are capable of doing, and not work which the Government declares them to be capable of. Africans want to be allowed to live where they obtain work, and not be endorsed out of an area because they were not born there. Africans want to be allowed to own land in places where they work, and not to be obliged to live in rented houses which they can never call their own. Africans want to be part of the general population, and not confined to living in their own ghettos. African men want to have their wives and children to live with them where they work, and not be forced into an unnatural existence in men's hostels. African women want to be with their menfolk and not be left permanently widowed in the Reserves. Africans want to be allowed out after eleven o'clock at night and not to be confined to their rooms like little children. Africans want to be allowed to travel in their own country and to seek work where they want to and not where the Labour Bureau tells them to. Africans want a just share in the whole of South Africa; they want security and a stake in society.

Above all, we want equal political rights, because without them our disabilities will be permanent. I know this sounds revolutionary to the Whites in this country, because the majority of voters will be Africans. This makes the White man fear democracy.

But this fear cannot be allowed to stand in the way of the only solution which will guarantee racial harmony and freedom for all. It is not true that the enfranchisement of all will result in racial domination. Political division, based on colour, is entirely artificial and, when it disappears, so will the domination of one colour group by another.

Extracts from a speech by Nelson Mandela made in his own defense at the Rivonia treason trial, South Africa 1964.

11

Southern Africa: Its Problems and Prospects*

MOSES E. AKPAN
South Carolina State College

The second half of the twentieth century has witnessed a spectacular change in the political history of Africa. This vast continent, known for centuries as the "Dark Continent"—not that the continent itself was as dark as was the European ignorance of it—which fell to European imperialism in the nineteenth century, has recently seen the emergence of a number of independent states. This event has been so dramatic in contemporary international politics that the year 1960, which saw seventeen African states being admitted to the General Assembly of the United Nations, has come to be known as the "Africa Year" in that august world body.

Today, as a result of this political awakening, almost every part of Africa, except Southern Africa, is free from colonial and settler rule. (Figure 11-1) The persistence of such regimes in Southern Africa has precipitated two important problems: the problem of minority rule and that of racial discrimination. The solution of these two problems is a matter of grave concern to Africans in Southern Africa, as well as to those in the independent African states. This essay is an analysis of these two problems and the prospects of their future solution.

MINORITY RULE

Although the regimes of Southern Africa often claim to be democratic, the popularly accepted principle of majority rule practiced by Western democracies, or what Africans usually refer

---

*Southern Africa, as used here and throughout this essay, specifically refers to those Southern African countries still under colonial and settler rule: Angola, Mozambique, Rhodesia, South Africa, and Namibia (formerly Southwest Africa).

191

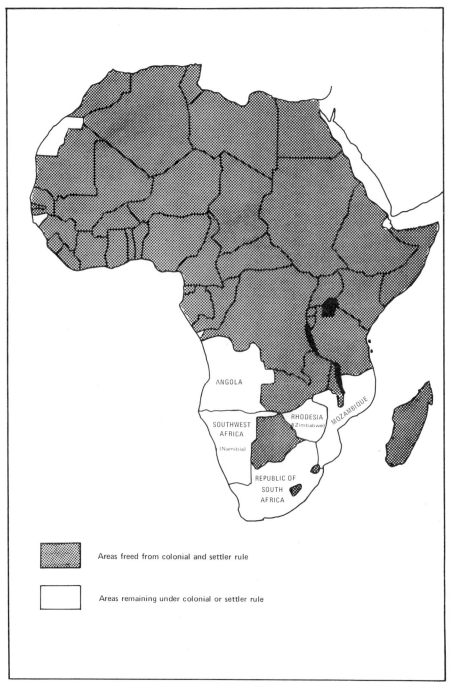

Figure 11-1. Status of Colonial and Settler Rule.

to as "one man one vote", is completely ignored. Instead, despite the existence of overwhelming African majorities, colonial and settler minority regimes appropriate political powers to themselves. In Angola and Mozambique, for instance, the government, irrespective of the recently announced so-called self government, is controlled by Portugal and administered by a few colonial officers with little or no participation of Africans in the decision making processes of their respective countries. Similarly, in Namibia – formerly Southwest Africa – the territory continues to be administered by the minority settler regime of South Africa despite the opposition of the United Nations.

In Rhodesia where there are 4 million Africans, the government is controlled by only 200,000 white settlers. Also, in South Africa, 13.5 million Africans are completely denied the right either to vote or run for seats in the South African national parliament while 3.5 million white settlers appropriate political power to themselves.

The Africans are opposed to minority rule in Southern Africa. They view it as undemocratic and a denial of their right to "national self determination" and have sought to eliminate it. However, the Africans' demand for majority rule and independence conflicts with the interests of the colonial and settler regimes of Southern Africa, hence the failure of these regimes to make concessions to the Africans.

Portugal, for instance, has incorporated its overseas territories, including Angola and Mozambique, into its national territory instead of granting them independence. In fact, Portugal sees its very existence tied to its African and other overseas territories. It was this fact which persuaded Commander Manuel Sarmento Rodriques in 1950 to comment that the "overseas expansion" started by Portugal five centuries ago is the most important reason for its "existence as a nation", and that no Portuguese "doubts that the guarantee of our independence and our future existence lie not in Europe . . . our main field of action lies overseas." (Kimble 1960:266) Thus, despite its recently announced intention to grant self-government to Angola and Mozambique, Portugal, has no intention of committing political suicide by voluntarily granting independence to its overseas territories.

The Republic of South Africa, holding mandatory power over Namibia, is primarily interested in annexing the territory instead of preparing its inhabitants for "national self-determination" as demanded by the African majority in the territory. In South Africa itself, the minority settlers have shown no interest in majority rule nor in acceding real political power to the African majority population. Instead, the settler regime has established special ethnic oriented African reserves, known as *bantustans* or homelands and set up psuedo-parliaments for the Africans. In theory, these pseudo-parliaments are supposed to be self-governing, but in practice the reverse is the case. Real decision making in South Africa still remains the primary responsibility of the national parliament in Pretoria, an organ exlusive to the minority settlers.

In Rhodesia the same situation persists; a settler minority holds power over an African majority. This prompted Ian Smith to reject the British five point proposal for Rhodesian independence which included an "unimpeded progress toward majority rule" (Young 1967:277) and to opt instead for the unilateral declaration of independence (UDI) on November 11, 1965.

RACIAL DISCRIMINATION

The focus of this problem is the policy of assimilation as practiced by Portugal toward Angola and Mozambique, and the policy of *apartheid,* or separate development, as practiced by the Nationalist government of South Africa.

Through the policy of assimilation, qualified Africans, the *assimilados,* who have adopted European culture and tradition, at the expense of their African inheritance, are accepted into a sort of pseudo-European society and are allowed certain social, economic and political rights.

Apartheid is an Afrikaans word describing the official policy of the government of South Africa with respect to race relations. It implies the separate development of racial groups. Apartheid, which became the law of the land in South Africa in 1948 following the emergence of the Nationalist Party as the ruling political party in that country, is enforced by a number of discriminatory laws: the Pass Law, the Group Areas Act, the Bantu Education Act, the Native Building Act, and the Industrial Conciliation Act.

SOUTH AFRICAN DISCRIMINATORY LAWS

The Pass Law is primarily aimed at restricting the movement of Africans in white areas. It requires each African, male and female, to carry a reference book containing his photograph, name, ethnic group, and place of work. It is regarded by the South African government as the "cornerstone" of apartheid. (McCellan 1963:57) The law controls everyday aspects of African lives in South Africa. Without the document being properly endorsed by a host of authorities, Africans cannot work, live in towns, or even walk on streets. Failure to produce the pass, upon request of a South African police officer, is a crime carrying a fine of £ 1 ($2.80) or two weeks' imprisonment. It was estimated in 1962 that "one out of every seven Africans in South Africa has been convicted for violation of the Pass Law." (UN Publications 1964:19)

The Group Areas Act is primarily aimed at separating African residential areas from white areas. Under the legislation, separate residential areas are reserved exclusively for each of the South African racial groups. 13.5 million Africans are restricted to about 13 per cent of the total land in South Africa while the white population of 3.5 million occupies the remaining 87 per cent. Furthermore, under this Act, the industrially developed part of South Africa is reserved for the settler elements while the Africans are primarily restricted to less developed areas and expected to develop the barren lands into fertile agricultural units.

The Bantu Education Act was initially adopted in 1953. It established separate educational systems for whites and non-whites in South Africa. Provisions of the Act make it inevitable that non-white education will remain inferior to white education.

The University Extension Act of 1959 extended this policy of separate and unequal education to all the universities and colleges in South Africa. Thus, universities in Witwatersrand, Natal, and Capetown which had been integrated became segregated and separate colleges reflecting the major African ethnic and linguistic groups in South Africa were established.

The Native Building Workers Act was first passed in 1951 and amended in 1955. The Act first limited employment of skilled African builders in urban areas. The 1955 amendment prohibited the employment of African workers except where the work is to be undertaken on the premises to be occupied by an African or his dependents. Thus, Africans are legally barred from encroaching on skilled jobs regarded as the "prerogative of Europeans" in South Africa.

IMPASSE

The government of South Africa regards apartheid as the only means of preserving the culture and traditions of both the European settlers and the "Bantu natives" of South Africa (Louw 1960). Above all, apartheid is seen as the only means of removing from the white settlers in South Africa the fear of "ultimate political domination" by the African majority population and Africans from the threat of perpetual "economic domination" by the minority white settlers. (Duplessis 1959:62)

Portugal, for its part, sees its policy of assimilation as a means to make Africans equal to the Portuguese by uniting them in "bonds of brotherly love." (Emerson 1962:266) Commenting on the position in 1960, Commander Rodriques remarked that the objective of the policy of assimilation has to "Christianize, colonize and civilize . . . in diffusing our blood, our language and our religion, our only purpose is that high aim of making others equal to us and uniting them in bonds of brotherly love." (Kimble 1960:266)

The Africans are becoming increasingly restive under this denial of their right to power and their right to retain their traditional culture. They have sought in the past, and continue to seek, through a number of strategies, to induce their adversaries to modify their positions.

TACTICS OF RESISTANCE TO POLICIES OF THE COLONIAL AND SETTLER REGIMES

The Africans, because of their frustrations with the failure of the colonial and settler regimes of Southern Africa to make concessions to their demands for majority rule and racial equality, have resorted to a number of positive actions aimed at inducing those regimes to modify their policies. Four of these actions deserve attention.

BOYCOTTS AND STRIKES

The Africans in Southern Africa frequently have resorted to boycotts as a resistance technique aimed at forcing their colonial and settler regimes to respect African views on social and political issues. In South Africa, for instance, two school boycotts were organized in April, 1955, by the African National Congress in protest against the Bantu Education Act. Some 5,000 students, mainly from the East Rand area participated in the first boycott. The second one, involving 7,000 students and 116 teachers, was more successful.

A most recent successful strike in Southern Africa occurred in Namibia where about 15,000 African contract labor workers in Ovamboland participated in a protest against the policy of the government of South Africa. Furthermore, in January, 1972, a strike by mine workers at Umtali was reported in Rhodesia.

These resistance techniques have shattered the myth of peace and tranquility, which was taken to indicate the acquiescence of Africans to the policies of the regimes in Southern Africa. Furthermore, the Ovamboland strike in Namibia has caused acute embarrassment to the South African government which would prefer the world to think the territory content under South African mandatory rule. In fact, it has been reported that the situation in Ovamboland resulted in "closing down of mines, construction jobs and other services" in the country. *(Southern Africa* 1972:12) However, none of these strategies has caused the regimes of Southern Africa to modify their policies on minority rule and racial inequality. On the contrary, they have adopted more repressive measures and sometimes used physical violence against the Africans in order to silence them.

PEACEFUL PROTESTS

Another technique of resistance used by the Africans is mass demonstration. The most dramatic one occurred in South Africa in 1960. It was organized by the Pan African Congress of South Africa in defiance of the Pass Law. Mass demonstrations occurred in many cities in South Africa, including Sharpeville, Orlando, and Capetown.

More recently, in Rhodesia, in 1972, Africans protested *en masse* the proposed settlement between the British government and the white minority government. It began on January 13, in Shabani, a mining town in the south, and finally spread, like wild fire, to Gwelo and Fort Victoria and to Salisbury, the capital. Over 10,000 persons participated in the Gwelo demonstration.

Like the strikes and boycotts, the mass peaceful demonstrations have failed to persuade the Southern African regimes to modify their policies. Rather, they have become more repressive and brutal in defense of the *status quo.* This is exemplified in the Sharpeville incident in South Africa in 1960 where police opened fire on African demonstrators, killing 72 and wounding 187.* A further example of white Southern African back lash is the shooting to death of 15 Africans by Rhodesian police officers during mass demonstrations in January, 1972. *(Southern Africa* 1972:12)

LIBERATION ARMIES

The third resistance technique used by Africans in Southern Africa is the organization of freedom armies whose aim is to harass the governments and force them to make some concessions to the

---

*Since the writing of this article a similarly dramatic and tragic demonstration for better working conditions took place at the Western Deep Levels mine, Carltonville, September, 1973. (editor)

Africans. As will be pointed out later in this essay, the freedom armies, despite their reported successes, lack the capability to challenge adequately the military might of the Southern African regimes, hence their failure to force these regimes to modify their policies.

OUTSIDE AFRICAN HELP

The Africans in Southern Africa, because of their failure to effect the desired changes have begun to turn to their fellow Africans in the independent black African states for assistance. Since their request correlates with the overall objectives of Pan-Africanism espoused by those African states, it has been received by them favorably. The independent black African states have consequently resorted to a number of tactics aimed at inducing the Southern African regimes to modify their polices.

DIRECT APPEAL

The pattern of their appeal was established in 1958 at the First Conference of the Independent African States held in Accra, Ghana. A special resolution was adopted appealing to the colonial and settler regimes of Southern Africa to respect the human rights of Africans in their territories as provided by the Universal Declaration of Human Rights and the Charter of the United Nations.

In the same Conference, a special resolution was adopted appealing to governments of Southern Africa to grant immediate independence to the Africans in their respective territories. The appeals culminated in the Lusaka Manifesto of 1969 which called for negotiated settlements to the problems of minority rule and racial discrimination in Southern Africa. A warning was sounded that should such negotiations fail, the African states would be left with no other choice than to support the liberation armies organized by African freedom fighters in Southern Africa. Direct appeals, as a resistance technique, have not succeeded; the white regimes of Southern Africa have ignored them.

LITIGATION

The second resistance tactic used by the African states in Southern Africa has been litigation. On November 4, 1960, formal contentious proceedings were filed in the International Court of Justice seeking to induce the government of South Africa to recognize its international obligation to Namibia and to prepare its inhabitants for national self-determination.

The South African government's response to the court proceedings was negative. It challenged the Court's authority, and
further insisted that the case be dismissed. The Court ignored this
appeal and assumed jurisdiction over the case. Despite this initial
legal victory by the African states over the government of South
Africa, the final decision on the case by the Court was very frustrating to them; on technical grounds, the Court, by a vote of 8 to
7, denied the right to Ethiopia and Liberia – the two states which
represented the African states in the case – to undertake such
legal action against the government of South Africa.

DIRECT SUPPORT

A third tactic used by the African states is direct support of
the freedom fighters of Southern Africa. Coordinated assistance is
channelled through the African Liberation Committee, an arm of
the Organization of African Unity, with headquarters in Dar es
Salaam, Tanzania. The strategy has resulted in a number of successful armed confrontations with the regimes of Southern Africa.
Today, parts of Angola and Mozambique have been liberated from
colonial minority rule, and are under the control of the African
freedom fighters. Regardless of these successful incursions, the
support to the African freedom fighters by the African states has
not brought about any significant changes in the policies of the
Southern African regimes. Rather, it has facilitated their consolidation into a sort of "unholy alliance" to suppress and contain
the freedom fighters.

The African states lack the material power, economic and
military, to support the liberation movements to the point that
they can pose any real threat to the normal functioning of the
Southern African regimes. According to 1969 estimates, the per
capita income in thirty five selected African states was only $114.
As a result, African states are weak militarily. In 1968, only nine
African states had forces over 10,000. The total armed forces of
African States south of the Sahara was placed at 150,000. The
combat aircraft totalled only 529. On the other hand, the estimated forces of the Southern African regimes totalled 275,000. In
the Republic of South Africa alone, aircraft numbered 300.

RESORT TO THE UNITED NATIONS

Prompted by their inability independently to force the Southern African regimes to modify their policies, the African states
finally have turned to the United Nations for diplomatic assistance. The resort to the United Nations for diplomatic leverage has

brought no substantive results because of the power politics which tends to dictate the result of issues raised in that organization. Certain states, because of their material power — economic and military — exercise greater influence in the organization than those states with limited material power. Consequently, weak states tend to achieve their goals in world affairs only when they do not conflict with the interest of the powerful states.

This situation is reflected in the Charter and functioning of the United Nations itself. The veto provided for in the Charter of the United Nations confers on the five most powerful states — the power to prevent any imposition of forcible actions which would conflict with their own interest or those of their friends and allies. In 1963, for instance, the British veto prevented the adoption of a resolution which could have conflicted with the interest of the Rodesian minority regime. In 1970, the United States vetoed a Security Council resolution which could have been contrary to the policy of the United Kingdom.

The power politics in the Security Council of the United Nations has forced weaker states, including the African states, to turn more to the General Assembly for adoption of resolutions relative to their interests in world affairs. The African states, because of their numerical strength in the General Assembly and because of the support usually given to them by some Asian and Latin American states, have successfully induced the Assembly to adopt a number of resolutions condemning the policies of the Southern African regimes. These diplomatic victories, however, have been mostly ineffective because they usually require the approval of the Security Council to give them force. There have been some significant actions by the United Nations with respect to the problems of minority rule and racial discrimination in Southern Africa.

U.N. ACTIONS AGAINST MINORITY RULE

In October 1966, the General Assembly of the United Nations adopted resolution 2142 (XXI) which formally terminated the Mandate of South West Africa (Namibia) and placed the territory directly under the administration of the United Nations. The resolution failed to resolve the Namibian question; the General Assembly is not empowered to enforce such resolutions. In March, 1969, the Security Council finally adopted a resolution on Namibia calling upon the minority settler government of South Africa to withdraw its administration from the territory. Although the Council adopted this resolution, it did not call for any forcible action against South Africa because such a measure was opposed by the United Kingdom and France.

An even more significant action on the part of the United Nations came in November, 1965, when the Security Council adopted a resolution calling upon all member states to break off all economic relations with the settler minority government of Rhodesia and not to recognize its Unilateral Declaration of Independence. It is significant that the adoption of this forceful measure came only when the United Kingdom had changed its 1963 policy on Rhodesia. The economic sanctions have not toppled the regime as hoped by the Africans. However, the United Nations action has caused considerable economic damage to the Rhodesian regime. Above all, it has helped to delay the recognition of the UDI by the international community. Rhodesia remains unrecognised as a nation-state.

U.N. ACTIONS AGAINST RACIAL DISCRIMINATION

Following the Sharpeville incident in March, 1960, the Security Council took up the apartheid question, consideration of which, prior to this time, had been opposed by Western powers, particularly the United Kingdom and France. The resolution characterized the policy of apartheid as a threat to international peace and security, and asserted the readiness of the Council to take positive action to prevent any further occurrence of disasters similar to that of the Sharpeville incident.

Furthermore, in November 1962, the General Assembly of the United Nations adopted a resolution imposing comprehensive political, economic and military sanctions on South Africa. This resolution required the approval of the Security Council to become enforceable. The Western powers opposed it there. Nevertheless, in 1963, the Security Council finally adopted resolution S/5388 (1963) which placed limited military sanctions on South Africa. The resolution, because of continued defiance by certain Western states, particularly the United Kingdom and France, has had little influence in inducing the South African government to change its policies.

In conclusion, therefore, the Africans have succeeded in dramatizing their opposition to minority rule and racial discrimination as practiced by the white southern African regimes. But none of their tactics has forced any of these regimes to modify their policies in any significant manner.

PROSPECTS FOR THE SOLUTION
OF SOUTHERN AFRICAN PROBLEMS

The failure of the African resistance tactics to cause Southern African regimes to respect African human rights raises the question of the eventual alternative strategy open to Africans for the elimination of minority rule and racial discrimination in Southern Africa. Four possible strategies deserve special attention.

WAITING FOR A CHANGE IN ATTITUDE

The first is to wait for a change in the attitude of the white Southern African regimes. Should they decide to moderate their policies either through changes in administration, goodwill, or pressure from the Western powers, there could be a partial or full solution to the problems of minority rule and racial discrimination in Southern Africa. However, the prospects for such a development remain remote. The regimes of Southern Africa have tended, if anything, to harden their positions.

Two "gestures" have recently been made by the racist regimes. Portugal has claimed to have accorded self-government to Angola and Mozambique. South Africa has opened up a "dialogue" with independent Black Africa. Neither of these moves has been accompanied by changes in official policy. Africans are almost totally excluded from the decision-making processes of Angola and Mozambique. The "dialogue" advocated by South Africa is merely aimed to promote her economic development, not to seek solutions for her internal racial problems. It can be seen that both these gestures were designed to create diplomatic reverses for the Africans who, until very recently, had been very successful in arousing world opinion against the policies of minority rule and racial discrimination. The prospects for the problems of Southern Africa being resolved through changes in the attitudes of the colonial and settler regimes remain as remote as ever.*

PRECIPITATING CHANGES IN WESTERN POLICY

Another factor that could further the solution of Southern African problems would be a change in the policy of the Western powers. Although the Western powers often have argued against the effectiveness of forcible measures, particularly economic sanctions, their positions seem to be dictated by their economic,

*Since this article was written a dramatic change in government and control in metropolitan Portugal has resulted in a "change in attitude" towards Portugal's colonial role in Africa. It remains to be seen whether the "change in attitude" will result in the granting of independence under majority rule in the three Portuguese colonies. (editor)

strategic and other interests in Southern Africa. The United Kingdom, France and the United States, for instance, have large investments in South Africa. Furthermore, the location of Southern African ports athwart the sea route around the Cape of Good Hope is of special logistic importance to the Western powers. Furthermore, the United States has space tracking facilities in South Africa, and the sudden interruptions of these facilities could affect the progress of her space programs.

Internal pressure may be building up in the Western world against policies which tend to favor minority rule and racial discrimination in Southern Africa. In the United States, for instance, groups such as the Black Caucus in the Congress have been taking positions against the United States policy toward Southern Africa. These activities culminated in a march on Washington on May 27, 1972 to dramatize support for the liberation movements of Southern Africa. Elsewhere, other Western powers have moderated their policies. In 1965, for instance, the British government reversed itself by supporting sanctions against the Rhodesian minority regime. Despite these gestures, Western powers seem unwilling to jeopardize economic, strategic and other interests in Southern Africa; they are not prepared to make changes in their policies that might bring about an open confrontation with the white regimes of Southern Africa.

AFRICAN DIRECT MILITARY CONFRONTATION

The third tactic which might resolve the Southern African problems is direct military confrontations between the white minority regimes and the African states. But the African states lack adequate material power to successfully undertake this type of adventure. Besides, direct military action by the African states might serve as a pretext for foreign intervention on one side or the other and could lead to all-out world war.

SUPPORT FOR THE LIBERATION MOVEMENTS

The last and potentially most successful tactic seems to be to increase support of the liberation movements in Southern Africa. This strategy could have both indirect and direct advantages.

The decision on the part of African States to see that adequate military and economic support is given to the liberation forces could have three indirect results. First, it could provide an extra incentive to the African states to strengthen, through their own initiatives as well as through assistance from external sources, their own economic and military capabilities. Such development could, in time, place the African states in a better position to offset the military imbalance presently existing between them and the Southern African regimes. The increased material power of the African states might serve as a warning to the Southern African regimes and might induce some changes in their internal policies. Secondly, a decision on the part of African states to increase their economic and military potential would provide more commercial opportunities in Africa for Western interests. This would help to distribute Western economic involvement in the continent more widely – balancing the economic concentration that exists today in Southern Africa. Finally, if African states increased their military might, Western states with sympathies for the liberation movements could channel aid to the movements indirectly via their commercial dealings within the African states.

The direct effect of adequate military and economic support of the liberation armies would be to increase the effectiveness of the resistance to such a point that it could disrupt the normal functioning of the established regimes of Southern Africa. This threat might induce those regimes to liberalize their policies toward their black populations, or it might lead them to greater repressions. This last, in turn, could generate more incidents like Sharpeville. Sharpeville-type incidents would almost surely arouse the concern of the Western powers because such incidents contain the very real threat of a racial war which could endanger the peace of Africa in particular and the world at large. The prospect of such a holocaust would surely focus the interest and the might of the major powers on efforts to solve the problems of minority rule and racial discrimination in Southern Africa.

PART TWO
Resources and Materials

12

What to Use?
Materials for Teaching About Africa

BARRY K. BEYER
Carnegie-Mellon University

A decade ago a conscientious teacher who wanted to teach a unit on Africa had to search long and hard to find any instructional materials. That situation no longer exists. In fact, it is reversed. Today, materials search out teachers. There are so many instructional materials on Africa produced by so many publishers that brochures advertising their availability fairly deluge teachers and administrators alike.

The problem of finding appropriate materials persists, of course. But now it is a different problem. Instead of trying to find just any piece of material that might resolve the problem, teachers now must cope with the problem of selecting, from among a multitude of colorful, appealing, exciting materials, the two or three or four that might best help them and their students accomplish their learning objectives. In some ways, the present situation is a happy one. But it is still a difficult one with which to cope.

THE PLACE OF MATERIALS IN TEACHING

Which materials, then, do I use to teach about Africa? As crucial as this question is, it is *not* the place to start planning for teaching about Africa. Before even dealing with this question, a teacher must understand four basic principles about any teaching, principles which are especially relevant to teaching about Africa: objectives, content, selectivity, and materials.

OBJECTIVES

The first basic principle is that objectives, not materials, come first. Objectives shape the kinds of content, materials and teaching strategies to be used; if the objectives are not clear or are not

207

worthwhile then the resulting learning experience is quite likely to be a meaningless hodgepodge of fact-memorizing or other useless exercises. As painful and distasteful as it may be, deciding upon and stating clear objectives is the first step in worthwhile, productive teaching and learning.

All too often materials serve as the tail that wags the dog; too many African units are planned around the kinds of materials seemingly available to teachers. The common perception of what materials are available is usually limited to textbooks or an old filmstrip or a few jungle books in the school library; this leads to teaching which is necessarily stultifying, confining and, frankly, dull and out-of-date. All too often, planning and teaching about Africa serve only to perpetuate the erroneous stereotypes and myths about Africa that already exist and that ought to be eradicated, and are, indeed, eradicated in more creative classrooms.

In addition to correcting false impressions and erasing erroneous stereotypes, a worthwhile unit on Africa can help students accomplish higher, broader objectives such as to develop concepts and generalizations; to refine and practice thinking, study and social skills; and to clarify and develop attitudes and values relative to other people as well as to themselves. Having multiple objectives such as these provides a teacher with a set of guidelines for selecting and using instructional materials as well as for planning daily learning experiences and evaluating these experiences.

CONTENT

To accomplish the types of objectives noted above requires a view of content that is not now common in many classrooms. Content, information about Africa, must be *used* as a vehicle to accomplish something broader or beyond itself rather than merely as an end in itself. This is to say that learning content *per se* should not be the sole objective of studying Africa. Instead, students should use this content—manipulate it, dissect it, pull it apart, refit it—to build relevant concepts and generalizations; refine social, study and thinking skills; and gain insight into themselves and the culture in which they live. In so doing, content will be learned. But this content will also serve larger ends and its relevancy will be enhanced far beyond the time and space dimensions in which it is used.

SELECTIVITY

If conceptual objectives like those mentioned above are to be accomplished by a study of Africa, sweeping coverage of information about all aspects of all of Africa must be replaced by in-depth study of selected aspects of Africa. Little if anything worthwhile is learned by *covering* something. A standard dictionary difinition of *to cover* is "to take in and hide from view!" And that is precisely what happens when teachers cover anything in the classroom. Useful insights are clouded rather than facilitated. The major purpose of a unit on Africa, as indeed of a unit on any topic, ought to be to *un*cover, not to hide from view.

In terms of studying Africa, selectivity simply means carefully picking and choosing content and topics that will help accomplish a few well chosen, worthwhile knowledge, skill and effective objectives. Such selection may mean studying only two or three representative countries in depth rather than a smattering about all the countries on the entire continent; it may mean studying how people live in one or two places rather than trying to study how all Africans live; it may mean finding out how representative Africans use their habitat in order that the teacher may focus on cultural beliefs and values. In sum, a worthwhile study of Africa clarifies rather than obscures, and clarification is more likely to result from in-depth, selective study rather than from sweeping coverage of everything.

MATERIALS

Many types of materials may be used in teaching about Africa. Some of these materials are produced by commercial publishers. Others, however, can be easily made by teachers from local resources and materials readily available to them. Unfortunately, many teachers seem to be unaware of the great range of these latter materials. Local resources, materials already in the typical school, and mass communications media offer potentially unlimited and inexpensive sources of learning materials for studying Africa if teachers can only become alert to them. Rather than neglect to teach Africa because "our district has no funds for materials" as is so often the excuse, teachers can design exciting learning experiences built around these readily available materials. Consideration of such materials should precede any survey of commercially produced, but often times prohibitively expensive, instructional materials.

SOME "NON-COMMERCIAL" SOURCES
OF INSTRUCTIONAL MATERIALS ON AFRICA

Classroom teachers have a wealth of often untapped resources on which to draw in teaching about Africa. Many of these are local and community resources while others are made by the teachers themselves from materials to which all teachers have ready access. Precisely which of these sources to tap or which materials to prepare depends in the final analysis on the objectives set for instruction, but awareness of the wide range of such sources available might well enable teachers to set and accomplish more and higher objectives than they otherwise would consider. Some of these sources are described here.

LOCAL OR COMMUNITY RESOURCES

What is there in an average community that may be used in teaching about Africa? Or, better yet, who is there in a local community that can help teach about Africa? People—outside speakers—with some knowledge of or experience in Africa may well live in any average American community today. Many of these people can be persuaded to meet with a class; to discuss their experiences and knowledge; and to show their slides and any carvings, clothing or other objects they acquired in Africa. Ministers with missionary experience in Africa, businessmen who travel to Africa or who do business with Africans, returned military personnel or Peace Corps volunteers, parents, teachers or students who have travelled there as tourists, professors in local colleges or universities—all or some of these people may be available to help teach about Africa. African students enrolled in local universities or colleges may also be enlisted in this effort.

Of course, resource people and their slides or "artifacts" are not the whole answer to the quest for teaching materials on Africa. They can be misused just as easily as a text or paperback. But if they are carefully selected, if the teacher integrates their presentations into a carefully planned sequence of learning activities—if, in a word, speakers are *used* just as a text or film or game might be used to provide some data which the students then can use to check out hypotheses or questions they are investigating— then such visitors can serve as exciting and worthwhile "learning materials" on Africa.

SERVICE AGENCIES

Teachers also frequently turn to local and other organizations and agencies for assistance in teaching about Africa. The African-American Institute* offers bibliographies of materials as well as

---

*Addresses for all publishers or sources of materials mentioned may be found at the conclusion of this chapter.

teacher "starter kits" and other resources which are of immeasurable value to the novice. Local tourist agencies often supply posters, travel guides and other typical tourist data which may be used to provide insights into various aspects of Africa's climate, topography, history, peoples and national development. Letters to UNESCO, the United States Department of State, embassies of African nations, and American airlines such as Pan American or Trans-World Airlines can bring free or inexpensive materials and, occasionally, speakers or films or recordings. Materials from sources such as these, although they usually take an inordinate amount of time to arrive, can be most useful in teaching about selected aspects of Africa.

MASS COMMUNICATIONS MEDIA

Probably no other newspaper in the United States provides better in-depth coverage of Africa than does the *Christian Science Monitor.* Over a period of several weeks this newspaper usually publishes a half dozen lengthy feature articles on such subjects as political events in Namibia (Southwest Africa) or Rhodesia, or social and economic conditions in Ghana, Nigeria or Kenya, and so on. A collection of such articles, mounted or perhaps duplicated, may serve as extremely useful sources of data on Africa. *The New York Times* annual economic supplement on Africa (usually published just after the first of each year) also provides a wealth of data about various African states. Television, too, offers increasingly more detailed and less "touristy" presentations on Africa, and teachers have been known to tape record the video and/or audio of some of these programs for later use in their own classes. The recording of *Whimaway,* so popular on the radio some months ago, could have been most useful in a study of Africa.

African English-language newspapers and magazines may also be used to great advantage in classroom teaching about Africa. In fact, an exciting instructional unit could be built primarily around a collection of such materials. Newspaper and magazine advertisements provide useful insights into the economy, international relations and cultural values of the various African nations and peoples, as do the feature articles, news articles, and other typical newspaper ingredients. A collection of papers from one city such as Accra or Lagos, or a few papers from several cities in different parts of Africa offer unlimited opportunities to learn about this part of our world. Use of African magazines such as *Drum** (an

*Approximately $18.50 airmail annually.

African monthly news magazine much like *Ebony*) and *Teen and Twenty**   (a monthly magazine written by Nigerian teenagers for Nigerian teenagers) offer similar possibilities. Library or teacher subscriptions to any of these or similar materials are inexpensive and, although three or four months should be allowed for surface delivery, will provide teachers with an extremely valuable teaching resource.

LIBRARY RESOURCES

Although school and local or travelling libraries frequently have only a few materials on Africa which can be used profitably by students, these resources tend to be more in number or kind than one might suspect. Virtually all libraries have several sets of encyclopedias and other reference books *(World Almanacs* and so on); non-fiction materials such as travel books, biographies and "story of" type books; collections of folklore or legends, some of which are African in origin; and periodicals which contain notice of current events in African states. These, too, may be tapped for use by students as the basis for oral reports, drawings, or displays. Excerpts are often made for use in large group situations. Collections of all these materials may even be carried into the classroom where students can use as many as they wish for a period of several weeks in their search for needed evidence about Africa.

TEACHER-MADE MATERIALS

Many teachers make their own instructional materials and some experts contend that use of such items makes for better learning than does use of the colorful, slick, and glossy commercially produced materials. Most teacher-made materials involve a minimal expense, usually borne by the teachers; they can also involve students in the preparation, and this in itself can be an exciting learning experience.

Numerous teachers today find the thermofax machine a useful aid because its ability to copy and make spirit masters of almost any printed material enables them to duplicate newspaper or magazine articles, cartoons, charts, maps, advertisements, and other documents related to Africa. Where multiple copies of any print source are not readily available, these teacher-made copies frequently offer a useful substitute.

---

*Approximately $3.36 surface, $14.28 airmail annually.

A camera—a simple instamatic or more complex 135mm out-fit—can and ought to be just as useful a teaching aid as the thermo-fax copier. Scores of teachers now create their own slide libraries by taking colored slides of photographs on Africa found in travel magazines, geographic magazines, books, atlases, and other similar sources. Copies of woodcuts, line drawings, and black and white photos from explorers' diaries, biographies, and old travel ac-counts often provide materials as useful in history lessons as the colored slides of geography subjects do in geography lessons. Such a practice not only makes available a large personal collection of visuals on which to draw, but also enables teachers to build dif-ferent slide "shows" by reshuffling the same slides. Where teachers find themselves all thumbs with a camera, school audio-visual directors and even student photography clubs have been known to provide the needed expertise.

Teachers can make picture card sets, too. Old issues of *Na-tional Geographic Magazine* and similar journals are often ripped up for their photos which can easily be mounted on cardboard and arranged in multiple sets for groups of students to use in their classroom study. Back issues of this magazine may be obtained from the society's headquarters but cheaper, if slightly worn, copies may also be secured from second-hand bookstores. Teach-ers who purchase four to six copies of the same issue can put together 4-6 sets of cards with each set containing the same photos. Where it is impossible to obtain copies of the desired journal, teachers often make black and white photos of the illus-trations they wish to use and then use multiple enlargements as picture cards. Such use of pictures provides not only a new type of medium for most students but also allows them to work in groups and to use manipulative materials, things that are notoriously lack-ing in most classrooms.

Teachers who find maps and charts they wish to use often re-draw these on acetates or on paper from which they make color transparencies. Students in art or mechanical drawing classes can be called upon to help. In fact, a few teachers organize their class study of Africa around locating certain visual aids relevant to their study. As their students search all possible sources for these aids, they not only learn about the subject under consideration, but they also develop basic thinking, study and social skills as well as certain desirable attitudes and values. The product of such an exciting, cooperative teacher-student search for and development of learning materials is often an entirely new—and refreshingly positive—outlook toward teaching and learning on the part of both teacher and students!

SOME COMMERCIALLY
PRODUCED INSTRUCTIONAL MATERIALS

When, in the mid-1960's, teaching about Africa suddenly became popular, commercial publishers rushed to fill the void in
teaching materials. Hundreds of filmstrips, paperbacks, films,
texts, recordings, transparencies, and similar materials suddenly
appeared. Most of these were colorful, attractively packaged, and
intriguingly titled. However, many were also hastily structured,
inadequately researched, outrageously priced and replete with bias
and gross distortions of reality. Most of these materials are still
available. But, fortunately, so are other, more recently published
materials* that bear the obvious marks of competent scholarship,
quality production and creative educational research. Some of
these latter materials deserve close consideration by teachers who
wish to help their students learn about Africa and, in the process,
develop conceptual knowledge, thinking skills and positive attitudes toward learning—not to mention also enjoy what they are
doing.

TEXTBOOKS

Most elementary and secondary school geography and history
texts contain something on Africa. But, to the best of my knowledge there is only one world history or geography text authored in
whole or part by a recognized Africanist. *The Human Achievement* (Silver Burdette Co.), coauthored by the internationally
respected scholar of Africa's past, Philip D. Curtin, is similar in
style, size and weight to other typical hardcover tenth grade world
history texts, but the section on Africa is worth examining, and,
for those students reading at grade level, worth using. A recent
hardcover text—more accurately a collection of readings woven
together by interpretation and sometimes exhortation—is Evelyn
Rich and Emmanuel Wallerstein's (a well known sociologist and
expert on African politics) *Africa: Tradition and Change* (Random
House).

Paperbacks outnumber hardcover texts on Africa, however,
and of all the paperback texts on Africa now available none can
compare to two very different such materials. Basil Davidson's
Discovering Our African Heritage (Ginn and Company) is by far

---

*A comprehensive, annotated listing of over 700 texts, filmstrips, and other instructional
materials on Africa may be found in Barry K. Beyer, *Africa South of the Sahara; A
Resource and Curriculum Guide,* New York; Thomas Y. Crowell Company, 1969. This
volume also includes guidelines for organizing units on Africa and pre and post evaluation instruments.

the most exciting interpretative paper-covered text on African history and culture to appear in the past ten years. Of course, it too, has its drawbacks. It tends to inspire more wonder than critical thought, sometimes gets much too preachy and is sometimes guilty of making generalizations of questionable accuracy. In spite of these occasional lapses, however, Davidson "puts it all together", up to and including the period of the Atlantic Slave Trade, better than any other author.

Discovering Our African Heritage makes connections that few other available texts make—how large scale production of food surpluses leads to more complex social organization, or how words in one language relate to words in another. It presents stimulating photos, maps and illustrations, and brings people and their culture into a recounting of African history and geography. An obvious attempt to promote a positive image of black Africa's history and to challenge racial stereotypes, this book could be a most useful text for tenth graders. In fact, teachers at any grade level, uninformed about African history and culture, would benefit greatly from a study of this text.

The second outstanding "text" on Africa is Leon Clark's set of multiple paperbacks (six titles in all) on African culture and history, *Through African Eyes: Cultures in Change* (Frederick A. Praeger Publishers).* Clark has woven together excerpts from African literature—biographies, poetry, novels—and from government documents, traveller's accounts, scholarly studies, newspapers, oral traditions and other sources to help junior high school students develop a firsthand feeling for the African experience today as well as in the past. The affective dimension of this series of inexpensive paperbacks (averaging a little over 125 pages each) coupled with the inquiry oriented teaching strategy outlined in his elaborate teaching guides offers teachers an unparalleled opportunity to get at Africa from the inside—through African eyes!

Other very useful, top quality paperbacks are:
Fred Burke, *Africa*. (Houghton, Mifflin Col, 1970) paper $2.20

> A survey of African history with chapters on habitat, ancient history, Sudanic kingdoms, central Africa, the slave trade, European penetration, and African independence.

*The complete list of titles is as follows:
I *Coming of Age in Africa, Continuity and Change;* II *From Tribe to Town — Problems of Adjustment;* III *The African Past and the Coming of the European;* IV *The Colonial Experience: An Inside View;* V *The Rise of Nationalism: Freedom Regained;* VI *Nation Building; Tanzania and the World.* The six paperbacks are also available in a single volume (hardcover, price $12.50).

Fred Burke, *Africa: Selected Readings.* (Houghton, Mifflin Co., 1969) paper $1.80

An annotated collection of excerpts from the writings of scholars, journalists, explorers, African leaders, and others on Africa's land and peoples, and various periods of African history.

Philip J. Foster, *Africa South of the Sahara.* (The Macmillan Co., 1968) paper

A survey of Africa south of the Sahara with emphasis on contemporary Africa and its people, history, traditional life, and geography as well as on changes in urban life, education, and other aspects of life.

Olivia Vlahos, *African Beginnings.* (The Viking Press, 1969) paper $2.45

A survey of the cultures of pre-European Africa south of the Sahara empasizing the traditional life of selected African peoples with some attention to contemporary life styles of the Kikuyu, Tonga, and other peoples.

MANIPULATIVE MATERIALS

Materials such as picture cards which students may handle and shuffle around offer fine opportunities not only for student learning but for relaxing the classroom atmosphere and for giving students a chance to move about, work in groups and talk informally among themselves—all essential features of a good learning environment. Use of both "artifacts" and maps also admirably fits these needs when studying about Africa.

"Artifacts" seem to be a popular teaching material when studying any culture group, and they are undeniably useful in helping students gain insights into a people's habitat, history, technology, and value system. However, their use is just as likely to reinforce erroneous stereotypes as it is to lead to more realistic understanding. To treat wood carvings prepared for the tourist trade as exemplifying basic African values may well be tantamount to using the souvenir knick-knacks any tourist can pick up at Niagara Falls or the Grand Canyon as keys to earlier American culture. Great care must be taken, in using any product of human workmanship such as automobiles and pairs of shoes as well as hoes, carvings and castings, to avoid creating the negative impressions. Careful teaching can avoid this pitfall, however, and teachers may involve students in eye opening learning experiences about Africa by giving them an opportunity to handle and examine various material examples of African cultures. ALVA Museum Replicas, Inc. have available a large collection of reproductions of typical traditional African works of art which may be well used to raise questions about and gain insights into African cultures, life styles and habitats.

Another type of manipulative material currently available for studying Africa is a set of maps called *Africa Inquiry Maps* (Thomas Y. Crowell Company, $43). A class set of these maps— thirty packets each containing a set of ten outline maps of Africa (showing vegetation, climate regions, selected cities, elevation above sea level, major bodies of water, selected ethnic groups, and other important data) printed in color on tough, see-through paper—enables students individually or in groups or pairs to over-lay one on another as they manipulate these materials to develop meaningful spatial and areal relationships among various data, to raise questions or to generate hypotheses for further investigation. A teaching guide with easily duplicated tear-out student activity guides accompanies this material and offers numerous suggestions for using these maps with any students from grades four through twelve in inquiry or other learning experiences.

Wall maps—three dimensional in effect—that should be con-sidered are:

> *Aero Raised Relief Map of Africa.* (A. J. Nystrom Com-pany) $49
> A flat multicolored 45" x 49" plastic coated map with surface features raised to represent varying elevations.
> *Wenshow Relief-Like Map of Africa.* (Denoyer-Geppert Co.) $27.25
> A pull down, multicolored 64" x 75" relief map with three dimensional effect showing surface features and elevation.

VISUAL MATERIALS – FILMSTRIPS

Where Africa is concerned, filmstrips of all degrees of quality abound. Three sets are particularly outstanding, however. One is a set entitled *Africa Speaks—I* (Doubleday Multi-media, $60) which consists of five, beautiful, color filmstrips with accompanying recorded narratives. Although some questionable over-generaliza-tions do occur in the narrative and maps, the content is well presented. Individual strips focus on geography, empires and kingdoms, the European colonial period, and two representative culture groups. The last two strips, in fact, make this set unique for they present case studies of the Ashanti of Ghana and the peoples of Tanzania.

A second outstanding set of filmstrips is *African Art and Sculpture* (Warren Schloat Production, $45) which, in three filmstrips with accompanying recordings, presents black African history and culture through a study of art and sculpture. This fascinating and fast moving series uses carvings, bronzes, masks, and other African works of art to reveal significant aspects of the African past and of present African cultures and value systems.

Zanj Africa (E.M.C. Corporation, $78) is another invaluable filmstrip-record set. This set consists of 6 filmstrips and records and is an audio-visual study by an anthropologist of the interaction of three neighboring peoples who live near or on Kenya's Indian Ocean coast. Although some of the concepts that can be developed through use of this set might be considered quite sophisticated, the basic picture it presents of life in East Africa may easily be used in junior high school and upper elementary grades.

All three of these filmstrip sets are excellent learning materials but they only scratch the surface of the many other sets available. Among the others teachers should consider are:

Africa: Land of Developing Countries. (Society for Visual Education, 1965) $39.75

A set of 6 filmstrips, 3 records and scripts.

The Living World of Black Africa. (Crowell-Collier-Macmillan Corp., 1969) $108.00

A set of 12 filmstrips, with records and scripts.

VISUAL MATERIALS: FILMS

Many different types of films on Africa exist including 8mm loops, 8mm sound cartridges, and 16mm narrated and non-narrated sound films. Doubleday Multimedia and Ealing Corporation produce excellent sets of super- and regular 8mm 4 minute loops on village life, city life, farming and other aspects of Africa. BFA Educational Media has produced two excellent narrated color films on life in West Africa and in East Africa (as well as corresponding sets of filmstrips). But of all the 16mm films on Africa now available those produced by the International Film Foundation are probably the most creative and potentially useful.

In addition to their outstanding quality and content, IFF films use a number of innovative techniques. *The Ancient African* (1970), the best available film on Africa's pre-colonial history, is a 25-minute narrated color film that uses split screen techniques and animation as well as a judicious mix of scenes of the present and past to present a vivid and accurate summary of the African past. The *African Village Life* series, on the other hand, consists of a number of non-narrated short 16mm films (5 to 15 minutes in length) depicting various aspects of the life of the Bozo and Dogon peoples of West Africa. *Building a House, Building a Boat, Herding Cattle, Onion Farming,* and *Fishing on the River Niger* plus *Bozo Daily Life* provide vivid pictures of the daily life of these people complete with on-the-scene recorded sound unbroken by interpretive narration.

Other films deserve special mention, too. One outstanding film is Gerald McDermott's animated interpretation of a famous Ashanti folk tale entitled *Anansi The Spider* (Texture Films, Inc.). This colorful, 10 minute, narrated film recounts one of Anansi's most celebrated adventures in a tale calculated by its African authors to help explain how things came to be the way they are. This film can be used by elementary, secondary or college students alike as a fine introduction to or example of the basic values and beliefs underlying African culture.

Iron-Making the Old Way (also Texture Films) differs from the preceding film in style and approach but not in quality. One of a series of similar films, *Iron-Making* graphically depicts the ironmaker at work in traditional African society as he makes his own charcoal and collects his own iron ore prior to combining them to produce iron in blast furnaces he has had built by his helpers. Short on interpretive narration and long on powerful photography this film, as others in the series, fairly puts the viewer into Niger and makes possible an affective understanding of life in Africa that most films fail to develop.* Of course, there are scores of other 16mm films on Africa but none are quite as striking or potentially useful in getting into African life and culture as those mentioned here.

There are other types of visuals available; picture cards, slides of African art, masks and sculpture, and overhead transparencies on African history, geography and cultures. Some of the best of these include:

> *African Arts.* (Robert Lowie Museum, University of California, 1968)
> Two sets, each of 25 color slides, of West African masks, sculptures, dolls, and other art objects, with detailed written descriptions of each – $15 per set.
> *Alpha-Map Transparencies: Africa* (Allyn and Bacon, 1967)
> A spiral-bound book of 33 multi-color single transparencies on the physical, economic, and cultural characteristics of Africa – $60.

*Another excellent film in this series is *Water on the Savanna*.

World Cultures – Unit 1: Africa. (Keuffel and Esser Company, 1966/71)

A book of masters for 30 sets of multiple overlay color transparencies on African geography, history, and culture – $39.95; pre-made copies of these transparencies are also available as Spectra Transparencies.

LITERATURE AND MUSIC

Teachers of Africa often tend to overlook African music and literature, contemporary as well as traditional, as materials that can be used in learning about Africa. This is unfortunate, for both are not only more relevant to students than are texts or paperbacks but also more fun to use and better written than the more traditional teaching materials.

A great deal of traditional African music is available from Folkways Scholastic Records, some with detailed explanatory notes for easy teacher-student reference. Phillips Records of England also distributes many of the more popular African hi-life and other contemporary records. Teachers should not forget that the lyrics of African music, especially the contemporary music, provide extremely useful clues to African culture and values.

African literature—novels, autobiographies, poems, plays, proverbs, folktales, and oral traditions—may also be used to learn about Africa and Africans. Novels are especially useful materials, and entire courses or units of study may be built around them.* Although Chinua Achebe's novels about political, social and cultural change in West Africa seem most popular with teachers of junior and senior high school studies of Africa, there are scores of other novels which may serve equally well and which have the advantage of representing other areas and peoples of Africa. Autobiographical accounts such as Camara Laye's *The African Child* (Fontana Books) and Mugo Gatheru's *Child of Two Worlds* (Doubleday and Company) are another type of literature that can serve as a useful learning resource. The Humanities Press distributes inexpensive copies of African English-language literature *(African Writers Series),* and multiple copies of a number of these titles would be a useful adjunct to any serious classroom study of Africa.

African proverbs, folktales, plays, and poems offer excellent insights into African culture, habitat, history, and life. Many school libraries already have one or two collections of these forms

---

*For a detailed discussion on the use of African literature in teaching about Africa see Chapter 13.

of literature from which teachers might excerpt especially relevant materials for student use. The Oxford University Press distributes two series of inexpensive, durable, paperbound booklets originally published by African authors for use in English speaking African primary and intermediate grades—the *African Junior Library* and the *African Readers Library*. Each series contains short adventure and humorous stories, true life accounts, reminiscences and school stories that can be used by elementary and junior high school students to gain insights into African life. Some additional useful collections of African literature are:

Langston Hughes, ed., *Poems from Black Africa*. (Indiana University Press, 1968) paper $1.75

Several hundred poems from various African nations.

Charlotte and Wolf Leslau, eds., *African Folk Tales*. (The Peter Pauper Press, 1963) hardcover $1.25

25 short folktales from all of Africa.

Rene Guillot, *Rene Guillot's African Folktales*. (Franklin Watts, Inc. 1964/65) hardcover $3.95

23 folktales from West Africa.

Jessie A. Nunn, *African Folk Tales*. (Funk & Wagnalls, 1969) hardcover $4.95

20 folktales from East Africa.

OTHER MATERIALS

Some useful multimedia kits on Africa also exist including *Ashanti Family of Ghana* (Selective Educational Equipment, $174) designed especially for use in primary grades (but equally well used by students of any grade level depending on their objectives). This kit includes an Ashanti handcarved *Owari* game and other Ashanti craft items such as a piece of kente cloth, a gold weight, and an Akuaba doll; large photograph-study prints; a tape recording of Ashanti songs and folk-lengends; masters for student handouts; 15 children's books about the Ashanti; two filmstrips and a teacher's lesson guide. Such a collection of materials offers an opportunity, superior to most other sets, to get inside a culture.

All kinds of other types of commercially prepared materials exist for use in studying Africa: records, slides, tapes, atlases, workbooks, ditto map sets, books of readings or primary sources, simulations, games, puzzles, workbooks, programs, and displays.* In addition, teachers may use their own materials—newspaper

*These materials, as noted above, may be found annotated in the author's resource guide *Africa South of the Sahara: A Curriculum and Resource Guide.* New York: Thomas Y. Crowell Co., 1969.

articles, recipes, slides, maps, letters, art objects, and local re-sources—to teach about Africa in their classrooms. But regardless of which materials are selected, teachers must select them according to the basic principles of good teaching outlined above.

USING INSTRUCTIONAL MATERIALS ON AFRICA

If there is one thing that is true of all the available instructional materials on Africa, it is that there is hardly one that doesn't suffer from at least one flaw or weakness. Yet, there is no such thing as a "bad" piece of instructional material on Africa. True, there are materials shot full of bias, of prejudice, of mis-representation, of factual error, and of poor quality.* If the contents of these materials are committed to uncritical memorization, the results may, indeed, be "bad"—that is to say students will learn or reinforce the very biases or erroneous knowledge teachers may be seeking to correct. Should this occur, however, it is not the fault of these materials; it is the fault of how they are used.

At the risk of repeating a very essential point about teaching about Africa—the way any particular piece of learning material is used by teacher and students determines its utility and value. A teacher aware of the flaws common to most materials on Africa—including those they make themselves as well as those commer-cially produced—may use them in very creative ways to stimulate learning, raise questions, test hypotheses, and test student knowl-edge. These materials may also be used to help students develop their intellectual skills in detecting bias, separating fact from opinion, identifying unstated assumptions, checking the logic of arguments or the kinds of evidence used to support opinions, and separating relevant from irrelevant arguments. These are all skills essential to further learning and to effective citizenship. If mate-rials on Africa are used to accomplish objectives such as these, the errors and biases will not be learned—they will be detected. The resultant learning will include not only a more accurate picture of the subject but also valuable thinking skills, attitudes and self-images.

Instructional materials on Africa cannot be selected without reference to the way they are to be used in the classroom. The way materials are to be used, in turn, depends on the objectives

*For a detailed analysis of such flaws in currently available instructional materials on Africa see Barry K. Beyer, "The Big Pitch – or, Selecting Materials on Africa Can be Sticky," in *Media and Methods*, April, 1970, pp. 45-47 *passim;* and Michael J. Fuller, "Africa as Seen by World History Textbooks," in *Social Education*, May, 1971, Vol. 35, No. 5, pp. 466-473.

sought by the teacher and students. Imagine the exciting learning experience on Africa's physical and human geography in store for a class which plans to:

1. Introduce a study of Africa by eating a typical West African meal of rice or fufu, with groundnut stew and the appropriate side dishes of peanuts, pineapple, bananas, shredded coconut, and other fruits (or study the recipe if preparation of such a meal is not possible) as described in Time-Life's *Foods of the World* books (1970) on *African Cooking* and *Recipes: African Cooking*, pp. 60-61;

2. Then list its impressions of (1) the habitat where the people who eat meals like this live and (2) the nature of their life style as well.

3. Then—in small groups, pairs and individually—check the accuracy of one or more of these impressions against information about Africa provided through:

   a) a set of picture cards of photos clipped from old geography magazines,

   b) a collection of newspaper clippings on life in this region of Africa,

   c) a talk by a fellow teacher who toured parts of West Africa last summer,

   d) a set of slides on life in this region made by the teacher from photos in magazines and books,

   e) materials in the school library—encyclopedias, travel books, explorers' records, primary sources, and old history books,

   f) maps of Africa, such as the *Africa Inquiry Maps,* and accompanying student activity guides,

   g) a filmstrip/recording about an individual who lives in this region such as the filmstrip from *Africa Speaks — I* entitled *People of Ghana,*

   h) a talk by a person from this region, presently a student at a local college or university;

4. Then, in small groups, evaluate the accuracy of their original impressions in terms of the evidence pulled from the information presented in all the above materials and draw appropriate conclusion;

5. Then, individually or in pairs, evaluate the accuracy of what their text says about this part of Africa by comparing what they have found out to what the text contains; and

6. Finally, to raise new questions for further study about how typical of all of Africa is this region with its peoples, about the relationship of a people's way of life to their habitat, and

about the spatial distribution, areal association and spatial interaction of selected features of Africa today and at selected times in the past.

Would such a series of lessons work with your students? Could you secure and use all or most of these materials or convenient substitutes? What objectives are implied by these materials and the sequence in which they are arranged? What content is implied? What could students get out of such a series of lessons? Where will these lessons lead—or what new doors to learning will these lessons open?

Teaching about Africa is no task for the unimaginative teacher who still clings to the single text book, lecture, and occasional sound film method of teaching. One central piece of material is no longer a sufficient fund of information about Africa. Worthwhile teaching and learning about Africa require purposeful use of a number of kinds of instructional materials, some teacher-made and perhaps some commercially prepared. There certainly is no dearth of either type of material today. Worthwhile teaching and learning about Africa also require teacher involvement in these materials—but involvement not in the sense of flipping through catalogs to find something that may be useful nor in the sense of criticising every piece of material with which one comes in contact. The involvement in materials that most directly enhances learning about Africa is that which comes from extensive experimenting with, developing of and rearranging of materials in classroom learning situations; it is the kind of involvement that makes one *feel* not only the media but also the subject. In the last analysis it is the purposeful selection, use and reuse of a wide variety of instructional materials that provide the key to worthwhile teaching and learning about Africa today.

SOURCES OF MATERIALS NOTED IN THIS CHAPTER

African American Institute
866 United Nations Plaza
New York, New York 10017

Allyn and Bacon
470 Atlantic Avenue
Boston, Mass. 02210

ALVA Museum Replicas, Inc.
30-30 Northern Boulevard
Long Island City, N.Y. 11101

BFA Educational Media
2211 Michigan Avenue
Santa Monica, Calif. 90404

Christian Science Monitor
Christian Science
   Publishing Society
1 Norway Street
Boston, Mass. 02115

Thomas Y. Crowell Company
201 Park Avenue, S.
New York, New York 10003

Crowell-Collier-Macmillan Co.
866 Third Avenue
New York, N.Y. 10022

Denoyer-Geppert Company
5235 Ravenswood Avenue
Chicago, Ill. 60640

Doubleday Multimedia
Doubleday & Co., Inc.
Garden City, N.Y. 11530

Drum
Woolworths Ltd.
P.O. Box 30184
Nairobi, Kenya

Ealing Corporation
2225 Massachusetts Avenue
Cambridge, Mass. 02140

E.M.C. Corporation
180 E. Sixth Street
St. Paul, Minn. 55101

Folkways Scholastic Records
50 West 44th Street
New York, N.Y. 10036

Fontana Books
Wm. Collins & Co., Ltd.
14 St. James Place
London, S.W. 1
England

Funk & Wagnalls
380 Madison Avenue
New York, New York 10017

Ginn and Company
Statler Building
Back Bay P.O. 191
Boston, Mass. 02117

Hayden Book Company
116 W. 14th Street
New York, New York 10011

Houghton Mifflin Company
110 Tremont Street
Boston, Mass. 02107

Humanities Press
303 Park Avenue South
New York, New York 10010

Indiana University Press
10th and Morton Streets
Bloomington, Indiana 47401

International Film Foundation
475 Fifth Avenue
New York, New York 10017

Keuffel and Esser Company
20 Whippany Road
Morristown, New Jersey 07960

The Macmillan Company
866 Third Avenue
New York, N.Y. 10022

A. J. Nystrom Company
3333 Elston Avenue
Chicago, Ill. 60618

Oxford University Press
200 Madison Avenue
New York, New York 10016

The Peter Pauper Press
Mt. Vernon, New York 10552

Phillips Record Company
35 E. Wacker Drive
Chicago, Ill. 60601

Frederick A. Praeger Publisher
111 Fourth Avenue
New York, New York 10003

Random House
School Division
201 E. 50th Street
New York, New York 10022

Robert Lowie Museum
103 Kroeber Hall
University of California
Berkeley, California 94720

Selective Educational
  Equipment, Inc.
3 Bridge Street
Newton, Massachusetts 02195

Silver Burdette Company
Morristown, New Jersey 07960

Social Studies School Service
10000 Culver Boulevard
Culver City, California 90230

Society for Visual Education
1345 W. Diversey Parkway
Chicago, Illinois 60614

Teen Topics Publications
P.O. Box 14
Ikeja, Nigeria
West Africa

Texture Films, Inc.
1600 Broadway
New York, New York 10019

Time-Life Books
Time-Life Building
Rockefeller Center
New York, New York 10020

The Viking Press
625 Madison Avenue
New York, New York 10022

Warren Schloat Productions
115 Tompkins Avenue
Pleasantville, New York 10570

Franklin Watts, Inc.
575 Lexington Avenue
New York, New York 10022

The Radiance of the King

Things Fall Apart

A Dream of Africa

Bound to Violence

A Grain of Wheat

The Wanderers

The Palm-Wine Drinkard

A Wreath for Udomo

God's Bits of Wood

The African

The Beautyful Ones Are Not Yet Born

The Interpreters

Boy!

Mine Boy

13

Contemporary African Literature:
An Untapped Source

NANCY M. HOON
Montgomery County Schools, Maryland

- How can American students get some feel for what it is like to live and be a part of a culture other than their own?

- How can they integrate their learning about the climate, topography, economy, and culture of a distant land into a coherent image of that land, the people and the texture of their lives?

- Bound as they are in an American classroom, how can students experience a distant culture, observe its inner workings, and seek its significant patterns?

Contemporary African literature forms a large, untapped source of materials that appeal to the senses and emotions as well as the intellect. An excellent, authentic novel or play lets the reader live in the society as it is represented to him by one of its members. The piece of literature integrates the separate elements of geography and culture into a holistic pattern; it personalizes the facts about the culture, and gives a human dimension to them. It reveals how the culture both sustains and limits the individual, how it relieves him of some anxieties and engenders others, how it tempers some interpersonal conflicts and intensifies others, how it gives a man a place in society and forces him to conform to it.

The growing body of literature written by Africans in English or French almost by necessity deals with two concepts that are of particular interest to social studies teachers: cultural contact and cultural change. African men and women who write of their African experience in the language and literary forms of Europe are themselves living embodiments of cultural contact.

SELECTION OF WORKS

The burgeoning literature of Africa offers such a number of titles that, at first glance, choice for classroom use seems difficult. Selection will depend on the context and purposes of the teaching, the reading abilities and interests of the students, the level of community acceptance, and the availability of inexpensive paperback texts.

For some courses one determinant will be the region being studied. It may be all important to a geography teacher that the work be set in East, West or South Africa. Sometimes it is possible to specify a particular nation or culture. Some cultures such as the Ibo and Yoruba of Nigeria have developed a vigorous literary tradition in the European mode. In other cultures the energies of the people are more engaged in other pursuits or their literary activity remains in the vernacular language and traditional modes—unavailable to the American student. Hence it is not always possible to find appropriate pieces of literature from a particular culture.

A more important consideration than the region may be the focus of the literary work, whether it is on traditional village life, on the colonial experience, or on life in independent Africa. East and West African literature may be conveniently divided into three categories: literature depicting traditional village life, literature depicting the colonial life and the modern city, and literature exploring contemporary political and social problems.

The literature of traditional village life is typified by Chinua Achebe's two novels, *Things Fall Apart* and *Arrow of God,* and by Camara Laye's autobiography, *The African Child.* These works evoke the patterns and values of a traditional Ibo village of Nigeria and a Malinke village of Guinea, but they also reveal the erosion of these cultures by contact with the English and French. Achebe's tone is both objective and angry; Laye's is more personal and suffused with a sense of loss. Both are popular with American students.

The novels of colonial life and the modern city reveal the impact of Western civilization on all facets of life but especially they portray the disruption of traditional values. They tend to portray the modern cities of Africa as moral wastelands. The hero or heroine often returns to the village of his birth seeking a virtue, health, and fertility that he wants but can no longer be a part of. Many of these works present a problem; in their unflinching portrayal of the loss of values, they may reinforce student stereotypes of the African as amoral or corrupt. These works often lack the rich texture of the literature of traditional life and are not generally as well liked by students.

Politics is not surprisingly the chief topic of many of the more recent novels from independent Africa. The authors have shifted from an attempt to portray the values of traditional life to an exploration of contemporary political and social problems. Like Robert Penn Warren's *All the Kings Men,* these works reveal the relationship between personal and political corruption. Most are infused with disillusionment and some, such as Ayi Kwei Armah's *The Beautyful Ones Are Not Yet Born,* so reek of filth and decay, that some readers find their language and imagery offensive. Although these works are not as popular with students as the literature of traditional life, they are of great interest to mature students who want to grapple with the social, economic, and political problems of contemporary Africa.

For a number of reasons, the novels of Chinua Achebe have been the most frequent choice of American social studies teachers. They are among the best written and therefore the most pleasurable to read. His four novels span three categories of modern African writing. *Things Fall Apart* and *Arrow of God* evoke traditional Ibo village life and chart the seeds of its disintegration under the British intrusion. *No Longer at Ease* follows the fortunes of the British-educated grandson of Okonkwo, the protagonist of *Things Fall Apart,* in Lagos, the capital city, under colonial rule. The political novel, *Man of the People,* examines some of the problems of independence. This novel was published just two weeks before the *coup* that it predicted, the *coup* that touched off the series of bloody incidents culminating in the Nigeria/Biafra Civil War.

SUGGESTIONS FOR TEACHING

Specific lesson plans will, of course, be dependent upon the specific purposes of the course, the abilities and background of the students, and the amount of time and other resources available. This unit for senior high school students is based on Achebe's *Things Fall Apart,* but most of the objectives and teaching strategies are equally applicable to other works of African literature.

OBJECTIVES

Upon completion of this unit, the student should be able to:
*   evaluate from internal evidence, using some commonly accepted criteria, the validity of a piece of writing as a source of geographic and anthropological data

- extract from a literary document relevant data on any of the major structures of a society such as subsistence patterns and technology or social and political organization
- explain orally how several parts of the culture are related to each other (e.g., family and kinship system to subsistence patterns)
- identify the traits of the Ibo culture that made it particularly susceptible to change as a consequence of contact with Western culture
- characterize the ideal Ibo male personality and explain its relationship to Ibo child rearing practices
- contrast the ideal Ibo male personality with the ideal American one
- compare and contrast the causes and effects of cultural change in an African and American society
- define at least three possible responses by individuals to rapid cultural change.

I. INITIAL ACTIVITIES

1. Begin a discussion with this question: Suppose you wanted to introduce American culture to someone who did not know anything about it. You couldn't bring the person to the United States—you had to send someone or something to him. Who or what would you send? Or pose the above question but limit it to a thing. Ask students to bring the thing—or, if this isn't feasible, a representation of it—to class. Have the students explain their selection. Keep returning to the question; what could the person learn from the thing?

2. If no student has brought up a book, play, television show, or film, ask which of these they might send. Ask, also, why such a choice might be more helpful than a manufactured object or some of the other suggestions.

3. Ask, if they could choose a representative person to send, who would it be? Richard Nixon? Archie Bunker? The principal of the school? Let the class decide whether it would be better to select an exceptional or an "average" person.

4. Assign the reading of *Things Fall Apart* while the above discussion is going on. Introduce the novel as an opportunity to look through a window into another culture and to take part, through the imagination, in other life styles.

5. Give the students a brief opportunity to respond to the novel spontaneously, to say what they liked or didn't like, etc. Use these comments as clues for further direction of class.

II. EVALUATION OF THE NOVEL AS A SOURCE OF CULTURAL DATA

1. Review: How do anthropologists gather data on contemporary cultures? Past cultures?
   Discuss: Is a novel a good source of cultural data? Is there any novel or play or film or television program you would recognize as a good source of data about the United States? How about *The Last Picture Show? All in The Family?*
   Bring out these points:
   a. All literary works would provide some data.
   b. Some would be better sources than others.
   c. It would be possible to create a work whose major purpose would be to present aspects of the culture imaginatively.
   d. Such a work might be a relatively good or bad source.
   e. Novels and other literary works tend to focus on the exceptional man in the culture. (Okonkwo, hero of *Things Fall Apart,* is a "super-Ibo.")
2. Ask: Is *this* novel a good source of data? How can we know?
   Bring out these points:
   a. We can look at internal evidence such as evidence from the text that Achebe expected non-Ibos to read his book (he defines terms no Ibo would need defined) and examples of practices such as the killing of twins that he knew would not be sanctioned today.
   b. From the novel itself, can we guess at Achebe's motives for writing it? (Compare, Chinua Achebe, "The Role of the Writer in a New Nation," in *Africa Is People,* ed. Barbara Nolen, New York: Dutton, 1967).
OR
3. For a more structured approach, introduce students to common standards to determine the credibility of a document. (See, for example, Louis Gottschalk, *Understanding History.)*
   a. Is the author able to tell the truth? Is he near in time and place? (See, Gerald Moore, *Seven African Writers* or Judith Illsley Gleason, *This Africa: Novels by West Africans in English and French.)*
   b. Is he willing to tell the truth? Is he biased? Is he too eager to please? Does his literary style make him change or gloss over things?
   c. Is he disinterested and objective? Does he, for example, provide evidence prejudicial to the culture?
   d. Can the information be corroborated independently?
4. Discuss: How much is *Things Fall Apart* a European rather than an African document? Bring out that the language and literary form are European, the title comes from William

Butler Yeats' poem "The Second Coming." (Some readers have compared the novel to a classical tragedy. Students who are familiar with this form might enjoy playing with this idea also.) Bring out that, in addition to being a picture of a traditional African society, the novel is also evidence of a newer, more generalized international African culture of men steeped in European culture but seeking to recapture and define their African heritage.

III. THE ACQUISITION OF CULTURAL DATA

1. Introduce the assignment:
    Now is your chance to try to work and think like an anthropologist. We have agreed that the novel is not a perfect source of information, but it is a pretty good one. Imagine that you were an anthropologist living in Umuofia during the time of Okonkwo. What could you observe about the Ibo culture? In order to work efficiently, you can divide into small groups of three to five students and each group may be responsible for one of the topics. Suggested list of topics:
    a. subsistence patterns and technology
    b. sex and marriage
    c. family and kinship
    d. status and role
    e. personality structure
    f. religion and the supernatural
    g. social and political organization
    h. proverbs and myths
    Give the groups time to meet and to write a brief generalized description of the part of the culture they are responsible for. Assemble and duplicate these descriptions for class distribution.

IV. ANALYSIS OF THE DESCRIPTIONS

1. Discuss: Are there any errors or omissions in any of the descriptions? Are they adequate descriptions of the culture? (Students may feel that the description of religion is thin. The novel has been criticized for slighting the role of religion in Ibo culture. Perhaps in response to this criticism Achebe wrote *Arrow of God,* a novel whose protagonist is an Ibo priest.)
2. Discuss: How are various parts of social structure and culture related to one another?
    e.g. family and kinship patterns to subsistence patterns

child-rearing practices to basic personality structure
religious beliefs and practices to social structure
subsistence patterns to social structure
geographical conditions to cultural patterns

V. FURTHER ANALYSIS AND COMPARISON OF THE CULTURE –
THE IDEA OF SUCCESS TO THE AMERICAN

1. Discuss:
    a. What is the Ibo idea of success? How is it marked? How is it earned?
    b. What statements does the novel make about success? What are its satisfactions? What is its cost to the individual, his family, and his associates? How can its pursuit be self-defeating? Does this judgment on success seem to be a part of the Ibo culture or does this judgment seem to be imposed by the novelist?
2. View the CBS News films "Sixteen in Webster Grove" or "Webster Grove Revisited," a popular film such as *The Graduate*, or a popular television situation comedy. Ask the same questions about success as for the Ibo culture.
3. List on the board the ideal Ibo and American male personalities. Compare them.
4. Discuss: What values in Ibo culture are most important? How might some of these values be achieved through alternate routes supplied by the imposed British culture? Note that the Ibo valued wealth as measured by the number of yams a man owned, but that the perishability of yams imposed some natural limits on the acquisition of this wealth. Speculate on what might happen when an imperishable form of wealth, money, is introduced.
5. Hypothesize: What aspects of the Ibo culture might make it particularly susceptible to influence from the British culture? (See Ottenburg, "Ibo Receptivity to Change" in Bascom and Herskovits, *Continuity and Change in African Cultures.*)

VI. THE INDIVIDUAL IN A PERIOD OF RAPID SOCIAL CHANGE

1. List on the blackboard many of the characters from the novel. Beside each write how they responded to the British intrusion. (Students may suggest three categories such as Reactionary—Okonkwo, Moderate—Obierika, and Radical—Nwoye; or some other classificatory scheme. Discourage them from making so many distinctions that the categories become useless. Ask: Why did Okonkwo react so violently against the British, and

Nwoye embrace them so eagerly? Why were Obierika and others middle-of-the-roadish?

2. Compare these reactions to the reactions of various adults to long hair or the student power movement.

3. Review what happens to some of the characters who reacted strongly either positively or negatively to the cultural change. What seems to be the novel's judgment about appropriate responses? Does this seem to be the judgment of Ibo culture or of Achebe alone?

VII. VERIFICATION AND EXTENSION OF KNOWLEDGE

1. Interview an Ibo informant. Invite Ibo students living in the United States to the class. Have each group prepare and ask questions to verify the data. (Thousands of Ibos are studying in the U.S. Contact the foreign student advisor of your nearest college or university for names and addresses.)

2. Read an anthropological study such as:

   Ottenburg, Phoebe V., "The Changing Economic Position of Women Among the Afikpo Ibo," in *Continuity and Change in African Cultures,* W. Bascom and M. Herskovits, eds., Chicago: University of Chicago Press, 1959.

   Ottenburg, Simon, "Ibo Receptivity to Change," in *Continuity and Change in African Cultures.*

   Uchendu, Victor, *Ibo of Southeastern Nigeria,* New York: Holt, 1965. Written by an American-educated anthropologist who is himself an Ibo.

3. Read another novel about the Ibo, such as:

   Achebe, Chinua, *Arrow of God,* New York: Doubleday, 1969. This novel gives a fuller picture of religion and family structure than *Things Fall Apart.*

   Nwapa, Flora, *Efuru,* London: Heineman, 1966. This novel gives a fuller picture of the lives of women than Achebe's novels do.

   Amadi, Elechi, *The Concubine,* London: Heinemann, 1966.

VIII. EVALUATION

Evaluation of the unit should, of course, be in terms of the original objectives. These objectives can be listed on a simple checksheet, with one checksheet for each student, as follows:

1. Evaluates from internal evidence the validity of *Things Fall Apart:*

- applies the four questions on the credibility of documents to the novel
- notes that Achebe was born after the events he writes of and had a European literary education
- cites evidence of Achebe's awareness of a non-Ibo readership
- identifies practices Achebe portrayed even though he knew they would be offensive to his readers
- identifies Okonkwo as an exceptional man in his culture

2. Extracts relevant data on the group topic:
   - identifies relevant passages
   - lists facts
   - interprets facts to build a coherent picture
   - identifies "unknowns"

An evaluation of this type can occur as the teacher observes the students working individually or in small groups. The important point is that such evaluation be a part of the on-going process of teaching, not just an activity at the end of the unit.

In this unit student groups are asked to write descriptions about the parts of the culture they are responsible for. These descriptions are one piece of evidence for evaluation. Students could also be asked to give other brief oral or written presentations on topics such as the inter-relationship between two major facets of the culture. It is important, however, that written assignments be more than a summary of class discussion. If students are asked to write about the individual in a period of rapid social change, they might be asked to construct a series of hypotheses and simply list after each of the characters in the novel who seem to conform to the hypothesis.

If the structure of the course permits, it will be useful to see if students can apply the skills and concepts they have developed in this unit. Do they, for example, apply the tests of credibility to new cultural documents? Do they continue to use the concept of cultural change and to observe its effects on individual men and women?

IX. SUGGESTIONS FOR FURTHER STUDENT RESEARCH

Students individually or in small groups may work on topics such as these and prepare demonstrations or reports to the class.

Ibo art—
> Beier, Ulli, *African Mud Sculpture,* Cambridge: Cambridge University Press, 1963
> other books on African art and slides from the African Art Museum, Washington, D.C.

Ibo dance—

Ibo music—
> Echezona, W.W., "Ibo Music," in *Africa Is People,* ed. Barbara Nolan, New York: Dutton, 1967. The author, an Ibo, is an American-trained musicologist.
> collections of African music

Women's rights and role in Ibo culture
> See sources listed in VII above

Background and causes of the Nigerian (Biafran) Civil War

The Ibo in the contemporary world
> Achebe, *No Longer at Ease,* Greenwich, Conn: Fawcett, 1969
> _____, *Man of the People,* New York: Doubleday, 1967.

X.   ADDITIONAL RESOURCES FOR STUDENTS AND TEACHERS

> Abrash, Barbara. *Black African Literature in English Since 1952: Works and Criticism.* New York: Johnson Reprint Corporation, 1967. A bibliography now somewhat out of date.
>
> Beier, Ulli, ed. Introduction to *West African Literature.* Evanston: Northwestern University Press, 1967. Excellent.
>
> Bohannan, Laura, pseud. Elenore Smith Bowen, *Return to Laughter,* New York: Doubleday, Natural History Library, 1964. One of our leading field anthropologists wrote this fictionalized account of her life and work among the Tiv people of Nigeria.
>
> Gleason, Judith Illsley. *This Africa: Novels by West Africans in English and French.* Evanston: Northwestern University Press, 1965. Plot summaries and excellent sociological and literary commentary.
>
> Heywood, Christopher, ed. *Perspectives on African Literature.* New York: Africana Publishing Company, 1972.
>
> Hoon, Nancy M. and Abell, Richard P. "The Classroom Potential of West African Literature," *Social Education,* 30:4 (April 1969), 418.
> Also contains suggestions for an English teacher using the Achebe novel in a multidisciplinary program.

Killiam, G.D. *The Novels of Chinua Achebe.* New York: Africana Publishing Company.

King, Bruce. *An Introduction to Nigerian Literature.* New York: Africana Publishing Company, 1969.

Larson, Charles R. *The Emergence of African Fiction.* Bloomington: Indiana University Press, 1971.

Leach, Josephine, "A Study of Chinua Achebe's *Things Fall Apart* in Mid-America," *English Journal,* 60:8 (November 1971), 1052. Further suggestions for a multidisciplinary humanities approach to the teaching of this novel.

Moore, Gerald. *Seven African Writers.* London: Oxford University Press, 1962. Still one of the best introductions to the subject.

Palmer, Eustace. *An Introduction to the African Novel.* New York: Africana Publishing Corporation, 1972. Excellent literary criticism by a Sierra Leonean of twelve African novels.

Pieterse, Osmo and Munro, Donald. *Protest and Conflict in African Literature.* New York: Africana Publishing Corporation, 1969. Very useful to the social studies teachers.

Roscoe, Adrian A. *Mother is Gold.* London: Cambridge University Press, 1971.

Zell, Hans and Silver, Helene. *A Reader's Guide to African Literature.* New York: Africana Publishing Corporation, 1972.

SELECTED LIST OF AFRICAN WRITERS
Fiction and Biography

CAMEROUN

Beti, Mongo
Dipoko, Mbella Sonne
Oyono, Ferdinand

ETHIOPIA

Sellassie, Sahle

GAMBIA

Peters, Lenrie

GHANA

Abruquah, James
Aidoo, Ama Ata
Armah, Ayi Kewei
Asare, Bediako
Awoonor, Kofi
Djioleto, Ama
Duodu, Cameron
Dzovo, E. V. K.
Hayford, J. E. Casely
Konadu, Asare
Selormey, Francis

IVORY COAST

Loba, Ake

KENYA

Gatheru, R. Mugo
Kariuki, Josiah
Khadambi, Asalache
Mazrui, Ali
Ngubiah, Stephen N.
Ngugi
Ogot, Grace
Wachira, Godwin

LESOTHO

Mofolo, Thomas

MALAWI

Kachingwe, Aubrey
Kayira, Legson
Rubadira, David

MALI

Ouologuem, Yambo

MOZAMBIQUE

Honwana, Luis Bernado

NIGERIA

Achebe, Chinua
Agunwa, Clement
Akpan, Ntieyong
Aluko, Timothy
Amadi, Elechi
Clark, John Pepper
Egbuna, Obi B.
Ekwensi, Cyprian
Fagunwa, D. O.
Ike, Chukwumeke
Munonye, John
Nwapa, Flora
Nwanko, Nkem
Nzekwu, Onuora
Okara, Gabriel
Okpenwho, Isidore
Soyinka, Wole
Tutuola, Amos
Ulasi, Adaora
Uzodinma, E. C. C.

RHODESIA

Samkange, Stanlake

SENEGAL

Diop, Birago
Kane, Cheikh Hamidou

Laye, Camara
Ousmane, Sembene

SIERRA LEONE

Conton, William
Easmon, Sarif
Nicol, Abioseh

SOMALIA

Farah, Nuruddin

SOUTH AFRICA, Republic

Abrahams, Peter
Brutus, Dennis
Head, Bessie
Hutchinson, Alfred
Kunene, Mazisi
La Guma, Alex
Matshikiza, Todd
Matthews, James

Mphahlele, Ezekiel
Modisane, Bloke
Nkosi, Lewis
Rive, Richard
Themba, Can

SUDAN

Salih, Tayeb

TANZANIA

Palangyo, Peter
Ruhumbiki, Gabriel

UGANDA

Kimenye, Barbara
Liyong, Taban lo
Oculi, Okello
Sentongo, Nuwa
Serumaga, Robert

(editors)

PART THREE
Approaches to Teaching

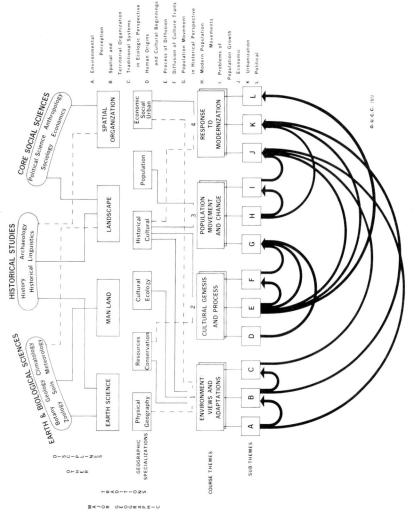

Figure 14.1. A Thematic Geography and its Supporting Fields.

14

Teaching African Geography as an Interdisciplinary Adventure

FRANK E. BERNARD AND BOB J. WALTER
Ohio University

> The trend toward interdisciplinary
> collaboration and coordination is
> irreversible . . . (Sherif and
> Sherif, 1969: 5)

In theory and in practice geography has always been an eclectic discipline. Instead of concentrating on a particular category of phenomena, geographers have chosen their material from a variety of sources. Unity in the discipline has been more in the viewpoint and methodology than in the objects studied. This has led others to be puzzled by the broad scope of the field. As Broek (1965:4) observes, workers in more specialized fields, "feel that the geographer seems to put his nose into any and every subject which is already taken care of by the specialized sciences."

Any geographer who knows his discipline can turn this pejorative image to his favor. He can argue that indeed geography does include diverse and apparently unrelated phenomena, but at the same time, he would surely point out that geography rarely studies these objects for their own sake. Instead geography attempts to understand their spatial characteristics and organization, or perhaps, to determine how they contribute to a better understanding of the character of a given place. To a degree, therefore, while many disciplines are spiraling toward higher and higher levels of specialization, many geographers still believe that an important value of their discipline is synthesis and integration of a wide range of subfields (Figure 14-1). By its very nature, geography, like history, has always sought to discover what today are called *interdisciplinary relationships.* Long before it became fashionable, geographers ranged widely through disciplinary borderlands and even occasionally crossed the boundary zones themselves.

245

It is the contention of this paper that high school geography on non-Western areas such as Africa must take advantage of this *natural* interdisciplinary character in order to survive. But it must do so using the concepts, generalizations, and themes developed in modern geography. In this way it will reach beyond its boundaries to provide a truly enlightening synthesis – a synthesis which will produce future generations of high school students with a far greater appreciation and understanding of Africa.

Secondary school teachers striving to achieve an interdisciplinary character to their social studies instruction may well feel at a loss concerning how to accomplish this. Advice on approaches which are *interdisciplinary* are plentiful (Miller, 1964; Shinn, 1964; Beyer, 1971; and Beyer and Penna, 1971). These cover a range of discipline-based outlines (anthropology, history, social psychology, etc.), emphasize concepts, and stress inquiry-teaching. One approach which has not been used widely in geography or in social studies, but which we feel has great merit, is the thematic approach. It offers a number of advantages for improving teaching in general, for using the interdisciplinary viewpoint, for incorporating the character of modern geography, and for teaching about non-Western areas such as Africa.

THE THEMATIC ORGANIZATION

The thematic organization enables a teacher to achieve a number of desirable educational goals. It provides an interpretative framework and is selective in detail rather than comprehensive or encyclopedic. Recurring themes create a basis for demonstrating the relationships among places, events, and problems. The thematic approach can utilize a current event classificatory scheme for placing in context – areal, historical, etc. – recent happenings. It can emphasize the problem approach and the inquiry method of teaching.

Most social studies teachers in secondary schools are not trained to teach from the interdisciplinary viewpoint even though they have a discipline specialty, usually history, which has an integrative character. Most recent social studies projects are discipline oriented. (Kennamer 1970) The thematic approach is valuable because it enables teachers to remove themselves from a strong discipline orientation. It encourages them to incorporate content and concepts from other social science disciplines, while providing a structured organization and a wide framework to accommodate these ideas. Teachers have the advantage of developing their own themes, drawn from their discipline background, relevant to their teaching situation, and focused on student interest. Moreover, themes give emphasis to general concepts common to all social sciences and allow students to study material from the disciplines through an integrated approach in a variety of ways.

For geography teachers, particularly those who focus on foreign areas, the thematic approach has similar advantages. It permits the inclusion of modern systematic concepts, especially those relevant to the region under consideration. It provides a dynamic spatial framework and emphasizes spatial processes, rather than form, static description, or factual information. Themes encourage consideration of the spatial aspects of human behavior such as resource exploitation, a recent development in the field.

Cross-regional, intercultural, and cross-areal studies can also benefit from the use of a thematic organization. Using a conceptual base drawn from the social sciences and emphasizing spatial processes of modern geography, regions or areas of differing characteristics—environmentally, culturally, politically, etc.—can be compared and contrasted within an integrative frame. Themes used in this way enable students to draw their own generalizations, and to demonstrate that they can *use* information rather than just learn it. This enables them to *think* rather than memorize about different world areas.

It has been argued that the thematic approach is alien to the secondary teacher's viewpoint, difficult to teach, and not practical since there are few textbooks organized in this manner. Insofar as few teachers are trained interdisciplinarily, it may be alien, but since the majority of secondary social studies teachers are from a broad integrative discipline, such as history, it really is not unfamiliar. With the thematic approach, the instructor trained in history can teach social studies using general concepts, rather than a junior scholar course in history. It may be difficult to teach in that it requires more knowledge of the subject and more planning on the part of the teacher in order to support the chosen themes and seek hypotheses for testing in classroom instruction. This is a positive element which should lead to better and more effective teaching. There are few thematic textbooks available, but this may be only a temporary situation. Furthermore, the lack of textbooks is a possible advantage since it forces the teacher to become more versatile in selecting material, to be more flexible in choosing concepts, and to be more open in teaching method. Fortunately, there is a plethora of material suitable for thematic organization, as is indicated later.

A THEMATIC CURRICULUM DESCRIBED

To demonstrate that teaching African geography can be an interdisciplinary adventure and to show the validity of the thematic approach, a curriculum project* (Bernard and Walter 1971) is described which was developed with the above goals in mind, and suggestions are made as to how it might be adapted to a high school geography course on Africa.

One of the most difficult tasks in the thematic approach is selecting themes. In order to select authentic interdisciplinary themes for Africa, a survey of geographical, social science, and Africa-related journals was conducted. After analyzing the kinds of studies in these journals and relating them to recent developments in geography, a selection was made of four themes and twelve subthemes (Figure 1). They are meant to furnish a geographic perspective to research trends of the other social sciences, an integrating function traditional in geography. Additionally, they are intended to provide a continental view of significant spatial patterns and processes. These are only some of the possible themes; they are used to indicate the potential of a thematic organization to an African geography course.**

THEME 1. THE ENVIRONMENT: VIEWS AND ADAPTATIONS

This theme begins with the assumption that an "objectively" described environment is often irrelevant to African human geography. Environmental descriptions written by observers outside the culture are really interpretations based on the culturally biased perceptions of the observers. The environment is considered here as a *milieu* that not only surrounds and supports African cultures, but also interacts with them. The environment is explored through the eyes of the local inhabitants, on the premise that every culture has a folk geography distinctive to its own values, beliefs, history, and environmental experience. Knowing what individuals in a culture think and feel about their surroundings leads to insights about their decision-making and other aspects of their behavior.

Territoriality—the way in which society's institutions are spatially organized—and culture ecology—the dynamic relationship

*We gratefully acknowledge the Institute of International Studies of the Office of Education for financial support in the development of our thematic curriculum.
**Others have suggested themes for geography (Anderson, 1965 and Kennamer, 1965) and for African geography (Stanley and French, 1972) or other world areas (*Intercultural Education,* 2, 1 (1970):19-20 and 2, 3 (1971):23-24). However, insofar as we are aware, this is the first time a comprehensive curriculum on African geography has been done completely on a thematic basis.

between man and land—are also examined in this first theme. The expression of territoriality is closely related to a society's system of social relations, the values that underlie these relations, and the views of a people about the boundaries and the sustaining qualities of their own country. The ecological perspective concentrates on process rather than form, focusing on the changing relationships between man and nature and attempting to assess the cause-and-effect linkages that flow back and forth between them within a systems framework.

THEME 2. CULTURAL GENESIS AND PROCESS

The second theme is built on the premise that a great thread of continuity may be found in African cultural evolution. To trace this thread is to shed light on the processes of modern cultural change, human occupancy, and spatial arrangement in Africa. Diffusion theory—the examination of diffusion as a dynamic spatial process—provides the framework for the discussion. Beginning with the origin and spread of man from humanity's original culture hearth, we examine various culture traits in a diffusion context (Figure 14-1). The origin and spread of agriculture, of the Bantu language family, and other cultural traits are used to demonstrate the utility of diffusion concept. A discussion of trade as a mechanism of diffusion is of considerable importance to this theme.

THEME 3. POPULATION MOVEMENT AND CHANGE

Theme three is concerned with population mobility and demographic change. The movement of African peoples, both now and in the past, is viewed as a significant integrating factor in African human geography. While most geography textbooks fail to give sufficient attention to population mobility and demographic change, studies made by historians and economists recognize population migration as a critical factor in the exchange of ideas and the modern development of the continent. Patterns and problems of population growth are also integral to this theme since the impact of increasing numbers of people on agricultural lands, on urban growth structure, and on economic development is pervasive throughout the continent.

THEME 4. RESPONSE TO MODERNIZATION

The last theme is focused on the transition from traditional life to modernity, occurring in varying degrees in every corner of the African continent. It emphasizes the processes of change that have been most significant in this transition: economic change, urbanization, and political modernization. In the discussion on economic modernization, the emphasis is on agricultural change and its concomitants and on the development of infrastructure, both of which are essential to development. The urbanization subsection deals with the draw of the city, the complex linkages between rural and urban areas, and the social and economic problems of African cities and urban systems. The analysis of political modernization describes contemporary trends in the perspective of time and space and examines the drive toward the creation of nation-states as the dominant theme in African polity.

We believe these themes bring new relevance to African geography and provide an integrating overview of the continent and its problems. They furnish cross-disciplinary links to other social sciences since numerous trends and concepts are drawn from them. They offer a set of specific concepts and models which students can apply in case studies. Finally, they allow students to draw a challenging set of generalizations within an interdisciplinary, interpretive framework.

IMPLEMENTING THE THEMES

Two writers have developed a useful model and a method of implementing these themes, or any others, using a problem-solving approach and the inquiry-teaching method. Fraenkel (1971:195) suggests a comprehensive curriculum model in which student activities can be seen as an integral part of a larger whole. The model is modified and expanded below:

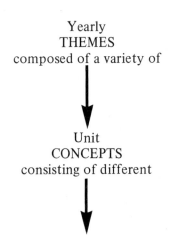

Yearly
THEMES
composed of a variety of

Unit
CONCEPTS
consisting of different

TYPES OF KNOWLEDGE
that include ideas and hypotheses
supported and exemplified by a number of specific facts

carried out by
ACTIVITIES
in which students engage in the major operations
which constitute rational inquiry

Gunn (1970:337) believes some of the best activities that can be conducted in the social studies classroom are simulation games, calling them "serious representations of social or physical systems." In demonstrating that one of our subthemes can be used as a classroom activity in a secondary social studies or geography class, we have chosen a simulation game. The outline below is merely that—an outline. It is meant to be suggestive of possibilities and indicative of procedures. We believe it is better for the individual teacher to work out detailed activities, suitable to specific classroom situations.

The game concerns rural-to-urban migration and is drawn from Theme 3, Subtheme H (Figure 14-1). The idea of people leaving the farm and moving to the city is one easily understood in this country; thus, the universality of the process allows secondary school students to identify with an increasingly common phenomenon in Africa. The overall goal is to show how the process works in a different cultural setting.

Gunn (1970:340-41) outlines a number of steps in simulation game design critical to making it succeed.* First is to identify the outcomes. This includes specifying time, place, functions, elements, and roles; i.e., the major components and variables of the game. Gunn (1970:340) states: "These items set the stage for significant decision-making, a stage that will represent a compromise between the reality being simulated and the degree of complexity permissible for the game." Second is planning the game in a step-by-step fashion. This permits stipulation of the relative importance of each role, of the possible interactions between players, and of the mechanics involved in the activity. Additionally, the sequence of events is fixed. Third is experimental playing to smooth rough spots, to tighten rules, and in general, to remove

---

*See also Chapter 18 of this book. (editor)

'bugs.' Fourth is provision for "a series of complications that make the game increasingly realistic for more experienced or more mature students." (Gunn 1970:341)

To implement the game of MIGRANT MOVE, some preparation of teacher and students is necessary. This preparation involves the reading of one or two novels—Ekwensi's *People of the City* and Abrahams' *Mine Boy*—and the viewing of two films—*Mandabi* and *Boom Town West Africa*. These give the participants a feel for the setting, a sense of the culture, and an understanding of the forces at work, important to all players no matter what specific role they assume in the game.

Mabogunje (1970a) provides the necessary information to carry out step one in the simulation game design and he does this within a conceptual framework—a system. In his systems schema, he specifies two major roles (potential migrant and urbanite), seven elements of the system (rural control subsystem, migration channels, etc.), forces at work (stimulus, etc.), and factors of the environment (technology, economic conditions, etc.). The latter three sets of components can accommodate several persons in each element, force, or factor, varying with the number of players available. Assignment of individuals to roles within the systems schema should be made with the novel and films in mind.

A second reading selection (Caldwell 1968) is necessary prior to attempting step two. In his discussion, Caldwell details specific determinants influencing the potential migrant and indicates their relative importance. He distinguishes major factors of village and household characteristics (four) and of individual nature (three) and minor factors of individual nature (three). Once a clear understanding of these is attained, the migration sequence can be fixed with different forces and interactions occurring at varying times and places.

The game can now be played as many times as necessary to make sure each player understands his role and with as realistic conditions as are feasible. Since educational simulations are means to an end, "decision-making for students in real-life situations" (Gunn 1970:352), the objective in MIGRANT MOVE is to have the students make decisions on whether or not to migrate to the city. A useful follow-up exercise is to compare the students' game experience with their perceptions of reality and redesign the game in light of their discussion. The depth and scope of the perceptions are often surprising. It soon becomes apparent that young students can handle complex simulations and come up with surprising decisions. (Gunn 1970:352)

This game of MIGRANT MOVE has been discussed only brief-ly.* While we emphasize the spatial dimensions of the migration process, it is of interest to many other disciplines of the social sciences—history, demography, economics, sociology. Therefore, playing the game even from a geographic perspective provides an interdisciplinary flavor to the educational feast and demonstrates how the thematic approach assists in producing that flavor.

With a plentiful supply of materials on Africa presently available, teachers can draw their own themes and design their own activities. The source materials range from those aimed at elementary and secondary schools (Kenworthy, 1965; *Grade Teacher,* 86, 2, 1968; Beyer, 1971; and *Social Education,* 35, 2, 1971) in which are found outlines, theme suggestions, concepts, teaching units, and teaching methodology to those designed for introductory college courses but adaptable to senior high school classes (Paden and Soja, 1970 and Walter and Wiley, 1973). In addition, there is now an abundance of suitable visual materials, from filmstrips, overhead transparencies, and slides to films. Beyer (1971) has a comprehensive list and there is a whole issue of *Social Education* (35, 2, 1971) devoted to Africa. It has an especially good collection of enrichment materials: novels, poetry, and audio-visual items arranged by grade level. Finally, Martin, Adams, and Weaver (1972), Paden and Soja (1970), and Walter and Wiley (1973) provide lists of films useful for thematic and interdisciplinary approaches.

CONCLUSION

This paper is meant to show how teaching African geography can be an interdisciplinary adventure in secondary schools. Given the eclectic nature of geography, the interdisciplinary trend in the social sciences, a thematic approach, and a social studies framework, the adventure can be a truly enlightening and educational one. For the student, it develops an appreciation of Africa, an understanding of the social science disciplines and their perspectives, and a knowledge of concepts and conceptual thinking. For the teacher, it can be an opportunity to see students grow intellectually, a fruition to the teaching endeavor, and an exciting and exhilarating experience. It is one that we highly recommend.

---

*For a fuller outline of it and other games, we refer you to the second phase of our curriculum development project, *Africa: A Thematic Geography, Volume IV – Teacher's Manual and Syllabus,* due for completion in June, 1973.

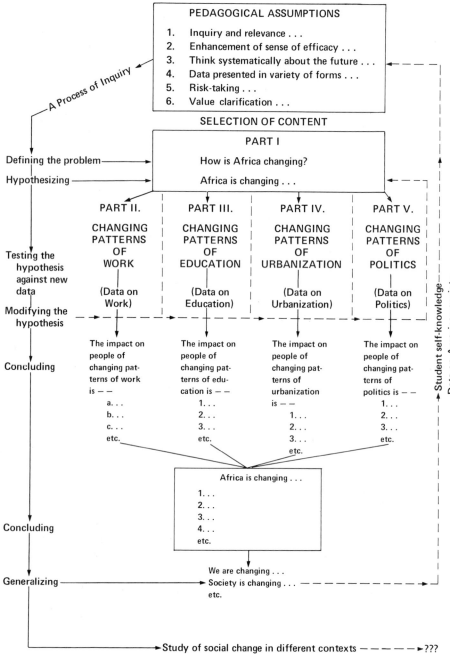

Frontpiece. Teaching about Social Change in Africa.

15

Teaching About Social Change in Africa

SVEN E. HAMMAR
State University of New York, Fredonia

PEDAGOGICAL ASSUMPTIONS

The following list of criteria for the design and evaluation of curriculum materials in the social studies is offered as an index of the pedagogical biases underlying this essay. Several of the criteria may be re-stated as testable hypotheses; however, the validity of these criteria must ultimately be determined by submitting them to the value judgments of society and the uncertain verdict of history.

Other things being equal, one activity is more worthwhile than others if:

1. Students are required to actively engage in inquiry into problems, processes, or ideas that directly concern them (rather than engage in passive activities such as listening to lectures, completing work sheets, or participating in routine teacher-led discussions).

2. The sense of personal efficacy of students is augmented by a) the acquisition of knowledge and skills that can be perceived as being useful in making decisions and influencing the actions of others, and b) being involved in learning situations where individuals of varying interests and abilities can reasonably expect to succeed.

3. Students are required to think systematically about the future by doing such things as identifying and projecting trends, devising and practicing solutions for existing or projected social problems, and by learning and exercising skills and techniques that are likely to be useful in the years ahead.

255

4. The information upon which student inquiry is based is presented in a variety of forms—books, handouts, visual aids, interviews, surveys, newspapers, etc.—and that students are required to work with the information in different combinations and settings, such as simulations, panels, individual research, committees, both in school and in the community.

5. Students and teachers alike are encouraged to depart from the safe, prosaic, non-controversial standardized social studies fare and investigate problems that are ordinarily not dealt with in "the book".

6. Students are required to deal systematically with values, both their own and the values of society, by identifying values, clarifying them, detecting inconsistencies, and by committing themselves through words and actions to the strengthening of values they feel are important.

The writer is more concerned with the concept of social change than with specific social science disciplines, more concerned with social change in its global context than with social change in Africa, and more concerned with how students learn than with what they learn.

WHY TEACH ABOUT SOCIAL CHANGE?

"A fish is the last one to know that he is swimming in water."

This pithy saying, which must be attributed to some nameless Asian sage, illustrates one of the persistent problems in teaching about social change. It is largely invisible, yet we are figuratively immersed in it and change affects all aspects of our lives.

It is virtually a truism that change is occurring more rapidly now than ever before, and that uncertainty and an almost perpetual sense of crisis are distinctive hallmarks of our age. It is doubtful that man has ever asked the questions, "What is happening to us?" and "Where are we going?" with more urgency than he does today. These are questions that high school students ask, though the forms in which these questions are posed rarely lead to satisfying insights or systematic inquiry. Answers—or rather the beginning of some answers—lie in the study of social change and it is important, both in terms of student interest and the needs of society, to introduce curriculum materials on social change that students can relate to their own lives. The assumption is that individuals and society must understand change in order to cope with it.

Social change is an integrative and correlative subject that cuts across the methodological and content area boundaries of the social sciences. Whereas the secondary curriculum is often fragmented and narrowly specialized, social change, as a field for student inquiry, "puts it all together". Very broadly considered, social change is not just one social science content area among others; it is all areas, a heading under which many disparate social phenomena can rationally be ordered and studied. Models of social change are models of social analysis; to know how an institution changes (be it a family, a government or a society) is to know how that institution functions.

The delimiting areas of social change to be studied vary with the interests and concerns of the investigators. Several scholars, most notably Freud, have regarded the individual personality as the most important property of groups and hence, the most important unit of change to be studied. On another level, social psychologists emphasize the individual in his social setting as the most significant unit of study. Sociologists view the group as the unit of analysis; their investigations stress conduct and thought forced, in a sense, on individuals through social action. Studies of such topics as bureaucracies, social class, crime, occupations and the like are characteristic of the sociological approach to the study of change. Anthropology emphasizes as its unit of analysis, *culture,* a concept that in many ways embraces more than the sociological concepts, *group* and *society,* inasmuch as culture is defined to include such components as symbols (language, rites, etc.) and artifacts (tools and technology).

History is essential to an understanding of social change because the transition from "what it was" to " what it is" takes place in the time dimension. The spatial dimension—movements of people, changing patterns of land usage, urbanization trends, etc.—are concerns of geographers. Political change usually comes under the heading of political science, and economists have the most to say about the process of industrialization and modernization. The concepts and research techniques of all of the social and behavioral sciences are combined in the study of social change; the subject is truly inter-disciplinary.

High school students are certainly not interested in debates over what constitutes the correct unit of social change to be studied, or the methodological devices to be employed. There can be no *right* answers in such a debate. Curriculum materials for an introductory unit on social change should offer an eclectic sample, a variety of emphases from which students can choose in accordance with their interests and the nature of the problems to be investigated.

WHY AFRICA?

Social change is normal. No culture—even among the most isolated peoples in the highlands of New Guinea—is exempt from the process of change. In pre-literate and pre-industrial society, change took place so slowly and life was so short that the people involved were largely unaware of what was happening. Functional roles and value systems could be painlessly adjusted to altered situations. Change was invisible.

It is in the modern world that the rate of change has accelerated to the point where it has become highly visible, and nowhere is this visibility more apparent than in Africa. Changes that took place in the western world over the last four-hundred years—the scientific, industrial, political and social revolutions—are occurring in Africa within the space of a few generations. The effect is analogous, perhaps, to time-lapse photography where the life cycle of an organism can be depicted in half an hour. The visibility of change allows study and an understanding of the process. Hopefully, with understanding will come new ways to manipulate change and to cope with it.

One of the assumptions of the preceding paragraph is that the process of change in Africa is very similar to the process we see operating in our own society, the differences being in the accelerative rate of change, its magnitude and emphasis. This assumption is important, for if it is true it means that a unit on social change in Africa can serve both as a *window* for viewing Africa and a *mirror* in which the student can see himself and his society. The utility of comparative studies is widely accepted. The identification of cross-cultural similarities and differences, with an analysis of causal factors, can provide understandings of social behavior which would otherwise be difficult to obtain. We are very much interested in what happens under the stresses of change to families, patterns of work, urban life, socialization of the young, values, status and the many other components that determine the style and quality of our lives. In Africa, these components stand out in bold relief and provide vivid contrasts to our own society. Our ethnocentric biases should not blind us to the possibility that the African response to change offers more than just an experiential record. As western culture has borrowed and adapted certain African forms in art and music, so might we borrow in other areas. In dealing with social change Africans have been quite innovative in such areas as developing institutions for meliorating the tensions of rapid urbanization, and it is certainly probable that other responses—planned or informal—might provide instructive models for western society to follow. Needed is a reversal of the stereotypic trend in the secondary social studies curriculum that views social change in Africa primarily in terms of the introduction of western technology and institutions, with perhaps a patronizing reference to such indigenous African institutions as the extended family and the tribe. Attention should be focussed not only on what African society can borrow from the West, but what the West can borrow from Africa.

Prior to a study of social change in Africa, it is desirable for students to have a knowledge of the process of acculturation (imperialism, colonial rule, missionaries, trade, migrations, and the like) and to know something about the development of indigenous African institutions. This can best be accomplished through an inquiry-oriented study of the history and peoples of Africa. Social change would thus be the content theme that would synthesize the student's knowledge of Africa and would make it a fitting springboard to the study of social change in a global context.

CONCEPTS

The justification for studying social change in the African context is ultimately derived, not from the uniqueness of the setting nor the special importance that Africa has assumed in world affairs, but from the contributions such a study can make to a more general understanding of the human experience. It is not difficult for students to see relationships between problems of rapid social change in Africa and similar problems as they appear elsewhere in the developing world. What is more difficult—perhaps not for students to see but to accept—is the idea that rapid social change is a global phenomenon and that the same processes that are operating in Africa are also present in our own society.

Four broad conceptual categories* of change can be examined in an introductory unit: work, education, urbanization, and politics. (Figure 15-1) Other categories of change (family structure, religion, technology—the list is encyclopedic) can be sub-

---

*Concepts are seen as situated in "clusters" (or "networks" or "webs")—the more complex the cluster, the potentially more potent the concept. The depicted concept clusters are tentative and suggestive; the re-ordering of existing data and/or the acquisition of new data will suggest additional sub-concepts and altered patterns of inter-relationships.

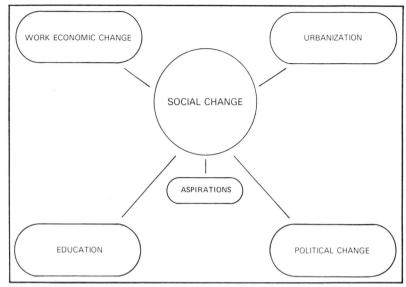

Figure 15-1. Broad Concept Development.

sumed under these broader headings. The model of concept development is quite simple: to realize their changing levels of aspirations, Africans must change their patterns of work (to get money), acquire formal education (to get work), live in cities (where Africans can more easily acquire formal education and find jobs in the money economy), and engage in politics (to provide a necessary degree of social control).

SOCIAL CHANGE

Social change in developing areas is most easily investigated under the rubric *modernization.* Broadly speaking, the goal of modernization is the transformation of a pre-industrial society into a society that is economically *advanced.* Models of modernization may be drawn from ideology (Marxism and its variant, Maoism, are examples) but our usual models are the prosperous and relatively stable nations of the West.

Modernization is usually studied in the context of economic development and industrialization. There are strong arguments that support this approach—most Africans and African nations regard a rising per capita standard of living as a given value—but it is misleading to consider economic development as the single most important factor in modernization. Several African nation-states (Tanzania is an example) give high priority to the political socialization of the masses, and the establishment of a new social order is an essential first step in any program of modernization. A list of the preconditions for modernization and economic development must include, in addition to purely economic factors, leadership commitment to change, rising literacy rates and the desire of broad segments of the population for a materially better life. In the absence of firmly accepted models of socio-economic development, the singling out of one factor or set of factors as being most important is misleading. However, *achievement orientation* —ambition for personal betterment—must be widespread if any impetus for modernization is to be sustained. An introductory curriculum unit on social change in Africa must focus on the varied aspirations of Africans. The question "What are Africans becoming?" cannot be examined without first asking "What do Africans want to become?"

Students can hypothesize about the aspirations of Africans and identify the more important elements of change by analyzing segments from novels, poetry and biographies written by Africans, African newspapers, case studies and sociological anecdotes. This type of data brings out the expressive element, the feelings, attitudes and, particularly, the motivations of people caught up in the process of change.

CHANGING PATTERNS OF WORK

Changes in patterns of work have a profound effect on other aspects of life. (Figure 15-2) The separation of the place of work from the place of residence alters in many ways the structure of

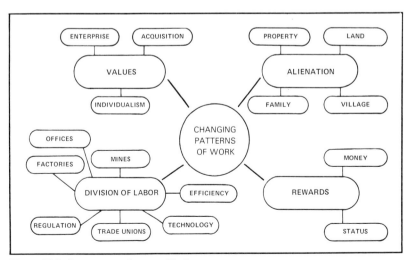

Figure 15-2. Concept Development-Work.

the family inasmuch as sons and daughters may be denied an association with their parents and are thus partially deprived of this model of adult behavior. Labor becomes mobile, a precondition for economic development, and mobility also breaks the chains of cooperation and obligation that bind families and villages together. Money and the things money can buy become the objects of work replacing the communal goals established by the village and the tribe. Money, as a means of determining status and social differentiation, competes with traditional systems of social stratification, and the new form of competition tends to produce a sense of dislocation and tension for those transitional people caught up in the change. People are free to become individuals, to pursue their own goals rather than the collective goals of the family and tribe, but freedom for the man in transition may also mean frustration, confusion and loneliness.

Changing patterns of work have not automatically meant *progress* for all Africans, at least in terms of the quality of their lives. The meliorist view, that the acceptance of Western religions forms, morals, and particularly work habits (grotesquely caricatured in the *white man's burden* argument for imperialism) would result in a better life for Africans has been challenged by another argument, that economic development is a kind of horrid machine that heartlessly destroys social organizations and leaves its victims demoralized, alienated, and empty. More recently, some scholars have asserted that modernizing institutions does not, in itself, generate greater psychic stress. The debate is unresolved. Students should have the opportunity to probe the profound problems of personal adjustment to changing patterns of work in Africa and, by so doing, make comparisons and develop insights about work that will apply to their own present and anticipated roles in life.

An understanding of how work is organized is essential for an understanding of the process of economic development, and a study of changing patterns of work can lead to understandings about other areas of change, namely economic and social organization and changes in demography and human ecology.

EDUCATION

A prominent feature of deliberate programs of modernization is an emphasis on formal education. Africans are particularly eager to acquire formal education and African governments regularly allocate a large percentage of their budgets to education. Ideally the curricula in developing African states are planned in such a way as to provide students with useful vocational skills and the attitudinal orientations necessary for adjustment to rapid social change. The structures of formal education—grades, clocks, schedules, teachers, classes, competition—conform in symbolic ways to the features of industralized society and its paradigm, the factory. Learning becomes rational and secular and students become more open to new experiences and innovations. The adult destinies of many Africans are radically different from those of their parents; their new skills, status and value systems set them apart from the generation of their parents and those without formal education. In short, through education men become more involved in the intricacies of modernization and social change. (Figure 15-3)

Undeniably, the style and quality of life for that minority fortunate enough to receive a formal education has improved. There are relatively few jobs in the money sector of the African economy where some sort of degree—a primary school leaving certificate, the West African School Certificate, a university degree—is not required. As social and economic institutions grow and as industrial technology becomes more complex, the needs of African society for professionally trained people will also grow. Despite all this, planned educational change in Africa often includes dysfunctional elements. Africa inherited the structure and content of the educational systems of the colonial powers which produced Latin teachers and government clerks whereas Africa had greater need of people with managerial skills and training in the more practical professions. Africans may borrow the educa-

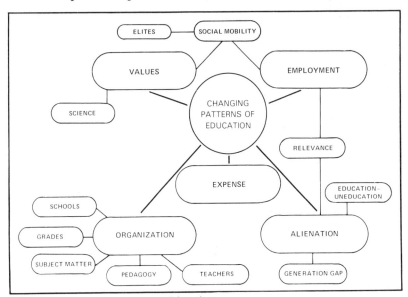

Figure 15-3. Concept Development-Education.

tional forms of the West, along with its technological and managerial know-how, but Western models (even assuming that they were originally useful) have a rapid rate of obsolescence as the Atlantic community evolves into the developmental stage labeled *post-industrial society.*

The cost of education is an additional dysfunctional element. Because money is limited, not all Africans who are qualified and who desire a formal education can find a school opening. Should priority be given to elementary education and the elimination of illiteracy, or should elementary programs be restricted and the money savings allocated to secondary schools and colleges? Money that is spent on education cannot be channeled into the economy. Without a reservoir of usefully trained people, economic development is hamstrung; without economic development, school graduates face unemployment and frustration.

URBANIZATION

The forces of social change in Africa converge with a sometimes shattering impact on cities. It is here that work is organized in factories and offices, and products and services are distributed. Schools and universities are located in the metropolitan centers as are the sprawling government bureaucracies (which in some African countries employ a majority of those in the money economy). The decision makers in Africa who are committed to modernization are not the intellectuals, the entrepreneurial elite, the new political leaders, they are all of these and urbanites as well. Social change and modernization cannot be studied outside the context of the city.

Africa has urban traditions that reach back to antiquity; traditions, moreover, that persist in many contemporary African cities. Urban traditions—the city as a market, the city as a religious center, the city as a traditional stronghold—may, and often do, clash with the modernizing concept of a city as an industrial, entrepreneurial, cultural and administrative center. Will the traditional market, with its noise, color, haggling, and richness of human interaction be replaced by an *efficient* supermarket? Will the structure of the extended family be altered by the construction of low-cost single unit dwellings? Traditions may act as a brake on accelerating economic development, but traditions may also serve as a rudder that helps to steer people through a new and ever-changing urban environment. A study of urban traditions in change must also lead to an examination of the complex interrelationships of urban living—the purposes that bring people together, the subtle webs of communication, the patterns of human

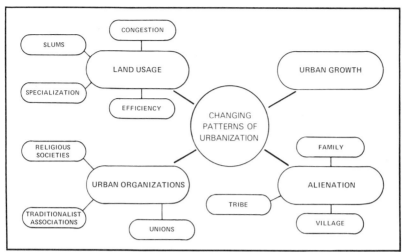

Figure 15-4. Concept Development-Urbanization.

movement and interaction—which are the elements that determine the style and quality of urban life. (Figure 15-4)

African cities are growing in population faster than cities anywhere else in the world. This rapid influx of people, drawn largely from the rural hinterlands, has exacerbated problems of urban sprawl, slums, crime and unemployment—the pathological symptoms of rapid social change found in virtually every urban area in the world. A form of *culture shock* occurs when people move from the leisurely pace of village life, where each person's role and status is known and where there are no strangers, to the impersonal and fragmented life of the city. For most of those who make the move, few have successfully made the transition from the traditional organization of agricultural life to the organization of labor in the more technologically sophisticated milieu of the city. For those without the skills or the psychic orientation necessary for urban survival, there is an almost inexorable drift to the slums—the shanty towns or *bidonvilles*—that ring every African city. Neither housed nor employed nor cared for, these urban displaced persons struggle for survival in a new world not yet prepared to accept them.

The harsher aspects of urban life are meliorated by volunteer associations—a unique feature of African cities. Tradition affords virtually every African city-dweller—through his membership in an extended family, tribe and religious society—membership in one or more associations; his job, neighborhood, age, marital status, and interests make him eligible for membership in many more. A variety of human needs—entertainment, security, companionship, political and economic leverage—are satisfied through membership in voluntary associations; participation also serves some of the broader needs of a society in transition. Government sponsored welfare programs are inadequate by almost any standards and voluntary associations must take up some of the slack. Unemployment compensation, health insurance, legal assistance, loans and housing assistance are just a few of the benefits that may be afforded members of voluntary associations. Political associations contribute to the political socialization of the masses, and trade unions—possibly the most popular and successful form of voluntary association in Africa—help to ease the tensions of a labor force in transition from a village economy to the monetary wage system of the city.

Urban problems (when viewed with a Western frame of reference) are of such a magnitude in Africa that the American urban crisis seems insignificant in comparison. Yet problems on the two continents are similar, if not in degree and emphasis, at least in form. Student investigation of both the problems of rapid urbanization and the African response can provide useful insights into the same problems as they appear in our own society.

POLITICAL CHANGE

The forces of political change in Africa are essentially the same forces at work elsewhere in the world. People are constantly on the move, new economic relationships are established, the primary ties that bind together families and kinship groups are loosened, and a new political institution, the nation-state, replaces local institutions as the instrument for the maintenance of social order and welfare. (Figure 15-5) A host of necessary functions, ranging from the conduct of foreign relations to national economic planning, cannot effectively be performed at the local or tribal level.

The transition from tribal to national politics (which has been going on in the Western world for at least four hundred years) has been happening in Africa for only a few generations and, furthermore, the transition is not occurring with the same intensity or at the same rate for all Africans, even within the same nations. It is a problem of synchronization or, rather, the lack of it; a ubiquitous problem in all changing societies, but one that is exacerbated in Africa by the extreme contrasts between *traditional man* and *modern man.* Individuals and groups that are politically effective within the context of the traditional social order may experience confusion and a sense of powerlessness when dealing with the nation-state. The opposite, of course, will also be true. This prob-

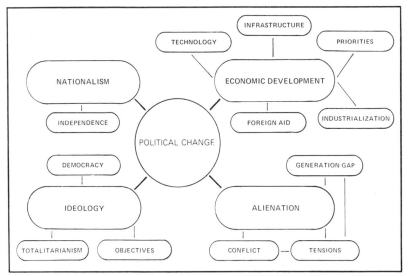

Figure 15-5. Concept Development-Political Change.

lem of non-synchronization also applies to generations; the values and political perceptions of one age group may be vastly different—much more so than if political change had occurred at a more leisurely pace. Viewed in the context of personal values, it is a situation where the felt relationship between some Africans and the new political order is clear; they see themselves as politically efficacious and have an understanding of the purposes and procedures of government. For other Africans, political perceptions are less clear; bureaucratic government is distant and abstract, and they feel a personal confusion about how to relate their lives to a political milieu they do not understand. It is often the poor peasantry, labor migrants, newcomers to the cities, school leavers and members of an older generation who were raised in a different tradition who have this feeling. What these Africans in transition feel is akin to the same sense of alienation and powerlessness that is felt by their counterparts elsewhere in the world, including America.

African governments must assume a special responsibility for facilitating the transformation of economically dependent colonial societies into nations that are politically stable and independently capable of generating economic growth. Unlike Western society during its industrial revolution, sub-Saharan Africa has no sizeable autonomous entrepreneurial class to finance its industrial revolution. As a consequence, economic development has largely become a state function. Resources are limited, and the expectations of Africans for a better life are high, thus creating a gap between aspirations and reality that is a pernicious source of social discontent and one of the main causes of the chronic instability of many African states. To grossly over-simplify, governments have two options: they may seek development capital from overseas—investments from foreign companies, loans and aid from foreign governments—and run the attendant risks of becoming *neo-colonial dependencies,* or nations may try to *go it alone* by generating their own growth capital by following policies of austerity, sacrifice, hard work and patience. The dilemma facing African nations is as elsewhere a problem of balance and priorities. Students should have the opportunity to wrestle with the problem, but only with the full understanding that their hypotheses cannot be verified in any book.

GENERALIZATIONS

Inquiry is, among other things, a type of teaching strategy that encourages students "to find out for themselves". What then might students find out after inquiring for several weeks into the nature of social change in Africa? There is reason to believe that they will know more about how to learn, not only refinements of what they have previously learned about the process of inquiry but more of the cognitive operations useful in ordering and evaluating data. Students will learn some facts and conceptual umbrellas under which facts are organized, and perhaps they will also clarify some of their personal values and values of society. A last stage in the process of inquiry is generalizing. The range of possible generalizations about social change is great, theoretically limited only by the availability and reliability of pertinent data and the agility of the students' minds. It is also possible that they will learn very little; there can be no guarantees when inquiry is open and students exercise choice about what is to be studied, and how. Learning is a very personal thing.

The following list of generalizations about social change is merely a *suggestion* of possible learning outcomes. There are no absolutes in the social sciences, and the absence of a generally accepted theory of social change makes these generalizations particularly vulnerable to modification and dispute. The social sciences are still waiting for their Newton.

1. Rapid social change generates conflicts and tensions that are socio-pathological, and these conflicts and tensions are visible both in the lives of individuals and in the larger context of groups and institutions. Change does not necessarily mean progress.

2. Not all components of man's social existence change at the same rate. This lack of synchronization of change tends to produce tensions and conflict.

3. Changes in any component of man's social existence, whether planned or spontaneous, generate counter-reactions to change. Not all segments of society benefit equally from change. Some may not benefit at all.

4. Change in one component of man's social existence leads to changes in other components and, therefore, social change must be viewed as a series of causal chains rather than events isolated by geographical area, historical time or social component. Change and the consequences of change are global.

5. All members of the human species (with a few exotic hold-outs) are in the process of becoming part of the same social system. The number of political, economic, and cultural linkages that are truly global continues to increase and to these visible linkages must be added a concomitant set of values (such as materialism and secularism) that are also becoming global.

6. As societies become more complex they also become more specialized and interdependent. Specialization occurs in two ways: individuals assume more specialized roles and they perform their role functions in more specialized settings. Specialization also means interdependence, the establishment of linkages between individuals, groups and institutions for purposes of maintenance and protection. A weakening of social linkages, either real or imagined, will produce tensions and conflict.

7. Increasingly, changes in specific components of man's social existence are the consequence of deliberate planning.

8. Historical accident, the complexity of man's social existence and the absence of a tested theory of social change limit man's ability to predict with any degree of precision the shape of society in the future.

9. The rate of social change continues to accelerate. The prospects for man, despite his adaptive skills and social ingenuity, remain uncertain.

16

The Case for an Economic Development Approach to Teaching About Africa

PETER C. GARLICK
State University of New York, New Paltz

An economic development approach to African studies at secondary school level has far greater possibilities than have been explored; it also has some important advantages over the predominantly anthropological and historical approaches offered by the usual textbooks on Africa. This approach, focusing on development, has a universality which might well appeal to teachers whose syllabus includes Asia as well as Africa, for all countries face economic development problems.

An economic development approach has a potential for involving students in immediate and recognizable situations; Africans are presented to them as contemporary people with familiar problems—fellow beings trying to make a living, though in less favorable circumstances than Americans or Europeans. Modern American youth is brought face to face with the problems of modern African youth. Young Americans and Africans can be seen to have problems in common; if American youth feels a generation gap, it should be possible to understand something of the gap between young and old in Africa; if American youth has difficulties in finding jobs, the problem is far greater in Africa.

A contemporary economic perspective on Africa carries with it less chance of an over-fascination with the exotic (to Americans) aspects of African societies and cultures which is a persistent danger of an anthropological approach. It is so easy to misunderstand the material or fail to realize that it may already be out of date. Further, adequate data for an economic approach at high school level are readily available and verifiable, whereas a historical approach must cope with vast areas where knowledge is uncertain, with the added complication of diverse and opposite interpretations of the facts that are known. A teacher concerned about his limitations and expertise in African studies knows that he can do positive harm in misinterpreting anthropology or distorting history. It is comforting to find that in the approach discussed here, a little common sense and a good article can make a good lesson or

271

two. Both history and anthropology require substantial experience of life, quite apart from what can be learnt from the literature, for any real understanding. The argument is not that we should try to do without some background in these areas, but that we can perhaps minimize the dangers of replacing a student's preconceptions with a new set of myths. This is not only a sound academic objective but it may also serve a useful social purpose at this stage in American history with its black-white social problems.

ECONOMIC DEVELOPMENT AND DATA

An economic development approach cannot depend exclusively on existing textbooks. There are some good ones on the market, but few contain much about economic growth, and in any case the facts of contemporary Africa in all areas are constantly changing. Development implies change, and in many African countries the rate of change is rapid. The example of Nigerian oil illustrates this: in 1959, exports of crude petroleum were worth 2.6 million Nigerian pounds (7.28 million U.S. dollars); by 1971, exports of crude petroleum were worth 416.2 million Nigerian pounds (about 1,175.4 million U.S. dollars)—one hundred and sixty times as much. Petroleum products from Nigeria in 1971 vastly exceeded in value all its other exports put together. Oil has greatly changed Nigeria's development prospects. (This particular example is cited because a teacher's manual, *Teaching About Africa,* published in 1970 by New York State, was immediately hopelessly out of date since it based some of its materials on the 1959 U.N. *Statistical Yearbook.)*

Statistics are constantly changing, and the teacher must keep abreast of new developments. (This is not an aspect of the economic approach alone; historical and political approaches must continuously be revised in accord with contemporary changes in Africa. A teacher's guide like *Teaching About Africa,* referred to above, must be used with great caution: it still refers to the "Belgian Congo," "French West Africa," and the "Federation of Rhodesia and Nyasaland".) A course which emphasizes African economic development always has an aspect of current affairs about it. The focus is always on contemporary Africa.

ECONOMIC GEOGRAPHY AND ECONOMIC HISTORY

The basis for an economic development approach at the high school level must certainly be economic geography. The economic activities of seventy per cent of Africa's population (the proportion varies from country to country) are in agriculture. Some acquaintance with climate, topography, soils, and vegetation is therefore essential in any approach to African economies. Some countries depend upon mineral production for their export earnings. Mineral deposits and new geological discoveries are therefore important. The vast hydroelectric power potential of the continent (estimated at about forty per cent of world potential) and the many new schemes to harness this power are relevant for new mineral exploitation, for new industries, and for domestic consumption. This list emphasizes natural resources, but economic geographers are, of course, also concerned with social and cultural phenomena.

Although economic development has its base in economic geography, it is difficult for a teacher to avoid some aspects of economic history. For instance, the "scramble for Africa" and the consequent contemporary political, strategic, and economic links with various European nations cannot be ignored. Similarly, patterns of transportation and communication have bases in the colonial period. The pitfall that exists in the study of the historical/economic consequences of European domination of the continent is to get bogged down in the question of European exploitation. This is a question with great impact on a world at present so consciously divided between rich and poor, black and white, and Western and non-Western. These questions need not be ignored, but the issues of colonial exploitation and of neo-colonialism are still very much in debate, and it is not wise to let them dominate a course in African studies at secondary school level.

THE ECONOMIC APPROACH TO AFRICAN STUDIES

The study of the economic development of less-developed countries includes the whole spectrum of economics as applied to those countries. At secondary school level, a little common sense and general knowledge will carry a class most of the way. Students quickly realize that they know quite a lot about the economic institutions of their own country: government taxing and spending; what the Federal Reserve (or "central") bank does, and how the commercial banks receive deposits and lend money; how people work to earn money to spend on commodities created by others; how economic activities might be divided between primary production, secondary production, and services, or between sectors, especially agriculture and manufacturing. A less-developed country tends to have fewer and less sophisticated economic institutions and (by definition) is poorer. But the basic economic problem exists for all countries, no matter what their level of development—how to make the best use of limited resources in relation to national objectives, and the consequent need to decide which areas are the most important: that is, the problem of identifying and selecting priorities.

It is possible to discuss a wide range of problems in general terms, and to relate them to individual countries or groups of countries as the course progresses. The subject matter suitable for secondary school students might well be limited to production—to the problems of achieving greater output, with special reference to the factors of production: labor, natural resources, capital, and organization and enterprise. A problems approach is likely to be more stimulating than description.

TERMINOLOGY

There are ten terms that students should have a working knowledge of:

Economic development: the process of increasing the output of goods and services over time, embracing the changes in technical and institutional arrangements by which that output is produced. It is the result of a combination of social, cultural, political, and economic changes, which in turn bring about further changes.

Less-developed (or *underdeveloped,* or *developing*) *countries:* a technical term to economists meaning poor countries in comparison with the countries of North America, Europe, and Australasia. It has nothing to do with "culture" or "civilization". It concerns only per capita income.

Infrastructure: those services or public utilities regarded as the essential basis for other production to take place. These include transport facilities (roads, railways, and ports), power (notably electricity), and communications networks.

Subsistence economy: pure subsistence is self-contained and self-sufficient, all production being consumed and none sold. Pure subsistence farming is rare. Most subsistence farming allows for a margin for market exchange (for the exchange or purchase of such items as salt, farming tools, and domestic utensils).

Exchange (or cash) economy: an economy (or society) in which there is exchange of goods and services. (Most transactions *by far* involve cash or money.)

Labor: all those human activities, mental and physical, used in the production of goods and services.

Natural resources: all the materials and all the forces provided by nature, that is, that have no original cost of production.

Capital: man-made goods produced for use in further production of goods and services.

Gross national product (GNP): the total market value of all final goods and services produced in the economy in one year.

Gross domestic product (GDP): the total market value of all production before allowance is made for net property income from abroad. Because of foreign investment, there is usually a net outflow of property income in less-developed countries. GNP is usually less, therefore, than GDP in Africa.

POVERTY AND DEVELOPMENT

It may be hard for most students to comprehend what poverty means. But while on the average people are poor in Africa, as in much of Asia and Latin America, there are Africans who are relatively well-to-do, well educated, well housed, and well fed. A stereotype of all Africans with little to eat or wear is not only disturbing to African observers, but is indeed a caricature with little more validity than a stereotype of all Americans loaded with cameras and dripping with dollars. But there is poverty in Africa which can be related substantially to geographical area and natural resource endowment. In the poorer savanna areas, for example, there is commonly among agricultural subsistence peoples a "hungry season" between the end of the food supplies from the previous season and the next harvest. If this poverty is self-perpetuating, it can be illustrated by a diagram (Figure 16-1) indicating the enormous (though seemingly simple) problems involved in change.

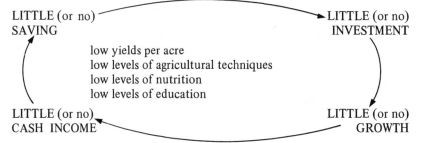

Figure 16-1. The Vicious Circle of Agrarian Poverty.

This diagram can be used to illustrate problems at the individual or family level and at national level.* At the individual level the description can be reworded:

poor diet → poor work effort → low output → low income → poor diet.

The problem is how to transform this circle into an upward development spiral. Three ingredients of economic development will be focused upon here: they are labor, natural resources, and capital.

LABOR

This term includes the quantity and quality of the work force. The growth of population is of current widespread concern and figures are readily available from the United Nations *Demographic Yearbook*. The problem of keeping pace in per capita terms with population growth is of profound concern. Changing attitudes to family size, and methods to control family and population growth go beyond what economics can tell us, but the topic is always of interest. No one can provide a timetable to show when and at what level population in African countries will become relatively stable, and pessimists (or realists?) may well pose some disturbing questions.*

A major point in the preceding paragraph may be developed. More people might be expected to produce more output so that total output (GNP) would increase, but unless there is increased productivity, living standards (or income per head) will not increase. In these terms, students can take up the problem of measuring income per head, and consider how, or how equitably, GNP is shared. Income per head is found by dividing GNP by the total population. But the arithmetic is not the problem. The answer cannot be correct unless both the numerator and the denominator are accurate, and the collection of these data is often difficult for less-developed countries. Incidentally, though rich and poor countries may be clearly distinguished, there is little sense in trying to make exact comparisons in per capita incomes between countries for a number of reasons, one of which is that demands (the "baskets of goods" bought) are different. A West African, for example, does not need central heating or winter clothes. Good national income figures are required by a government, however, so that changes from one year to another can be measured.

Quality of labor involves education and health. One of the major expenditures of African governments is on education. Such

*For a fuller list of the characteristics of less-developed areas see Leibenstein (1957: 40-41) or Higgins (1959: 11-13).

*These questions are discussed in Chapter 4. (editor)

an expenditure is commonly thought of in terms of investment—human investment—intended to increase the number of educated and skilled workers for the work force, thus promoting and sustaining economic development. But job opportunities do not keep pace with the numbers of people seeking employment. The enormous problem of providing positions for the rapidly-growing school leaver* population (Callaway 1963: 351-371) has led to a rethinking of what education should try to accomplish in African countries. Unemployment figures suggest that the expenditure on education could be put to better use. From the writings of Hunter (1967) and Lewis (1969) the problem facing African governments might be summarized in the following way (Figure 16-2):

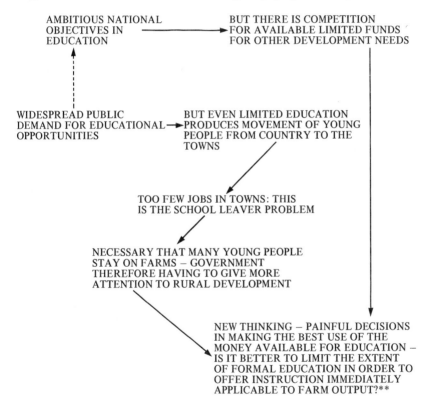

Figure 16-2. Problem Facing African Governments.

*The term "school leavers" includes school dropouts (among them those whose relatives can no longer afford to keep them at school), but, much more important, it also includes students who have gone through the school system.

**Teachers may wish to refer, in particular, to Nyerere's policies in Tanzania.

A feature of the African labor scene, particularly in parts of western, eastern, and southern Africa, is the migration of workers (Spengler 1964, Hance 1970). In western Africa the movement has been from the poorer inland savanna areas to the richer agricultural forest areas and the towns nearer the coast. In eastern and southern Africa this movement has been towards the richer mining and farming areas. Labor migration occurs among regions within a country, as well as across nation-state boundaries. In recent years some African states have expelled Africans of other countries partly in an attempt to deal with unemployment problems.

Figure 16-3 shows the movement of labor from poorer subsistence areas towards job possibilities in three main directions:

Figure 16-3. Labor Migration.

The components of movement can be summarized under *push* and *pull* factors.

Push Factors
Economic
☐ absence (or diminution) of income and of other opportunities at home (population pressures, soil deterioration, etc.)
☐ need for cash to pay taxes
☐ desire to buy products of industry (clothing, bicycle, farm implements, etc.)
Non-economic
☐ avoidance of traditional obligation or conflict with authorities (family, elders, chief)

Pull Factors
Economic
☐ greater opportunities elsewhere
☐ cash income (perhaps to meet family obligations)
Non-economic
☐ lure of towns
☐ a period of work away from home may have become an accepted part of a young man's life (said in some areas to be almost an "initiation rite" − an indispensable stage in the process of growing up)

NATURAL RESOURCES

Economic development can take place without the presence of natural resources, but in these circumstances the other factors of production must be adequate to outweigh this initial disadvantage. No African country, with the possible exception of South Africa (which built its present strength on its mineral deposits) is at present in a position to outweigh any such disadvantage. But agricultural development is possible for most African countries, and, indeed, is now seen to be the key to economic change. Basic problems are increased productivity, increased diversity of output, and sustained adequate price levels for agricultural products on the world market. It must be appreciated that the "green revolution" is not markedly apparent in Africa (maize in Kenya is one exception), and that food imports are still high in many countries. Indeed, according to F.A.O. *Annual Reports,* agricultural output per head actually declined slightly in Africa in 1969, and has shown no improvement through 1972.

A number of countries in Africa have substantial mineral resources, and recent developments (for example, Nigerian oil, and

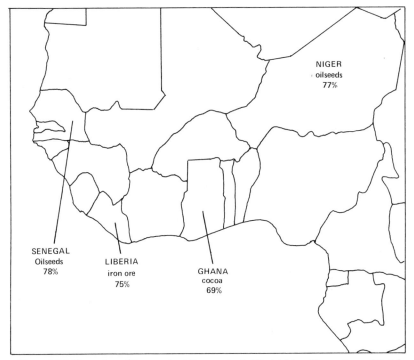

Figure 16-4. Examples of One-product Economies in West Africa. (Percentage of Total Exports)

new discoveries in Botswana) indicate that there is still much to hope for from further geological exploration. Mineral wealth, like agricultural export crops, can provide the foreign exchange for needed capital imports and constitute the "leading sector" or the "engine of growth" to get the economy moving.

Africa South of the Sahara 1972 (*Europa,* 1972) contains details of African economies—output of the various sectors, GNP, budget, trade figures and the like. It is possible to compile maps of Africa from tables in the book showing the major exports of African countries and their frequent dependence upon one or two commodities. (Figure 16-4 and Figure 16-5)

The many hydroelectric power schemes can be shown in similar fashion. A teacher may wish to develop the story and discuss the purposes of one of the schemes, the completed Volta River Project in Ghana (Hance 1967), or examine the problems of financing and building the Cabora Bassa Dam in Mozambique. The

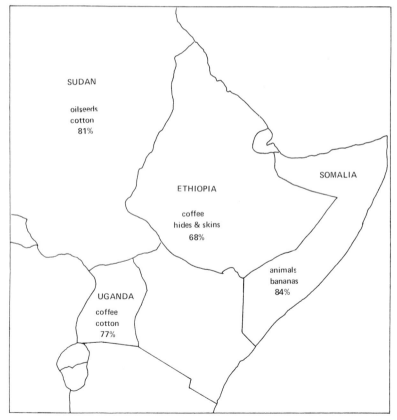

Figure 16-5. Examples of Hydro-electric Power (HEP) Schemes in Southern

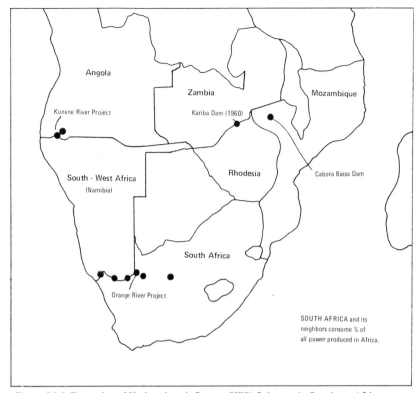

Figure 16-6. Examples of Hydro-electric Power (HEP) Schemes in Southern Africa.

political ramifications of some of the schemes in southern Africa could be of great interest in the classroom. (Figure 16-6)

The study of schemes such as these might be concerned with the following:

hydroelectric power
water shortage in the dry season
urban water supplies
flood control
irrigation
fisheries
inland waterways suitable for transport
disease control (river blindness – Volta Dam, Ghana)
(HEP is particularly important for Africa because there are few deposits of coal outside South Africa. South Africa is also building nuclear power plants.)

CAPITAL

If an African country has a strong private enterprise base in its developed or modern sector, the economy might grow through profits being plowed back. If the sector is small, capital accumulation through this means (which has accounted historically for the development of the western world) will be low. If the industrial sector is foreign-owned, it may wish to remove its profits from the country. If indigenous industry is weak, or if foreign capital is hard to attract or unwilling to reinvest, it seems that the government has no alternative but to play an important part in saving for, and itself undertaking, investment. In any case, there is some spending which only the government is likely to undertake because it is not profitable for private enterprise to do so. Such expenditures on infrastructure – on ports, roads, power, and so on – are an essential foundation for the production of goods and services. Without them, costs will be too high, and businesses will not invest except in exceptional circumstances, such as a major mining enterprise.

So governments not only build infrastructure, but may have to participate in, or themselves develop, manufacturing enterprises if these are to exist at all. This role of governments in development is accepted by development economists, but it may still give rise to discussion among students who have been brought up with fairly solid beliefs in private enterprise.

If business, or a middle or entrepreneurial class, is not saving for investment, where can an African government obtain funds to promote its investment objectives? In answer to this question one might construct a diagram (Figure 16-7) about the possibilities of capital formation.

Many people think of capital investment solely in terms of factories and machines, but perhaps a quarter of all new investment in a rapidly urbanizing country goes into urban housing (Lewis 1955). Towns represent enormous investment and the growth of towns, or of a particular town, is a topic with great socio-economic content likely to attract student attention.

It is important to remember that we are speaking about countries which are predominantly agricultural. A major emphasis is on progress in agriculture which implies substantial investment in the rural areas: the importance of this cannot be emphasized too strongly. However, economic development tends to promote growing urbanization and a demand for jobs in industry. Another major objective is to increase industrialization. Note that industrialization tends to absorb substantial amounts of investment while providing relatively few jobs. This not only presents a problem in allocating funds for development, but also indicates the need for careful "balance" between sectors, since the provision of employment is an objective in development planning.

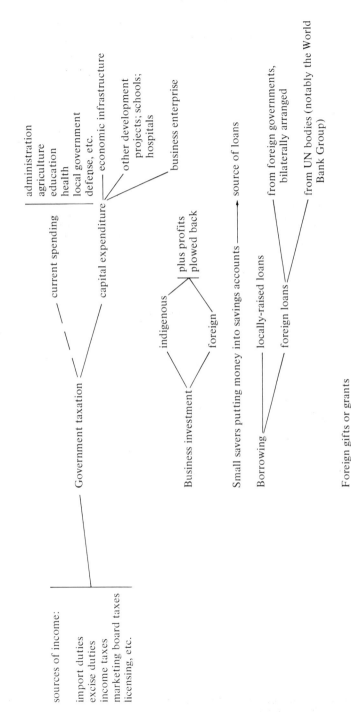

Figure 16-7. Capital Formation.

Figure 16-8 describes the relationship between agriculture and the rural areas and industrialization (or manufacturing) and the urban areas.*

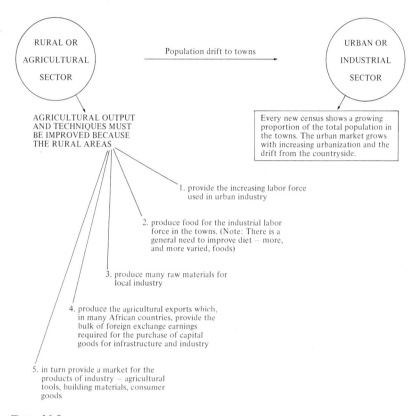

RURAL OR AGRICULTURAL SECTOR

Population drift to towns

URBAN OR INDUSTRIAL SECTOR

AGRICULTURAL OUTPUT AND TECHNIQUES MUST BE IMPROVED BECAUSE THE RURAL AREAS

Every new census shows a growing proportion of the total population in the towns. The urban market grows with increasing urbanization and the drift from the countryside.

1. provide the increasing labor force used in urban industry

2. produce food for the industrial labor force in the towns. (Note: There is a general need to improve diet — more, and more varied, foods)

3. produce many raw materials for local industry

4. produce the agricultural exports which, in many African countries, provide the bulk of foreign exchange earnings required for the purchase of capital goods for infrastructure and industry

5. in turn provide a market for the products of industry — agricultural tools, building materials, consumer goods

Figure 16-8.

*This figure is based upon Chapter 1 of *Agriculture and Industrialization,* U.N. Food and Agriculture Organization, Rome, 1967.

The material covered here has been concerned with production and the factors of production. The major points about production have been expressed in general terms, and are summarized in Figure 16-9:

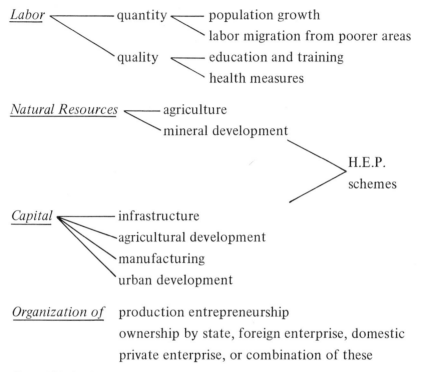

Labor — quantity — population growth
             labor migration from poorer areas
        quality — education and training
             health measures

Natural Resources — agriculture
             mineral development
                          H.E.P.
                          schemes

Capital — infrastructure
        agricultural development
        manufacturing
        urban development

Organization of production entrepreneurship
                   ownership by state, foreign enterprise, domestic
                   private enterprise, or combination of these

Figure 16-9. Production

There is much more to economic development than has been glimpsed in this paper. Vast areas of economics are omitted, including consumption, distribution, and exchange (including international trade) to use old divisions of the subject which development economists still often emphasize as convenient to their framework of analysis. The emphasis has been simply on basic approaches to how to increase national output (or national income), or, put in other terms, how to increase income per head or living standards. This may well be as much as any teacher would wish to attempt, though current events in African countries or newspaper accounts of United Nations reports or conferences (FAO, GATT, or UNESCO, for example) might lead into other areas of discussion.

ECONOMIC DEVELOPMENT
AND OTHER AREAS OF INTEREST:
Suggestions for Study

ECONOMICS AND SOCIAL CHANGE

The study of economic development through the process of increasing the output of goods and services is closely related to other aspects of social change. A society, or a nation, or a state — call it what you will — is a complex of forces. The social sciences look at society from different points of view because society is too complex to comprehend without analysis or dissection. But, of course, society is one and indivisible. It means little to talk about building a nation in the absence of economic foundations and supports. The relationship between these various aspects of social change might be developed by attempting to assess some particular patterns of social change brought about by economic change, and the effects in turn of those changes upon the economy and future economic prospects. Assess, for example, the immediate and the longer-run effects of the building of a railway or a new port, or of the introduction of a new cash crop. The tendency is for students to develop a "model" likely to be over-optimistic in its representation of achievement both in scale and in time. Achievement may be phenomenal in oil and possibly other mineral production, but for most other production it is not.

ECONOMICS AND WORLD RELATIONS

A teacher may wish to select a topic from international trade relationships — the one- or two-commodity export problem; the difficultites of developing trade between neighboring African countries which produce much the same commodities; the association of many countries with the European Common Market; or the terms of trade. The poorer countries of the world are growing richer more slowly than the richer countries which grow still richer, and thus the gap between them widens in per capita terms. Attempts by African countries to obtain price agreements for their major commodities could be a useful topic for the classroom. However, the terms-of-trade argument, which is often used well beyond economic considerations to criticize trading relationships between rich and poor countries, is controversial and has to be handled with care, and up-to-date statistics are essential.

ECONOMICS AND THE SIZE OF NATION-STATES

One topic of enormous importance in Africa, a consequence of its colonial heritage, is the size and shape of countries. Only seven or eight countries in Africa south of the Sahara have populations of over 10 million. About twenty-six countries have populations of under 5 million, including several with fewer than 1 million. The size of a national market (the product of population size and purchasing power per head) is thus very small for most countries and considerably inhibits opportunities for industrial growth. How can these small countries – micro-states as Leopold Senghor has called them – survive? The Economic Commission for Africa (ECA) in Addis Ababa, one of the regional commissions of the United Nations, has been working on the problem for several years. It attempted to persuade countries to associate more closely in their economic activities by grouping into "sub-regions" – north, west, east, and central (there was no southern group). However, the ECA is now working much more through associations of African countries which developed independently of ECA's efforts. The objective is much the same – to improve their economic condition through customs unions and co-operation in a number of areas.*

A study of this problem of size of countries could lead to an examination of the ECA itself. It is interesting that there is usually little or no mention of the ECA in school textbooks though the Organization of African Unity (OAU) receives attention. The ECA certainly deserves fuller consideration than the textbooks accord it. As a subject area, the ECA links up with the United Nations and its various agencies, with other U.N. regional commissions (useful to teachers dealing with other continents), and ultimately with the major national contributor to U.N. activities, the United States.

CONCLUSION

The economic development approach to teaching about Africa would seem to have advantages over other approaches in terms of the universality of the problems that it examines. Its demands on teachers are not excessive. Indeed, a journal article can often form the basis for one or more lessons.

---

*Examples are UDEAC, OCAMM, the Conseil de l'Entente, the East African Community, and the West African Economic Community (which replaced UDEAO in 1970). *(Africa 1972,* Europa, and *Africa Contemporary Record.)*

Much depends upon access to good current materials. Two journals likely to be of use are *Africa Report* and *African Development.* The latter provides the possibility of case studies from its monthly economic surveys. There are advantages in looking more closely at a country's economy, supplementing an article with information from a recent reference volume. This is a long way from Mansa Musa's pilgrimage to Mecca or age groups among the Kikuyu. A teacher must judge for himself what, in the limited time available, is likely to provide not only a "rounded" presentation of Africa but one as accurate as he is capable of making it. It is possible that the economic approach has not been used, simply because the textbooks have largely been written by historians, political scientists, anthropologists, or sociologists, and that their presentations have come to be accepted.

The contemporary nature of economic development has been stressed. While teaching at Howard University the writer learnt from a distinguished colleague a useful approach or technique which helps stimulate student interest. Occasionally, a lesson may be allowed to develop from it. This approach is called "Keeping up with Africa" (or KUWA), and it may be played almost as a game. Current news items about Africa from the better newspapers and magazines are introduced in class, and students are encouraged to contribute items that they have "discovered". Many of the items may be political, but there is a lot of economic material, and many of the political items can be shown to have economic aspects. The writer's own preference is to limit KUWA to perhaps ten minutes of classroom time unless it fits into a prepared structure, since KUWA can seem to be only disconnected bits of news, and both teachers and students tend to feel easier if they have a feeling for the course as a whole.

One way to plan such a course is select topics from Andrew M. Kamarck's *The Economics of African Development.* Such a selection can relate to a teacher's interest, and supplementary materials from journal articles and reference volumes can often easily be found. That still leaves the teacher with the job of transforming what he has selected into lessons. It is hoped that some of the ideas in this paper might help him.

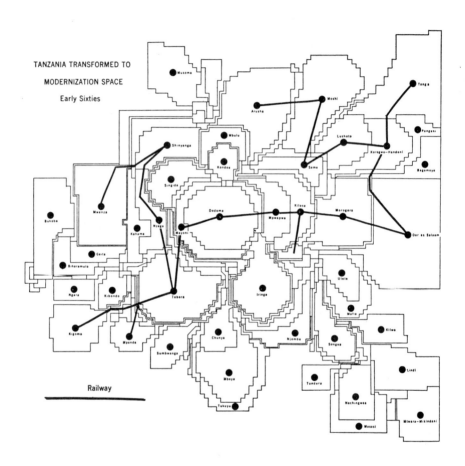

TANZANIA TRANSFORMED TO

MODERNIZATION SPACE

Early Sixties

Railway

17

Applying the *New Geography* to the Teaching of Africa

RICHARD R. BRAND
University of Rhode Island

> . . . my own experience suggests,
> that students are often more
> ready to receive new ideas than
> we are ready to teach them . . .
> Peter Haggett

In recent years the High School Geography Project has demonstrated the possibility of enriching geographic instruction in the schools by introducing organizing concepts and methodologies in problem solving frameworks. The focus of the *new geography* is on the analysis of the patterns and processes that arise from the study of spatial organization. Area studies have revealed relationships and processes not seen before and these are proving to be of practical use in development planning. This essay seeks to show the relevance of spatial analytical approaches to several broad problems of modernization in Africa.

The volume of geographic research on Africa is imposing but only a fraction of this is analytical in approach. In contrast with the bulk of the existing human-geographic literature, therefore, the *new geography* in Africa tends to extend description into analysis and to search for causal relationships through the use of cartographic and quantitative manipulation. Not every article that smacks of *spatial analysis* is appropriate reading material for the teacher, however, much less for direct classroom use. On the other hand, the studies chosen for exposition here are thought to be particularly clear in presentation, yet they incorporate modern analytical methods. Hopefully, they will strike a responsive chord among those seeking examples of the *new geography* in African studies.

291

The discussion is organized around three principal themes: spatial distributions, interaction, and perception. The first is essentially static and deals primarily with the delineation of formal regions, thus producing answers to the geographer's *what* and *where* questions. The second is concerned with forms of movement over a surface, and the dynamic functional linkages that constitute the geographer's nodal region. The last deals with influences that condition people's spatial consciousness and preferences, a process-oriented enquiry into behavioral geography.

While the study of spatial distributions and interrelations is scarcely new to geography, the METHODS used to identify and structure the phenomena of interest here are relatively recent additions to the literature on Africa. Nevertheless, we are dealing with the traditional geographic question, "Why are spatial distributions structured and patterned the way they are?" Within such a process-oriented framework the *new geography* views regionalization as a means to an end – the spatial classification step in the scientific method – rather than an end in itself. Further, the behavioral approach to environmental imagery and mental map formation represents an exploratory attempt to understand the process by which space preferences are formed. Here, both the subject matter and the analytical methods are relatively recent departures in African geography.

SPATIAL DISTRIBUTIONS AND INTERRELATIONSHIPS

The on-going concern of geographers for observation, orderly description, and explanation, so well exemplified in the French *regional-ecological* tradition, is perhaps the most popular approach used by teachers of Africa today. Indeed, the importance of accurate description is not to be minimized even in geographic research. In the words of Peter Gould (1970: 150):

> It is difficult to see how we can write good theory illuminating the process of modernization before we have good descriptions of the basic spatial patterns that ultimately must be linked together through time . . . our knowledge of such sequential patterns in Africa is slight while our understanding of process is virtually nonexistent.

While acknowledging the importance of orderly description, however, let us not lose sight of the potential benefit to be reaped if the location and distribution of phenomena are viewed as stepping-stones to the more substantive questions of interrelationship and causality. All too often we examine the elements of a region as separate and distinct entities, paying only lip service to the way in which phenomena interact in space. We acknowledge the importance of systems formulations (Carey, 1970; Mabogunje, 1970a, yet most textbooks and lesson plans continue to recite the familiar litany of man, the land, transport, agriculture and so forth with little attention to their complex interrelationships and the processes regulating these systems.

AN EXAMPLE FROM KENYA

Edward Soja's study of modernization in Kenya (Soja 1968) offers interesting methodological illustrations of several contemporary geographical approaches to the complex processes of change in less developed countries. It is discussed here to illustrate how spatial perspectives are used first, in identifying PATTERNS of development indices and their change over time, and then in structuring the basic relationships between these indices so as to gain insight into the PROCESS of modernization itself.

The pre-European space-economy of Kenya was characterized "by islands of dense agricultural settlement in a sea of pastoralism." The cultural landscape which emerged after the European penetration "was one of clusters of islands, both agricultural and pastoral, embedded in a matrix of European alienated land" (Soja 1968: 23). Asian traders, restricted as they were from the European-controlled highlands, became townsmen who dominated the retail trade and lower echelons of the administrative hierarchy. The imposition of boundaries made for increased tribal insularity and many agriculturists began to identify with the new political subdivisions. A major reorientation of the space economy occurred with the rise of selected highland regions in the interior at the expense of the formerly prosperous coastal regions. In response, a general redistribution of population from the coast to the highland growth poles took place, and no tribe gained more than the Kikuyu who were proximately situated with respect to Nairobi and the European farming areas around Nakuru.

Professor Soja found the development of communications in Kenya to correspond to a descriptive model of transport expansion previously formulated in West Africa. Through the use of sequential maps he showed the growth and diffusion of the road network and the importance of the towns served by both rail and road. Other indices of modernization such as traffic flows, railway passengers and postal facilities tend to reinforce the generalization about the dominance of highland nodes. Regardless of the index chosen, the single-feature maps highlight the overbearing importance of Nairobi and the major axis of development northwestward to Nakuru.

In coming to grips with the *what* and *where* questions about development in Kenya, a traditional cartographic approach mapping one element at a time was adopted as a research strategy. What then distinguishes this study from the traditional approach? The innovation lies in using these individual distributions to serve a higher end; they are presented as descriptive preludes to the development of a composite picture of modernization. This strategy places the emphasis not on individual features of the historical geography of Kenya, but on their interrelationships.

While such an approach may sound straightforward enough the consideration of the multiplicity of linkages in the Kenyan space-economy is a task far too complicated for traditional cartographic display and verbal analysis. Imagine the number of interrelationships that must simultaneously be considered; consider also that the indices contribute differentially to the overall pattern. Without doubt the capacity of language and the map to express these multivariate relationships is limited.

In the face of such tasks recourse was sought in quantitative methods designed for the task. The technique chosen by Soja was principal components analysis, a mathematical model designed to reduce an array of measures to a smaller number of independent clusters of closely associated dimensions. The contribution of each variable to each component, or the component loadings, determine the structure of the new dimension and are used in interpreting the component. Mapping the weighted components facilitates the construction of multiple-criteria uniform regions which then become the basis for interpretation of spatial variations in the impress of modernization.

The first question answered by the algorithm is one of simple statistical association. When the thirty-six administrative districts of Kenya (Figure 17-1) receive scores on twenty-five indices of development, the task becomes one of determining how any or all of these measures co-vary with each other. Soja determined these interrelationships through a rank correlation procedure which yielded a matrix of correlation coefficients. A partial version of Soja's bivariate correlation matrix is reproduced here to illustrate the potential for introducing such output in the classroom.

TABLE 17-1
MATRIX OF RANK CORRELATION COEFFICIENTS (MODIFIED)

Variable	1	2	3	4	5
1 European Population	–	.76	.46	.81	.81
2 Urbanization		–	.33	.84	.75
3 Post-secondary education			–	.29	.73
4 Per capita postal traffic				–	.59
5 African cash income					–

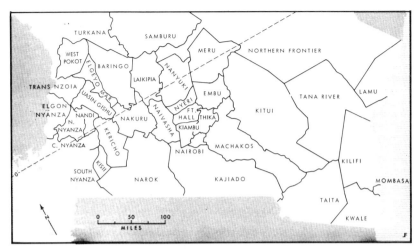

Figure 17-1. Administrative Districts Before 1963.

Reading across row one it can be seen that the European population is strongly associated with urbanization, postal traffic, and African cash income. From these high positive coefficients indicating strong relationships among several of the indices, it is clear that a certain amount of redundancy is present in the original data. Several of the variables appear to be measuring the same underlying dimension, development. With this as a lead, the question naturally becomes one of determining which other clusters of variables seem to be measuring different dimensions of variation. The solution to such a query is beyond the range of the desk calculator; computer assistance is necessary.

When the correlation matrix is subjected to a principal components analysis, the effect is to collapse the twenty-five columns of the data matrix into a smaller number of independent dimensions (principal components) which parsimoniously summarize most of the variation in the initial data. The first unrotated dimension was found to be composed of indices suggestive of general development, with the communications variables associating or loading most highly. As expected in districts scoring highly on this dimension, there were large Asian and European populations, a well-developed transport network linking urban centers, high rates of literacy and economic participation, and a profitable agricultural base. When mapped the spatial pattern of this dimension was readily interpreted. Figure 2 shows Nairobi, Mombassa and Nakuru standing out as the leading growth poles. Subsequent analysis showed Nairobi to be the unparalleled core area of the

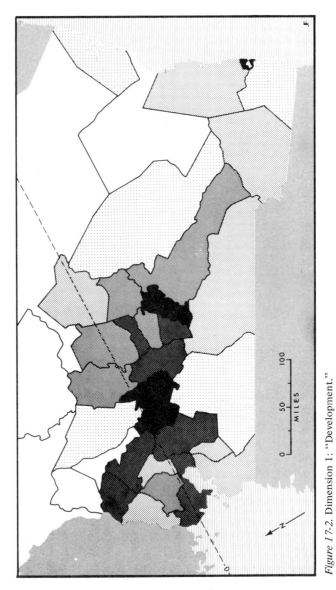

Figure 17-2. Dimension 1: "Development."

country followed by Mombassa and Nakuru, capital of the "White Highlands." The choropleth map of scores on the first component represents not only a partial answer to the geographer's "what" and "where" queries, but summarizes a number of highly significant relationships as well. The mathematical algorithm produced an empirically derived multiple-criteria uniform regionalization of the country on the basis of the component scores.

The Soja study goes on to extract and interpret other important dimensions which refine the meaning of the first component
by distinguishing between the indigenous and expatriate sub-
systems. It concludes with a cartographic representation of the
core area of Kenya and its outlying appendages. Viewing the
highly nucleated pattern of development leads one to appreciate
the geographic implications of a highly imbalanced space-
economy, a common characteristic of nation-states in the early
stages of economic development.

ADDING A TEMPORAL DIMENSION

Whereas Soja's study of Kenya derived a set of empirically
derived multiple-criteria uniform regions, the analysis was essentially static since the data apply to one point in time. It is possible,
however, to add a dynamic element by performing similar analyses
for several points in time.

In a study of Tanzania (Gould 1970: 149-170) such a tempo-
rally oriented research design was adopted. The country was covered with a grid containing 289 cells, allowing for the assignment
of data at a relatively fine scale of measurement and insuring the
consistency of observational units over time. Once again a principal components model was used to abstract the underlying
dimensions of modernization, this time at five points in time beginning with the 1920s and terminating in the early 1960s. In lieu
of plotting the derived *modernization scores* in choropleth fashion
as was done by Soja, contour maps were produced with modernization isolines interpolated from the grid cells at each point in
time.

With the passage of time two salient features were revealed:
the modernization dimension was consistently strong, and the
original *islands of development* or *growth poles* enlarged and began to coalesce as development progressed. By comparing the
patterns on successive maps, one is able to interpret the expansion
of the modernization surface in spatial and temporal terms. Interestingly enough, areas barely affected by winds of modernity, as
measured by the input data, changed very little over the forty year
period. Much more noticeable, however, was the intensification of
development in the existing growth poles, particularly those
urbanized places along the railway from Dar es Salaam inland
(Figure 17-3). The message offered here reinforces our awareness
of the indispensable roles played by towns in Africa. This understanding was underscored by a cartogram in which Gould converted the areas of the grid cells into sizes proportional to their

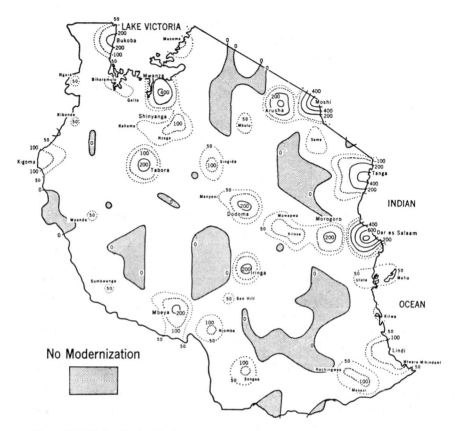

Figure 17-3. Modernization Surface.

modernization scores (Figure 17-4). "Particularly striking is the dominance of the urban nodes and the collapse of the interstitial areas. When we speak of modernization we are clearly discussing an emerging and strengthening urban system." (Gould 1970: 169)

Once again there is the possibility of translating the results of quantitative geographic research into instructional terms. Gould's sequence of maps could, for example, be compared with maps of the Tanzanian road and rail networks to demonstrate the central importance of accessibility as a conditioner of development. Students whose experience is limited to highly mobile societies are unlikely to have an intuitive feeling for the conditions of relative isolation exemplified in many developing economies today, thus, the importance of teaching about modernization in comparative spatial terms.

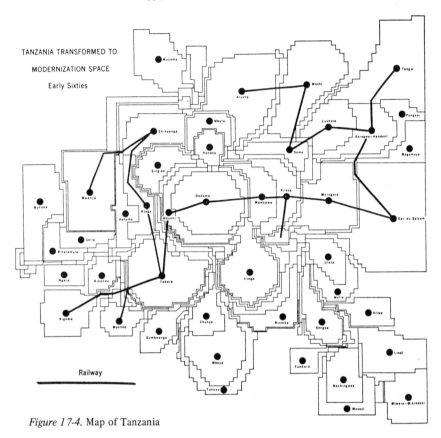

Figure 17-4. Map of Tanzania

MOVEMENT AND INTERACTION

From the foregoing examinations of spatial distributions and interrelationships it is clear that transportation is a particularly important input in the process of nation-state development. Much of the areal differentiation of *colonial* landscapes resulted from the spatial inequalities introduced by transportation networks (McNulty 1972). In a real sense these systems structure the space-economy. Mining towns, administrative centers and the coastal ports become foci not only of high order economic functions, but also of cultural and political activity as well. Rates of urban growth can be directly related to changing levels of accessibility and communications.

Transportation may be generalized, however, beyond its

normal connotation to the circulation of people, ideas, goods and other phenomena over the surfaces of national territories. When considered in these terms, colonialism established the conditions conducive to vast increases in human interaction; law and order were enforced, basic infrastructure was introduced, and urban growth poles were established and maintained. Of all the forms of interaction in Africa one of the most important has been the movement of people through time and space. Moreover, the study of migration and human interaction is bound to become increasingly important in the years ahead as agrarian societies accelerate the pace of urbanization and begin to industrialize. Heretofore, few geographers have attempted to study the PROCESS of migration in Africa though many have described in great detail actual population movements (see Hance 1970: 128-208).

One of the first attempts at the spatial analysis of the migration process in Africa is that of J. Barry Riddell who treated the movement of people and institutions in Sierra Leone as behavioral responses to changes in the national space-economy over time (Riddell 1970). To a certain extent, the medium (or methodology) employed by Professor Riddell is the message. His reasons for breaking with the traditional descriptive approaches to the study of migration might well be taken in a broader sense to represent the scientific approach to problem solving characteristics of the *new geography* in Africa. In his words:

> Thus, the study of migration and its causes in Europe and Anglo-America has focused largely on inductive generalization, quantitative model construction, and attempts at testing hypotheses and proto-theories. In contrast, African migration research has emphasized unique studies in specific, temporal, geographic, and methodological contexts, seldom seeking general and comparative relationships; irrationality and interpersonal and intertribal differences were seen as preventing general statements from being formulated, and the lack of hard quantitative data precludes attempts at model building . . . Further, prominent Africanists have criticized model-building and theory-testing in African studies because it is said that the assumptions used in the social sciences and economics are of relevance only to Western societies.
>
> It is in the light of the findings of the Western migration studies, and with an appreciation of the African situation, that the study of the pattern of migration to Freetown, the capital of Sierra Leone, is undertaken. (Riddell 1970:100)

The author goes on to construct a research design intended to answer a *why* question, that is, what are the foremost influences conditioning the intensity and spatial variations of migration?

Drawing from evidence produced elsewhere in Africa, a set of likely influences were identified. Distance was hypothesized to be inversely related to migration; the population size and educational level of the sending areas positively so. Also, the extent of urbanization in a chiefdom was expected to exert a strong positive rather than negative influence on the volume of movement to Freetown.

While an interpretation of Riddell's analytical techniques may be left to the interested and equipped reader, his approach to the formulation (and reformulation) of a mathematical model of migration rests on the assumption that

> movement is the resultant of many factors, which at times operate separately, but most often in combination. Thus, the effects of urban influence on migration are not independent of distance, and the impact of education will partially depend upon the degree of modernization. (Riddell 1970: 116)

Once again there is need for multivariate statistical techniques to parcel out the relative influence each independent variable has upon migration. The set of explanatory variables was reduced to a smaller number of uncorrelated components which then became surrogates for the larger set. The first and strongest of these was a general urban dimension, which, once mapped, identified the growth poles associated with colonial administration, mining districts and other highly accessible nodes served by the railway. Using values for this and three other derived constructs as inputs into a multiple regression model with migration flows to Freetown as the dependent variable, urbanization and distance were found to be the two most important determinants. The consistently important role of urban places and relative accessibility asserted themselves again, just as they did in Kenya and Tanzania. It was also found that those places first linked to the capital by the communications network "established and maintained a lasting flow of people to Freetown. There is, in effect, a feedback mechanism, with movement leading to more and better information, which in turn leads to further movement." (Riddell 1970: 125)

Perhaps the most significant of Riddell's findings for the research geographer and the educator alike was that "the provincial towns act as catalysts to movement from rural areas to the large cities rather than as alternatives." (Riddell 1970: 130) This process, which has come to be called *step-wise migration,* progresses upward through the urban hierarchy and stands in opposition to the classical view of migration as postulated by Ravenstein

(1889) in which intervening opportunities absorb rural migrants and diminish the flow to the largest cities. According to Riddell

> The migration process cannot be controlled by government policy or programs other than the strictest imposition of police-state restrictions on movement. Improvements in the rural areas and provincial towns will not stem the flow, but serve to increase it. Migration must be recognized as an increasingly important component of the evolving modernization process and its consequences must be provided for by increased efforts in urban housing, sanitation, food supply, and employment opportunities. (Riddell 1970: 127)

By no means, however, are these conclusions parallel to research and planning everywhere in Africa. In fact the trend in recent national development plans is to limit attempts to expand the economic bases of the large cities in favor of rural-based development schemes (Taylor 1972). According to Mascarenhas and Claeson (1972), the second Tanzanian Five Year Plan (1969-74) explicitly seeks "to disperse total urban population amongst a number of towns to maximize the development impact of rural areas." The policy of UJAMAA VIJIJINI as elaborated in Nyerere's *Socialism and Rural Development* thus aims at rural transformation. Concern and precious capital are being committed to the lower and middle range of the urban hierarchy in an effort to *anchor* the rural population and thereby reduce the pressure on the growth poles at the upper end of the system. The recently announced decision to allow regional autonomy in Tanzania is a dramatic step forward in President Nyerere's campaign to decentralize authority and promote a more equitable regional development surface. While the goals of more broadly based development capture the imaginations of many, the task of developing a hierarchy of central places is a vexing one whose success hinges on more than ideology and administrative fiat. Tanzania is and will continue to be a desperately poor country (in monetary terms) for many years to come.

The basic differences between Professor Riddell's conclusions and the assumptions underlying UJAMAA VIJIJINI in Tanzania provide ready made material for a class investigation of regional development strategies in Africa. Role-playing might be introduced, for example; one group might represent the interests of the traditional village elders in the areas of emigration; another, the migrants themselves; a third, colonial decision-makers; and a fourth, post-independence government planners. In preparing for such group assignments, students would come to see the conflicts of interest and different alternatives involved in policy-making in a spatial context.

ENVIRONMENTAL PERCEPTION

Research on the behavioral processes that condition the way people see their surroundings is indicative of a deeper search for explanation characteristic of the *new geography*. Recently published exploratory studies of personal attitudes and space preferences (mental maps) in Africa and elsewhere suggest that the geographical analysis of aggregate spatial preference data has direct value to government planners seeking to iron out existing regional inequalities.

In Gould's study of space preferences in Tanzania, a small sample of students supplied information on their choices of locations for a civil service assignment. A map of space preferences produced from these responses "matches to a remarkable degree a surface of modernization, constructed quite independently as a composite expression of twenty-six variables." (Gould 1969: 30-31) Figure 17-5 shows broad troughs along the coast, in the south and toward the interior, all of which are poorly developed relative to the Tanzanian surface as a whole. When preferences

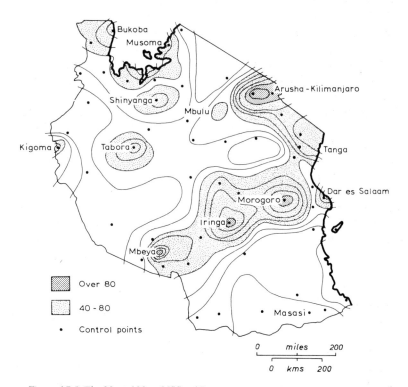

Figure 17-5. The Mental Map, MSS p 17

were measured according to attitudes toward people in various parts of the country, Masailand (the trough between Arusha and Musoma in Figure 17-5) was perceived as a most unlikely place for the groups of educated respondents to feel comfortable. A general dichotomy of preferences was also evident between northern coastal and interior locations.

When the districts were mapped according to scores on perceived accessibility (travel scale), those with rail and first class road service were accentuated. However, all districts having commensurate levels of rails and roads were not equally represented on the preference scale; those with well known towns such as Tabora, Kigoma (on Lake Tanganyika), Mwanza, Arusha and Moshi "are all seen as more accessible than some of the intervening areas with equally strong rail links." From each of the urban centers with high preference scores a great deal of communication, or information flow, reached the capital with the result that popular awareness of these locales was heightened.

Armed with the knowledge of some of the spatial dimensions involved in the search behavior of potential migrants, the social scientist is better equipped to interact with the planner. It is critical, for example, for the development strategists in Kenya and Tanzania, where bold new plans are now in force, to know the attractive and repellant migrant destination nodes. Incentives could then be offered to attract qualified personnel into the less preferred areas. In Gould's parlance this would smooth out the surface of space preferences.

Another exploratory study of perception deals with residential desirability in western Nigeria (Gould and Ola 1970: 73-87). Here, an attempt is made to probe how mental maps are formed and how they change from childhood to maturity. It was found that the perceptual ties of Nigerian thirteen year-olds to their local areas were much weaker than those of British youngsters of the same age. Knowledge of distant urban areas in Africa is apparently gained at an earlier age, and these stand far above the rural parts of the perceptual surface. Interestingly, the maps of the preferences of other age groups (fifteen, eighteen and twenty-three year olds) were extraordinarily consistent. "No matter which age level is taken, the same basic configuration appears again and again." (Gould and Ola 1970: 76) There was, however, a spatial concentration of preferences for urban centers that intensified with increasing age.

The analysis then proceeded with a preliminary attempt to isolate some of the sources of information that condition geographic space learning. Important among these are migration travel experience and information coming from members of one's extended family. When the data on visits to relatives, length of stay and number of relatives were used as predictors or independent variables with perception scores as dependent variables and a multiple regression analysis performed; "between 84.3 and 87.6 percent of the variation in the perception scores is accounted for by these variables together." (Gould and Ola 1970: 78)

Apart from the technical complexity of the mathematical and statistical algorithms used in perception studies, one can find a good deal of geographic content and methodology that is of use at the secondary school level. The question of the concentration or diversification of development strategies is a prime example. To add realism to such a classroom enquiry one could consider the concepts of information flows, directional biases, feedback mechanisms, intervening opportunities, barriers and linkages; on the response side there would be the space preferences of rural and urban populations, the set of destination nodes, the actual migration or interaction streams, and finally the modernization surface with its pits and peaks. The range of spatial concepts and process-oriented methods of enquiry that could be introduced is much broader than those described in this essay, and the venturesome teachers willing to experiment are encouraged to use other studies. Presenting material in terms of a modern spatial perspective involves the familiar uniform and functional regionalization, but it goes deeper to tap the notion of spatial processes. Involved here are the scientific concepts of dependence and independence, probability and determinism, induction and deduction. These could be introduced to more advanced students in problem-oriented contexts thereby enriching the traditional approaches to area studies.

CONCLUDING REMARKS

When the High School Geography Project embarked on its program a fundamental assumption was that if the *new* geographic perspectives were to receive a wide adoption in secondary schools they would have to be presented by teachers with little formal training in spatial analysis. The same is true if concepts of the *new geography* are to be infused in secondary school programs in African studies.

The hope for an infusion of the *new geography* into existing secondary school African courses is not as remote as one might think. Teaching materials incorporating many contemporary geographic concepts (Walter and Bernard 1971) are currently being used by the author with introductory level college students, and these can be modified for use in the high schools. What is needed at this juncture is a cadre of *risk takers* — teachers having some familiarity with contemporary geographic methodology who see enough potential transferability in the materials cited in this chapter to go out and evaluate them.* This phase of intellectual curiosity must then be followed by a phase of greater risks, those of instructional experimentation and implementation. While the latter phase may, in many cases, be beyond reasonable expectation in the short run, there is even reason to hope that those aware of the progress made by contemporary research geography will take up the challenge of continuing self-education. An unstructured diffusion process of the *new geography* in the classroom is bound to follow.

*See Chapter 21 for a sample teaching module developed by Richard Brand. (editor)

PART FOUR
Teaching Strategies

18

The Design and Use of Simulations to Teach African Studies

PETER L. FRENCH
St. Lawrence University, New York

The primary obligation of non-Western studies programs in secondary schools is to teach our young people about the nuances of cultures so that as future adults they will interact more effectively with alien societies. In teaching about Africa, it is necessary to convey understanding of value perspectives that contrast sharply with American value systems. The task involves far more than mere description of exotic environments, unfamiliar customs, pre-industrial economies, and political amalgams that link antiquity with universal suffrage and the ballot box. Standard African materials provide limited understanding to students raised in the competitive, post-industrial consumer society that is America. In *People of Plenty* (Potter 1954) the thesis is developed that American values, democratic form of government, and social institutions have all been shaped by the abundance of the physical environment. This relationship between values and the environmental setting may be arguable, but it is fair to state that American culture has been perceptibly influenced by unparalleled abundance, unbridled optimism in the potential of technology and aggressive individual achievement motivation. How deeply embedded are those characteristics is apparent today as individuals attempt to reconcile the ambiguity of this historic value perspective with incontrovertible evidence that the environment has limits to its bounty, that technology cannot resolve all problems, and that rugged individualism may be both costly and detrimental to society.

By contrast, much of Africa's historical experience has been remote from the characteristic American experience. Therefore, what the instructor must try to convey to students is an awareness of the way harsh physical conditions have forced societies to survive in marginal conditions that engender revelationary belief systems to the discouragement of even low level technologies. The integrity of social behavior has been maintained by uncompromising obligations to consensus and cooperation rather than encouragement of individual initiative. Today, the pace of economic change over a quarter of a century is subjecting those old beliefs to searching reappraisals, but it is foolish to suggest to students that this fleeting impact with Western technologies has modified attitudes built over centuries. Even in those regions long exposed to colonial rule the pace of culture modification is slow, uneven, and frustrating to new political elites who would hurry their people forward into the technological world.

Given the reality of an observable disparity between American and non-Western value perspectives, the thesis developed here is that African studies courses are materially benefited through the use of carefully defined role-play simulations: that in seeking to fulfil legitimate goals of African studies programs, such simulations can show the student how culture impinges on decision-making. Furthermore, when exposed to a series of such teaching formats in combination with other materials, it is possible to perceptibly raise effective orientations to a more positive regard for Africa's peoples and cultures.This conviction is based on extended experience in the use of simulation games to teach African studies.

Making the case on a substantive level, however, is only half the battle in suggesting the viability of simulations as a useful educational tool. The latter portions of this article deal with a number of the practical considerations in the design and operation of simulation exercises. This commentary with its volume of impressionistic insights is derived from five years of experience in the construction, modification, and operation of four interrelated simulations.* These exercises have been tested and refined to a point where they presently constitute a set of core materials that could be used for an African studies course of four to six weeks' duration. While writing and testing such materials one becomes intimately aware of the apprehension such exercises generate in the minds of teachers. Also, one becomes cognizant of the importance of making such materials compatible with mandated curriculum requirements. The experience, however, has produced the conclusion that such materials can be designed with the requisite simplicity so as not to intimidate any instructor while preserving the substantive contextual value of the exercise.

---

*These simulations are referred to without footnoted reference throughout this article. Collectively, they have been titled *The Africana Simulations,* and individually the titles are *Kutiisha, Kisasa, Uhuru,* and *Maneno.* The set consists of four *Player Books* and *The Director's Manual.* For further information on these simulations, write the author at The Department of Government, St. Lawrence University, New York, New York.

DESIGNING SIMULATIONS FOR AFRICAN STUDIES

To introduce the special qualities of non-Western simulation exercises, a few brief comments are offered on simulations in general. These operating models of physical and social situations seek to represent reality in "model" form by reducing reality to manageable proportions. This is done through selective incorporation of those elements of reality which the designer deems relevant to his purpose. Thus, simulation of a social setting is more than mere role play because the participant is forced to make his actions correspond to the functioning of some real social system.

How students learn from simulations will vary with the exercise used and with the control maintained by the simulation director, but at least two main sources of student learning are recognizable. One, students may learn directly as a result of their experience in the simulation. For example, students playing decision-makers in a relatively poor country have a heightened awareness of the difficulty of attempting to meet societal demands in the midst of economic poverty. The *Uhuru* simulation sets as a basic goal the teaching of the difficulty of maintenance of civilian democracy in poor African states. During an early run of the simulation, the student playing the role of the president showed his awareness of the problem by requesting information on how to turn the country into a dictatorship when beset by a flood of demands from the other players. In such a context, the simulation has functioned as a teacher. The second source of learning is the post-simulation discussion in which role-play becomes a take-off for examination of the reality that has been simulated. This process has two pay-offs. One, it prompts students to make more explicit their beliefs about referent reality. And secondly, it affords the instructor an opportunity to ferret out mis-conceptions and mis-information.

In developing simulations dealing with Africa, certain modifications in format are necessary in order to achieve the benefits described above. Because students possess very little in the way of referent reality about Africa, it is necessary to make role descriptions, background information, and operating scenarios much more comprehensive than would be the case if one were simulating a more familiar setting such as a court room or local town council meeting. It is not sufficient to indicate to a student that he is a tribal elder or that he lives in a small village. He should be given the following type of information:

> You are an elder of the Killuk tribe, the pastoralists of Bahati. Your tribe is more loosely organized than the Bantu Zuni or Bandari, and

the tribe has less occasion to gather for discussion of tribal business. Perhaps the most inportant feature of your responsibilities lies in organizing the initiatory rites when young men are taken into adult life in the tribe. . . (from *Kutiisha: Colonial Rule in Bahati*)

Background settings should incorporate such features as:

Kisasa is a tiny village located in the western highlands of the country and inhabited by people (who) compose one patrilineal and partilocal clan. . .The villagers have good reason for leaving the flood plain untouched. First, the climate in the hills is cooler and the water is clear, and in the plain are often stagnant pools that breed malarial mosquitoes and other diseases. But most importantly, the people do not go to the plain since it is the place of the ancestral clan burial grounds. (from *Kisasa: Learning New Ways in a Bahati Village*)

The scenario also must be more explicit, providing the participant with sufficient information to permit him to carry out his role with reasonably high expectation that his performance will approximate the reality being simulated. A scenario ought to include such technical description as the following:

The basic problem for the government in drawing up its new budget is to have sufficient resources to meet demands being made. . . . For the coming year, the Upesi government is faced with more serious problems. This year it will receive only 3.5 million from the British government. . . . It is anticipated that the government will need to expand its budget by at least 15%. . .This means the government needs a potential revenue of 28.5 million dollars. (from *Uhuru: Problems of Independence in Upesi*)

This development of sharply defined role descriptions, backgrounds, and scenarios has a dual purpose. The additional information allows the students to bring added integrity to their performance in the simulation. But, of equal value, incorporation of a volume of information into the simulation itself drastically expands the base from which the teacher can generate discussion in teaching about Africa. For example:

One resource shared by both countries is the Tsava River which flows down the Kongoni Mountains and out over the broad plateau area before dropping over the escarpment and forming the delta area at the coast. . . . (from *Maneno: The Arts of Diplomacy in the New African States*)

The instructor can use this information to review student knowledge of African geography, including discussion of the plateau form of the continent, the narrow coastal plain, the absence of good harbors, the many impediments to the navigability of rivers, and the potential for development of hydro-electric power. This leads naturally to further elaboration on the problems of hydro-electric power created by intermittent rainfall and reference to such functioning projects as Kariba, Jinja on Lake Victoria, and the High Aswan. Through such use of the materials, simulations become integral parts of the whole curriculum rather than adjuncts to be employed only when time permits.

The second major modification in the development of non-Western simulations is the construction of bargaining procedures that encourage cooperation and reduce competition. Since awareness of different value perspectives is a fundamental rationale for African studies programs, it is totally consistent to provide simulation procedures that encourage consensus rather than promote conflict, antagonism, individual achievement motivation and zero-sum game strategies. Most simulation exercises in use are designed to permit evaluation on the basis of winners and losers, and part of their appeal to students stems from the competitiveness built into the simulation context. Whether diplomatic, political, economic, social, or military, these formats are designed to teach understanding of multi-variate interaction through the use of conflict role-play. There is nothing inherently wrong with this basic design, and it is acceptable since the student immediately recognizes acceptable forms of behavior that he can practice within the simulation format, but such formats do not aid in exposing students to value patterns which contrast with their own values.

Therefore, the designer of non-Western simulations ought to make a conscious effort to incorporate rules, scenarios, roles, and bargaining processes that pay dividends for compromise, and teachers should emphasize these characteristics of the simulation. No role-play simulation can eliminate the dynamic of conflict without compromising the integrity of the exercise, but the emphasis on winning can be profitably reduced. This can be done by drawing up outcomes where conflict produces no real winners. The following example demonstrates how limitations can be placed on winning. The list notes few winners with the possible exception of the military officers.

To reinforce the significance of differing value perspectives, the rewards and penalties can be made more Western as the context of the simulation becomes Western. In the second stage of *Kutiisha,* the role descriptions and bargaining options are more Western in content and provide the Africans real leverage in influencing decisional outcomes. This change is in sharp contrast with stage one where traditional values leave the Africans virtually helpless to gain redress of grievances from their colonial rulers.

TABLE 18-1
RESULTS OF BARGAINING ROUND TERMINATION BASED ON
VIOLENT CONFLICT IN STAGE 1 OF THE KUTIISHA SIMULATION

"B. Full Scale Use of Military Force If Two 'Tribes' Are Involved:
1. 60% of missionary facilities destroyed.
2. 40% of military forces destroyed, but senior officers win distinction and promotion for gallantry in service to the King.
3. Governor is able to maintain control, but he has to inform the Colonial Office that he will be unable to generate local funds for administration and therefore the colony cannot be self-sustaining.
4. Trader's Association loses all annual revenues and 40% of cash investment in the colony is destroyed.
5. Colonial Office reduces administrative and military personnel by 33% leaving colony in a more precarious position for any subsequent rounds of bargaining.
6. The two tribes involved lose 35% of their male warriors; villages are 70% destroyed; cattle confiscated; family life is destroyed; unable to consider warfare in subsequent bargaining rounds."

From *The Director's Manual, Africana Simulations*

THE UTILITY OF SIMULATIONS FOR AFRICAN STUDIES

The educational benefits of classroom simulations can be limited by a number of identifiable factors, and if the role of simulations as teaching tools is to be expanded, then simulation design must be responsive to these limiting factors. African studies simulations bear the additional burden of dealing with unfamiliar substantive content, giving even greater emphasis to the need for careful formating if African or non-Western simulations are to receive full productive use. The three major considerations that appear to govern simulation use are the following. One, the limits of time imposed by mandated curriculum requirements critically determines whether an instructor will seek to incorporate a simulation into his syllabus. Two, the attitude of the instructor toward the use of non-traditional teaching materials helps determine if simulations will be used even when time and materials are available. Three, the students who are the potential users of simulations must be able to benefit regardless of classroom performance levels, academic proficiency, or background preparation.

SIMULATIONS, TIME, AND THE MANDATED CURRICULUM

Many simulations currently in use appear to have been developed as adjuncts to the regular curriculum materials rather than as an integral part of the syllabus. As highly interesting supplements, they are viewed by instructors as "intrusions" on the "real" business of teaching, and when judged from that perspective it is a logical consequence for instructors to be reluctant to use materials that cut into precious teaching time. If simulations are ever to realize their full potential, they must be designed so that they become easily coordinated with other materials as standard parts of the syllabus. To do so, the following facts are of primary importance.

Realistically, an Africa unit in the average American secondary school consists of between 400 to 800 minutes of effective teaching time. This is estimated on the basis of 2½ to 5 weeks for the unit with the realization that a certain amount of time is going to be lost with unscheduled assemblies, teacher institutes, meetings, yearbook pictures, band rehearsals and snow days. To use more than 20% of that time for a single simulation that is not directly related to the basic curriculum may be considered an imposition on the teacher and the students. A more realistic approach is to develop a simulation that may use as much as 40% of the time allowed for the Africa unit and then guarantee an integral relationship between simulation and the other materials being used. This would give the teacher approximately five to ten classroom periods to play one simulation in an extended form or perhaps two in a shortened version of each. If this is done, then the simulation loses its extracurricular appearance and becomes much more than a time-consuming educational gimmick.

There are two useful strategies that can be used to meet the problem of the time-mandated curriculum problem. The first is to develop formats that fit comfortably within even the most limited timeframes. The *Kisasa* simulation with its simple design and limited run-time demonstrates that this is clearly possible. The actual play of the exercise centers around a tribal council meeting in which the players defend their individual interests on the issue of traditional values versus economic development. The issue is resolved with a concluding referendum, and the instructor can quickly move to the post-simulation discussion and evaluation.

The second strategy is to design simulations that have a geographical focus in Africa while incorporating conceptual materials with relevance to all of the "Third World." This can then be used in year-long curricula such as the ninth-grade syllabus in New York State which is devoted to the non-Western world. Simulations similar to *Uhuru* and *Maneno* can be made to deal with the problems of internal development, international relations, and political modernization. The instructor is then provided with the option of using several simulations for an extended period of time and tying them in to units with differing geographic foci.

SIMULATIONS AND THE TEACHER

The encouragement of simulation use must be only a slightly easier task than getting older faculty to voluntarily learn computer skills. Simulations, by their very nature, tend to generate apprehension if not fear. Once a simulation is under way, the characteristics traditionally associated with a "model" classroom break down and disappear. Noise replaces quiet. Chaos appears to triumph over order. Movement becomes contagious. Quickly, the instructor realizes he has been removed from his role of judge and jury. As students pursue simulation activities and form their own independent judgments, the line of communication becomes circular within the group rather than linear, and some instructors appear to resent the shift from first string quarterback to head linesman.

Simulations dealing with Africa or Asia then introduce even higher levels of anxiety through the added uncertainty of dealing with a subject area in which most teachers have been inadequately prepared. The expansion of curriculum requirements to include non-Western studies has forced many teachers to retool and develop these new competencies. And, with a linking of African studies to the Afro-American heritage, mere factual knowledge is often not sufficient. The demands for relevance insist that the teacher engage in a cross-cultural exercise where he must teach Black studies or African studies with both competence and feeling.

Since simulations on Africa ought to expose students to a set of values that contrast with values acquired in most American homes and schools, the instructor's mastery of the content and procedures of the simulation materials is crucial. If the instructor understands the materials completely and shares the goal that simulation forces students to abandon standard American values for a few brief hours, then the simulation can be a success. If the teacher does not accept such a belief, then the effectiveness of the exercise will be compromised—no simulation is "teacher-proof."

THE STUDENT AND THE VALUE OF SIMULATIONS

The value of using simulations is primarily to benefit the student, and the standard values derived from such experiences are learning about competition, cooperation, empathy, and historical influences on society. However, it should not be assumed that students are cognizant of these values when they begin play or desire to participate in simulations with equal degrees of expectation. It is not uncommon to have few volunteers for leadership roles since students do not perceive themselves as leader types. Once involved, students learn that simulations are serious, require considerable amounts of paper work, outside reading, and can be frustrating because of the limits imposed by the bargaining controls. Contrastingly, other students seem to grow tremendously in terms of individual confidence about personal judgments. Released from the image of how they think they are viewed by their peers, students suddenly exhibit personality strengths previously not apparent. It is frequently observed that relatively shy students begin to exert extraordinary political leverage in their roles because they feel secure in the cloak of the role-description and are no longer constrained by the way they are viewed in the "real" world. Suddenly transformed from a reticent member of a class into a powerful tribal elder, they become momentarily different people who are apt to marvel at their own performances when discussing later the play of the simulation.

Who do simulations help most? It is clear from having conducted simulations with all age groups from intermediate schools to college level classes that nearly everyone can benefit from the use of simulations. It is also apparent that bright students absorb the essentials of simulations very rapidly and explore the relationship between simulation and reality at a faster pace than do other students. It is also true that the brighter student will exhaust his interest in a particular simulation much more rapidly than other students. These facts are set forth to indicate that simulations can be highly educational to all students. It is the experience of the past five years, however, that the student who may derive the greatest satisfaction from simulations is that student who is reading below grade level and otherwise might be described as either a "slow learner" or "disadvantaged".

This latter type of student presents the greatest challenge in terms of encouraging an interest in simulations, for even the reading of the short instructional *Player Book* may be difficult. The effort to stimulate such a student, however, is clearly worthwhile, for such students often turn out to be very effective players.

It is an established fact that students described as "disadvantaged" display skills in terms of the following characteristics:
1. Physical and visual rather than aural.
2. Content-centered rather than form-centered.
3. Externally oriented rather than introspective.
4. Problem-centered rather than abstract-centered.

5. Inductive rather than deductive.
6. Spatial rather than temporal.
7. Slow, careful, patient, persevering (in areas of importance), rather than quick, clever, facile, and flexible. (Riessman 1962: 72-73)

Riessman also noted that with these characteristics, potential creativity of such persons often fails to materialize because of verbal difficulties. With reference to the items above, many can be related to simulations, notably items one through six. Moreover, students who possess these characteristics often feel oppressed by the tedium of a school environment where nearly all criteria of achievement are based on symbolic learning and the ability to comprehend the printed page. The obligation to read simulation instructions is no different, but if that hurdle can be successfully met, the student has opportunity to do what he may most desire — to be someone else, somewhere else doing something else. Involved in a role that he understands, the student can exercise skills and latent ideas in a non-literary context that bring recognizable rewards from his peer group.

All students seem to eventually make their way to similar discoveries about the roles they play, the decisions to be rendered, the strategies to be developed, and the value of pre-planning in seeking to implement a particular idea. The pace of discovery does present some problems, for there seems to be an inverse relationship between the length of time a simulation can be profitably run and the standardized or normative performance levels of the students involved. The more academically oriented students get to the objectives quickly and can become bored with further extension of the simulation run. Others go more slowly, but they derive equal benefit and enjoyment. If there is a rule of thumb, it is more valuable to attempt to get round the boredom and frustration of an able student than to terminate a simulation too quickly.

When a simulation run is finished, a perplexing question remains to the teacher. Has the simulation had any impact on student values? It would be facetious to anticipate a thoroughgoing transformation of attitudes as a result of playing only one simulation or even several interrelated simulations. But the volume of comments collected over a period of years indicates that students do experience identifiable challenges to reassess previous ideas and come to a more positive regard for African peoples. The potential for such change is greatest when the instructor conducting the simulation pursues a meaningful discussion of culture norms by integrating the simulation experience with other materials on

Africa. If such discussion stresses the contrast between Africa and America the pay-off is much greater. The conclusion is that building cultural limitations into the simulation stimulates student perception of how the values of African culture both enhance and restrict the responses that the non-Westerner can make to social situations requiring a decision.

THE CONTENT OF AFRICAN STUDIES SIMULATIONS

The curriculum used to teach about Africa must, of necessity, be selective. The limits of time do not permit instructors to explore all the facets of African life except in narrowly defined and rigorously demanding graduate seminars. The challenge is to make the curriculum comprehensive without being superficial yet still remaining meaningful within the limits of time allowed. Curriculum materials must, therefore, be chosen so that they provide conceptual knowledge about Africa and its peoples. This conceptual knowledge must then be made intelligible to students through reference to the student's own awareness of reality.

Experimentation and considerable frustration eventually led to the elaboration of the following list of subject areas that could be effectively incorporated into *The Africana Simulations*

1. Climate
2. Colonialism
3. Colonial conflicts
4. Economy – modern
5. Economy – traditional
6. Foreign policy
7. Geography
8. Military affairs
9. Racialism
10. Relation of Africa to America
11. Religious traditions
12. Social systems organization

It is believed that this list or one roughly similar, if built into a simulation, and if absorbed by the student, would offer a reasonably good grasp of both the indigenous and external forces that have shaped present African social, economic, and political environments. Observed sequentially, students can learn how climate and geography influence the ordering of social systems, religious beliefs and traditional economies. This can lead to discussion of why African societies proved relatively weak in reacting to colonial intrusions and colonial policies. The adoption of Western beliefs via missionary religious training and modern economic enterprise helped create the conflicts that culminated in independence. The latter stage was assisted through the intervention of foreign policies of other nations. In the modern era, strategic considerations, foreign policy, and economic development continue to influence Africa along with the old social systems, tribal conflict and belief systems of pre-colonial days. The one topic not fitted in precisely is "relation of Africa to America" in which the teacher uses the concept of America as "the first new nation" from which to draw parallels between the United States and the new states in Africa.

The manner in which a student is introduced to these various topic areas was described earlier when discussing the need to provide a volume of information in the simulation context. If an instructor plays but one simulation, nearly all of the above topics could be introduced. The value of playing several simulations lies in the reinforcement of knowledge by overlapping ideas about Africa. To assist the teacher in identifying where overlap and the opportunity for reinforcement occur, simulations ought to include an instructional manual that identifies references from *Player Books* of different simulations under a specific topic area of discussion. Using the example shown in Table 18-2, it is evident that all four references discuss the role of a cash economy and its impact on African life.

To develop the appropriate discussion for the references noted, the instructional manual accompanying a simulation should also provide an outline of major points to be brought to a student's attention. Then after drawing a reference to a group of

TABLE 18-2:
PLAYER BOOK REFERENCES FROM THE "AFRICANA"
SIMULATIONS FOR USE IN POST-SIMULATION DISCUSSIONS

Simulation:	Marginal Color-coded Reference:	Simulation Excerpt
KUTIISHA	41	". . . You are now wage-earning, tax-paying urbanites."
KISASA	15	"for this work you have been paid in money, a strange new thing for you, but you have quickly found out what that money will buy. . ."
UHURU	35	". . . your fathers required you to earn money so that younger brothers and sisters could go to school. . . In five years your income has risen from $70 to $400. . ."
MANENO	6	"One of the reasons for the need of development funds is that the Baseru in Upesi want the government to have an 8% a year growth rate. . . ."

From *The Instructional Manual* and the Player Books for the "Africana Simulations" phrases in one or more simulation player books, the instructor has ready access to a discussion note similar to the following:

> A student should be aware of the outcomes of economic change introduced by Europeans. As Africans were forced to labor for low wages in a money economy while experiencing a growth in the desire for Western goods, they found they could not force wage increases without organizing into unions. This was particularly the case after World War II when inflation was world wide and cost of living indexes rose tremendously for Africans entering the wage economy. With independence, the burden of economic development shifted to the national leaders with too little money, too few natural resources, inadequate power resources, and demands from a rapidly growing population, more than half under the age of 20. For each leader there is the choice between welfare or industrial development. This is absolutely essential since internal resources rarely generate more than enough revenues to meet recurrent expenditures alone. To make available funds go further, national leaders have laid great stress on the need for cooperation and the institution of co-operatives as a means of speeding development. (from *The Director's Manual*)

If all the ideas in the above paragraph were effectively communicated to a student, his understanding of problems of modernizing economies would be quite good. The greatest value of having readily available discussion outlines for topics about Africa is that the instructor need not play every simulation if time does not permit. Students could play one simulation to get the feel of a particular set of roles and then just read the other accompanying *Player Books* which describe different simulations and provide a volume of information to be used in classroom discussion. In this way, simulation materials are part of the basic curriculum whether the simulation is actually played or not.

AFRICAN STUDIES SIMULATIONS
AND OTHER CURRICULUM MATERIALS

A final consideration in the discussion of simulations as tools for teaching is the relation of such exercises to other curriculum materials. In this area, the instructor has virtually unlimited latitude, though much is dependent on the grade level being taught. If the simulations are meant to be used at the ninth grade level, the non-Western studies year in New York state schools, for example, then the accompanying materials can be a relatively simple type of standard textbook. As students at higher levels become involved, instructors could usefully employ Bohannan and Curtin's *Africa and the Africans,* Hodgkin's *Nationalism in Co-*

lonial Africa and perhaps Wallerstein's *The Politics of Independence.* The introduction of other types of materials is also easily accomplished, and previous experience has shown that the use of the simulations in conjunction with the Achebe novels, *Things Fall Apart, No Longer at Ease* and *A Man of the People* provides an especially rich field for discussion and commentary.

At the college level, the employment of more sophisticated texts would be standard. The use of Doro and Stultz, *Governing in Black Africa* and Apter's *Politics of Modernization* can be integrated effectively with the content of simulation materials. Each level of instruction governs the degree of analytical complexity that will be introduced. For example, a ninth grade teacher might use a simulation like *Kisasa* only to stress certain aspects of communal life. At the college level, the same simulation can be used as a take-off for discussion of agnatic descent, lineage relationships, ascription versus achievement in traditional societies and the contrast between segmental, pyramidal, and hierarchical systems of social organization. In this sense, simulations are both teachers of all levels and ability groups and catalysts for learning a great deal about Africa.

THE CONSTRUCTION OF
AFRICAN STUDIES SIMULATION MATERIALS

The designer of simulations confronts a series of critical questions as he sets about his task: these questions and their answers will significantly influence the utility of the final product. In designing and testing simulations for African studies, it was determined that these tools should be useful to various ability levels starting at the ninth grade. Experience had shown that college students did not resent the simplicity of simulation designs constructed for lower level students, and that even these simple formats could be effectively used to initiate the most complex type of discussion. This focus on the secondary level was also selected to relieve some of the major criticisms about simulations that are expressed by high school teachers.

The potential audience is the key to successful simulation construction when resolving questions on the level of complexity to be built into the rules of the simulation. For example, the *Inter-Nation Simulation Kit* (Science Research Associates) is listed as being for high school students and adults, and it is excellent for college level classes. But it is an extra-ordinarily daring high school teacher with the brightest of students who would attempt to use it at the secondary level. In its present form, the simulation would be shunned by the vast majority of social studies teachers and could not be considered for use by students reading behind grade level. This one example has relevance to all simulations, and generates the guideline that if a simulation cannot be easily and confidently used by an instructor to teach students about a portion of the real world, then the design should be reconsidered.

REAL OR HYPOTHETICAL ENVIRONMENTS

A simulation designer can choose either to simulate reality or abstract from reality certain descriptive features. Since most secondary school Africa units do not have time for analysis in depth, hypothetical formats that incorporate many facets of Africa are more appropriate. With college level students it might be possible to simulate the Congo-Katanga crisis, the Biafran War, the Unilateral Declaration of Independence in Rhodesia or any of a number of events, but for students who must learn many concepts in limited time frames, a hypothetical format is more useful.

If the designer is constructing a series of interrelated simulations, as was the case with the *Africana Simulations,* it is useful to construct a single game board that can be used for all the simulations in the set. For the "disadvantaged" learner with his visual physical strengths, this is a helpful tool. The accompanying map (Figure 18-1) describes the condition of two imaginary countries, Upesi ("hurry up") and Bahati ("tranquility"). In this case personal familiarity with East Africa builds in a geographic bias of physical features suggesting a combination of Kenya, Uganda, Tanzania, Malawi, Zimbabwe, and Zambia. It is a recognized deficiency that the simulations do not incorporate the distinctive physical characteristics of the Guinea Coast of West Africa. However, even this hypothetical environment permits introduction of discussion on geographic formations, climate, ecology, and the resultant influence on social organization. Also, the choice of a not too thinly disguised East African focus of the equatorial region encourages discussion of mixed ethnic stocks and varied patterns of segmental and monarchical social organization. Simply, the area is attractive for hypothetical simulation.

HOW MANY ROLES?

The number of people to be involved is a choice that is conditioned by the average size of the social studies class. Eighteen to twenty-five players is suggested with fewer being more advisable. Limiting the number of roles offers the instructor several advan-

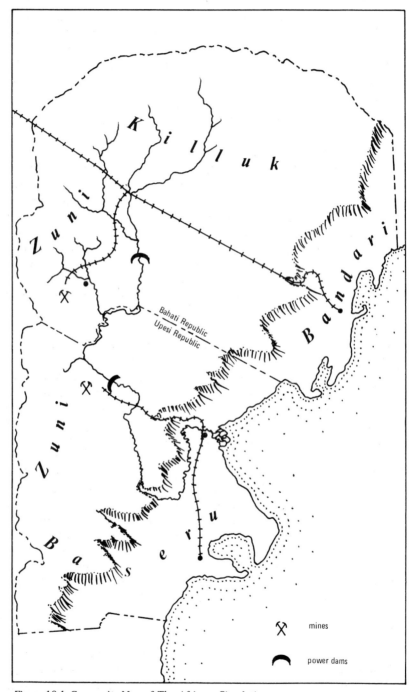

Figure 18-1. Composite Map of *The Africana Simulations.*

tages. Extra students can be used as observers recording the play of the various participating groups actively involved in the simulation. Other students can be used by the instructor to help run the simulation. Both assistants and observers often have a great deal to contribute to post-simulation discussion since they may have been aware of what was actually happening while individual players could only see their specific interests. These additional students are also useful as a reservoir of understudies who can step into various roles when key players inevitably become ill or do not attend school during a crucial part of the simulation run. Someone is always getting his yearbook picture taken, or having a special dentist appointment. Accounting for this contingency in advance pays great dividends, and usually a student who has been a reporter/observer of a set of roles can step into active participation without difficulty.

In establishing the individual roles for the simulation, it is useful to put players in groups of at least two, as indicated in Table 18-3. This permits students to work out strategy jointly, with some feedback on their ideas while playing the simulation. Also, it permits one of the group to move about conducting the bargaining while his counterpart enters into negotiation with players that may come to their assigned place in the simulation room. Use of individuals acting alone tends to fragment communication within the simulation-run and results in a loss of information as to what actually happened when students start to discuss the simulation at the conclusion of the run.

CONTROL OVER SIMULATION OPERATIONS

Simulation designers can create highly active and dynamic formats, or limit the actual movement of the players greatly. Move ment permits player inter-action and is thought to be valuable. However, requiring one player in each two person group to be

TABLE 18-3:
LISTING OF ROLES FOR "STAGE II" OF THE KUTIISHA SIMULATION

Colonial Governor	Council of Clan Elders (3)
Chief Native Commissioner (optional)	UN Trusteeship Council
Minister for the Colonies	Representative
Secretary of State for the Colonies	Bahati African Democratic
Major General of the Army	Union Officers (2)
Lt. Colonel of the Army	Bahati Trade Union Congress
European Traders Association (2)	Officers (2)
Missionary Alliance (2)	Bahati League of Urban Welfare
	Officers (2)

always at his assigned place reduces confusion. The reporter/ observer assists the instructor at this point in insuring that players conform to this rule. It is this one rule which is most difficult for students at any grade level to obey. The excitement and urgency of the simulation causes them to forget to report back to their counterpart as enthusiasm for negotiation mounts. Their concern for the substance of decision overrules interest in simulation regulations, and the instructor and his aides must exercise strenuous efforts to control this aspect of the action.

How much movement is built into the simulation is important in encouraging teachers to even attempt simulations. Amidst virtually uncontrolled movement, the classroom appears to be in chaos (actually it is not), and is seen by the teacher as the antithesis of what a classroom ought to look like. Striking an effective balance on movement and restraint to make the simulation orderly while not compromising its substance is a valuable goal of the simulation designer.

LENGTH OF SIMULATION OPERATIONS

If the instructor is only going to spend a maximum of 40% of his instructional time conducting a simulation, this means the design of the simulation must permit it to be played within roughly 160 to 320 minutes, or five to ten class periods. This assumes a class period of approximately fifty minutes where experience has shown that absolutely nothing happens during the first ten minutes of the class. The exhilaration of changing classes, talking in hallways and interrupting routine guarantee this irreducible minimum of lag time before the instructor can take up the business of teaching. It may be possible to play simulations without interruption, but the standard procedure will probably dictate use of normal class time; run-time for a simulation should account for the realities of life in the schools.

The sequences for the minimum playing times of the four African studies simulations are shown in the following table. It is believed that spending any less time would result in not deriving substantial benefit from the simulation. It is possible to design mini-role plays that can be conducted in the space of a single class period, but the level of interaction among players is greatly reduced and only a tiny fraction of "reality" is thus "simulated." With the possible exception of the *Kisasa* simulation, it is felt that the playing times listed below should be doubled in conducting the simulation and some additional time should be given to post-simulation evaluation.

TABLE 18-4
MINIMUM TIME SCHEDULES FOR THE OPERATION
OF FOUR AFRICAN STUDIES SIMULATIONS

	Kutiisha-I	*Kutiisha-II*	*Kisasa*	*Uhuru*	*Maneno*
Orientation	40 min.	40 min.	40 min.	40 min.	40 min.
Playing Time	40 min.	80 min.	80 min.	80 min.	80 min.
Evaluation	40 min.	40 min.	40 min.	40 min.	40 min.
	120 min.	160 min.	160 min.	160 min.	160 min.

The times which simulations list for orientation are really the tip of the iceberg. It takes only a few minutes to distribute Player Books and assign the various roles. After several days, a full class period can be devoted to clarifying roles and procedures in the simulation. But students should be aware that much study must be given to the simulation prior to commencement of play. This raises the issue of pre-simulation communication among the players. Since it is inevitable, it is better to build that feature into the simulation and then capitalize on it by reminding students that if they are not really prepared when the simulation starts, some of the other players will overwhelm the lazy ones through the implementation of fully developed strategies.

The post-simulation evaluation and discussion should be as rich or richer than the simulation exercise itself in terms of developing student understanding of the environment just portrayed. This, of course, depends on the instructor. Since the simulations are part of the basic curriculum, the discussion could run longer than the minimum time that might be suggested for the whole operation. Instructors should be encouraged to make this period as long as time permits or until ideas and insights developed in the simulation have been fully explored.

THE CHOICE OF BARGAINING SEQUENCES

There is no more challenging aspect of simulation design than the development of bargaining procedures and the elaboration of the rules of the game. If the designer hopes that a simulation will have wide utility, he should opt for maximum simplicity so that students can work comfortably within the simulation format and so that the instructor conducting the simulation will not feel threatened by extraordinarily complex rules which both inhibit play and cause students to raise questions that the teacher is not prepared to answer.

The key to the bargaining procedure is the choice of the bargaining unit. The dynamic element of simulation arises from differing interests among the players. Each player or group of players is attempting to gain either voluntary compliance toward or coercive respect for a particular set of interests. In the "real" world, the ways of doing this are multiple, but in the select portion of reality that exists in simulations, a unit of exchange has to be created. It can be money, points, or any symbolic commodity, but it must be there, easily identifiable, and made valuable through the rules built into the game. The votes, dollars, points or units should be easily exchangeable and, if necessary, convertible into alternative forms. For example, if the prime bargaining unit is "points" and the simulation also permits use of dollars, then the basic conversion ratio should be explicitly established.

A demonstration of the types of bargaining procedures that can be used in simulation development is contained in the four *Africana* simulations. *Kisasa* involves discussion with a voting referendum at the conclusion. *Uhuru* uses points as a bargaining unit which can then be voted either in support of or opposition to the head-of-state.* *Maneno* employs a multi-purpose, convertible "unit" that determines outcomes along with voting by the players in the game.** *Kutiisha* does not utilize a specific unit, rather it tightly controls player decision options, proceeds along a "decision tree" and culminates with the instructor's announcement of decision outcomes.*** The latter format has a special appeal in allowing the instructor to retain a position of great significance in the simulation through announcement of "bargaining round termination outcomes" which the players will not have known in advance. Only at that point are students made aware of the full consequences of their decisional choices.

The conclusion on bargaining procedures is that with modest effort it is possible to create meaningful bargaining rules that will not intimidate the potential user. The easier the bargaining procedure is to deal with, the more enjoyable the simulation becomes, and the full potential of the content of the simulation stands a greater likelihood of being realized. The simulation exercise where the bargaining procedures impede fulfilment of the goals fails in its primary educational purpose. Preservation of simplicity is paramount to effective use of simulations at the secondary level.

---

*The bargaining procedures for *Uhuru* are a simplification of some of the processes used by Scott, Lucas, and Lucas in "Simuland". See their *Simulation and National Development,* (New York: John Wiley and Sons, 1966)

**Maneno* involves a drastically simplified version of the *Inter-Nation Simulation Kit* in terms of "unit" convertibility with consequent increase in the complexity of player "voting" to build in reference to ethnicity. See *Internation-Simulation Kit.* (Chicago: Science Research Associates)

***Kutiisha* has been designed using the decision-tree format with the intent that at some point it can be rewritten into a computer based game for one player in the role of a Colonial Governor.

EVALUATION OF SIMULATION EXPERIENCES

Since the subject of Africa is so completely new to most students, the designer of such simulations is well-advised to limit the goals he seeks to fulfil through use of any one simulation exercise. Three or four primary goals for an individual simulation are sufficient. For example, the *Uhuru* simulation has only three basic goals: (1) to demonstrate how ethnic (tribal) conflict can inhibit development, (2) to demonstrate the burdens sustained by new rulers in resource-short countries of Africa, and (3) to demonstrate the difficulties of seeking to maintain civilian democracies in the new states of Africa. The simulation designer can help the teacher by incorporating explicit lists of goals and offering suggestions how post-simulation discussion can insure these goals are fulfilled. Undoubtedly, the instructor will discover socio-psychological by-products of the simulation experience, particularly for the "disadvantaged" learner, but the primary thrust of the evaluative period will be adequately served if the instructor can have some assurance that at least the basic goals have been met.

CONCLUSION

While this discussion has given perhaps inordinate reference to personal experiences in the use of simulations to teach African studies, it is felt that this was the most useful method of building a case for the expanded utilization of simulations in non-Western studies. By drawing attention to the important problems that compromise the use of simulations, other simulation designers can avoid the mistakes that have been made in the past. The building into a non-Western simulation of a volume of substantive materials is necessary for the players and encourages the use of simulations as integral curriculum components rather than supplements. It is appropriate to speculate that the simulation package of several exercises could be employed usefully to provide teaching tools on North Africa, the Middle East, South Asia, Southeast Asia, East Asia, and Latin America. Once students experiment with simulations as a tool of learning, they will readily involve themselves in these exercises, and instructors can anticipate a shortening of orientation time and a rising level of smooth sophisticated simulation play.

The experience of five years has demonstrated that no one need feel afraid of using such materials, that teaching can be more effective through their use, and that students are exhilarated by the introduction of such exercises. Given the student's need to know about Africa and other non-Western areas of the globe, a need that combines factual understanding with affective sensitivity, the use of the well-designed simulation presents an extraordinarily useful tool for getting past the limitations of one's own value perspective to a fuller appreciation of the world's which most Americans have only recently discovered.

19

What are the Needs of Modern Manufacturing in Africa South of the Sahara? A Geographically Based Inquiry Unit

JACK M. SHERIDAN
University of Houston

INTRODUCTION

An inquiry unit usually begins with a question or problem relevant to student interest and ability. Students next list possible solutions, answers, or hypotheses and then collect and interpret information to test these tentative ideas. Their original notions are restated according to the collected data, and as such, can be tentative conclusions. Given new information, conclusions are further modified and ultimately developed into abstractions which can be used to explain and predict events or situations.

Hence, one general objective of the inquiry unit is to help students learn a rational means of developing validated thought. The learning environment is arranged so students use a systematic process to answer questions and solve problems. As there is continued use of the process, they acquire a deeper understanding of it and there is transfer of the operation to everyday life situations. Maintenance of our society requires individuals to be critical thinkers and effective decision makers—qualities which are fostered through the use of the inquiry-centered unit.

A parallel objective to process development is a deeper understanding and broader application of subject matter. Teachers will use inquiry because there is a deeper student involvement with content. Students must use facts and ideas to test hypotheses and draw conclusions, and under such circumstances, they see the meaning of factual data. Then they are more apt to apply this data again in new situations.

333

DEVELOPING A QUESTION FOR CLASSROOM INQUIRY

One of the teacher's first tasks in planning an inquiry unit is that of developing a question or problem for directing investigation, while keeping general goals in mind. At this time, many teachers reflect on what students have already studied and attempt to build a situation in which previously drawn conclusions can be applied or further tested. The following statement by a teacher illustrates this building notion:

> During our study of the United States and Canada, we found much of the population oriented to waterbodies and rivers. Do you suppose this idea holds true for other places in the world? What about Africa? Do most of the people in each country live close to rivers and coastlines? Where do the people live?

One inquiry unit is designed to logically follow another, and a final unit in the sequence takes students to a level of formulating generalizations based on all their experiences. More will be said later about structuring inquiry units.

Often a question or problem for inquiry develops as the instructor reads in the subject matter he will be teaching. Many times this is the case when a teacher, planning an inquiry unit for the first time, is not sure of the order of things to follow. Interesting information or a discrepant event raises a question in his mind, and he then refines that question for classroom use.

The question for this unit was developed in such a manner. While reading on tropical Africa, the writer became intrigued with how the individual countries are pressing for their own modern economic development. There is a desire to produce more of the commodities they now must import. They want to be less dependent on foreign production and exploitation. Equally of interest is the idea that the process of modernization there cannot be any duplication of what has happened in countries like Britain or the United States. Next came this thought and question: Given (1) a desire for modern economy and (2) physical and cultural differences which negate implementation of foreign modernization models, what should be the nature of future manufacturing development in Africa? Ensuing personal investigation led to the decision of restating the question for directing class inquiry. The specific question for students, then, became as follows:

> What are the needs of modern manufacturing in Africa south of the Sahara? (Exclude the state of South Africa.)

The stated question has relevance for student inquiry in geography classes. The question is timely in terms of current interest in ecology and the concern of some over the possible outcomes of the world movement toward industrialization. Through data collection, students will encounter information and ideas drawn from physical and cultural geography. Specifically stated, students will develop increased knowledge relative to these topic areas:

1. The economic and non-economic factors of the geography of manufacturing
2. The physical geography of Africa south of the Sahara
3. The available resources for economic development in the region
4. The present levels of modernization in the region
5. The patterns of spatial interaction within the region
6. The procedure for drawing a valid conclusion.

As a result of their total research activity, the students can make the following abstractions:

1. The countries of tropical Africa lack in terms of the basic needs for developing large scale modern manufacturing.
2. High level production of manufactured goods will be dependent on improved conditions with respect to fuel and power sources, markets, skilled labor, capital, and transportation and communication.
3. In order to achieve these improved conditions, special means or new kinds of economic institutions may need to be developed.
4. The nature of these unique ways may vary from place to place, depending on specific and general needs.

DEVELOPING THE INQUIRY UNIT

The specific objectives are built into the following section, which is a step-by-step account of how the unit can be developed. The procedure is organized according to an inquiry process. Little reference is given to lengths of time, for experience has shown that time varies with individual groups of students. To further clarify the nature and the scope and sequence of the unit, a brief statement for each phase is given here:

1. In the introduction—motivation phase—students are introduced to some concepts pertaining to the geography of manufacturing. Students develop an understanding of these ideas as they consider the possibility of a new manufacturing facility in their own area. Concept development is fostered as they discuss the advantages and disadvantages of locating the firm in their locale. After this discussion the teacher begins to have students focus on modern

manufacturing in less-developed nations. The purpose of this initial phase is to arouse interest and build background for the upcoming problem.

2. During the second phase, actual inquiry begins with a definition of the problem and the statement of hypotheses. Students switch their attention from the needs of manufacturing in their own locale to a consideration of needs that will have to be met as tropical African nations press for home-owned modern manufacturing. They hypothesize as to the needs of modern manufacturing if the nations are to have increased production of consumer type goods.

3. In the third phase students must test their hypotheses. This is accomplished by having students determine which hypothesized needs remain apparent as they choose locations for some given manufacturing facilities.

4. In the fourth phase students conclude as to the general needs of modern manufacturing in tropical Africa. They change verified hypotheses into conclusions.

5. Finally, in the fifth phase students are given new data through a case study. Their ideas regarding modern manufacturing in tropical Africa are modified according to this new data and they begin to think in terms of specific needs for specific places.

INTRODUCTION–MOTIVATION AND BACKGROUND PHASE

Teacher	*Students*
1. Begin by asking, "If a steel manufacturing firm is contemplating the building of a branch plant near our area, what are some things (factors) their officials may need to consider before they make any serious efforts toward actual construction?"	Students may respond with ideas such as availability of land, adequacy of transportation and attitudes of local citizens. (At this time it is not necessary for them to state all factors relative to the geography of manufacturing.)
Note: The teacher may choose to start with something other than steel manufacturing, depending on the	

nature of the local situation. (There already may be a steel mill in the vicinity.) It might be best if the teacher chooses a hypothetical facility that is not present in their locale: auto assembly, mobile home construction, etc.

2. Introduce concepts relative to the geography of manufacturing. Rather than a straight lecture, one can say, "If a large manufacturing firm is considering a move to our area, here are some points they will need to think about."

They compare the given ideas with their ideas stated earlier regarding the steel mill.

Relate and discuss the following:
Proximity to production materials
Proximity to market
Proximity to fuel and power
Proximity to transportation routes
Availability of manpower and skills
Availability of capital.
Here are additional concepts often given:
Availability of adequate water supply
Availability of land
Taxation policies
Cost of living
Disposal of waste
Subsidies
Needs and interests of the people.

3. Given the above back-
ground concepts, let them
discuss how they would feel
toward the development of
a major steel works in their
town.

They have an open discussion
and informal debate regarding
the issue. (A number may be
negative toward having more
industry in their area.)

4. Point out that in spite of
current conservation interests, a number of countries
are pressing for modernization through increased
economic production. They
are seeking better living
through industrial growth.

Students may react with statements and questions. Some of
the statements may express
concern with regard to disrup-
ting environment and culture.

Exemplify briefly by noting
the Volta River Project
sixty miles north of Accra
in Ghana. The project has
involved the construction of
a dam, powerplant, a trans-
mission grid, and a related
aluminum smelter for ex-
ploitation of nearby extensive bauxite deposits. It represents a massive effort toward achieving modernity.

DEFINING THE PROBLEM AND HYPOTHESIZING

Objective:
    Given geographical data on Africa south of the Sahara, stu-
    dents can hypothesize the needs of modern manufacturing in
    that part of Africa (i.e., there is need for a larger number of
    skilled laborers.)
Materials:
    Open to any resource materials which give accurate physical
    and cultural data on Africa (See the following development for
    specific kinds of materials which can be used.)

Teacher

Students

1. State that developing modern manufacturing in Africa

is not simply a matter of introducing Western technology and know-how. Point out, for example, some of the many problems which are related to manufacturing in tropical realms: (1) copper circuits tend to corrode rapidly, (2) most lubricants used in machinery need a higher melting point and (3) micro-organisms quickly infest stored goods. Air conditioning is possible; however, it alone adds considerably to the cost of operation and hence to the cost of goods.

2. Next ask, "If African nations are to have increased manufacture of consumer type goods, which needs will first have to be met?"
or
"What are the needs of modern manufacturing in Africa south of the Sahara?"

3. The first step after definition of the problem is to have students secure information about the land and people of tropical Africa. This information will be necessary data in the process of building hypotheses regarding the needs of manufacturing. Having students gather the information can take place in many ways, using a variety of source materials.

Students secure and record information. Some may choose to organize the information through the use of broad headings:

Physical realm
Cultural realm

Other students may prefer a more definitive system of keeping their information organized. One such system is according to the transparency topics seen on the left.

The writer has relied on transparencies and overlays for helping students acquire knowledge and ideas.* The following transparencies appeared to be most useful:

Relief and landforms
Natural vegetation
Climate
Soils
Political
Population
Diets and health
Literacy
Minerals
Railroads
Highways
Agriculture
Industry

Each transparency reveals certain factual information, and through interpretation, additional information becomes available. For example, one transparency reveals that subsistence and semi-subsistence forms of agriculture are still prevalent over very large areas. Ensuring interpretation and research by the class led them to relate such forms of agriculture to low per capita income and insufficient crop yields.

The teacher may present additional information through lectures and read-

Some information can be recorded on outline maps.

Note: Interest can wane quickly if the instructor insists on a strict, rigid system of gathering and organizing information. In the end, it may work best if the students have a "loose" body of information. They will not need a massive block of data that takes six weeks to collect. Experience has shown (1) that this information gathering step should proceed rather rapidly (four to eight days) and (2) that interaction between teacher and students is necessary for giving certain factual data more meaning.

*Lawrence Latour, *Alpha Map Transparencies: Africa,* (Boston: Allyn and Bacon, Inc., 1967). See also Chapter 12 (ed.)

ings. For example, the writer directed a question relative to the nature of African rivers and then read a short passage telling about them. (Murphy 1971:477) With the use of a rail network transparency, more data was given as to how Africans have attempted to cope with the fact that most of their rivers are broken by falls and rapids.

Allow time during class periods for students to report information they have secured on their own time in the library or outside of school.

4. Having secured basic information, students convene as a large group and infer or hypothesize the general needs of modern manufacturing in Africa south of the Sahara, excluding South Africa.

As a class group, students discuss, further interpret, and analyze the data so they can hypothesize the needs.

Example: The group has found that per capita income is low by U.S. standards; hence, they infer that money probably is not available to spend for large amounts of consumer goods. From this they hypothesize that there is a need for creating local markets for goods manufactured in tropical Africa.

After several class meetings, a list of hypotheses may appear as follows:

1. There is need for improved transportation and communication.

2. There is need for additional power sources.
3. There is need for a larger supply of skilled labor and clerical workers.
4. There is need for new sources of capital.
5. There is need for creating markets for the goods.
6. There is need for improving the quality and efficiency of agriculture. (They must be able to feed more people, secure money for industrial investment, and release people from land to work in industry.)
7. There is need for means of informing the people as to the total meaning and impact of massive industrial development.

Note: The above list is according to one group of students. Another group may develop a slightly different listing. There is no magical number of hypotheses; however, experience has shown that students invariably hypothesize needs regarding fuel and power sources, markets, skilled labor, capital, and transportation and communication.

TESTING THE HYPOTHESES

Objectives:

Given a map of Africa south of the Sahara, each student can mark a specific place which he considers the most ideal for a chosen manufacturing facility.

At the same time, each student can indicate in writing which of the hypothesized needs are apparent at the place he has marked.

Materials:
Open to any resource materials which give accurate physical and cultural data on Africa.

Teacher	*Students*
1. To test the hypotheses, assign the following task to each student: According to your personal interests, choose a manufacturing facility listed below and locate it at a specific place somewhere in Africa south of the Sahara, excluding South Africa. Try to find what you believe is the most ideal site for your facility.	The student now inquires into the physical and cultural geography of each country so that he can find the most suitable place for his chosen manufacturing facility. A criterion for choosing the best place can be the given list of factors pertaining to the geography of manufacturing. It may be difficult to find an ideal place for any one of the given facilities.

a. Manufacture of career apparel for management personnel and factory workers. (Think in terms of large quantity production.)
b. Manufacture of household items made of wood (furniture, kitchen aids, etc.).
c. Manufacture of internal combustion engines to power construction equipment (actual manufacture and assembly).
d. Manufacture of rail transport devices (signal equipment, switches, couplers, etc.).
e. Manufacture of simple toys (building blocks, cloth dolls).

In order to secure information regarding specific places, the student may need to bring many sources together. At this time the classroom probably should be open and less structured, for it is necessary that the student be allowed to move about in search of specific information.

Example: After examining a map of Africa, a student decides to explore his notion that Matadi (Zaire) may be the best place for locating an assembly plant for sub-compact autos and mini-trucks. He may start with encyclopedic sources, general reference works, and periodicals (*National Geographic, Journal of Geography,* etc.) in the school library. Back in the classroom

f. Assembly plant for subcompact autos and minitrucks (parts from European manufacturer).

Consider that initial financing may come from outside sources; however, plan so the facility eventually will be locally owned and operated. The market for the produced items is to be mainly in tropical Africa.

After you have selected the most ideal place, list any needs or shortcomings which are evident. Develop your list of needs in the same manner as our earlier stated hypotheses (i.e. lack of local markets for the manufactured goods).

he joins in a small group that is once more going through the transparency sets. The student decides to consider another city after he notes there is a larger market in West Africa. Also, his instructor's college text indicates a shortage of level ground for industrial development.

The student finds the place he believes most suitable and then identifies the hypothesized needs which are evident at the place.

Example: A student may choose Point Noire in the Republic of the Congo as a site for the manufacture of wooden household items because there is a nearby source of wood. Point Noire also is a shipping port for logs and there are some wood processing plants in the vicinity; therefore, an adequate labor supply may be present. On the other hand, an adequate power supply will be a problem, at least until the proposed dam is constructed on the Koulilou River. A market for household items may exist throughout tropical Africa; however, literature indicates that surface transport presently is inadequate for shipment of bulk goods.

The student's work verifies two hypotheses which have been stated:
There is need for improved transportation and communication.
There is need for additional power sources.

2. During the above individual inquiry, the teacher can opt to have students base their locational decision to some extent on C.E. Black's schema for determining a nation's level of modernization. Black discusses four phases of modernization through which societies pass. (Black 1967:67-68)

"the challenge of modernity —the initial confrontation of a society within its traditional framework of knowledge, with modern ideas and institutions, and the emergency of advocates of modernity.

the consolidation of modernizing leadership —the transfer of power from traditional to modernizing leaders . . .

economic and social transformation —the development of economic growth and social change to a point where a society is transformed from a predominantly rural and agrarian

Using Black's schema may help some students decide whether or not they would locate their manufacturing facility in a given country.

Example: A student may decide against locating the facility in a country which is in the *challenge of modernity stage.* Such a nation probably is lacking in terms of market, labor, energy, and transportation.

way of life to one predominantly urban and industrial

the integration of society —
the phase in which economic and social transformation
produces a fundamental
reorganization of the social
structure throughout the
society."

On pages 90-94 in his book,
Black categorizes each
country according to the
above descriptions.

DRAWING CONCLUSIONS

Objective:
    Following their individual work in testing hypotheses, students
    reconvene as a large group and draw conclusions as to the
    general needs of modern manufacturing in tropical Africa.
Materials:
    Those materials students have found most useful in their in-
    dividual efforts.

Teacher	*Students*
1. Begin by asking, "As a re-sult of your individual re-search, what can we con-clude about the needs of modern manufacturing in Africa south of the Sahara?"	In the large group, each stu-dent reports the needs which are evident at the place he has located for his manufacturing facility.
	They compare individual find-ings to determine which needs stand out or are evident in most cases.
	Students then draw conclu-sions as to the general needs. Their concluding statements may appear much like the first two abstractions given earlier:

1. The countries of tropical Africa lack in terms of the basic needs for developing large scale modern manufacturing.

2. High level production of manufactured goods will be dependent on improved conditions with respect to fuel and power sources, markets, skilled labor, capital, and transportation and communication.

DEVELOPING ADDITIONAL IDEAS IN LIGHT OF
CONCLUSIONS AND NEW DATA

Objective:

Given a case study of the actual development of a manufacturing facility in Uganda, each student can identify in writing specific operations or institutions which would have to be implemented to insure economical, high level production in the facility he located.

Note: This final episode can also serve as an evaluation segment of the unit. Each student applies his understanding of (1) the needs of modern manufacturing and (2) the geography of a specific place in proposing operations or institutions which will make production feasible in the plant he has located.

Materials:

Basic reference: Larimore (1964:146-153) Those materials students have found most useful in their individual efforts and a large detailed map of Africa.

Teacher	*Students*
1. Relate information about the Nyanza Textile Mill at Jinja, Uganda, at the source of the White Nile River:	Students take notes on how the Nyanza operation was developed so that certain needs were met.
In 1949 the Nyanza Textile Industries was organized to	They will note that the Jinja situation is an illustration of

manufacture cotton fabrics for local consumption. Initial financing was through a British firm, with the Uganda Development Corporation (a government agency) contributing a lesser amount. By 1957 the British investors had sold out to the Uganda agency because of continued financial losses. Actual production began in 1956, and by 1959, three-shift continuous production was attained. Accumulated losses of one million dollars were paid off by 1961.

To insure that the mill would benefit local economy, the following conditions were established:

a. The firm would use only Uganda grown cotton.
b. Only African labor would be recruited.
c. The factory would be located on the highway and the railway which link Jinja with points in Kenya and Tanzania.
d. The factory would be built near the Owen Falls Power Station, which would supply electric power at a special rate.
e. The mill would have unlimited use of water from the White Nile.
f. In East Africa only the Nyanza firm would be licensed to manufacture the special means or new economic institutions implemented to insure economic production. Without these added features, the basic needs would remain. Students may view some of the features as being contrary to free enterprise.

cotton. (Since 1959 this is no longer true.)

g. The East African Common Market would be open to all products from the Nyanza firm, and special tariffs would protect against cheap imports.

To attain local financing, the government secured control over export earnings from the sale of cotton and coffee. Following World War II, the prices of these two commodities had risen steadily on the world market; however, the government did not allow the farmers' income to rise with world prices. Thus, the government accumulated surplus monies for investment in manufacturing.

2. Given the Nyanza Textile Mill situation, have each student (1) analyze the place he selected for his manufacturing facility and (2) decide what specific features or institutions can be implemented to insure high level production at his facility.

The student again studies the physical and cultural geography of the area in which he located his facility. In writing, he then specifies conditions which may need to be established if his firm is to have continued high production. He can take ideas from the Nyanza situation and modify them for his own situation.

Example: A student has chosen Kamina (Zaire) as a site for the manufacture of rail transport devices. To insure high level production, the following special conditions were proposed:

1. There should be reciprocal trade agreements among tropical African countries. Such agreements would favor the exchange of locally produced goods at prices which are lower than world exchange prices. Zaire then could purchase iron ore (West Africa) and coal at special rates, and would in turn, reduce prices on the transport equipment.

2. There should be a small steel mill constructed. This mill would produce steel for use in making the transport devices and for other industries in tropical Africa. Developmental costs for the mill would be very high; however, special trade agreements similar to the above could be arranged. With steel and rail device production, there would be two-way movement of goods: raw materials (coal and iron ore) moving in and finished materials (steel goods) moving out.

3. There should be a committee formed for extensive planning of an expanded rail transport system throughout tropical Africa. The Kamina industry could then plan their production in accordance with present and future needs.

4. There should be an intensive program for training

supervisory personnel drawn from the local population.

5. There should be special housing provided for workers. The housing should be more than adequate so that workers will want to stay and will take interest in changing to a more industrial society.

3. One way of assigning grades is to divide the class into groups of three and have each group evaluate three papers belonging to other class members. Cut names off of all papers.

The final grade on each paper will represent a group decision.

Student groups will evaluate the feasibility of the ideas expressed by the individual student. Judgments will be made according to how well they believe a student's proposed ideas meet pressing needs. They will consider the "sensibility" of an idea—that is, can the idea actually be implemented? Said another way: Is the proposed idea reasonable in terms of our (the students') knowledge?

At this time the last two abstractions listed earlier will become apparent to the students:

1. In order to achieve improved conditions for modern manufacturing, special means or new kinds of economic institutions may need to be developed.

2. The nature of these unique ways may vary from place to place, depending on specific and general needs.

EXTENDING INQUIRY DEVELOPMENT

This unit leads to a natural development of certain inquiry skills. In the hypothesizing and testing of hypotheses stages, students usually need help in securing information or data. Specific aid needs to be given in terms of using the *Readers' Guide to Periodical Literature,* the card catalog, and the various forms of book indexes. Additional time must be spent in guided reading, for some students still are learning to read for specific information. Students also require time spent in learning to use maps as data sources. The teacher definitely should allow time for this skill development, as there will be loss of interest and frustration when students are rushed.

It is often assumed that the value of inquiry will be cognized as students go through the process. Experience has shown, however, that care should be given in communicating the process as students are using it. The idea is not so much to sell them on a method of inquiry as it is to help them see a means of drawing supported conclusions. To communicate awareness, the instructor can occasionally review what has been happening and then can project ahead to the next operation. An additional means of building awareness is to accept no concluding statement unless the student can support it with data.

Perhaps the best way of advancing the use of process is to provide practice through a series of related inquiry units. When inquiry units are constructed together, students also have a setting in which they can continually test and apply the same ideas; hence, there is a higher level comprehension of subject matter. Beyer (1971: 131-158) indicates three ways of tying inquiry units together so there will be greater understanding of process and content: (1) the additive inquiry structure, (2) the cumulative inquiry structure, and (3) the sequential inquiry structure. The following paragraphs relate examples of each structure, using the above unit as a basic reference.

The additive inquiry framework includes the articulation of a problem; a series of independently taught units in which students apply the inquiry process to that problem; and a final unit in which they generalize in light of findings from each of the units. To exemplify this structure, one can have an introductory unit with a problem such as, "What are the needs of modern manufacturing in less-developed nations?" Then would come the unit given in this paper: "What are the needs of modern manufacturing in tropical Africa?" This same question would be used for regions in Latin America, Southeast Asia, and the Indian Subcontinent.

Finally, students would bring all their findings together and generalize the needs for regions included in their study.

For the cumulative framework there is a succession of units, each building on the one before it and all together culminating with a synthesis of accumulated ideas. In this case, students could start with the question of manufacturing needs in less-developed regions; proceed to the unit on Africa where they would hypothesize and test ideas; continue to other units (Latin America, India, Southeast Asia, etc.) where they would modify, reject or add to the ideas developed in the Africa unit; and finally, end with a unit in which their tested ideas are restated as generalizations.

In the sequential inquiry framework, students first define a problem and examine data so they can hypothesize, test solutions, and develop some possible conclusions. Next small groups of students investigate new data for purposes of further testing the class-drawn conclusions. They reconvene and generalize according to the findings of each small group.

Here the question of the needs of modern manufacturing in tropical Africa could be the main problem. After their intensive study of one area (the Congo Basin) in Africa, students post tentative answers to the question. In small groups they test their tentative notions through studies of other African areas (West Africa, East Africa, etc.). When they feel there is enough supportive data, their tentative answers are changed to generalized statements.

In order to tailor a course of study for a particular group, the instructor can vary any one of the given structures. The main idea is to choose questions or problems which ultimately lead students to more effective thinking and a deeper understanding of pertinent content.

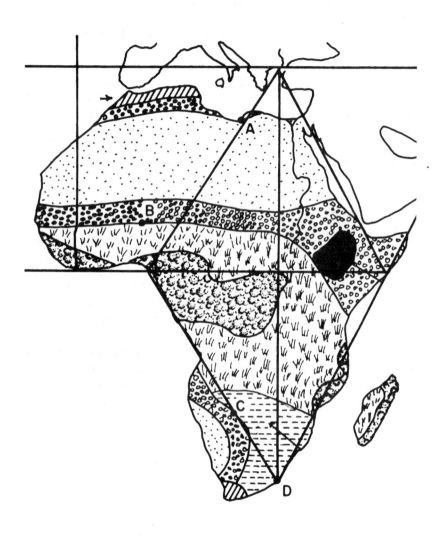

20

The Use of Sketch Maps in Teaching About Africa

JOHN H. WISE
Lakehead University, Ontario

> *So geographers, in Afric-maps,*
> *With savage-pictures fill their gaps;*
> *And o'er uninhabitable downs*
> *Place elephants for want of towns.*
> *Jonathan Swift*

The drawing and use of sketch maps by the teacher and by the individual student can play a very important role in teaching and studying geography. Although the idea is not new, it is especially appropriate to the stimulation, presentation and geographical interpretation of data and ideas concerning Africa during the last quarter of the twentieth century.

A study of professional journals, resource books for geography teachers, and other materials published in the English language throughout this century strongly suggests that the sketch map has increasingly become a distinctive feature or, at least, a desired facet of school geography in several countries, particularly in secondary schools. Generally, however, this has not been the case in American schools. The reasons for this are complex and need not concern us here. Suffice it to say that they probably are linked with: (1) the overall neglect of geography in schools; (2) little sketch map use in many university geography courses; and (3) what McNee (1955:416) has called "a misplaced reverence for the mathematical and mechanical exactness of maps" coupled with "the mistaken belief that great drawing ability is necessary."

THE VALUE OF SKETCH MAPS

The value of sketch maps in geographical education may be associated with seven closely related aspects:

355

(1) sketch maps can be a most concise and effective means of expressing or summarizing certain data, ideas, concepts, relationships or patterns in geographical terms;

(2) sketch maps can be seen to be within the essence of geographical thought and understanding;

(3) the continual drawing of useful sketch maps throughout the grades can save a considerable amount of time which might otherwise be wholly spent upon written or oral expression;

(4) the drawing and use of sketch maps can allow a maximum of individual student involvement, firmly based on the principle of learning-by-doing;

(5) the drawing of effective sketch maps demands that the main points of a topic or problem under consideration be clearly perceived and interpreted geographically;

(6) sketch maps can be an attention-gaining means of reflecting and interpreting up-to-date and reputable newspaper reports, statistics and other material associated with current problems such as the revolution in colonial Guinea-Bissau, the patterns of *apartheid,* or Zambia's access to ocean ports;

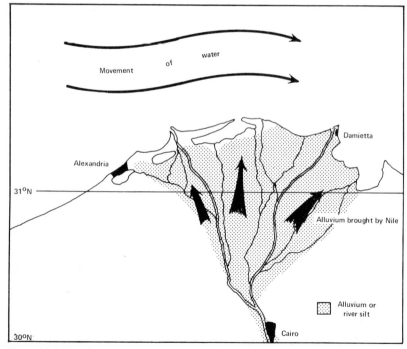

Figure 20-1. Sketch Map to show the Position of Alexandria in Relation to Off-shore Currents near the Nile Delta.

(7) sketch maps, by their very nature, lend themselves readily to relatively recent visual teaching techniques such as the overhead projection of several transparencies placed on top of one another.

CHARACTERISTICS OF AN EFFECTIVE SKETCH MAP

Six inter-related characteristics of an *effective* sketch map are:
(1) A sketch map should be easy to read and simple, emphasizing one geographical point, idea or theme. It should neither be cluttered with irrelevant data, nor be overcrowded in design. An example is seen, for instance, in a map that shows the position of Alexandria in relation to the directions of alluvial deposition and prevailing off-shore currents (Figure 20-1). Good sketch maps need little explanatory writing.

(2) A sketch map should be the outcome of thought to which the map-drawer has contributed, and it should be an adequate instrument for further useful thinking. There is little educational value in a student's copying a textbook or other

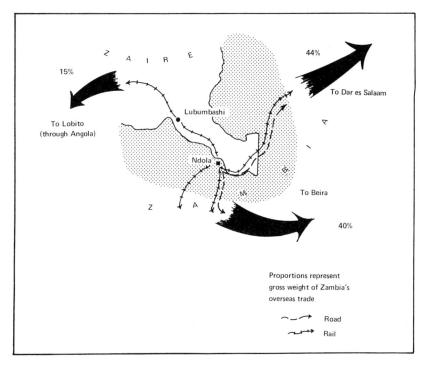

Figure 20-2. Diagram to Show the Export Routes from Zambia to the Coast, 1969.

prearranged sketch map unless, perhaps, it be done upon a transparency or chalkboard for the purpose of class discussion.

(3) A sketch map should have a scale and compass direction. No sketch map can be said to be *like* a map if these two attributes are omitted. Figure 20-2, then, is in fact a diagram. Apart from this omission, it bears the qualities of an effective sketch map. Often the drawing of a linear scale can be time consuming. Two correctly labelled lines of latitude will imply not only a scale but also the north and south directions (Figure 20-1).*

(4) A sketch map should have a title and, where appropriate, a key.

(5) Where possible a sketch map should be drawn in at least three colors. While it seems true to say that a map's appearance should be reasonably attractive to the eye as well as to the mind, the use of color is solely to establish certain spatial relationships, rather than to decorate or to embellish. (The days of a person's placing symbolic elephants "o'er uninhabitable downs," or symbolic cherubs with puffed cheeks blowing winds over a mapped Bight of Benin, have passed long ago!)

(6) A sketch map, although simple and quickly drawn, should not be misleading. It is essential that the positions of physical and human phenomena are fairly accurately depicted. This point may seem platitudinous but it can be frequently overlooked.

Common errors detracting from the essence of a sketch map's meaning include: (a) a confusion of lines, such as isotherms, drawn in the same color or with the same symbol; (b) an incorrect marking of a city's position in relation to a river or a coastline; and (c) the drawing of an area in isolation. An example of each of these errors, together with appropriate correction, is given in Figure 20-3.

USES OF THE SKETCH MAP

From the above discussion, possible uses of sketch map drawing become apparent. Three are emphasized. First, the drawing of a sketch map in a student notebook or on a large chalkboard can be a step-by-step record of the main points discussed in a lesson. The map, then, is a convenient geographical *shorthand* summary of the work done. Figure 20-1 is an example

---

*We are reminded that one degree of latitude is approximately equal to seventy miles.

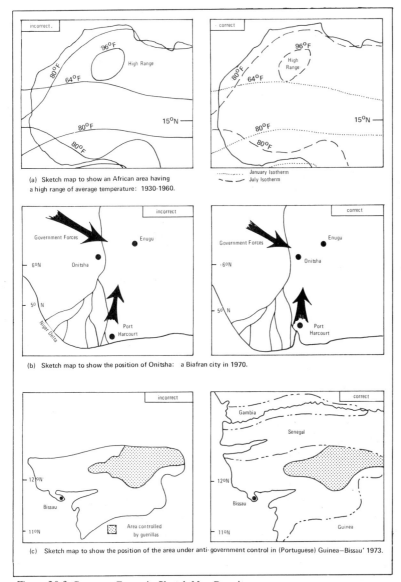

Figure 20-3. Common Errors in Sketch Map Drawing.

of a lesson that may begin with a classroom study of a projected satellite-photograph of the Nile delta, and with some references to the once flourishing Ancient Greek port of Damietta — now defunct. After studies of an appropriate large-scale map of the Egyptian coast and of statistics regarding the Nile's fluctuating

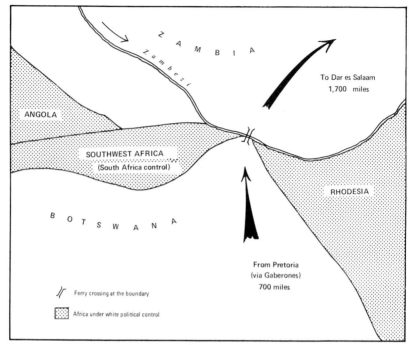

Figure 20-4. Diagram to show the Zambia-Botswana Boundary.

volume, the lesson ends with a consideration of why Alexandria through the centuries has survived as a port. A major factor allowing such survival, it is reasoned, may have been the favorable association of off-shore currents tending to divert alluvial deposition beyond the delta toward the east. Damietta has a shallow harbor.

Second, a sketch map can be used to highlight or to dramatize visually the current significance of places and events that are not always evident in small scale maps found in school materials. For instance, a class can discuss the political significance of the 200 yard narrow strip of boundary line shared by Zambia and Botswana along the Zambesi River (Figure 20-4).

Three, the sketch map can provide succinct data that may usefully form the basis of evaluatory or recapitulatory tests. One approach, for example, might employ the familiar patterns of a vegetation sketch map that has already been "built up" in a lesson-unit (Figure 20-5).* Having just added the positions of

---

*The somewhat geometrical initial guidelines for drawing the major outline of the vege-tation regions maps have been kept in Figure 20-5. They may provide a guide in the drawing of areas where undue distortion can lead to difficulties.

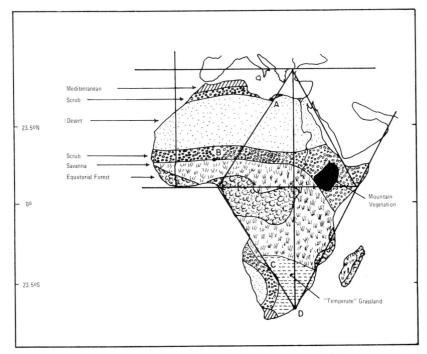

Figure 20-5. Sketch Map to Show the Major Vegetation Regions of Africa.

stations A, B, C, and D to an overhead projected version of the unit summary map, an high school teacher might say:

Look at the map and look at these climate statistics. They refer to one of the four places I have marked. Which is the place and what is the reason for your answer?

	J	F	M	A	M	J	Jy	A	S	O	N	D	Total
Av. Temp.	75	75	74	71	66	63	63	63	66	68	71	73	°F.
Av. Rain. (inches)	4.3	4.8	5.1	3.0	2.0	1.3	1.1	1.5	2.8	4.3	4.8	4.7	39.7

(If the question is suited to the average stage of conceptual understanding, it seems likely that few would have difficulty in noticing that the temperature figures suggest a Southern Hemisphere station. Whether it be C or D may demand greater effort.)

Within the compass of the third emphasized possible use of sketch maps is the matter of a student's or a teacher's designing frameworks for simulation and problem-solving games. An example that can contribute toward the playing of a *Railway Pioneers Game* of the kind posed by Walford (1969: 64-76) is seen

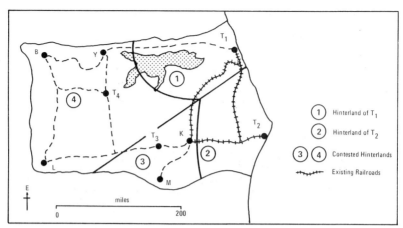

Figure 20-6. Sketch Map for an African Railroad Game.

in Figure 20-6. It is given that the depicted country is located somewhere between the two Tropics and that it already has railroads from seaports T_1 and T_2 to city K. Competing railroads are to be built further inland. One problem might be: "Will city L become wholly within the hinterland of seaport T_2?" Not until the game is in an advanced stage, perhaps, will many realize that the country is not altogether hypothetical. (Hilling 1966: 119)

At this point, we can perceive three main kinds of sketch map: (a) descriptive; (b) analytical; and (c) facilitative. The descriptive ones range from a cartographic *potpourri* (Figure 20-7a) that merely transcribes a written extract to one that descriptively portrays a geographical analysis (Figure 20-2; *Zambia's Export Routes)*. It may be noted that, by itself, Figure 20-7a has scarcely any central point or theme, unless it be that the represented data happen to be located in or near the Nile Basin. Thus, according to criteria mentioned above, Figure 20-7a is not *effective.* Yet it need not be fully discredited. When placed alongside a tabular record (Figure 20-7b) it can serve as an integral part of a lesson-unit's *unmapped* summary. In function, Figure 20-5 *(Vegetation Regions)* is a descriptive map standing so-to-speak centrally between Figures 20-2 and 20-7a. Analytical sketch maps or diagrams are represented by Figures 20-1 *(Alexandria's Position)* and 20-4 *(the Botswana-Zambia "Gateway")*. Figure 20-6 *(African Railroad Game)* is in the facilitative category. If sketch maps are to be mainly descriptive, rather than analytical or facilitative, many can play a vital role if they refer to matters likely to be in the headlines of tomorrow's *New York Times.*

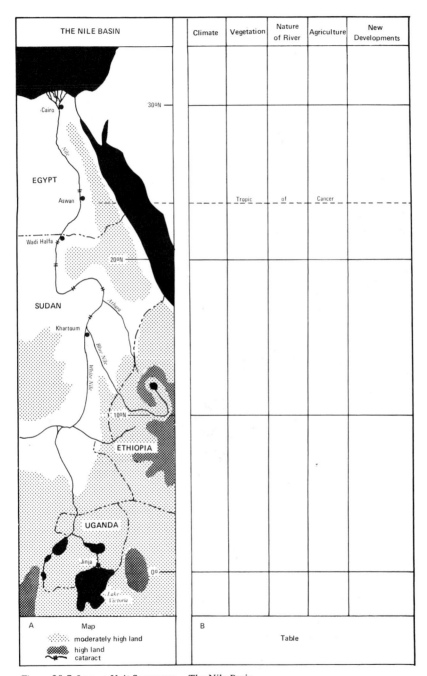

Figure 20-7. Lesson Unit Summary – The Nile Basin.

From the point of view of substance, three kinds of map, again, are perceived, namely: those especially emphasizing (a) patterns; (b) distributions; and (c) inter-relationships. An example of each is seen, for instance, in Figures 20-3a (*Northwestern Africa Isotherms*), 20-5 and 20-1, respectively. But it appears that there are many maps that cannot be categorized in this fashion. If true, this is hardly surprising, for it could be strongly argued that, no matter how many definitions there be of *geography*, these three words—*patterns, distributions,* and *interrelationships*—should be, at least implicitly, evident in each of them. From the point of view of suitable data for sketch map drawing, all is relevant provided that it can be expressed in spatial terms. Nevertheless, in reflecting upon the apparent heritage of sketch map drawing in the school geography of several countries, one is

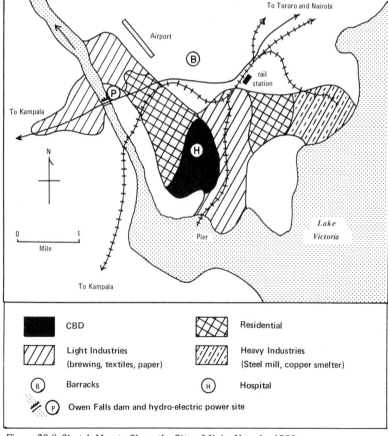

Figure 20-8. Sketch Map to Show the Site of Jinja, Uganda, 1973.

led to the inescapable belief that the physical components—especially relief and landforms—have been frequently overly stressed. Recommendations for the future keep this point in mind. A tendency toward an anthropocentric approach is suggested: one that records in simple form the patterns of land use and possible social and economic development such as, for instance, the kind based on a large scale map and seen in Figure 20-8. (Hoyle 1967: 64-67) Other possibly useful studies might be concerned with the spatial distribution and diffusion of cultural ideas and attitudes. Sketch-maps could be drawn to show not only the distribution of industrial plants and of multipurpose development schemes linked with rivers, but also of schools, hospitals, and libraries—that is, areas with more than one teacher, doctor or librarian per unit number of persons. Must geography teachers in school always await the findings of research in the field? Not always. In the case of sketch mapping, much that can be done by the teacher may be reliant upon his intuitive judgement—a judgement hopefully based upon wide reading in which the headlines of a reputable newspaper can play their useful part. If if is true that in the last quarter of the twentieth century "children should [still] constantly draw maps", a well-known French geography-educator's remark holds a key for us all: "The example of the teacher constantly drawing on the chalkboard will convince pupils that they themselves should learn to draw [diagrams and sketch maps]". (Hanaire 1965: 143)

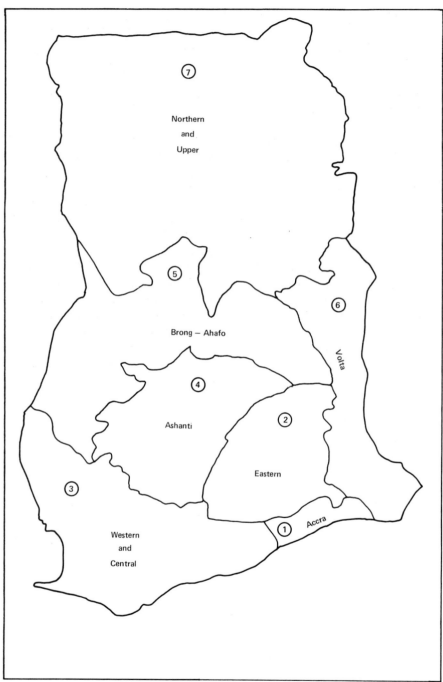

Figure 21-1. Ghana Administrative Divisions, 1960.

21

Structuring Geographical Relationships in Africa
An Instructional Module

RICHARD R. BRAND
University of Rhode Island

INTRODUCTORY INFORMATION

Grade level: advanced classes of college-bound students

Length: variable according to instructor's preferences (approx. 3–4 classes)

Overall objectives:
1. Methodological – an awareness of and appreciation for the value of the scientific method as an approach to explanation
2. Skill oriented – a familiarity with the combined use of elementary statistical and cartographic techniques in search of geographic relationships
3. Content oriented – an exposure to rural and urban landscapes in West Africa; and an understanding of the relationships between the growth of cities and other correlates of modernization

Implementation: the exact place of this module within a course on Africa depends largely upon the preferences of the instructor. In terms of the objectives, however, it is important to preface the module with a brief overview of an idealized progression of steps in the scientific method such as those outlined here:
1. identification of an appropriate geographical problem
2. formulation of an hypothesis or set of working assumptions
   _____ expressing a relationship between phenomena
   _____ considering single and multiple factors
3. selection of relevant facts
   _____ determination of appropriate scale of observation
   _____ delimitation of a time span

367

4. description of relevant data
   _____ operational definition of terms
   _____ measurement
5. data manipulation
   _____ generalization through classification
   _____ search for patterns via mapping
   _____ regionalization
   _____ comparison of simulated and actual distributions
   _____ cause and effect relationships require invariant occurrence and proof of logical relationship
6. laws, theory, and models

The material in this module is concerned primarily with phases 1 through 5 of the progression outlined above. Although no technical expertise is presumed students should be prepared with some familiarity with the Ghanaian space-economy and a beginner's knowledge of the spatial perspective of geography.

Instructor's reading:

S. Gregory, *Statistical Methods and the Geographer* (London: Longmans, 1964) pp. 167-208.

Ronald Abler, John S. Adams and Peter Gould, *Spatial Organization, The Geographer's View of the World* (Englewood Cliffs, N.J.: Prentice-Hall, 1971), Chapter 2, "Science and Scientific Explanation," Chapter 3, "The Science of Geography" and Chapter 5, "Structuring Geographic Relationships."

Bert F. Hoselitz, "Generative and Parasitic Cities," *Economic Development and Cultural Change,* Vol. 3, No. 3 (1955) pp. 278-294.

Students reading:

E.A. Boateng, *A Geography of Ghana* (2nd ed. N.Y.: Cambridge University Press, 1966), pp. 3-11.

Harm J. de Blij, *A Geography of Subsaharan Africa* (Chicago: Rand McNally, 1964), pp. 346-362.

THE MODULE

STEP 1: *Identifying a Geographical Problem*

A debate rages among social scientists and government planners as to the real contribution of cities to the overall growth of regional economies in developing nations. With the mounting interest in regional development schemes it becomes more important to determine in what ways it is proper to call these nodes "growth poles." It is also desirable to learn how variations in the level of urbanization affect other indices of development.

ACTIVITY: (30-45 minutes) Show film strips or color slides of modes of rural occupance in West Africa and contrast these with scenes from modern commercial and industrial towns and their hinterlands. Stress the concept of the, "growth pole" and solicit comments about its components.

STEP 2: *Hypothesis Formulation*

Develop the notion of an hypothesis as a "working assumption" or "likely answer" to a problem. Provide cues evoking responses as to the relationship between urbanization and other facets of economic standing. Suggested hypothesis: More urbanized regions will be more advanced on other measures of development than less urbanized regions.

ACTIVITY: (20-30 minutes) To stimulate thinking about the various correlates of development and their variability in space present the following tabular data and suggest that students compare the data with descriptions found in reference books in an effort to establish generalizations about the correlates of economic development.

STEP 3: *Selection of Facts and Description of Data*

Stress the need to aggregate additional information concerning the foregoing data. From a geographical point of view there are certain generalizations that apply to the regions of Ghana which help to explain the observed variations in both literacy and urbanization. Included here might be the location relative to European contact, the physical base, the history of indigenous political-economic organization, and other factors which students might enumerate.

Group reading assignments might be arranged in advance with attention directed to the following:

Kwamina B. Dickson, *A Historical Geography of Ghana* (New York: Cambridge University Press, 1969), pp. 269-291.

E. A. Boateng, *A Geography of Ghana* (2nd ed.; N.Y.: Cambridge University Press, 1966), pp. 143-201.

Point out the importance of using existing theory to guide the search for relevant facts. Rather than sending groups off using a "hunt and peck" approach, the array of possible data should be limited to those indices which have previously been shown to be important contributors to regional differentiation in developing countries. In this way theory can be shown to be very valuable as a feed-back mechanism within the scientific method.

Important terms should be defined. The term "urbanized" as defined by Webster is not precise enough for scientific purposes of measurement and comparability, thus the need for an *operational* definition. In the Ghanaian context an urban place is one with a nucleated population greater than 5,000 persons.

Indicate the advantages of measurement. The phenomena selected for examination should, whenever possible, be scaled or measured for reasons of precision and comparability.

STEP 4: *Data Manipulation*

Often it is difficult to perceive statistical or spatial trends in data in tabular form. Classifying and mapping data is an elementary operation that often aides generalization and may even facilitate the discovery of latent spatial patterns.

ACTIVITY: Have the students select appropriate class intervals and prepare a choropleth sketch map of the distribution of "literacy" and "urbanization" on the blackboard. The base map provided here (Figure 21-1) may be duplicated and used by the students as they participate in the exercise.

Point out that the maps do not reveal much about the statistical relationships between the two distributions. Suggest a graphical approach, e.g. a scatter diagram of Urbanization against Literacy using data from Table 21-1 (Figure 21-2).

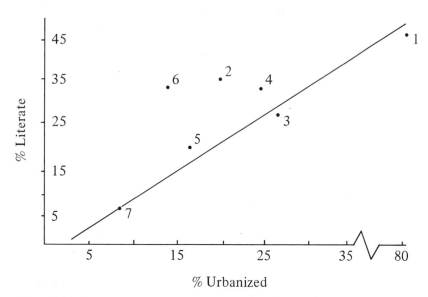

Figure 21-2. Scatter Diagram of Urbanization against Literacy.

TABLE 21-1
REGIONAL VARIATIONS IN LITERACY
AND URGANIZATION IN GHANA, 1960

Regions (Figure 21-1)	% literate	% urbanized
1. Accra Capital District	47	80
2. Eastern	35	20
3. Western & Central	28	27
4. Ashanti	33	25
5. Brong-Ahafo	20	16
6. Volta	34	13
7. Northern & Upper	6	8

From the evidence now available what generalizations can be made about the statistical relationships involved? ... the geographic relationships? Have the students list the facts that can be gleaned from the maps and the graph. What are the likely explanations for the observed structure and pattern?

ACTIVITY: The students have now seen the demonstration of a relationship between a measure of development and that of urbanization, but how strong is this relationship? The following practical exercise demonstrates how students can approach such a question by manipulating data using correlation analysis.

Scenario —

The Ghanaian Ministry of Economic Affairs finds it necessary to evaluate the extent to which urban places may properly be termed "growth poles" in the country. The only data available for the task is on the level of urbanization, school attendance and value added in manufacturing and construction.

From the available literature it is determined that a positive relationship exists between urbanization and measures of resource development. Urbanization is thus considered as an independent or predictor variable. By convention it is plotted on the horizontal or "X" axis of a scatter diagram. "School attendance" and "value added" are taken as measures of resource development and plotted as predicted or dependent variables on the verticle or "Y" axis. Since there are two dependent variables two scatter diagrams are required.

When the data on the two graphs are plotted, lines of best fit approximating the trend of the distribution of points should be drawn by hand. Two variables are said to be in direct relationship and thus positively correlated if increases in the value of one variable are accompanied by increases in the value of the other. An inverse or negative relationship would result if an increase in one were accompanied by a decrease in the other. In the former case the line of best fit has a positive slope upwards and to the right; a negative relationship would produce a line sloping from the upper left to the lower right. A horizontal or verticle line would indicate the absence of any relationship.

One set of computations can be worked out on the board. Students can then be assigned to plot the remaining set of data on "urbanization" and "value-added" for homework. They might also be assigned several pages of reading wherein the meaning of the coefficient of correlation is explained. Two such sources are S. Gregory, *Statistical Methods and the Geographer* (London: Longmans, 1964), pp. 167-84; and W.H. Theakstone and C. Harrison, *The Analysis of Geographical Data* (London: Heinemann Educational Books 1970), pp. 74-79.

SAMPLE COMPUTATION OF THE COEFFICIENT OF CORRELATION

In order to calculate the degree to which changes in direction (plus or minus) and magnitude in one set of data (urban population) are associated with comparable changes in another set (school attendance), the data tabulated in Table 21-2 are applied to the following formula which results in a single value called the Product Moment Correlation Coefficient

TABLE 21-2
STATISTICAL DATA FOR THE NINE REGIONS OF GHANA, 1962

Region	Urban Population[1]%	School Attendance[2]%	Value Added[3] (£G millions)
Western	20.1	29.8	6.7
Central	22.3	28.0	2.3
Accra C.D.	82.0	51.3	22.9
Eastern	12.8	40.1	4.8
Volta	5.4	36.5	2.1
Ashanti	24.0	34.0	7.5
Brong-Ahafo	6.4	18.9	1.5
Northern	6.0	5.6	1.6
Upper	5.7	7.4	1.3

1. Percentage of regional population in towns having more than 10,000 population
2. Regular school attendance of girls ages 6 to 14 years
3. Value added in manufacturing and construction

$$r = \frac{\frac{1}{n} \Sigma (a-\bar{a})(b-\bar{b})}{\sigma_a \cdot \sigma_b}$$

where a = urban population
$\bar{a}$ = average urban population
$\bar{b}$ = school attendance
b = average school attendance
Σ = "take the sum of"
n = number of regions
σ_a = standard deviation (a) is
calculated as $\sqrt{\dfrac{\Sigma (a-a)^2}{n-1}}$

The calculation proceeds as follows:

a	b	(a-ā)	(a-ā)²	(b-b̄)	(b-b̄)²	(a-ā)(b-b̄)
20.1	29.8	- .4	.16	2.2	4.84	- .88
22.3	28.0	1.8	3.24	.4	.16	.72
82.0	51.3	61.5	3782.25	23.7	561.69	1457.55
12.8	40.1	- 7.7	59.29	12.5	156.25	- 96.25
5.4	36.5	-15.1	228.01	8.9	79.21	- 134.39
24.0	34.0	2.5	6.25	6.4	40.96	16.00
6.4	18.9	-14.1	198.81	- 8.7	75.69	122.67
6.0	5.6	-14.5	210.25	-22.0	484.00	319.00
5.7	7.4	-14.8	219.04	-20.2	408.04	298.96
ā=20.5	b̄=27.6		Σ=4704.30		Σ=1810.84	Σ=1983.38

$$\sigma_a = \sqrt{\frac{\Sigma(a-\bar{a})}{n-1}} = \sqrt{\frac{4707.30}{8}} = \sqrt{588.41} = 24.25$$

$$\sigma_b = \sqrt{\frac{\Sigma(b-\bar{b})}{n-1}} = \sqrt{\frac{1810.84}{8}} = \sqrt{226.35} = 15.04$$

Then, the correlation coefficient (r) =

$$\frac{1}{n} \frac{\Sigma(a-\bar{a})(b-\bar{b})}{\sigma_a \cdot \sigma_b} = \frac{1983.38/_8}{(24.25)(15.04)} = \frac{247.92}{364.72} = .68$$

COEFFICIENT OF DETERMINATION (r^2)

When the correlation coefficient (.68) is squared and multiplied by 100 it gives a value known as the COEFFICIENT OF DETERMINATION (46.23%) which indicates that the percentage of variation around the mean in one variable is "explained" by variation in the other. On this basis we have "explained" less than half of the variation in percent urban population on the basis of school attendance, and vice-versa. Conversely, more than half the

variation is unexplained. What then can be said about the significance of the spatial relationship?

A TEST OF SIGNIFICANCE

The correlation coefficient must be tested to see whether or
not a chance occurrence of this magnitude is likely on the basis of
the size of the initial data set. This can be done by means of the
student's t test. Figure 21-3 is based on the t distribution and
allows the significance level to be read directly from the graph.

In our case the nine regions of Ghana yield (n-2) seven degrees
of freedom; thus the correlation coefficient must be above +.75 or
below -.75 before it can be considered as statistically significant at
the .05 level (ie., within a five percent probability of error). Since
the correlation coefficient (.68) falls below the threshold it cannot
be concluded that a significant relationship exists between percent

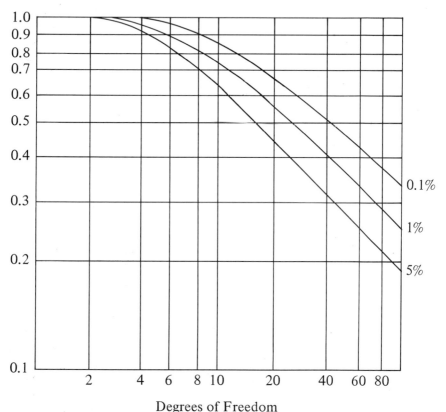

Degrees of Freedom

Figure 21-3. Significance Levels for Correlations Coeffients Using the Student's
Distribution.

urban and school attendance as they have been measured in Ghana. The lesson to be learned here is that however large the coefficient of correlation may be, it must be interpreted in terms of its statistical significance which is a function of the number of observations involved. The correlation coefficient is a relative value and large values are not necessarily significant.

HOMEWORK ASSIGNMENT

Have one half of the class calculate the coefficient of correlation between "urban population" and "value added." The coefficient of correlation that should result is .86 which accounts for 73.95% of the variability. It is significant at the .01 level. The remaining students could write up a summary statement of their findings about the role of "urbanization" in Ghana and its spatial relationship with "school attendance."

REFERENCES CITED

Abrahams, P., 1970, *Mine Boy.* Collier, New York.

Africa South of the Sahara, 1972, Europe

Anderson, R. C., 1965, "The Role of Human Geography in the Study of Emerging Nations," *Social Education, 29.*

Apter, D., 1965, *Politics of Modernization,* University of Chicago Press, Chicago.

Balogh, T., 1966, "Introduction" in R. Dumont, *False Start in Africa,* Praeger, New York.

Benveniste, G., and W. Moran, 1962, *Handbook of African Economic Development.* Praeger, New York.

Bernard F. E. and B. J. Walter, 1971, *Africa: A Thematic Geography, Volume I – Themes, Volume II – Readings, Volume III – Bibliography.* Office of Education, Washington.

Beyer, B. K., 1969, *Africa South of the Sahara: A Resource and Curriculum Guide.* Crowell, New York.

Beyer, B. K. and A. N. Penna, (eds.) 1971, *Concepts in the Social Studies,* National Council for the Social Studies, Washington, D. C.

Beyer, 1971, "Africa Through Inquiry," *Social Education, 35.*

Biebuyck, D., (ed.), 1963, *African Agrarian Systems,* Oxford University Press, London.

Black, C. E., 1967, *The Dynamics of Modernization.* Harper and Row, New York.

Bohannan, P. and P. Curtin, 1971. *Africa and Africans,* Natural History Press, New York.

Boserup, E., 1965, *The Conditions of Agricultural Growth.* Aldine, Chicago.

Bretton, H. L., 1966, *The Rise and Fall of Kwame Nkrumah: A Study of Personal Rule in Africa.* Praeger, New York.

Broek, J. O. M., 1965, *Geography: Its Scope and Spirit.* Charles E. Merrill, Columbus.

Busia, K. A., 1967, *Africa in Search of Democracy,* Routledge and Kegan Paul London.

Caldwell, J. C., 1968, "Determinants of Rural-Urban Migration in Ghana," *Population Studies, 2.*

Callaway, A., 1963, "Unemployment Among African School Leavers," *The Journal of Modern African Studies, 1, 3.*

Carey, G. W., 1970, "Systems, Model Building and Quantitative Methods," *Focus on Geography: Key Concepts and Teaching Strategies,* (ed.) P. Bacon, National Council for the Social Studies, Washington, D. C.

Clark C., 1967, *Population Growth and Land Use.* St. Martin's Press, New York.

Davidson, B., 1966, *African Kingdoms,* Time-Life Books, New York.

deSchlippe, P., 1956, *Shifting Cultivation in Africa: The Zande System of Agriculture,* Humanities, New York.

Doro, M. E. and M. M. Stultz, 1970, *Governing in Black Africa: Perspectives on New States,* Prentice-Hall, Englewood Cliffs.

Dumont, R., 1966, False Start in Africa, Praeger, New York.

Duplessis, C. W., 1959, "Highway to Racial Harmony," *First Paper 69, Supplement to the Digest of South Africa,* Pretoria.

Ekwensi, C., 1954, *People of the City.* Humanities Press, New York.

Emerson, R., 1962, *From Empire to Nation,* Harvard University Press, Cambridge.

Evans-Pritchard, E. E., 1967, "The Nuer of the Southern Sudan," in M. Fortes and E. E. Evans-Pritchard, (eds.), *African Political Systems,* Oxford.

Fanon, F., 1963, *The Wretched of the Earth.* Grove Press, New York.

Fraenkel, J. R., 1971, "A Curriculum Model for the Social Studies," *The Social Sciences and Geographic Education: A Reader,* (eds.) John M. Ball, John E. Steinbrink, and Joseph P. Stoltman, Wiley, New York.

Frankel, S., 1960, "The Tyranny of Economic Paternalism in Africa," Supplement to *Optima,* Johannesburg.

Gluckman, M., 1967, "The Kingdom of the Zulu of South Africa," in M. Fortes and E. Evans-Pritchard, (eds.), *African Political Systems,* Oxford.

Gould, P. R., 1969, "The Structure of Space Preferences in Tanzania," *Area* 1, London.

Gould, P. R., 1970, "Tanzania 1920-63: The Spatial Impress of the Modernization Process," *World Politics* 22.

Gould, P. R. and D. Ola, 1970, "The Perception of Residential Desirability in the Western Region of Nigeria," *Environment and Planning,* 2.

Grade Teacher. 1968, 86, 2.

Greenberg, J. K., 1966, *The Languages of Africa.* Indiana University, Bloomington.

Gunn, A. M., 1970, "Educational Simulations in School Geography," *Focus in Geography: Key Concepts and Teaching Strategies,* (ed.) P. Bacon, National Council for the Social Studies, Washington.

Halliman, D. M., and W.T.W. Morgan, 1967, "The City of Nairobi" in W.T.W. Morgan, *Nairobi, City and Region,* Oxford University Press, Nairobi.

Hanaire, A., 1965, "Teaching Material" in B. Brouillette (ed.) *UNESCO Source Book for Geography Teaching,* Longmans/Unesco, London.

Hance, W., 1967, *African Economic Development.* Praeger, New York.

———, 1970, *Population, Migration and Urbanization in Africa,* Columbia University Press, New York.

Hanna, W. J., and J. L. Hanna, 1971, *Urban Dynamics in Black Africa,* Aldine, Chicago.

Higgins, B., 1959, *Economic Development.* Norton, New York.

Hilling, D., 1966, "Tema – The Geography of a New Port," *Geography,* 51.

Hodder, B., and D. Harris (eds.), 1967, *Africa in Transition,* Methuen, London.

Hedgkin, T., 1957. *Nationalism in Colonial Africa,* New York University Press, New York.

Hoyle, B. S., 1967, "Industrial Developments at Jinja, Uganda," *Geography,* 52.

Hunter, G., 1962, *The New Socieities of Tropical Africa.* Oxford University Press, London.

Hunter, G., 1967, *The Best of Both Worlds.* Oxford University Press, London.

Intercultural Education, 1970 2, 1 and 1971 2, 3.

Jones, W., 1961, "Food and Agricultural Economics of Tropical Africa," *Food Research Institute Studies,* Vol. 2, No. 1 Stanford, Cal.

Kamarck, A., 1967, *The Economics of Africa Development.* Praeger, New York.

Kay, G., 1969, "Agricultural Progress in Zambia" in M. Thomas and G. Whittington (eds.), *Environment and Land Use in Africa,* Methuen, London.

Kennamer, L., 1965, "Improvement of Instruction in Geography." *Social Education,* 29.

Kennamer, L. 1970, "Emerging Social Studies Curricula: Implications for Geography." *Focus on Geography: Key Concepts and Teaching Strategies,* (ed.) P. Bacon, National Council for the Social Studies, Washington, D. C.

Kenworthy, L. S., 1965, *Studying Africa in Elementary and Secondary Schools.* Columbia University, New York.

Kimble, G., 1969, *Tropical Africa,* Vol. 1, Land and Livelihood, Twentieth Century Fund, New York.

_____, 1960, *Tropical Africa,* Vol. II Society and Polity, Twentieth Century Fund, New York.

Larimore, A. E., 1964, "Nyanza Textile Industries Ltd.: A Modern Producer of Cotton Fabrics in an Underdeveloped Economy", in R. S. Thomam and D. J. Patton (eds.) *Focus on Geographical Activity: A Collection of Original Studies,* McGraw Hill, New York.

Leibenstein, H., 1957, *Economic Backwardness and Economic Growth,* Wiley, New York.

Lewis, W. A., 1969, *Some Aspects of Economic Development.* Ghana Publishing Corporation

_____, 1955, *The Theory of Economic Growth.* Allen and Unwin, London.

Lugard, Sir F. D., 1902, *Colonial Annual Reports No. 346,* Northern Nigeria, His Majesty's Stationery Office, London.

Louw, E., 1960, *Statement Before the General Assembly of the United Nations,* GAOR, 15th Session, A/PV 1033 October 15th.

_____, 1968, *Urbanization in Nigeria.* Africana Publishing Corporation, New York.

Mabogunje, A. L., 1970a, "Systems Approach to a Theory of Rural-Urban Migration," *Geographical Analysis,* 2.

_____, 1970b, "Urbanization and Social Change" in J. Paden and E. W. Soja, *The African Experience,* Vol. 1, Northwestern University Press, Evanston.

Martin, J. W. Adams, and H. Weaver, 1972, Africa Projected: A Critical Filmography, *African Studies Newsletter,* 5, 2:

Mascarenhas, A. C. and C. F. Claeson, 1972, "Factors Influencing Tanzania's Urban Policy," *African Urban Notes,* 7.

Mazrui, A. A., 1970, "The Common Man's Charter and The Three Faces of Socialism," *Makerere Political Review,* Vol. 1, No. 2

_____, 1972, *Cultural Engineering and Nation-Building in East Africa* Northwestern University Press, Evanston.

McCellan, G., 1963, *South Africa.* Praeger, New York.

McNee, R. B., 1955, "On the Value of Sketch Maps," *The Journal of Geography,* 54.

McNulty, M. L., 1972, "African Urban Systems, Transport Networks and Regional Inequalities," *African Urban Notes,* 7.

Miller, S. C., 1964, "The Interdisciplinary Approach to Teaching Social Studies," *Social Education,* 28.

Murdock, G. P., 1959, *Africa: Its Peoples and Their Culture History.* McGraw Hill, New York.

Murphy, R., 1971, *An Introduction to Geography.* Rand McNally, Chicago.

Nyerere, J. K., 1966, *Freedom and Unity.* Oxford University Press, London

Obote, M., 1968, *The Common Man's Charter.* Government Printer, Entebbe, Uganda.

_____, 1970, *Document No. 5,* Ugandan Parliament, July 17.

Oram, N., 1965, *Towns in Africa.* Oxford University Press, London.

Paden, J. N. and E. W. Soja, 1970, *The African Experience, Volume I – Essays, Volume II – Syllabus, Volume IIIa – Bibliography, Volume IIIb – Guide to Resources.* Northwestern University Press, Evanston.

Peil, M., 1971, "The Expulsion of West African Aliens," *The Journal of Modern African Studies,* Vol. 9, No. 2.

Porter, P. W., 1970, "The Concept of Environmental Potential as Exemplified by Tropical African Research," in Wilbur Zelinsky, Leszek A. Kosinski and R. Mansell Prothero, *Geography and a Crowding World,* Oxford University Press, New York.

Porter, P., 1969, "Research Directions and Needs in African Rural Geography," in N. Miller (ed.), *Research in Rural Africa,* East Lansing, Michigan.

Potter, D., 1954, *People of Plenty.* University of Chicago Press, Chicago.

Riddell, J. B., 1970, *The Spatial Dimension of Modernization in Sierra Leone.* Northwestern University Press, Evanston.

Riessman, F., 1962, *The Culturally Deprived Child.* Harper and Row, New York.

Sherif, M and C. W. Sherif, (eds.) 1969. *Interdisciplinary Relationships in the Social Sciences.* Aldine, Chicago.

Sithole, N., 1959, *African Nationalism,* Oxford University Press, London.

Shinn, R. F. 1964, "Geography and History as Integrating Disciplines," *Social Education,* 28.

Social Education, 1970, 34, 4.

Social Education, 1971. 35, 2.

Soja, E. W., 1968, *The Geography of Modernization in Kenya: A Spatial Analysis of Social, Economic and Political Change,* Syracuse University Press, Syracuse.

Southern Africa, 1972, Vol. 5 (March)

Spengler, J. J., 1964, "Population Movements and Problems in Sub-Saharan Africa" in E.A.G. Robinson (ed.), *Economic Development for Africa, South of the Sahara,* MacMillan.

Stanley, W. R. and K. E. French, 1972, "Studying the Human Geography of Sub-Saharan Africa in the High School and College," *Journal of Geography,* 71.

Taylor, D. R. F., 1972, "The Role of the Smaller Urban Place in Development – A Case Study from Kenya," *African Urban Notes,* 7.

Tordoff, W., 1968, "Provincial and District Government in Zambia," Part II, *Journal of African Administration,* Vol. VII, No. 4.

Uganda Government, *Parliamentary Debates,* Vol. 23.

United Nations Economic Commission for Africa, 1969, "Size and Growth of Urban Population in Africa," G. Breese, (ed.), *The City in Newly Developing Countries: Readings on Urbanism and Urbanization,* Prentice Hall, Englewood Cliffs.

United Nations (F.A.O.), 1967, *Agriculture and Industrialization,* Rome

United Nations Office of Public Information, 1964, *Apartheid in South Africa,* U.N. Publications, New York.

Walford, R., 1969 *James in Geography,* Longmans, London.

Wallerstem, I, *Africa: The Politics of Independence,* lands in Marss, New York

Walter, B. J. and F. E. Bernard, 1971, *Africa: A Thematic Approach,* 3 vols. U.S. Office of Education, Institute of International Studies, Washington, D.C.

Walter, B. J. and D. Wiley, eds., 1973. *Selected Syllabi for Introductory, Interdisciplinary Courses on Africa,* Foreign Area Materials Center, Intercultural Studies Information Service, New York.

Young, K., 1967, *Rhodesian Independence.* Heinemann, New York.

Zartman, W., 1966, *International Relations in the New Africa.* Prentice Hall, Englewood Cliffs.

SELECTED READINGS

ANTHOLOGIES: SELECTED READINGS

Burke, Fred. *Africa: Selected Readings* (Boston: Houghton Mifflin Company, 1969)

Cartey, Wilfred and Martin Kilson. *The Africa Reader: Colonial Africa* (New York: Vintage, 1970)

_____, *The Africa Reader: Independent Africa* (New York: Vintage, 1970)

Clarke, Leon E. *Through African Eyes: Cultures in Change* (New York: Praeger, 1971)

Drachler, Jacob. *African Heritage* (London: Collier-MacMillan, 1969)

Moore, Clarke, D. and Ann Dunbar. *Africa Yesterday and Today* (New York: Bantam Pathfinder, 1970)

Moore, Jane Ann. *Cry Sorrow, Cry Joy: Selections from Contemporary African Writers* (New York: Friendship Press, 1971)

Nolan, Barbara. *Africa is People* (New York: E. P. Dutton, 1968)

Nyerere, Julius K. *Uhuru Na Ujamaa: Freedom and Socialism* (New York: Oxford University Press, 1970)

Wallbank, T. Walter. *Contemporary Africa: Continent Transition* (New York: Van Nostrand, 1964)

_____, *Documents in Modern Africa* (New York: Van Nostrand, 1964).

ATLASES

Fage, J. D. *An Atlas of African History* (London: Edward Arnold Publishers, 1963)

Fordham, Paul. *The Geography of African Affairs* (Baltimore: Penguin, 1965)

Fullard, Harold. *Modern College Atlas for Africa* (London: Phillips & Sons, 1965)

Gailey, Harry A. *The History of Africa in Maps* (Chicago: Denoyer-Geppert, 1967)

Oxford Regional Economic Atlas (Oxford: Clarendon House, 1970)

BIBLIOGRAPHIES

Four recent reliable bibliographies are:

Bederman, Sanford, H. *A Bibliographic Aid to the Study of the Geography of Africa: A Selected Listing of Recent Literature Published in the English Language.* 2nd ed. Atlanta: Bureau of Business and Economic Research, Georgia State University, 1972.

Bernard, Frank E. and Bob J. Walter. *Africa: A Thematic Geography – Bibliography.* Vol. 3. Washington, D. C.: Office of Education, Institute of International Studies, September 1971. Accompanies two other volumes in the set of curriculum materials which include a basic text and a set of correlative interdisciplinary readings.

Paden, John N. and E. W. Soja. *The African Experience.* Vol 3a (Evanston: Northwestern University Press, 1970)

Library of Congress, African Section. *Africa South of the Sahara: Index to Periodical Literature, 1900 – 1970.* 4 vols. Boston: G. K. Hall, 1971.

ECONOMY

Allan, W. The African Husbandman (Edinburg: 1965)

Bohannan, Paul and G. Dalton, eds. *Markets in Africa* (Evanston: Northwestern University, 1962)

Dumont, Rene. *False Start in Africa* (New York: Praeger, 1966)

Green, Reginald H. and Ann Seidman. *Unity or Poverty?* (Baltimore: Penguin, 1968)

Hance, William A. *African Economic Development* (New York: Praeger, 1967)

Kamarck, Andrew M. *The Economics of African Development* (New York: Praeger, 1971)

O'Connor, A. M. *The Geography of Tropical Economic Development* (New York: Pergamon Press, 1971)

Soja, E. W. *The Geography of Modernization in Kenya,* (Syracuse: University Press, 1968)

Yudelman, Montague. *Africans on the Land* (Cambridge: Harvard Universities Press, 1964).

GENERAL BOOKS

Bernard, Frank E. and Bob J. Walter. *Africa: A Thematic Geography:* Vol. 1 – Themes, Vol. II – Readings, Vol. III – Bibliography. (Washington: Office of Education, 1971)

Bohannan, Paul and Philip Curtin. *Africa and the Africans* (New York: Doubleday, 1972)

Brokensha, David and M. Crowder. *Africa in the Wider World* (New York: Oxford University Press, 1967)

Paden, John N. and E. W. Soja. *The African Experience* Vol. 1 – Essays, Vol. II – Syllabus; Vol. IIIa – Bibliography, Vol. IIIb – Guide to Resources. (Evanston: Northwestern University Press, 1970).

Taylor, Alice, ed. *Focus on Africa South of the Sahara* (New York: American Geographical Society/Praeger – forthcoming)

GEOGRAPHY TEXTS

Carlson, Lucille. *Africa's Lands and Nations* (New York: McGraw, 1967)

Fordham, Paul. *The Geography of African Affairs* (Baltimore: Penguin, 1972)

Grove, A. T. *Africa, South of the Sahara* (New York: Oxford University Press, 1970)

Hance, William A. *The Geography of Modern Africa* (New York: Columbia University Press, 1964)

Harrison Church, R. J. *Africa and the Islands* (New York: Wiley, 1971)

Hodder, B. W. and D. R. Harris, eds. *Africa in Transition* (New York: Barnes and Noble, 1972)

Stamp, L. Dudley and W. T. W. Morgan. *Africa: A Study in Tropical Development* (New York: Wiley, 1972)

HISTORY

Ajayi, J. F. A. and Ian Espie. *A Thousand Years of West African History* (London: Nelson, 1965)
Collins, Robert O. *Problems in African History* (Englewood Cliffs: Prentice-Hall, 1968)
————, *Problems in the History of Colonial Africa* (Englewood Cliffs: Prentice-Hall, 1970)
Davidson, Basil. *Africa: History of a Continent* (New York: MacMillan, 1966)
Davidson, Basil. *African Kingdoms* (New York: Time-Life Books, 1966)
July, Robert W. *A History of the African People* (New York: Scribners, 1970)
Oliver, Roland and J. D. Fage. *A Short History of Africa* (Baltimore: Penguin, 1962)
Oliver, Roland and Anthony Atmore. *Africa Since 1800* (Cambridge, England, University Press, 1967)
Rotberg, Robert I. *A Political History of Tropical Africa* (New York: Harcourt, Brace, Jovanovich, 1965)
Vansina, Jan. *Kingdoms of the Savannah* (Madison: University of Wisconsin, 1966)

NOVELS

Abrahams, Peter. *Mine Boy* (New York: Collier, 1970)
Abrahams, Peter. *A Wreath for Udomo* (New York: MacMillan, 1971)
Achebe, Chinua. *Arrow of God* (New York: Doubleday, 1969)
Achebe, Chinua. *Things Fall Apart* (Greenwich: Fawcett World, 1970)
Amadi, Elechi. *The Concubine* (New York: Humanities, 1966)
Armah, Ayi Kwei. *The Beautiful Ones Are Not Yet Born* (New York: MacMillan, 1969)
Beti, Mongo. *Mission to Kala* (New York: Humanities, 1966)
Conton, William. *The African* (New York: Humanities, 1966)
Ekwensi, Cyprian. *Burning Grass* (New York: Humanities, 1966)
Ekwensi, Cyprian. *People of the City* (Greenwich: Fawcett World, 1969)
Laye, Camara. *A Dream of Africa* (New York: MacMillan, 1971)
Mazrui, Ali. *Trial of Christopher Okigbo* (New York: Third Press, 1972)
Ngugi, James. *Grain of Wheat* (New York: Humanities, 1968)
Ngugi, James. *Weep Not Child* (New York: MacMillan, 1969)
Rive, Richard. *Emergency* (New York: Collier, 1965)

POLITICS

Davidson, Basil. *Which Way Africa* (Baltimore: Penguin, 1971)
Doro, Marion E. and Newell M. Stultz. *Governing in Black Africa* Englewood Cliffs: Prentice-Hall 1970)
Emerson, Rupert and Martin Kilson, eds. *The Political Awakening of Africa* (Englewood Cliffs: Prentice-Hall 1965)
Emerson, Rupert. *From Empire to Nation* (Cambridge: Harvard University Press, 1960)

Gibson, Richard. *African Liberation Movements* (New York: Oxford University Press, 1972)

Markovitz, Irving Leonard, ed. *African Politics and Society* (New York: Collier-Macmillan, 1970)

Mazrui, Ali A. and Hasu H. Patel. *Africa in World Affairs: The Next Thirty Years* (New York: Third Press, 1973)

Mazrui, Ali. *Cultural Engineering and Nation-Building in East Africa* (Evanston: Northwestern University Press, 1972

Nyerere, J. K. *Freedom and Unity* (New York: Oxford University Press, 1966)

Post, Ken. *The New States of West Africa* (Baltimore: Penguin, 1968)

Sithole, Ndabaningi. *African Nationalism* (New York: Oxford University Press, 1969)

Touval, Saadia. *The Boundary Problems of Independent Africa* (Cambridge: Harvard University Press, 1972)

Wallerstein, Immanuel. *Africa, The Politics of Independence* (New York: Vintage Books, 1961)

SECONDARY SCHOOL BOOKS

Burke, Fred. *Africa* (Boston: Houghton Mifflin Company, 1970)

Kolevzon, Edward R. *the Afro-Asian World: A Cultural Understanding* (Boston: Allyn and Bacon, 1969)

Murphy, E. Jeffersen. *Understanding Africa* (New York: Crowell Company, 1969)

Rich, Evelyn and Immanuel Wallerstein. *Africa: Tradition and Change* (New York: Random House)

SOCIAL/CULTURAL/HUMAN

Caldwell, John C. and Chukuka Okonjo, eds. *The Population of Tropical Africa* (New York: Columbia University Press, 1968)

Gibbs, James L., ed. *Peoples of Africa* (New York: Holt, Rinehart and Winston, 1965)

Greenberg, J. K. *The Languages of Africa* (Bloomington: Indiana University, 1966)

Hanna, W. J., and J. L. Hanna. *Urban Dynamics in Black Africa* (Chicago: Aldine, 1971)

Hance, William A. *Population, Migration and Urbanization in Africa* (New York: Columbia University Press, 1970)

Herkovits, Melville J. *The Human Factor in Changing Africa* (New York: Random House, 1967)

Hunter, Guy. *the New Societies of Tropical Africa* (New York: Praeger, 1968)

Lloyd, P. C. *Africa in Social Change* (Baltimore: Penguin, 1967)

Maquet, Jacques. *Civilizations of Black Africa* (New York: Oxford University Press, 1972)

Prothereo, R. Mansell, ed. *People and Land in Africa South of the Sahara: Readings in Social Geography* (New York: Oxford University Press, 1972)

Turnbull, Colin M. *The Lonely African* (New York: Simon and Schuster, 1962)

NOTES ON CONTRIBUTORS

MOSES E. AKPAN

Professor and Chairman, Department of Social Sciences; and Director, Teacher Training in Developing Institutions (TTDI) Graduate Fellowship Program on Integrated Social Studies at South Carolina State College, Orangeburg, South Carolina. Main interests are in the fields of Political Science, particularly in African Politics; and Education, mainly in preparing teachers for Black Studies and Civic Education.

FRANK E. BERNARD

Associate Professor of Geography and Director of African Studies. Teaches Africa, cultural geography and resource management. Primary research interests are population growth, resource management and utilization, and agricultural change. Author of *East of Mount Kenya: Meru Agriculture in Transition*

BARRY K. BEYER

Associate Professor of History and Director of Graduate Studies in History, Carnegie-Mellon University, Pittsburgh, Pennsylvania; formerly Director of Project Africa; developer of numerous instructional materials on African geography and history – co-author of transparency series *World Cultures: Africa* (Keuffel and Esser) and *Africa Inquiry Maps* author of *Inquiry in the Social Studies Classroom: A Strategy for Teaching.*

RICHARD R. BRAND

Assistant Professor of Geography, University of Rhode Island. Formerly lecturer in Geography, University of Cape Coast, Ghana. Research interests and published articles guest editor of *African Urban* in urban development processes in Africa.
Notes (4: 1972)

JOSEPH BROWNELL

Professor and Chairman, Department of Geography, State University of New York, Cortland. Specializes in the teaching of map skills and the regional geography of Canada.

BARRY FLOYD

Former acting head of the Geography Department at the University of Nigeria, then head of Geography at the University of the West Indies, Dr. Floyd is now on the staff at the University of Durham in England. His interests lie in the problems of rural land use in the tropics, with special reference to small farmers. Author of *Eastern Nigeria: A Geographical Review.*

PETER L. FRENCH

Assistant Professor of Government at St. Lawrence University, Canton, New York, where he teaches Political Science. Main interests lie in the fields of African area studies, race relations, international politics and educational innovation in instruction.

HARRY A. GAILEY

Professor of History and Director of the African Studies Program, California State University, San Jose. Area specialization is West Africa with concentration on interaction between British Administration and African cultures in the 20th century. Author of *A History of the Gambia, The Road to Aba, The History of Africa in Maps, A History of Africa from Earliest Times to 1800,* and *A History of Africa from 1800 to the Present.*

PETER C. GARLICK

Professor of Economics, Department of African Studies, State University of New York at New Paltz. He has lived for twelve years in Africa, ten of them in Ghana. His most recent publication is *African Traders and Economic Development in Ghana.*

SVEN ERIK HAMMAR

Assistant Professor of Education at the State University of New York, College at Fredonia, where he teaches methods courses. His professional interests include international education, field-centered preparation of teachers and social studies curriculum design.

WILLIAM A. HANCE

Professor and Chairman of the Department of Geography at Columbia University. He has been specializing in the economic geography of Africa since 1947 and is the author of 5 books and numerous articles concerned with economic development, population and urbanization. Most recent publication: *Population, Migration and Urbanization in Africa.* He is currently President of the Council of the American Geographical Society.

NANCY M. HOON

Teacher Specialist in the Department of Curriculum and Instruction, Montgomery County (Maryland) Public Schools. Main interests lie in development of multi-disciplinary curricula in the arts, sciences, and social sciences. She is presently working on a project for secondary schools in Science, Technology, and Society.

AKIN L. MABOGUNJE

Professor of Geography at the University of Ibadan, Nigeria and currently Vice-President of the International Geography Congress. His special research interests deal with urbanization and problems of economic development. Publications include *Yoruba Towns* and *Urbanization in Nigeria.* He is also co-editor of *The City of Ibadan.*

ALI A. MAZRUI

Professor of Political Science at Makerere University, Kampala, and currently Fellow at the Center for Advanced Study in the Behavioral Sciences, Stanford. His interests include problems of national and cultural integration, with special reference to Africa. Publications include *Towards a Pax Africana, Essays on Independent Africa* and *The Trial of Christopher Okigbo.*

J. H. NKETIA

Director of the Institute of African Studies and Professor of Musicology, University of Ghana. Held the Horatio Appleton Lamb Visiting Professorship at Harvard University 1971. Publications include: *Funeral Dirges of the Akan, African Music in Ghana* and *Ethnomusicology in Ghana.*

DENT OCAYA-LAKIDI

Lecturer in political science, Makerere University, Kampala, Uganda where he teaches political theory and traditional political systems. He is editor of *Perspectives on Politics and Government in Uganda* (East African Literature Bureau). Was recently nominated as the Uganda national editor for the Encyclopaedia Africana.

JOHN PADEN

Associate Professor of Political Science at Northwestern University. Author of *Religion and Political Culture in Kano,* and co-author of *The African Experience,* and *Black Africa: A Comparative Handbook.* He has done research in northern Nigeria and Hausa speaking areas of West Africa.

JACK M. SHERIDAN

Associate Professor of Curriculum and Instruction at the University of Houston, Houston, Texas, where he teaches world regional geography and social studies methods. His main interests are in developing inquiry centered learning units and strategies. He contributed to the 1972 NCGE Yearbook, *Metropolitan America.*

ROBERT W. STEEL

John Rankin Professor of Geography, University of Liverpool, since 1957. He has had a long association with geographical research in the Third World, principally in tropical Africa, and was President of the African Studies Association of the United Kingdom in 1971. His interest in the teaching of geography at all levels is reflected in his current presidency (1973) of the Geographical Association.

REED F. STEWART

Assistant Professor of Geography and Anthropology at Bridgewater State College, Bridgewater, Massachusetts, teaching with an emphasis on the geography and cultural anthropology of Africa. Research deals with the Mande-speaking peoples of West Africa.

DERRICK J. THOM

Assistant Professor of Geography at Utah State University, Logan, Utah. His research interests are in political geography, population and settlement, and West Africa. He is currently serving as the Secretary-Treasurer of the Western Association of Africanists.

COLIN M. TURNBULL

Professor of Anthropology at Virginia Commonwealth University. Formerly head of the Department of Ethnology at the American Museum of Natural History in New York. Has spent many years in the field as an anthropoligist in Africa particularly with hunters and gatherers. Books include: *The Forest People, The Lonely African* and *The Mountain People*.

BOB J. WALTER

Associate Professor of Geography at Ohio University, Athens. Teaching African, political, and cultural geography. Main interests in spatial aspects of political modernization, migration process and flows, population growth and change, and incipient urbanization.

JOHN E. WILLMER

Professor of Geography, State University College of New York, at Cortland. Formerly Senior Lecturer at the University of Nigeria. Teaches cultural and political geography. Main interests lie in geographic education particularly in preparing teachers for non-Western world studies.

JOHN WISE

Associate Professor of Education at Lakehead University, Ontario, Canada, where he provides initial and in-service methodology courses for secondary school geography teachers who hold degrees in the discipline. His main interests are directed toward the history and nature of geography education in English-speaking countries, and toward aspects of regional geography.

CREDITS: PHOTOGRAPHS AND ILLUSTRATIONS

Page 2 top right courtesy of the Uganda Tourist Board.

Page 48 courtesy of the United Nations.

Page 104, Page 150 and Page 270 courtesy of the Agency for International Development.

Page 206 courtesy of the Museum of African Art, Washington, D.C.

Page 332 courtesy of the Tanzania Information services.

Page 190 quotations from *No Easy Walk to Freedom* by Nelson Mandela (Heineman, 1965) pp. 184-5 top; 187 middle; 188-9 bottom.

Remaining photographs: J. and J. Willmer

All original maps drawn by Joseph Brownell

Photographic consultant: Bill Clymer

Cover design: Buckner Winston